Medical Family Therapy and Integrated Care

Second Edition

Medical Family Therapy and Integrated Care

Second Edition

Susan H. McDaniel, William J. Doherty, and Jeri Hepworth

American Psychological Association • Washington, DC

Published by
American Psychological Association
750 First Street, NE
Washington, DC 20002
www.apa.org

To order
APA Order Department
P.O. Box 92984
Washington, DC 20090-2984
Tel: (800) 374-2721; Direct: (202) 336-5510
Fax: (202) 336-5502; TDD/TTY: (202) 336-6123
Online: www.apa.org/pubs/books
E-mail: order@apa.org

In the U.K., Europe, Africa, and the Middle East, copies may be ordered from
American Psychological Association
3 Henrietta Street
Covent Garden, London
WC2E 8LU England

Typeset in Goudy by Circle Graphics, Inc., Columbia, MD

Printer: United Book Press, Inc., Baltimore, MD
Cover Designer: Mercury Publishing Services, Inc., Rockville, MD

The opinions and statements published are the responsibility of the authors, and such opinions and statements do not necessarily represent the policies of the American Psychological Association.

Library of Congress Cataloging-in-Publication Data

McDaniel, Susan H.
  [Medical family therapy]
  Medical family therapy and integrated care / Susan H. McDaniel, William J. Doherty, and Jeri Hepworth. — Second edition.
     pages cm
  Revision of aut
  Includes bibliographical references and index.
  ISBN 978-1-4338-1518-8 — ISBN 1-4338-1518-4 1. Family psychotherapy. 2. Family medicine. 3. Sick—Family relationships. 4. Sick children—Family relationships. I. Doherty, William J. (William Joseph), 1945- II. Hepworth, Jeri, 1952- III. Title.

  RC488.5.M3928 2014
  616.89'156—dc23
                                              2013005537

British Library Cataloguing-in-Publication Data

A CIP record is available from the British Library.

Printed in the United States of America
First Edition

http://dx.doi.org/10.1037/14256-000

This book is lovingly dedicated to our families,
close and extended, and especially
from Susan to David, Hanna, and Marisa Siegel;
from Bill to Leah Doherty, Eric Doherty,
and Elizabeth Doherty Thomas; and
from Jeri to Robert, Jon, and Katie Ryder

CONTENTS

FOREWORD

By the early 1990s, a generation of medical practitioners had responded to the crippling problem of fragmentation in our health care system, which partitioned people into ever smaller parts, organ by organ, for treatment by specialists and subspecialists. These practitioners had responded by creating and then practicing primary care, which was supposed to heal this fragmentation by practicing in breadth, across these fractures and rifts. Fifteen years earlier, George Engel had introduced the biopsychosocial model, which established a firm conceptual basis for understanding and treating people as whole persons— bodies, minds, families, communities, and all. In 1994, the Institute of Medicine published a defensible definition of primary care, described to be "practiced in the context of family and community." Yet this ideal was mostly beyond our reach. We were training and practicing with behavioral teachers and clinicians, with psychologists and psychiatrists and family therapists, but the clinicians, teachers, and scientists on each side of this chasm found the concepts and methods of the other to be strange and difficult to use. So many medical problems were so obviously affected by psychological and family factors! So many family predicaments and psychological problems were accompanied by physical symptoms! And yet the seamless integration of each into the other eluded us.

We could make good use of each other, but we weren't actually standing and working on common ground.

Then the first edition of *Medical Family Therapy* appeared in 1992, and it was a revelation. For the first time, therapists could see how "their" concepts and principles of treatment could be applied to medical problems. And conversely, physicians could see for the first time how psychological and systemic family concepts and principles of treatment could be incorporated into the fabric of the care they rendered. This book made it possible for these disciplines to find each other and to forge a partnership that immensely improved the care that was possible. Primary care was augmented. Medical care in general was broadened. Family therapy and medical psychology found potent new applications. The book enjoyed a well-deserved worldwide success and is in widespread use today.

But the world has changed in two decades. Researchers have extensively studied the interplay between the biomedical and the psychosocial domains; they have learned many new things about family influences on health, and vice versa. We know much more about the details of molecular, genomic, and genetic medicine, and the workings of the brain, than we did 20 years ago. We also see new fractures between members of health care teams, between the health care system and the communities in which patients live, and between patients and the larger health care system. These divides could benefit from the same principles that bring medical and psychological clinicians together. We live in a different world today, one in which the cost of care, the value of care, the health of communities, and the patients' active participation in their own health care decisions have assumed new salience. As the world has changed, so have the three scholars who wrote the original *Medical Family Therapy*—they have grown with the times and have written a new, better *Medical Family Therapy*.

This second edition is a radically different book. It has been extensively rewritten—in some places, newly written. It is still a book written principally for psychotherapists who are interested in integrating the mind–body split, family therapists and those practicing from the psychosocial side of the river; it is still a book that hews more to general principles than specific theoretical orientations; it is still a book that heals fragmentation. But this edition addresses modern and emerging problems such as genetics, brain function, and the health care crisis and the reform efforts afoot. It interprets the recent evidence bolstering the clinical, economic, and population bases for integration and community engagement.

And just as in 1992, *Medical Family Therapy* is a revelation today. It borrows and repurposes modern strategies, skills, and techniques and applies them across a clearly demarcated zone of emphasis, so that practicing therapists can apply these principles immediately and intelligently, and so that educators and learners can easily translate current theoretical orientations into useful skills. But as before, there is much here also for the practicing "medical" clinician. Here he or she will find a justification for thinking systemically, a reason for considering factors outside the patient's skin as important as those inside, an impetus for working collaboratively in teams, an inspiration to expand one's personal skill set beyond the biomedical, and an actual blueprint for what must be done to transform our broken health care system into something whole and healthy. Virtually every patient with a chronic medical illness will benefit from the principles elaborated here, and from the services of a medical family therapist. The medical family therapist can be a guide for navigating the complex health care system, and an interpreter of it. But this book is not just a manual for how to practice better health care; it is also a contribution to the transformation of medicine. This is an enormous gift to the field of medicine and the world of health care. Thank you.

Frank V. deGruy, MD, MSFM
Professor and Chair of Family Medicine, University of Colorado at Denver; President of the North American Primary Care Research Group

Macaran Baird, MD
Past President of the Society of Teachers of Family Medicine; Professor and Chair of Family Medicine, University of Minnesota

Thomas Campbell, MD
Past President of the Association of Departments of Family Medicine; Professor and Chair of Family Medicine, University of Rochester

Robert Cushman, MD
President of the Collaborative Family Health Care Association; Professor and Chair of Family Medicine, University of Connecticut

PREFACE TO THE FIRST EDITION

In this book, we propose a new paradigm for the biopsychosocial treatment of patients and their families who are dealing with health issues. Our commitment to the practice we now call "medical family therapy" dates back to the late 1970s and early 1980s. During that time period, we all worked to apply the systems concepts, developed in family therapy to the world of modern medical care. In addition to being involved in family therapy training, each of us was teaching through the 1980s at a medical school in a department of family medicine. Much of our attention focused on expanding the view of the family physicians we taught and helping them to incorporate the needs and concerns of families and other relevant systems (such as other medical specialists or social agencies) into their thinking and patient care. In this book we turn our attention to our fellow therapists by offering a new model for working with the impact of health problems on patients and families. This is the first book for therapists that describes a family systems approach to a broad range of medical issues that occur at the interface between biology and family dynamics.

This book extends our prior work into the arena of family therapy. William Doherty's collaboration with family physician Macaran Baird resulted in the landmark 1983 book, *Family Therapy and Family Medicine*. Susan McDaniel, family physician Thomas Campbell, and family therapist David Seaburn worked especially to develop the pragmatics of family-oriented medical care. This resulted in a 1990 book for medical providers, entitled *Family-Oriented Primary Care*. Jeri Hepworth has developed important ideas about collaboration between physicians and therapists, which have been published in journal form. She also started a family therapy internship in her family medicine department. This experience, and those shared by Susan and Bill in their training capacities, led to our desire to develop our ideas about family systems, medical illness, and the medical system specifically for other therapists.

Our experiences as both medical educators and family therapy trainers have allowed us to identify the unique opportunities for family systems-oriented therapists to assist families with health problems. The audience for this book consists of family therapists, psychologists, behavioral medicine specialists, medical and psychiatric social workers, psychiatric nurses, and psychiatrists. Although primary care physicians and nurses may benefit, the strategies and techniques are intended primarily for therapists who are fully trained in family systems therapy.

Some colleagues and trainees have reacted to our interest in this area with caution and not a little skepticism. When one of us accepted a job in family medicine, more than one therapist colleague said, "Why in the world would you want to go and hang out with all those doctors?" When it comes to trying to collaborate with a physician on a case, the common complaint by therapists is that these doctors can never be reached and seem uninterested in coordinated treatment plans. The fascinating experience for each of us is that physicians make the same complaints about working with therapists! Some of these physicians do question whether psychotherapy does anyone any good, but most all of them complain that therapists are unresponsive to referrals. ("We never hear one word from them after we send a patient.") Hearing these two sides of the story is something like hearing from one spouse and then another, in a marital dispute.

What is not disputed is the need for patients and families to receive better and more comprehensive medical care. Soaring costs and the advent of new technologies for diagnosis and treatment have resulted in fragmented, specialized, and impersonal care in too many circumstances. Patients and families often feel lost in the maze of the medical system at a time when they feel the most vulnerable. Consumer groups have become increasingly vocal in their complaints. In response, the primary care disciplines of pediatrics, internal medicine, and especially family medicine have begun to develop a biopsychosocial approach to the common medical concerns of their patients. While these medical groups have groped their way towards a biopsychosocial framework, many therapists have lagged behind, staying focused on issues narrowly considered "psychosocial". This book is designed to help therapists advance with this broader movement in health care.

As we discuss in the early chapters of the book, family therapists have a tremendous opportunity to play a significant role in the changing world of health care delivery. When patients and their families face problems like chronic illness, infertility, or cancer, collaboration between family therapists and medical providers can result in more personal, more effective, and more comprehensive care. We hope this book will open dialogue and focus more attention on how therapists can productively participate in and influence the health care system. We want to encourage more research on the interaction between emotional and interpersonal process and biomedical events. And, finally, we seek to stimulate more innovation and clinical study of how people respond to illness and how they might use it, as family therapist Donald Williamson suggests, as a "call to consciousness" (1991, p. 229).

A word about the term "medical family therapy". We use the word "medical" to convey a focus on health problems such as chronic illness, disability, and health behaviors. We use "family therapy" to emphasize the family systems framework that informs our model. This label is consistent with other disciplines such as "medical anthropology" or "medical social work". However convenient and descriptive, the label is not without ambiguity. We do not wish to convey that medical family therapy is ordinarily practiced by physicians or that it necessarily involves prescribing medications. Nor do we wish in any way to exclude our family nursing colleagues who do not identify with the word "medical". ("Health care family therapy" seems cumbersome and ambiguous.) So, we conclude that "medical family therapy" is the best term to define what it is we do.

This book represents a genuinely collaborative project. We jointly planned and brainstormed about the contents of each chapter, debated ideas, and took individual responsibility for first drafts of different chapters. We reviewed, revised, and enlarged on each others' chapters, which often resulted in another round of excitement and debate that allowed us to define our joint vision. As an aside, this level of collaboration would have been impossible for three people living in New York, Minnesota, and Connecticut before the advent of electronic mail. We "spoke" to each other an average of once a day, and often more, during the project. This communication allowed us to attend to the details of writing, as well as the development of ideas in a way that was practical, effective, efficient, and, we might add, fun.

Thanks to our families who understand our enthusiasm for this work and cheer us along from the sidelines. We want to extend particular thanks to the medical providers with whom we have shared joys, tears, and challenges, and the patients and families who allowed us into their lives during painful times. It was these two groups, the medical providers and the families, who taught us what we now know about medical family therapy.

PREFACE TO THE SECOND EDITION

Two years after our book *Medical Family Therapy: A Biopsychosocial Approach to Families with Health Problems* came out, the United States plunged into the troubled waters of health care reform.[1] It was 1994, the year in which the U.S. Congress deliberated on Hillary Clinton's health care plan, and there were high expectations across the land that the nation's fractured health care system would be overhauled, expanded to include everyone in the country, and generally fixed.

On a cold January day in 1994, the three of us sat in front of the huge, two-story fireplace in the warm living room of Wingspread, a Frank Lloyd Wright–designed house-turned-conference-center in Racine, Wisconsin. We were talking excitedly with a dozen or so other therapists, physicians, and health care administrators who had convened for the Wingspread Conference on Collaborative Health Care. We were plotting a radical new way to take care of sick people—one that married modern medicine with the interpersonal

---

[1]Ideas in this preface first appeared in "Fixing Health Care: What Role Will Therapists Play?" by W. J. Doherty, May–June 2007, *Psychotherapy Networker*, 46, pp. 24–31.

skills of psychotherapy for improved outcomes at lower costs—and it seemed that the revolution was upon us.

We had been working with primary care physicians for more than a decade. In crossing the ocean from family therapy to the land of primary care medicine, we had discovered something that never came up in our training: People have bodies. We knew, of course, that people came with penises and vaginas (sex therapy was a required course), but even the brain was more the province of psychology than biology. Other organs such as livers, lungs, and hearts—well, these never came up in our PhD programs. When we did family genograms, we documented every cutoff and enmeshment known to Murray Bowen but left off the cancers and heart attacks passed down through the generations. In short, we never met a medical diagnosis in school or in early practice.

Another shock from working in a medical setting was that patients often don't get better, no matter what the treatment. We recalled a case with a frustrated medicine resident in which therapy helped a young woman with serious Crohn's disease handle her disease more constructively and develop a better relationship with her family. Ultimately, the patient did get along better with her family, and she did take better care of herself, but she died anyway. The therapist remembered his dismay when her mother called him to give him the news. He felt like a failure until the mother told him that the last months of her daughter's life were the most peaceful she'd spent in many years, thanks to the therapy, and that she and her husband were grateful that their frayed relationship with their daughter had healed before she died. The therapist was relieved to hear all of this, yet couldn't stop thinking about that old line: The surgery succeeded, but the patient died. Nonetheless, he became a different therapist that day, a more humble one. Up until then, he had thought that therapy, especially systems therapy, could "cure" anything—school-refusing kids would go to class, a depression would lift, and a couple would find sustained happiness.

THE BENEFITS OF INTEGRATIVE, SYSTEMIC HEALTH CARE

Nonetheless, from the beginning of our work as medical family therapists, we saw everyday benefits—and sometimes dramatic payoffs—from considering ailments from both a psychosocial and physical perspective. There was a 9-year-old boy with severe headaches who had received every diagnostic test in the world, yet no cause had been discovered. One of us met with his parents and physician to explore the context of his attacks. More history revealed that the headaches came on when he was worried or frustrated within his peer group. The tension left the room with this revelation. The therapist gave them a few tips about how the son could notice and manage his feelings and how the parents could help him talk about his inner experience so he didn't have to communicate through headaches, and that's all it took for attacks to disappear. Jay Haley would have been proud! But this was one of the rare, uncomplicated cases.

Most people who frequent medical clinics live with problems that are permanent companions, not episodic visitors easily banished. Along the way, they pick up a gaggle of health care providers who are often frustrated because these patients don't take care of themselves well enough, take up too much time, and cost too much money. We learned that the biggest thing we could do for patients was to help them live better with the hand of cards they'd been dealt. We also learned that the biggest thing we could do for physicians was to help support them in their stress so they could acknowledge their common humanity with their patients and help them be on the same team.

Most of us working in medical family therapy in those days had the luxury of being in academic centers and, therefore, buffered to some extent from the financial constraints of everyday medicine. In this hothouse environment, we knew we had developed a great new way of working in collaboration with medical and nursing professionals but sometimes wondered whether it could succeed in the real world.

But by 1994, medical family therapy was being well received, and a bright future was unfolding in local initiatives across the country, in places like HealthPartners in Minnesota, with its integrative care system, and the Cooperative Care Clinic of the Permanente Medical Group in Colorado, with its group medical visits. We were creating a new combination of steel and soul, joining the dazzling technologies of scientific medicine with the more nuanced power of behavioral and family systems approaches. Many of the beneficiaries were patients whose chronic problems—diabetes, cancer, obesity, asthma, chronic pain, and fibromyalgia—straddled the threshold between the physical and emotional worlds. Others faced terminal illnesses, and, there, too, the evidence was mounting that psychosocial interventions could improve physical health. We knew, for example, about research at Johns Hopkins showing that a family intervention improved blood pressure control and reduced mortality (Morisky, Levine, Green, Shapiro, Russell, & Smith, 1983) and improved diabetic control (Gilden, Hendryx, Casia, & Singh, 1989). We also knew about Regier's classic finding that primary care is the de facto mental health treatment system in the United States because it's where most people with mental problems go (Regier, Narrow, Rae, Manderscheid, Locke, & Goodwin, 1993; see updated review by Kessler & Stafford, 2008). Armed with this hard-earned knowledge, we now had good reasons to hope for major changes, which would extend far beyond our own limited experiments with integrated, systemic care. It was becoming increasingly obvious that the technology-driven, highly medicalized system as it existed was badly broken. Health care costs were inflating by double digits per year in the early 1990s. Yet there were nearly 40 million people with little or no access to basic medical health care and another 70 million with inadequate insurance. Individual citizens were spending about 14% of their income on health care—up from 9% in 1970 and nearly twice what citizens of other developed countries were spending. Americans were spending the most for medical care of any developed country without showing greater benefits in key indicators, such as infant mortality and life expectancy (Starr, 2011). There seemed to be a general consensus that our "health care system"—an unsystematic, partially regulated hodgepodge of government programs, private insurance, and free market anarchy—was cracking under the weight of high costs and fragmentation.

Democrats and Republicans agreed on the need for an overhaul, and 2 months before our conference at Wingspread, Hillary Clinton's health care bill had finally been presented to Congress on the last day of the session. Significant national change was on the way.

At the Wingspread conference, we were ebullient. Those of us who'd worked for years at the interface of medicine and psychotherapy were sure a new age was dawning. Not only would we soon see a new kind of system emerge—universal and integrated, patient and family centered, delivered by teams of therapists, physicians, nurses, and other professionals—we'd also help end the stifling, insurance-dominated approach to healing that combined the disadvantages of capitalism (hypercompetition, profits over people), with socialism's lack of competition, cost controls, and accountability. Our new model, we were sure, would keep people healthier—and at a far lower cost—than what had come before. We remembered Lyman Wynne, one of the founders of family therapy, saying at the final session of the conference, "I haven't felt this way since those first conferences in the 1950s when family therapy was being created." It all made perfect sense, and it was bound to sweep away all the obstacles in its path.

THE RUDE AWAKENING

Then we had our pie-in-the-face moment. By September 1994, Hillary Clinton's health care reform plan, fashioned by the best and brightest minds in health care and mandating universal coverage through the private sector, crashed and burned. The debate had been extensive and extreme (like the 2010 debate on health care reform would be more than a decade later). And then, of course, there were the infamous Harry and Louise ads developed by the health insurance industry's lobbying arm, the Health Insurance Association of America, which eroded the public's support for the proposed reform. In his postmortem, Paul Starr (2004), a key developer of the plan, summed up the roller-coaster experience: "It was one year from euphoria to defeat. . . . The collapse of health care reform in the first two years of the Clinton administration will go down as one of the great lost political opportunities in American history" (pp. 20–21).

In November 2004, a new conservative majority in Congress came in with a goal of limiting government and decreasing industry regulations. Right in step, HMOs and managed care companies threw their energies into cost containment, separating, as usual, mental and physical health. Instead of folding mental health care into physical health care to create an entirely new and effective healing system, the health industry outsourced—or "carved out"—mental health care to control costs. Mental health care was increasingly defined by payers as a nice, but not strictly necessary, frill that might improve quality of life or enhance the marriages or personal growth of those who could afford it, but it certainly didn't have much to do with real, life-and-death medical matters, like liver transplants, dialysis, or the amputation of the gangrenous limbs of people with diabetes.

Physicians, particularly primary care physicians who don't make much money on tests and procedures, became increasingly embattled and discouraged. Many abandoned private practice when large health systems made them offers they couldn't refuse. Physicians' incomes lost ground to inflation while expectations for productivity (patients per hour) increased. Starting in the mid-1990s, all but one family practice group in Minneapolis sold itself to a larger care organization because they couldn't sustain the expenses of practice in an era of reduced compensation. The one holdout, by the way, was the happiest group of practitioners on the scene, but they too succumbed to the cost pressures in 2010 and joined a large system.

Meanwhile, people with chronic diseases continued to receive expensive, high-tech, but often subpar care. Their medical illnesses like diabetes were often accompanied by depression and "problems of compliance"; they didn't change their diets, monitor their blood sugar, and make other changes that their doctors recommended. Typically, these noncompliant patients became depressed, continued to eat badly, watched their blood sugar skyrocket, started to lose their toes, and finally were referred to therapists who might help with the depression but knew nothing about managing diabetes. The result of this piecemeal care was that patients might feel less depressed, but their diabetes usually got worse, eventually costing the care system and the economy tons of money in progressive surgeries, heart attacks, amputations, and intensive treatment for eyes going blind.

All of this led to higher health care costs and to additional efforts to curtail costs in the system, especially for the poor, by cutting services. The uninsured remain out in the cold entirely, until they show up in emergency rooms with severe, sometimes terminal, and always costly complications from their undertreated or entirely untreated chronic conditions.

With the federal government on the sidelines from 1994 to the 2010 health care reform law, the pharmaceutical industry became the dominant player in health care, without, by the way, producing much in the way of true innovation. In their 2005 book, *Selling Sickness: How the World's Biggest Pharmaceutical Companies Are Turning Us All Into Patients,* Moynihan and Cassels joined a chorus of critics arguing that in looking for ways to maximize markets, pharmaceutical companies "redefine more and more healthy people as sick" (p. 3). They argued that this is accomplished through an informal alliance between the drug companies and some medical and patient advocacy groups who want to legitimize the conditions they care about.

Big Pharma has made big money in two other ingenious ways: by keeping drugs on patent by changing a molecule or two of an old formulation and then slapping a new name on them, and by direct-to-consumer advertising of prescription drugs: The breakthrough purple pill advertisement with the woman dancing around with the colorful scarf turned out to be for Prilosec (for acid reflux), which soon became one of the top three prescription drugs in the country. Or consider the hunky-looking middle-aged guys in TV ads improbably suffering from erectile dysfunction and craving Viagra, not to mention the dramatic increase in psychotropic prescriptions for preschoolers during the early 1990s (Zito, Safer, dosReis, Gardner, Boles, & Lynch, 2000).

With most mental health treatment occurring in primary care medical offices, time-starved physicians were reaching for the prescription pad when in doubt about how to respond to the complex behavioral problems of children and adolescents. As the old saying goes, when your only tool is a hammer, you see a lot of nails.

Thus did the counterrevolution win out before the first shot was fired in the battle to change U.S. health care in the 1990s. The goal of medical family therapy to integrate health care struggled against the political and market pressures to fragment that care. In 2005, after reviewing the early failed attempts at health care reform, the Nobel Prize–winning economist and columnist Paul Krugman and his colleague Robin Wells summed up the situation: "The evidence clearly shows that the key problem with the U.S. health care system is its fragmentation" (Krugman & Wells, 2006).

A DREAM REBORN

The promise we felt at the 1994 conference at Wingspread lived on in small pockets around the country and is now gaining political and economic momentum. The big difference today is that marketplace forces are calling for change and the U.S. federal government finally acted through the 2010 health care reform legislation, the Patient Protection and Affordable Care Act. Research is beginning to undercover the mechanisms by which the mind affects the body and relationships affect the immune system.

An unmistakable earlier signal of change occurred in 2005 at a small meeting of HMO leaders, state officials, and business executives in Seattle, Washington. At this meeting, sponsored by the Collaborative Family Healthcare Association (the organization launched at Wingspread), a benefits executive from Starbucks told the group, "This year we spent more for health care than for coffee beans." There were suppressed gasps in the room from everyone except the other benefits officers in attendance, who were nodding in agreement. Instead of being defensive, the HMO leaders concurred that their costs were out of control. The state officials, focused on both economics and public health, were as unhappy about the situation as the Starbucks executive.

What was remarkable wasn't the collective moaning but that all present agreed on the main problem: a care system that carves up people into pieces that separate professions or institutions are expected to treat, combined with a massive tilt toward expensive medical treatments. They also agreed that the large number of uninsured Americans was unconscionable, on both ethical and economic grounds, and that simply universalizing a flawed health care system would not solve the deeper problems.

Since then, companies such as General Motors have pleaded with Republican lawmakers for help with out-of-control health care costs, just so they can compete with industries in more enlightened countries with national health insurance. Employers, it turns out, never signed on to be the pack mules carrying skyrocketing health care costs; it happened almost by accident in the early years of World War II, when a few companies got around mandated wage freezes by offering health insurance to their employees. The trend established in those years didn't start reversing until the mid-2000s when blue states such as Massachusetts and red states like Tennessee began experimenting with forms of universal health care, this time in a much simpler form than the Clinton plan. In February 2007, Walmart CEO Lee Scott and Service Employees International Union President Andrew Stern held a press conference calling for the virtual scrapping of the employer-based health care system, accompanied by the development of a universal health care plan.

It isn't just private business and states worrying and agitating for change. The federal Medicare program faces a crisis acknowledged by liberals and conservatives alike. This tsunami is just offshore: the baby boom generation began to turn 65 in 2011, and the fastest growing age group in the country is those ages 85 and older. Medicaid, administered by the federal and state governments, is also heading for major problems because of long-term care of the elderly.

Another impetus for change is that we are now seeing a public backlash against the biggest single source for escalating costs: Big Pharma, the most profitable business in the United States and the most profligate contributor to political campaigns (Angell, 2004; Kassirer, 2005). Ironically, just when some therapists were coming to accept the hegemony of the pharmaceutical industry, the public has started to sour on the promise of a pill for every problem. The public's disillusionment with the pharmaceutical industry may have started because more people are becoming aware of just how much they're being exploited for profit. According to a Harris Interactive poll, public confidence in drug companies is extremely low, in the ballpark with that in tobacco and oil companies (Taylor, 2010). Note the discontinuation of hormone-replacement therapy for women following the revelation that the medicines were linked to breast cancer (Chlebowski et al., 2010), and the decline in SSRI prescriptions for children and adolescents after reports that they caused increased suicidal thinking (National Institute of Mental Health, 2012).

The second monster wave on the health care horizon, in addition to the aging population, is the growing obesity problem among children and youth and its devastating health consequences. What used to be called *adult-onset diabetes* is becoming a disease of the obese young, with potentially grave consequences for their future health (e.g., potential blindness, limb amputations, and kidney failure before they reach middle age). If we do not figure out a way to quell the spread of obesity in our children, they could comprise the first generation in modern history to live shorter, less healthy lives than their parents.

By around 2006, the tide was clearly turning on health care reform (Starr, 2011). A combination of frustration with the current health care system and worry about the future led to the Accountable Care Act, the federal health care legislation of 2010, which passed with an intensely divided Congress and country. It was not until the presidential election of 2012 that it became clear the health care reform law would remain in effect. However, even universal health care plans, vitally important for social justice, won't work well or efficiently if they only bring everyone into another version of the expensive and fragmented system we now have, which neglects whole persons in favor of their disparate parts. The challenge for the new health care reform environment is to create a new care-delivery model, not just a new payment model.

One promising development that is likely to have legs in health care reform is the *patient-centered medical home* (also called the *medical home* or *health care home*, our preferred term). This is an approach to primary care in which generalists and specialists, patients and families work in partnership to improve health outcomes and quality of life for people living with chronic health conditions and disabilities. These health care homes will involve close coordination among providers and with patients and families, with payment models providing incentives for integration instead of fragmentation. They are envisioned as a principal means to deliver on what Berwick has famously called the "triple aim" of health care: improved population health, lower per capita costs, and improved individual patient experience of health care (Berwick, Nolan, & Whittington, 2008). Although currently the health care home model has not emphasized integrated behavioral health services like medical family therapy, it will have to if it is to live up to its promise (Edwards, Patterson, Vakili, & Scherger, 2012).

RETOOLING FOR THE NEW HEALTH CARE SYSTEM

So how can an enlightened therapist hook up with the new promise for the health care system that will be taking shape over the next 20 years? A first step is getting ourselves educated on the pressure points in health care—the intractable problems such as high costs and low overall quality about which there's an emerging consensus that collaborative teams of medical and mental health professionals can make the kind of difference that may save the entire health care system (Edwards et al., 2012). The next step is to network in our local communities. This book aims to help therapists with the transition that will take us from being pigeonholed as mental health providers into being vital members of health care teams.

This new edition of *Medical Family Therapy* is a different book from its predecessor, given the many developments in the field in the 20 years since we wrote the first edition. Foundational chapters were redrafted from scratch, with older material retained only if it was equally relevant to the current clinical environment. These include the overview of the field (Chapter 1); clinical strategies (Chapter 2); collaboration (Chapter 3); health behaviors (Chapter 7); pregnancy loss, infertility, and reproductive technologies (Chapter 9); children (Chapter 10); somatizing patients (chapter 11); and caregiving and end of life (Chapter 13). New chapters include the shared experiences of illness when therapists have personal or family experience with the illness of their patient (Chapter 4), community engagement (Chapter 6), medical family therapy with couples (Chapter 8), genetics and genomics (Chapter 12), and the future of medical family therapy (Chapter 14). A new appendix profiles the practices of a number of medical family therapists.

Regardless of the next phase of health care planning and reform, learning about society's health care pressure points and developing collaborative relationships with medical professionals can't possibly hurt any therapist's practice. And it just might mean a new, flourishing career on the creative edge of health care. This book is our contribution to that hope.

ACKNOWLEDGMENTS

First, we would like to thank Susan Reynolds, who first took this project on and shepherded it through at APA Books. Special thanks to our reviewers, Jennifer Hodgson, Angela Lamson, and Nancy Ruddy, and our editor, Tyler Aune, whose suggestions contributed to improving this volume.

Along the way, many people helped us put the book together. We thank Susan McDaniel's assistant, Jeanne Klee, who helped (amazingly) with both the first and the second editions. We are indebted to Jennifer Samson for her outstanding work putting together the references for this second edition.

As always, we thank our patients and families, our colleagues, and our students, who helped to shape the ideas represented here, as well as our own families, who supported us through the years we've spent revising this text.

A special note to acknowledge what a stimulating treat it is to work together over these many years as we've identified medical family therapy and seen the approach blossom and grow. Continuity matters in relationships, whether it is psychotherapy, medicine, or scholarship. For this continuity, we are all grateful.

Medical Family Therapy and Integrated Care

Second Edition

I

FOUNDATIONS OF MEDICAL FAMILY THERAPY

1

AN OVERVIEW OF MEDICAL FAMILY THERAPY

The fundamental assumption behind medical family therapy is that all health and relationship problems are biological, psychological, and social in nature. There are no psychosocial problems without biological features, and there are no biomedical problems without psychosocial features. Stated differently, all therapeutic issues involve complex systems dynamics at the biological, psychological, interpersonal, institutional, community, societal, cultural, and environmental levels. However, health care professionals are generally trained to look at problems through a narrower lens—their favorite system, as it were—leading to fragmented, ineffective, and less humane care.

Medical family therapy tries to break out of five "ecosystemic splits" that have hampered health care. The first split is between the mind and body— that is, mental health and physical health. The science showing the linkages between the brain and the rest of the body, and between psychosocial stress and support and a wide range of medical conditions, is now overwhelming

http://dx.doi.org/10.1037/14256-001
Medical Family Therapy and Integrated Care, Second Edition, by S. H. McDaniel, W. J. Doherty, and J. Hepworth

(Cohen, Janicki-Deverts, & Miller, 2007; Fagundes, Bennett, Derry, & Kiecolt-Glaser, 2011). Any professional who fails to appreciate the interconnections between, say, diabetes and depression or trauma and chronic pain is not practicing 21st-century health care. Unfortunately, most therapists are still trained narrowly in the mental health sphere and enter practice with little understanding of the vast interplay between medical problems and mental health.

The second split is between the individual and the family (or the sphere of intimate relationships). Many therapists who accept the unity of the mind and body and the inseparability of physical health and mental health, operate with little understanding the importance of families in health and illness. They see the family mainly as a context for the individual patient as opposed to a powerful interpersonal force field within which the patient lives and functions. At the clinical level, many therapists receive little systematic training to work with families. Once again, this split does not do justice to the science showing the strong links between family and other social relationships and nearly every dimension of health, illness, and health care (Cohen, 2004; Glaser & Kiecolt-Glaser, 2005), and the care of patients suffers when it is disconnected from their intimate sphere.

The third split is between the individual and family and institutional settings, especially health care systems. A systems-trained therapist understands that when someone has a chronic illness, the patient and family also have a chronic relationship with health care professionals. Furthermore, they understand that dynamics occurring within families, such as secrets and triangulation, can also play out in the relationships between families and health care teams (Imber-Black, 1988). Likewise, families can be caught up in disconnects and rivalries between health care professionals, but most therapists are not trained to assess how the dynamics of the provider system interact with family dynamics to create cooperation or impasses in treatment. Even systems-trained family therapists often do not have enough understanding of the medical provider system to collaborate with providers and families.

The fourth split occurs among the clinical, financial, and operational worlds of health care, reflecting the lack of what C. J. Peek (2008) called a "three-world view." Most health care professionals are trained in the clinical realm—what is clinically appropriate and effective for the people with whom we work. We leave the operational world—how the care system functions to deliver clinical services—to the managers. And we leave the financial world—how to pay for this work and keep the practice economically sustainable—to the CEOs and the accountants. Of course, private practice professionals have always had to attend to all three worlds, but employed clinicians tend to have a one-world view, as do managers and accountants.

Peek made the increasingly influential case that lasting health care innovations must reflect the demands and constraints of these three worlds or they are doomed. He also argued that at the clinical case level, the same principle applies: Effective care involves "clinical quality, good operational excellence, and good resource stewardship" (Peek, 2008, p. 25). The implication for medical family therapists is that they must take a truly systemic view of the health care settings they practice in and not assume that the logistical domains of health care are somebody else's business.

The final split is the fault line between the often insular world of clinical health care and the larger community world that includes neighborhood, culture, and larger institutions. Health care professionals tend to operate with limited knowledge of and capacity to work with "nonhealth" institutions, such as social services, cultural organizations, faith communities, and government and private insurance systems. Even systems-trained therapists are apt to see these groups mainly as influences on the individual patient and family and not as active participants in every aspect of health care in the community (Doherty & Mendenhall, 2006). Although more and more therapists are trained to be culturally sensitive, there is a big difference between appreciating, for example, how a Hmong patient and family might think about surgery and knowing which Hmong clan leaders to meet with during a late-term pregnancy crisis when the providers want to do a Cesarean delivery but the family sees this as a violation of the human body.

With all of these bifurcations in the world of health, the problem is both conceptual and pragmatic: How broadly and deeply do therapists and other health professionals *understand* a patient's problem and treatment options, and what *skills* do they bring to working across the domains of mind, body, family, health team, and community? Few therapists nowadays subscribe conceptually to the splits we have described; a moment of reflection suggests that health and illness are complex. The challenge for professionals is to develop clinical knowledge and practice skills across domains. Of course, no individual professional or professional specialty is going to be highly knowledgeable and skilled across all the domains we have outlined. To reduce the complexity of these issues to manageable levels, it's necessary to create areas of focus in professional work. Thus, most physicians will focus their energies more on biological issues than on family problems, most therapists will focus more on the psychosocial side of clinical problems, and most managers will know more about operational efficiency than therapy. Similarly, we will continue to make distinctions between family problems and psychological problems and physical problems. As practical as these distinctions may be for everyday discourse, they only represent ways that we "punctuate" the seamless web of human life; physical and psychosocial problems do not exist as discrete, boundaried domains of reality. Nor does culture exist outside of embodied individuals and families that create and transmit it. As Gregory Bateson (1979) emphasized, the map is not the territory.

The practical challenge, then, is not to create a superprofessional who can do it all but rather to *stretch all health professionals* to take into account the important roles of all domains of the human reality from cells to culture and beyond and to create *health care teams* that have the capacity for complex understanding and sophisticated skills across the domains. One of the aims of this book is to help therapists understand what it takes to work successfully in the emerging health care world of collaborative teams. However, much of the material we present will also be relevant to therapists working in typical mental health practices.

We wrote this book for therapists who want to be more intentional about how they incorporate into their clinical practice the experience of medical illness and their interactions with the medical treatment system. Hence the term *medical* in the title. For us, treating people with health challenges cannot be done without attention to the family system. Hence, the term *family* in *medical family therapy*. Medical family therapy is fundamentally a systemic, holistic approach that asserts that mind, body, relationships, and community all interact and affect one's health. In medicine, this approach is labeled *biopsychosocial*.

Medical family therapy as described here is a metaframework instead of a particular theory or model of therapy. That means that therapists will use their preferred clinical models (e.g., systemic therapies, cognitive behavior therapy, problem-solving therapy, emotion-focused therapy) within the principles and practices of medical family therapy. The case studies in the book illustrate only a subset of the techniques and skills that are possible within medical family therapy. While acknowledging that there is a growing number of professionals whose primary identity is that of *medical family therapist* because of their degree training, we use the term here in an inclusive way for any therapist who wants to take seriously the health and relational aspects of their patients' lives. Medical family therapists can have any license or title as long as they identify with the biopsychosocial, systemic approach we describe in this book. With this orientation, medical family therapists are especially suited for the emerging health care world with its emphasis on integrated, team-based care with shared systems and facilities. The patient is seen in the context of the family, the provider in the context of the larger team and the health care system, and all of them in the context of the wider community and culture.

In the rest of this chapter, we lay out the foundations of medical family therapy, touching on issues and themes to be elaborated more fully in the rest of the book.

FOUNDATIONS OF MEDICAL FAMILY THERAPY

As we have noted, medical family therapy is a form of professional practice that uses the biopsychosocial model and systemic family therapy principles in the collaborative treatment of individuals and families dealing with medical problems.

The Biopsychosocial Approach

In his classic article in the flagship journal *Science*, Engel (1977) threw down a gauntlet to the medical field by arguing that the biomedical model was unscientific because it lacked complexity. On the basis of general systems theory, the biopsychosocial model acknowledges the hierarchical, interdependent relationships of the biological, psychological, personal, family, and community and larger systems (see Figure 1.1). Not only does any medical condition affect multiple levels in the systems hierarchy, every treatment, even if it focuses on one level, reverberates across multiple systems. Heart bypass surgery, for example, focuses on the organ system, but the surgery also affects lower systems (tissues, cells) and higher systems (the person, the social system of the patient, and the institutional systems that pay for the surgery). When any part of a complex human system is treated with regular and systematic disregard for its relations with the rest of the system, then there is poor scientific understanding and grave problems in delivery health care (Doherty, Baird, & Becker, 1987; Engel, 1980). In addition to outlining the hierarchy of systems involved in health care, Engel suggested that there are similar systemic processes (isomorphisms) occurring across levels. In speeches, he would tell the personal story of how the disruptive biology of his own chronic medical condition was parallel to his psychological distress related to an earlier death in his family.

Since Engel's original formulation, a lot has been learned scientifically about how the mind and body interlock and influence each other. We now know how psychological stress influences cortisol levels, which in turn influence heart disease; we even know how stress translates at the cellular level into poorer immune functioning (Cohen et al., 2007). Similarly, marital functioning has been found to be connected to parameters of the immune system (Kiecolt-Glaser et al., 2005). At broader systems levels, social class and educational attainment, in particular, are now known to be strongly associated with physical health and mortality (Sturm & Gresenz, 2002). Essentially, we now know that Engel was right in broad outline; the work remaining is to develop more knowledge of the mechanisms of the connections across systems levels and to learn how to bring the biopsychosocial perspective more fully into the practice of health care.

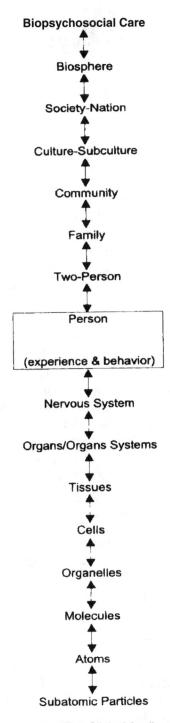

Biopsychosocial Care

↕

Biosphere

↕

Society-Nation

↕

Culture-Subculture

↕

Community

↕

Family

↕

Two-Person

↕

Person
(experience & behavior)

↕

Nervous System

↕

Organs/Organs Systems

↕

Tissues

↕

Cells

↕

Organelles

↕

Molecules

↕

Atoms

↕

Subatomic Particles

Figure 1.1. Systems Hierarchy. From "The Clinical Application of the Biopsychosocial Model," by G. L. Engel, 1980, *American Journal of Psychiatry, 137,* p. 537. Copyright 1980 by American Psychiatric Publishing. Reprinted with permission.

Systemic Family Therapy Principles

Medical family therapy is distinct from other forms of biopsychosocial practice by its use of *systemic family therapy principles* to understand and treat problems. If Engel's main contribution was to bring general systems theory to the broad spectrum of health care, the founders of family therapy in the 1950s applied general systems theory (von Bertalanffy, 1976) to the understanding of mental health and family relationships. They developed a rich set of systems concepts and clinical strategies that we assume are known to the reader (see Doherty & McDaniel, 2010, for a primer). Before the 1980s, there was relatively little scientific research on the fundamental tenets of family systems theory. Since then, however, researchers have begun to develop better measures of family systems dynamics such as cohesion, adaptability, alliances, coalitions, boundary problems, and other family dynamics related to well-being of individuals (Sperry, 2011). In particular, family systems theory has become a fertile ground for developmental psychologists in understanding how interactions at the family level influence adjustment at the individual level (McHale & Lindahl, 2011).

A more recent variant of systems theory is chaos theory or dynamical systems theory (Thelen & Smith, 1994). In addition to the standard systems idea of multiple interacting influences and emerging patterns, dynamical systems theory stresses the concept of nonlinear change—something major and sudden occurring that was not simply a function of a steady or linear change in a certain parameter. (A simple example of a *nonlinear* process is when water, which gradually heats at successive increases in temperature, suddenly boils at 99.97° Celsius.) Dynamical systems theories view persons and groups of person as complex systems like other complex turbulent systems in nature, such as weather patterns, the precise configurations of which cannot be fully predicted in advance. Medical family therapists who work with turbulent, complex family and provider systems find this kind of thinking appealing at an intuitive level. Among other things, awareness of nonlinear change can lead to not assuming major family pathology when families unravel after one more stress or "kick" in their system that sets them over the edge and to hope about possibility of sudden improvement in stuck family systems when they run into a patch of turbulence in their environment.

The core family therapy principle is a systems view of people and their relationships rather than a head count of the number of family members in the treatment room (Doherty & McDaniel, 2010). Family therapy brings concepts and treatment strategies that translate the sometimes-abstract world of general systems theory and the biopsychosocial model into terms that clinicians can apply in everyday practice. For example, a medical family therapist brings a unique set of conceptual and tactical tools to a situation when anxiety is reverberating back and forth between a patient and the family, and between the family and the physician, with the patient not sharing concerns directly with the physician who sees the family as critical and overreacting and then worries about being sued. Applied within an awareness of all levels of the biopsychosocial hierarchy, family therapy principles are a core dimension of medical family therapy.

Collaborative Care

Medical family therapy is inherently a *collaborative form of treatment*, even in situations in which the therapist is mainly working alone in providing therapy. Of course, it is collaborative with the patient and family who are the main agents of their own care. In addition, the medical family therapist is always aware of, and seeks to collaborate with, the other players in the life of a person with medical problems, including the health care professionals involved in the case. Nowadays these may be physicians, nurse practitioners, physician assistants, clinical pharmacists—whoever is actively involved in the care of the patient and family. In practice, this collaboration may range from simple information exchange to full team meetings. No professional has a complete perspective or full tool kit to deal with complex health problems, and without collaboration, patients and families get pulled, pushed, excluded, and often undermined in today's health care system (Blount, 1999).

Medical family therapists work with *individuals, couples, families, and extended family or intimate networks*. As we have emphasized, they see themselves as working systemically with individuals rather than taking off their medical family therapy "hat" because they are seeing an individual patient. When working with individuals, of course, they are apt to use tools from individual psychotherapy—for example, cognitive-behavioral therapy and hypnosis—but they are also operating with sensitivity to family and other systems. They look for opportunities to interact directly with those larger systems when it can benefit the patient. Of course, the hallmark of medical family therapy is the set of skills for convening and working collaboratively with families to promote the healing of the patient and the well-being of all family members.

Emphasis on Medical Problems

Finally, medical family therapy focuses on *medical problems*. Here we return to the problem of language. We are not suggesting that medical problems are a clear-cut category that differs from other problems that therapists treat. Everything is connected with everything else. However, *medical* is a commonly used term for conditions that with a strong biological base. People say, "I have a medical problem" for different issues than "I have a lot of emotional stress in my life" or "I have a family problem." To demarcate a zone of emphasis for medical family therapy (so that we don't suggest it is treatment for all human problems), we stress that medical family therapy focuses on problems traditionally treated by physicians and nurses who work in medical facilities, as opposed to mental health problems treated mainly in specialized mental health settings. In practice, the lines are more blurry, as when a medical family therapist works with individuals with schizophrenia who are also dealing with medical problems.

Overarching Goals for Medical Family Therapy

Much of the work of any therapist is to help clients achieve their particular goals for therapy. In medical family therapy, these idiosyncratic goals might take the form of better coping with a chronic illness or disability, less conflict about handling a medical regimen, better communication with physicians, more acceptance of a medical problem that cannot be cured, or help with making lifestyle changes. Underlying these particular goals are two more general objectives for medical family therapy: promoting agency and communion. These terms were first coined by Bakan (1966) in his book *The Duality of Human Existence* to denote two fundamental aspects of the human experience: the importance of the individual autonomy and self-assertion on the one hand and the importance of attachment and connectedness on the other.

Totman (1979) first used *agency* as a way to describe active involvement in and commitment to one's own health care. We expand it to mean the activation of the individuals and families to meet their needs related to health, illness and the health care system, and to contribute to their community. A strong sense of agency means making personal choices in dealing with illness and the health care system, both of which often contribute to feelings of passivity and lack of control. For professionals, promoting agency involves helping the patient and family set limits on the amount of control the illness or disability has over their lives, as in a decision to proceed with holiday celebrations despite the partial incapacitation of a family member. Other times it involves helping the family to negotiate for more information or better care arrangements with health professionals, hospitals, or insurance providers. Within the family itself, the therapist can promote the agency of the patient vis-à-vis other family members. This can take the form of boundary setting on family members' helpfulness or assertively asking for help, as when the caretaker of a person with Alzheimer's disease is coached on insisting on assistance from other family members. In a broader context, medical family therapists also promote the active involvement of individuals and families in their larger communities as contributors or citizens and not just recipients of services (see Chapter 7).

Communion refers to the emotional bonds that are often frayed by illness, disability, and contact with the health care system. It means the sense of being cared for, loved, and supported by family members, friends, and professionals. The quality of these social relationships appears to be the most powerful psychosocial factor in health and illness (Ranjan, 2011; Uchino, 2004). Serious illness or disability is an existential crisis for many people that can isolate them from those who care for them. One of the chief reasons for emphasizing the *family* part of medical family therapy is that serious illnesses and disabilities provide an opportunity for levels of healthy family bonding that the family may never have experienced before. Particularly during the acute phase of a life-threatening illness, family members may be emotionally available to one another in unaccustomed ways. However, during the chronic phase, many families deteriorate in their sense of common purpose and feeling. One of the medical family therapist's most important tasks is to help family members band together to cope with an illness and to do so within the context of allowing the patient maximum feasible autonomy and agency. Similarly, families who are dealing with catastrophic medical stressors, such as a child with a fatal form of degenerative muscular dystrophy, often need help in finding support groups of other families experiencing their problem. The sense of communion these groups provide cannot be matched in any other relationship. Sadly, however, parents are not generally given assistance in dealing with their own extended families, many of whom misunderstand and turn away emotionally from families with disabled or seriously ill members. Medical family therapists are ideally positioned to help with the sense of interpersonal communion among these families.

In a valuable extension of Bakan's original work on agency and communion, Helgeson (1994) argued not only that agency and communion are each necessary for human flourishing but also that when one exists in the absence of the other (lots of agency but little communion, or vice versa), negative health outcomes are the result. Helgeson summarized research related to gender differences to support the case that men tend to suffer negative health outcomes from exaggerated agency, and women, from exaggerated communion. As family therapists have argued for more than six decades, it is the balance of individuation and connection that promotes human well-being.

Because the health care system often strips patients of their sense of control over their bodies and behavior, it is important that medical family therapists hold the patient's autonomy as a high priority, even if the patient's decision is not to cooperate with treatment. However, this commitment to personal choice must be balanced with the relational nature of human life and illness: We do not live for ourselves alone, and personal agency is only one string on the musical chord that also contains communion with others. Medical family therapists who work every day with patients, family members, and health care professionals are well situated to advocate for the kind of balance in health care that the modern era makes so difficult to find.

The goals of agency and communion reflect our core value commitments as therapists. This work is not just about treating health problems; it's a way to approach human suffering. Any extended health crisis stirs up uncertainty and ambiguity and calls on the human capacities for agency and communion. The medical family therapist helps people respond to this call in the context of close relationships.

THE KNOWLEDGE BASE OF MEDICAL FAMILY THERAPY

Because medical family therapists operate in the biomedical–psychosocial overlap area of professional activity, they must acquire knowledge that is not generally accessible in their psychosocial systems training. Acquiring this knowledge in turn involves active learning from the work of other health professionals, biomedical scientists, and social scientists. Furthermore, because knowledge is changing rapidly in the biopsychosocial area, medical family therapists must be ongoing collaborators with physicians and other health professionals who were absent from their socialization as therapists, and ongoing readers of different kinds of professional literature, such as that in behavioral medicine. Next, we outline several areas of knowledge specific to medical family therapy.

Major Chronic Illnesses and Disabilities

Although medical family therapists are not expected to have detailed knowledge of the major chronic illness and disabilities, they should have an adequate working knowledge of basic biomedical facts and the resources to learn more when faced with specific cases. For the therapist to work meaningfully with families' medical problems, these problems must be more than "black boxes" to the therapist. Medical family therapists should become as informed as motivated patients are about their diseases. The list of diseases and disease complexes to be familiar with is not long; a basic list would include the following: diabetes; heart disease; hypertension; lung diseases such as asthma and emphysema; the major cancers; plus the most common degenerative diseases, such as Alzheimer's disease, multiple sclerosis, and the muscular dystrophies. Beyond these and several common disabilities such as cervical spinal cord injuries, the therapist should expect to read and consult with medical and nursing colleagues about the particular problems involved in specific cases. In addition to being acquainted with common medical problems, the medical family therapist should be informed about the major treatments and their psychosocial implications. The following statements illustrate the kinds of information that we believe a medical family therapist should have about common medical problems:

1. Hypertension generally has no symptoms and is therefore easy to ignore. Certain antihypertensive medications cause erectile dysfunction.
2. Diabetes mellitus Type I, which generally has an acute onset in childhood and adolescence, involves the failure of the pancreas to produce insulin, requiring lifelong insulin shots and careful attention to diet. It is often diagnosed in an emergency situation requiring hospitalization that is stressful for families.
3. Diabetes mellitus Type II used to be called *adult onset diabetes*, but that nomenclature changed with the rise of obesity among children and adolescence. It may or may not require supplementary insulin injections and can sometimes be controlled by weight loss and diet along with oral medications.
4. Multiple sclerosis often involves repeating periods of relapse and remission, and it involves emotional lability that may be independent of the patient's social situation at the moment.

To repeat an important point, a medical family therapist is not expected to have expert knowledge about common diseases but must know enough to be to work realistically with patients and families experiencing these problems. What a medical family therapist needs to know can be obtained from three overlapping sources: instruction from a physician or nurse, reading in medical encyclopedias and continuing education articles intended for primary care health professionals, and learning from patients and families, many of whom become quite expert on their health problems. For example, it was a woman with multiple sclerosis who first taught one of us about weepiness as part of the disease. "These tears are my disease talking," she said. "I'm actually doing pretty well today." Similarly, reading about genetic predispositions to breast cancer can disabuse a therapist of a simplistic belief that such cancers are caused mainly by a "cancer-prone personality."

Research in Behavioral Medicine and Other Social Sciences

Behavioral medicine has produced a significant body of research knowledge about health and illness since emerging as a specialty in psychology in the 1970s. Also called *health psychology*, this field, in combination with other traditional disciplines such as social epidemiology, medical sociology, medical anthropology, and nursing, offers bedrock information and perspectives for medical family therapy (Suls, Davidson, & Kaplan, 2010). Following is an outline of several areas that are particularly relevant to medical family therapy.

Stress and Illness

There is a voluminous body of literature attesting to the deleterious effects of psychosocial stress on physical illness (Antonovsky, 1979; Cohen et al., 2007). Fortunately, this body of work seems to have permeated the larger culture enough that patients and families are more apt to make the connection between life stress and biomedical problems.

Social Support and Health

As far back as the 1980s, House, Landis, and Umberson (1988) concluded in their review in the journal *Science* that there was enough research evidence to assert with confidence that social relationships are a central factor in health and mortality. In fact, the authors concluded that poor social support is a stronger predictor of mortality than cigarette smoking. The research has grown even stronger and more complex in subsequent decades (Uchino, 2004; Umberson & Martex, 2010).

Health Behaviors

Behavioral medicine and other researchers have documented the powerful role of health behaviors such as exercise and cigarette smoking in overall health and specific diseases (Glanz, Rimer, & Viswanath, 2008). A large number of main causes of deaths each year—heart disease, cancer, strokes, and pulmonary disease—are preventable with lifestyle changes (Danaei et al., 2009).

Cooperation With Medical Regimens

Lack of patient compliance with (or adherence to) medication and other prescribed regimens is a major cause of illness and mortality. A World Health Organization report (2003) concluded that "adherence to long-term therapy for chronic illnesses in developed countries averages 50%. In developing countries, the rates are even lower. It is undeniable that many patients experience difficulty in following treatment recommendations" (p. xiii). Behavioral medicine researchers have examined this issue in depth from psychological and behavioral perspectives.

Gender Issues in Health

Psychosocial issues in women's health became a major research interest in the 1970s and 1980s (Blechman & Brownell, 1988), followed by interest in men's health beginning in the 1990s (Payne, 2006). Women and men have special health issues and concerns about sexual and reproductive health, cancer, alcoholism, cigarette smoking, and care for ill family members. Lucy Candib (1999) and others (McDaniel & Cole-Kelly, 2003) have used a feminist perspective to examine the treatment of women and their families in the health care system.

As mentioned earlier, although behavioral medicine researchers have contributed substantially to the understanding of individual behavioral factors in health and illness, they have not paid as much attention to family issues. We now turn to the family research and theory literature, which offers the third base for knowledge in medical family therapy.

Family and Health Research

There is now a substantial body of research about families and health. In their book surveying this literature, Doherty and Campbell (1988) used the *family health and illness cycle* as a model for organizing the large body of work of research on families and health. The cycle delineates the phases of a family's experience with a health problem, beginning with family health promotion and risk reduction and moving to family adaptation to illness or recovery. Here we briefly outline the areas of research on families and health area that correspond to the phases of the family health and illness cycle.

Family Health Promotion and Risk Reduction

There is now widespread consensus that most health lifestyle behavior patterns are learned and sustained in families. Take the example of cigarette smoking: Smokers tend to be married to other smokers and to change their smoking patterns together (Franks, Peinta, & Wray, 2002). Furthermore, quitting smoking has been found to spread as a position social contagion through families and social networks (Christakis & Fowler, 2007). In terms of readiness to change a variety of health behaviors, spouses are more confident if their partner is also more confident about the change each wants to make in areas such as weight loss and exercise (Franks et al., 2012).

Family Vulnerability and Illness Onset or Relapse

The most widely used measurement of psychosocial stress, the Holmes–Rahe Social Readjustment Scale (Holmes & Rahe, 1967) contains a weighted list of 50 stressful events that require life readjustment by individuals.

No fewer than 10 of the 15 most stressful events are family events, such as divorce, death of a spouse, and major change in health of a family member. Biopsychosocial research has begun to find biological markers for family stress. Kiecolt-Glaser et al. (2005) found that lower marital satisfaction is associated with poor immune system responses. As documented in a review by Troxel and Matthews (2004), there is increasing evidence that marital stress and conflict lead to physiological changes that are associated with increased illness. In a classic early study of this phenomenon, Gottman and Katz (1989) showed that children's stress hormone levels (specifically, cortisol levels) were calibrated to the level of marital distress in their parents.

Family Illness Appraisal

In the family sciences, more and more attention has been paid to families' beliefs about health events. Families tend to have their own "epidemiology," based on their experience with certain illnesses, their relationship with the health care professionals, and their level of education about health issues. Family health activities such as visiting a physician tend to flow from complex consultative processes in which family members share their beliefs and expectations about a family member's symptoms. Since the first edition of this book, there has been important work on health beliefs and their role in healing families and illness. Wright, Watson, and Bell (1996) examined the interacting roles of patient beliefs, family beliefs and health care professional beliefs in shaping the experience of illness and the possibilities of healing. Others have focused on the intersection between family beliefs and culture (Marshall et al., 2011).

Family Acute Response

Family acute response refers to research on families' reactions to the immediate onset of a disease or disability, such as a heart attack, a diagnosis of cancer, or a cervical spinal cord injury. Families at this stage of a serious illness tend to become more cohesive immediately following a potentially fatal episode of a family member (Steinglass, Temple, Lisman, & Reiss, 1982). This is a time in which medical family therapists sometimes become involved with the family, especially if the therapist is working directly in a medical setting where the acute reaction is occurring. Because of difficulties getting access to families in the acute stage, there is little research to guide clinical interventions.

Family Adaptation to Illness or Recovery

This is the phase that medical family therapists are most apt to become involved with. Whereas many families handle the acute phase of an illness well, they are apt to find the chronic, readjustment phase more problematic. A large body of research has examined how families cope with realigned roles, new interaction patterns, changed social support, and the ongoing stressors of family life (Patterson & Garwick, 1994). For example, Rainville, Dumon. Simard, and Savard (2012) documented the levels of distress among adolescents of parents with advanced cancer. Recent research has focused on family strengths and resiliency while living with illness (Buchbinder, Longhofer, & McCue, 2009). Understanding the constraints and opportunities faced by families with chronic illness is a cornerstone of medical family therapy.

This section has summarized the areas of empirical research that undergird medical family therapy. The next sections cover several of the major theoretical models that have provided foundations for medical family therapy and emerging developments in other areas that have an impact on the work of medical family therapists.

Systems Theories About Families and Health

We begin with the pioneering contribution in family systems and medical issues, Minuchin, Rosman, and Baker's (1978) psychosomatic family model. This work was based on structural family therapy theory and clinical and research observations of families of children with uncontrolled childhood diabetes for whom "organic" explanations had been ruled out. Minuchin's team proposed that these psychosomatic families were characterized by patterns of enmeshment, overprotection, rigidity, poor conflict resolution, and triangulation of the child. Although this model has sometimes been misunderstood to imply that the family patterns "cause" the disease, the psychosomatic family model posits a circular process in which the family patterns and the disease mutually maintain each other (B. Wood et al., 1989). This model was given initial research support in a study by Minuchin et al. (1978), which showed a link between family interaction and blood glucose levels in certain diabetic children. Although there were methodological problems with this original study, Wood and colleagues (1989) later found support for some elements of the psychosomatic family model, particularly triangulation and marital dysfunction, in accounting for disease activity in children with Crohn's disease.

A second area of theory for medical family therapy derives from the work of David Reiss, Peter Steinglass, and colleagues at George Washington University. With theory and research that began with mental illness and the hospital environment and alcoholism, these scholars have shown how families become organized around health problems. Reiss (1981) and Reiss, Gonzalez, and Kramer (1986) described how the family's paradigm for coordination is an important factor in its ability to handle serious illness and relationships with the health care system. *Coordination* refers to the family members' level of readiness to experience themselves as a single unity, especially in times of stress. Steinglass's model of the alcoholic family (Steinglass, Bennett, Wolin, & Reiss, 1987) has proved useful in conceptualizing how families with other chronic illnesses can fail to buffer their daily routines and rituals from the illness, thereby allowing the illness to become an organizing principle of the family system.

A third piece of theoretical work underlying medical family therapy is John Rolland's (1984, 1988) psychosocial model of illness type and family life cycle. In his 1984 article in *Family Systems Medicine*, Rolland made the case for a typology of illness that would facilitate the examination of individual and family dynamics in chronic disease—in other words, a psychosocial typology of chronic illness. His proposed typology used four categories: onset, course, outcome, and degree of incapacitation. For the purposes of a medical family therapist, these dimensions, because they directly affect the family's everyday experience, are likely to be more important than the particular pathophysiology of specific diseases. For example, both Parkinson's disease and rheumatoid arthritis have a gradual onset and a progressive course, are nonfatal, and are incapacitating. Families with these illnesses will have a different set of challenges than if they had members with illnesses showing a different psychosocial profile, such as ulcerative colitis, which is a relapsing disease that does not follow a constant progressive course. Rolland (1988) integrated this illness typology with phases of the family life cycle, showing how the interaction between the characteristics of an illness and the family's developmental needs can derail a family from its natural course. For example, a cervical spinal cord injury to a parent can make it difficult for a young adult child to leave home physically and emotionally. Later, we discuss Rolland's more recent work on genetics and family relationships.

A fourth theory for medical family therapy is the family adjustment and adaptation response (FAAR) model (McCubbin and Patterson, 1982; Patterson, 2002), which combines family stress theory and family systems theory. Applied to medical problems, the FAAR model emphasizes the adjustment and adaptation phase of the family health and illness cycle. The model examines families' efforts to manage the demands of chronic illness and disabilities, in light its resources, coping patterns, and beliefs. The outcome of this coping process is a level adjustment or adaptation. The FAAR model has been operationalized by a number of self-report instruments and has been applied successfully in research on how families cope with chronic and disabling medical conditions (Patterson, 1989).

The final theoretical model to be described is the family fundamental interpersonal relations orientation (FIRO) model, an extension of Schutz's fundamental interpersonal orientations model (Doherty, Colangelo, &

Hovander, 1991). Originally developed by Doherty and Colangelo (1984) for family therapy, the family FIRO model was later applied to the family dynamics of health behaviors and chronic illness. The model offers three core dimensions of family interaction: inclusion (structure, connectedness, and shared meaning), control (power and influence), and intimacy (close personal exchanges). Publications on cigarette smoking (Doherty & Whitehead, 1986; Whitehead & Doherty, 1989), obesity (Doherty & Harkaway, 1990), and chronic illness (Doherty & Campbell, 1988) have postulated that health behaviors and disorders can serve as ways for families to be included or excluded from one another's lives, to create battlegrounds for control, and to open or close opportunities for intimacy.

In sum, a promising body of family systems theories offers a significant beginning theoretical foundation for medical family therapy's knowledge base.

Medical Family Therapy and the New Genetics

Since the first edition of this book appeared, there has been an explosion of knowledge about the human genome and a proliferation of genetic tests for a wide array of diseases—not only the causes of diseases but also susceptibility and resistance to disease, progression of disease, and responses to treatment. As McDaniel and Rolland (2006) argued, the impact of this new knowledge on patient and family systems can be enormous over the life course. Ethical and clinical challenges abound as family members decide whether to be tested, whom to tell of the results, and what decisions to make after the findings. These challenges are inherently family ones, calling for a delicate dance of agency and communion. In addition to being sensitive to these psychosocial challenges, medical family therapists must understand the psychosocial aspects of genomic disorders over time. Rolland and Williams (2005) developed a useful guide to the psychosocial types of these disorders, their time phases, and family functioning related to them. Chapter 12 in this book takes up these and other issues.

The New Brain Research

Along with the aforementioned advances in knowledge about the human genome, there have been fascinating scientific developments in the social dimensions of the human brain. We know in deeper ways that we are hardwired for social connections, and that relationships affect the brain along with the brain affecting how we relate to others. An example at the level of neuroanatomy is the discovery of mirror neurons that activate when we observe others and identify with what they are experiencing and when we read their emotions or intentions (Goleman, 2006). As developmental scientist Daniel Stern (2004) observed when reflecting on mirror neurons as part of new body of research on interpersonal neurology, "our nervous systems are constructed to be captured by the nervous systems of others, so that we can experience others as if from within their skin, as well as from within our own" (p. 76).

Daniel Siegel's interpersonal neurobiology has become a prominent guide for therapists who are working to apply this new science to working with clients. Interpersonal neurobiology attempts to understand human development and well-being by focusing on the importance of relationships in shaping the brain so that the mind develops resilience. The main tenet of this model is that the triangle of human experience has three irreducible points—relationships, mind, and brain—which share energy and information flow. Relationships are how energy and information are shared between and among people (Siegel, 2010). Clinical applications of this work have been slower to develop than the theory and basic science, but there are promising developments in areas ranging from trauma to couple problems. Medical family therapists embrace this new brain research for its consistency with systems theory and its support for communion as a core goal of their work.

Families and the Health Care System

Doherty and Baird (1983) maintained that the minimal fundamental unit of health consists of a triangle that includes a clinician, a patient, and a family. In Rolland's (1988) view, the illness and its psychosocial characteristics become an additional part of the treatment system. Thus, he expanded the therapeutic triangle into the *therapeutic quadrangle* consisting of the health care team, patient, family, and illness. If we further divide out the medical family therapist from the rest of the health care team, a pentagon is created, with the therapist needing to attend to issues involving the illness, the patient, the family, and the rest of the health care team.

For people dealing with chronic illness or disability, relations with health care professionals, HMOs, insurance providers, and government agencies are often among the most stressful aspects of their situation, and thus medical family therapists need a working knowledge of these health care and community systems to help families. During the 1980s, the field of family therapy began to attend directly to families' relationships with larger systems, as seen in the work of Imber-Black (1988) and Wynne, McDaniel, and Weber (1986). The central notion for medical family therapy is that the unit of assessment and treatment must include the family's and the therapist's relations with the relevant health care system. Reiss and Kaplan De-Nour (1988) explicitly dealt with relationships with the health care team. These authors showed how medical staff, family, and patient are linked together in a social system that goes through identifiable phases, each with its own developmental tasks. The phases are as follows: acute, chronic/maintenance, and terminal/bereavement. The central task of the acute phase is *assessment and support*, whereas the central task of the chronic phase is *vigilance versus burnout; maintenance of morale, development, and rehabilitation*. For the terminal phase, the central task is *comfort and composure*. Reiss and Kaplan De-Nour described how roles and interactions among patients, medical staff, and families change during these phases and proposed that the caregiving system's success in coping with later states depends on success in earlier phases.

Since the early 1990s when the first edition of this book was published, there has been an upheaval in how health care is delivered in the United States. As we described in the preface to this edition, health care reform efforts of the early 1990s failed, and the early promise of collaborative care stalled. Large insurance systems and provider systems now dominate, and the ranks of the uninsured continue to grow along with the public and private costs of health care. Accountable care organizations (groups of providers and hospitals working together to provide integrated services to a Medicare population) and Health Care Homes are being called on to deliver the "Triple Aim" mentioned in the preface, consisting of population health, cost containment, and a good patient experience (Berwick, Nolan, & Whittington, 2008; Edwards, Patterson, Vakili, & Scherger, 2012). Medical family therapists in the 21st century must make themselves knowledgeable about the current complexities and future prospects for the health care system and indeed become active participants in shaping its future.

KNOWLEDGE OF SELF FOR THE MEDICAL FAMILY THERAPIST

Over the years since the first edition of *Medical Family Therapy*, we have become more acutely aware of the importance of issues associated with the medical family therapist's knowledge of self. The personal and family of origin work expected of therapists often does not deal adequately with some of the unique issues that medical family therapists face every day. These include *medical family of origin issues* relating to the therapist's family experience of illness, health behaviors, health beliefs, and interactions with physicians and other health professionals. Because every family has a health history that is loaded with feeling and meaning, it is important for medical family therapists to sort out and come to peace with these issues. A useful training technique is to have trainees do a "health and illness" genogram focusing on how their family responded to medical problems and crises.

A second area for personal development work is *the therapist's personal history with illness, health behavior, and health care professionals*. A therapist who is ashamed of his or her own stress-related physical problems will not work effectively with patients who have similar problems. A therapist who has survived cancer will have both special empathy and possible bias when dealing with cancer patients and their families. A therapist who struggles with a sense of being overweight or who smokes cigarettes must sort through the meaning of these issues when working with health behavior problems. Similarly, a therapist who has had negative personal experiences with physicians must work through these feelings to be able to collaborate with physicians in medical family therapy.

A third area of personal concern for medical family therapists is *anxiety when dealing with the physical aspects of illness and treatment:* blood, needles, wounds, deformities, smells, body fluids, and an assortment of other assaults on one's sensitivity. This is particularly an issue for therapists who work in acute care and rehabilitation hospitals but it must be faced as well by medical family therapists when families discuss how they deal with cleansing large wounds, replacing ostomy bags, and dealing with the public embarrassment of visible symptoms. Some therapists say that they avoided medical school precisely because they don't like "blood and guts." To do medical family therapy well, these therapists will have to become desensitized to the physical processes of disability, illness, and treatment.

The final general area of personal work for medical family therapists concerns *power and status issues vis-à-vis physicians.* It is not uncommon to hear therapists express resentment and even hostility toward physicians as a group. Although some of this reaction is understandable because of particular negative experiences, we believe that working with physicians also stirs up whatever personal ambivalence therapists have about their own status and power as professionals and as people. The twin temptations are to treat physicians as authority figures instead of collaborators, or as figures of contempt or avoidance. Negative attitudes toward physicians clearly compromise the therapist's ability to do medical family therapy.

Having started out with high-level theory and the general knowledge base for medical family therapy, we turn immediately to the practical: the clinical strategies that make this work unique and energizing for practicing clinicians.

2

CLINICAL STRATEGIES FOR MEDICAL FAMILY THERAPY

Medical family therapy attends to emotionally complex aspects of patients' and families' lives. Therapists must have clinical sophistication in knowing how to facilitate useful discussions and plans. Like all therapy, there is strategy, and there is art; there is research, and there is clinical judgment. Medical family therapy integrates all these perspectives to help families have safe, honest, difficult, and also inspiring conversations.

In this chapter, we present the core systemic strategies of medical family therapy and discuss examples of implementation. The range of clinical strategies reflects the multitude of topics that can be addressed, depending on the needs of each patient and family. Strategies do not reflect any particular psychotherapy model but include ways to facilitate family communication, connection, collaboration, and creative adaptation to chronic illness. Therapists from many theoretical orientations can adapt the interventions to enhance patient and family agency and communion. It is unlikely that a therapist

http://dx.doi.org/10.1037/14256-002
Medical Family Therapy and Integrated Care, Second Edition, by S. H. McDaniel, W. J. Doherty, and J. Hepworth

will use all clinical strategies with any particular family. Instead, the clinical strategies can be considered a toolbox for helping families sort through the complex feelings and decisions that result with any health crisis.

Although medical family therapy occurs with patients and families facing acute or terminal illnesses, the most frequent referrals come from patients and families who are coping with chronic illness. These families have lengthy or dramatic experiences and are likely to recognize that they can use additional support or are willing to consider referrals from their clinicians. Therefore, this chapter draws its examples from families coping with chronic illness and from those clinical strategies that are useful for many chronic illnesses. The case of the Ellman family is used throughout the chapter to exemplify how clinical strategies are implemented. Several other brief cases are interspersed throughout the chapter to demonstrate the use of clinical strategies that were not a predominate part of the treatment of the Ellmans.[1]

Bill Ellman, age 53, was a successful attorney who litigated many cases of medical disability. As an adolescent, he was diagnosed with diabetes, and he became very educated in and involved with his care. Throughout his life, he carefully monitored his diet, insulin levels, and physical responses. Nevertheless, he had many complications, including circulatory problems leading to coronary bypass surgery, great toe amputation, and erectile dysfunction. More recently, his diabetes resulted in kidney failure requiring dialysis, with the possibility of kidney transplantation.

Bill's wife, Carol Ellman, a 49-year-old clinical social worker, was in good health and worked part time in the local children's hospital. When she was in her early teens, her father had a debilitating stroke, and her mother cared for him at home for 6 years until his death. Carol and Bill's children, Tara, age 23, and Michael, age 21, were in college but maintained fairly close contact with their parents (see genogram, Figure 2.1).

Carol initiated therapy for herself. She had coped well with Bill's illness for a long time but became overwhelmed by the increasingly serious medical crises, frequent hospitalizations, and reminders of her parents' experiences. She was concerned that her husband was becoming depressed and withdrawing emotionally from her. As she worried more, she found herself becoming both more resentful about caring for him and simultaneously guilty about those feelings. She wanted to continue to be supportive of her husband and still find ways to feel that she had some joy in her life. Although primarily interested in her own therapy, Carol was willing to include her husband and children as needed.

---

[1]All of the cases in this book have been camouflaged to protect the anonymity of our patients. The substance, however, is accurate and true to the dynamics of the family and the experience of the medical family therapist.

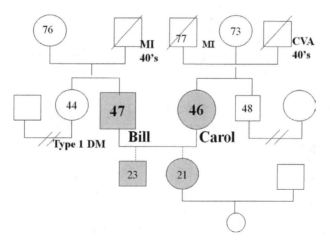

Figure 2.1. The Ellman family.

THE PREVALENCE OF CHRONIC ILLNESS
AND ITS FAMILY IMPACT

Chronic illness generally comes on gradually. People vary in how they respond to initial symptoms. Some seek care at the first recognition, and others avoid care while their family members worry or perhaps nag them to visit a health care professional. There are often lengthy periods of testing or multiple visits with different kinds of clinicians. Meanwhile, the person with symptoms and their family members create hypotheses about what may be occurring, which they may or may not share with one another. In retrospect, many describe the often lengthy time of uncertainty before diagnosis as a more difficult period than when they can finally name their disease.

Once a diagnosis is made, the person becomes a patient. Chronic illness demands new ways of coping, changes in patient and family self-definitions, and perhaps periods of adaptation. Over time, the patient realizes multiple losses, including physical health and functioning, loss of roles and responsibilities, loss of dreams, and the possibility of decreased life span. Families also experience losses and may begin to define themselves as a "family with cancer or diabetes," a "family with bad luck," or a "family who is no longer 'normal and healthy.'" Even when diagnoses become certain, uncertainty and ambiguity linger.

Medical family therapists help families realize that their complicated feelings are normal responses to a difficult crisis (see Chapter 4). This occurs when we help them honestly discuss their concerns, validate their experiences, and confirm that their responses are shared by others who face these difficult situations. Medical family therapists help families work effectively with their health care teams and respond to the illness. This means helping them acknowledge their strengths and their losses, as well as their positive achievements in the face of their disappointments.

Many of the arguments about health care reform cite the growth in the number of families projected to cope with chronic illnesses. The National Center for Health Statistics (Centers for Disease Control, 2008b) reported that 12% of all Americans are limited in their activities by a chronic medical condition. The percentage whose activities are limited by their chronic disease increases to 17% for those ages 45 to 64 and 42% for those older than 75 years. These percentages become more real with an example from a talk by medical ethicist Daniel Callahan (1991), who described how cemeteries reveal the history of modern medicine. He noted that until the 19th century, people of all ages arrived at the cemeteries but that late 20th century cemeteries are primarily full of people who died at an older age. Callahan suggested that the price to be paid for medical technology and curing is increased chronic illness.

Chronic illness accounts for a massive percentage of health care costs with generally unaccounted costs for families who provide varying levels of care. Management of chronic illnesses requires that patients, families, and health care systems work together. The long-term nature of care results in an ongoing relationship between the patient and at least one physician, characterized by Doherty (1988) as a "chronic relationship with the healthcare system" (p. 194). Families may be directly involved with frequent interactions with medical systems, often including multiple clinicians across multiple settings; indirect relationships occur when families are not invited into the "chronic relationship" between patient and physicians but must infer information from what the patient communicates. Whenever a patient returns home from a clinical visit, for example, families almost always ask the same question: "What did the doctor say?" The possibilities for misunderstanding and miscommunication are endless.

Medical family therapy requires therapists to evaluate their own views about how families have an impact on illness experiences. Steinglass and Horan (1988) described a distinction between resource or deficit views of families. In the *resource* model, positive family functioning and social support are presumed to buffer the severity of the illness. In the *deficit* model, family stress and interaction patterns are seen to exacerbate illness and impede optimal care. This simplistic distinction, however, does not account for the complicated family patterns that influence the ways families try to provide support and how patients understand the support. Past family patterns, good intentions gone awry, and miscommunications about what support is needed or desired result in misguided and sometimes harmful family support patterns (Ell, 1996). Although there is a paucity of research about how these family interactional patterns influence the course of illness and recovery (Campbell, 2003), clinical work should help families consider how they wish to provide care.

Families generally try to provide support, but sometimes the support looks like overprotection or intrusion. Other families, who value patient autonomy, may look like they are not sufficiently caring or involved with their family member. In most cases, a diagnosis of chronic illness hits families like a tornado that crashes through their lives. It is unexpected and leaves long-lasting devastation and debris. The varying patient and family responses can be equally unsettling and difficult.

The scene is also set for misunderstanding or conflict when families and health care systems share responsibility for care but do not have ways to clarify their roles or expectations for that care. Miscommunication is likely, particularly when patients and families are frightened and not knowledgeable about the illness or medical system. A medical family therapist is a welcome resource to help clarify the misunderstandings, help families obtain information and resources, decrease role strain for both family and health care systems, and help families and clinicians create more compassionate and sustainable systems of care.

CHRONIC ILLNESS: ILLNESS CHARACTERISTICS

Every new diagnosis is a unique experience for the patient and for their family. They have much to learn about the illness, how best to provide care, and how the stress will affect their relationships. Though the experiences are new to the families, many complain that they are treated, for example, as "just another cancer patient." The recognition of unique experience has led health care systems to advertise how they tailor treatments and environments to the unique needs of each patient and family. Medical family therapy provides an additional resource to help families consider these new experiences. While recognizing variability among families, there are still common characteristics of both illnesses and families that may help predict responses and encourage helpful interventions.

Course and Outcome

Illnesses create unique strains for patients and families depending on the degree of incapacitation, the visibility of the illness to others, whether it leads to death, and what meanings are associated with it. Family psychiatrist John Rolland (1994) created a useful typology with classifications including illness onset, course, outcome, and degree of incapacitation. The typology helps clarify why diseases that are progressive, fatal, and incapacitating, such as severe lung cancer, will have different implications than diseases that are acute and not fatal or incapacitating, such as a mild myocardial infarction (heart attack). These factors help explain why diseases such as lupus or Parkinson's, which are biomedically quite different from one another, can lead to similar psychosocial effects on families. Both of these illnesses have variable prognoses, and patients and families are never sure when or if exacerbation or additional symptoms could occur.

Onset of illness can be either acute, like a stroke (cerebral vascular accident), which occurs without warning, or gradual, such as cardiac disease, in which patients and families have time to become familiar with the disease and treatment. The course of disease can be progressive, constant, or relapsing–episodic. Alzheimer's disease is considered progressive, a spinal cord injury may be constant, and asthma represents a relapsing illness. *Outcome* refers to the expectation of whether the disease will shorten the life span. Disease outcome can be classified as *fatal*, such as many metastatic cancers; *possibly fatal*, such as cardiovascular disease; or *nonfatal*, such as arthritis. The fourth characteristic of Rolland's typology, *incapacitation*, reflects degree of disability. Degree of incapacitation is complicated by how visible the disease or condition is to others. There is significant variability in illness expression for each person, but in general, an illness is categorized as either *incapacitating*, such as Parkinson's, or *nonincapacitating*, such as hypertension.

Bill Ellman's diabetes had a gradual onset, with minimal impact when he was a young man. In his 30s, his diabetes became progressively worse. Each hospitalization for heart arrhythmia or surgery and eventually amputations became a new crisis. Hospitalizations became a more regular feature of their life, and this led to the expectation that further medical crises would ensue. The progressive nature of the illness meant that each new crisis resulted in somewhat more disability and a slightly altered quality of family life. The family worried about every event, and the hospitalizations became markers that the illness was becoming more severe, incapacitating, and moving toward the terminal phase.

Phase of Illness

Chronic illnesses develop over time, resulting in stages of illness analogous to individual or family developmental stages. Rolland (1994) distinguished the crisis, chronic, and terminal phases of illness and identified family concerns and tasks for each of these phases. Reiss and Kaplan De-Nour (1989) had previously labeled these stages as *acute, chronic,* and *terminal* phases, noting that adaptive coping patterns for one stage may not be functional at another stage.

The acute or crisis phase often begins before diagnosis, when the family senses that something is wrong. Once there is a diagnosis, or medical tests and visits to determine one, the family responds to the new information. Often, families temporarily reorganize to meet immediate needs, and family members begin the psychosocial tasks of accepting the illness, finding ways to provide care, and dealing with uncertainty. Although families may experience conflict about which treatment options to pursue or how to provide care, most families tend to pull together during the acute stage of an illness (Steinglass, Temple, Lisman, & Reiss, 1982).

The shift to the chronic phase varies with each illness (Reiss & Kaplan De-Nour, 1989) and occurs when patients and families accept that the illness in some form will be a part of their lives. During the chronic phase, which often includes periods of new exacerbations and crises, patients and families accept that there are permanent changes, grieve for their pre-illness identity, and negotiate roles for chronic care. At this stage, families generally become more informed and active participants in caring for the ill member and attempt to balance caregiving needs with other family needs.

The terminal phase, discussed in detail in Chapter 13, occurs in those chronic illnesses that lead to death, when the inevitability of death looms. The terminal phase may or may not be acknowledged by families. If recognized, the terminal phase allows for possibilities to deal with separation and mourning, create opportunities to discuss unresolved concerns, help the dying person to address concerns and wishes, and to say goodbye.

Cases referred when in acute crisis, either at the time of a disturbing diagnosis or when a patient enters a terminal phase, require active structuring to lower the level of anxiety in the family before people can effectively speak and listen to each other. Families referred in a chronic phase often have developed dysfunctional ways of coping with the illness and may require techniques that facilitate the patient and family becoming "unstuck." In all phases, the following clinical strategies (see Exhibit 2.1) can provide a

EXHIBIT 2.1
Clinical Strategies for Medical Family Therapy

1. Recognize the biological dimension.
2. Elicit the family illness history and meaning.
3. Respect defenses, remove blame, and accept unacceptable feelings.
4. Facilitate communication.
5. Attend to developmental issues.
6. Reinforce the family's nonillness identity.
7. Provide psychoeducation and support.
8. Increase the family's sense of agency.
9. Enhance the family's sense of communion.
10. Maintain an empathic presence with the family.

template for helping families enhance their relationships with one another and the health care team.

CLINICAL STRATEGIES FOR MEDICAL FAMILY THERAPY

1. Recognize the Biological Dimension

Medical family therapists must learn to feel comfortable with the physical domain and be curious about the biological health of the patient and sometimes that of other family members. We learn where and from whom our patients receive their health care, and how to get information to educate ourselves and our patients. These needs require that we discuss the role of family therapy within the health care process.

Focus on the Patient

Some traditional models of family therapy avoid labeling one distressed family member as "the patient." In medical family therapy, however, there is a patient: the person with an illness. Therapy includes consideration of the coping strategies of all members of the family who are being affected by this illness, but it begins with a focus on the patient. Other family members are best approached as consultants in helping the patient deal with the illness (Wynne, McDaniel, & Weber, 1986). For the behavioral and relational issues that therapists routinely treat, families may be encouraged to share responsibility for the problem, so they can all participate in whatever change will help reduce the undesired symptom. In therapy dealing with medical problems, families can feel blamed for their loved one's illness, a feeling the therapist definitely does not want to exacerbate.

Explain the Difference Between Psychotherapy and Other Medical Encounters

Patients in medical settings meet many kinds of health care providers, and it may not be clear why they are seeing a medical family therapist. They are primed for certain kinds of interactions: children may expect to get shots, adults may expect to get pills, and all patients expect to get answers and advice (Seaburn, Lorenz, Gunn, Gawinski, & Mauksch, 1996). From the first interaction, the medical family therapist begins the process of shifting the expectations of medical treatment to expectations useful for therapy. Useful questions include the following: "What do you expect from therapy?" and "What are your goals for treatment?" Time is well spent describing the nature of the collaboration, especially the sharing of information between the therapist and other clinicians and staff, the role of the therapist as facilitator or coach, and the ways in which patients and family members will be urged to use their wisdom and resources to face their challenges.

Solicit the Referring Clinician's Explanation of the Illness

As is discussed in Chapter 3, ideally, the therapist should obtain the medical provider's perspective about the patient's illness, prognosis, and special circumstances through an electronic letter or a referral letter, rather than receive medical information only from the family. With complicated cases, this conversation may occur in a family meeting or speaker-phone meeting so that physician, therapist, patient, and family all hear the same information. In the therapeutic triangle between the medical system, the therapist, and the family, the therapist communicates directly with the medical system and with the patient and family to avoid any splitting or unhealthy coalitions.

Maintain Humility About the Possibility of Biological Change

Sick people search for hope and for answers. Therapists help the patient and family cope with their particular problem: They do not, however, predict the effect of psychotherapy on the course of a particular illness. Each patient and family can be encouraged to carry out their own "research project" to track what seems to be helpful or unhelpful and to work with clinicians to devise a treatment plan with the greatest likelihood of successful physical and emotional outcomes.

2. Elicit the Family Illness History and Meaning

As with any family who comes to therapy, the therapist first gets to know members apart from the presenting complaint. Who are these people? Who works outside the home, and what is the nature of their work? What hobbies do they enjoy? How do they spend their couple and family time together? The family's ability to answer these early joining questions without moving into detailed discussion of the illness is an indicator of the extent that the family organizes itself around the illness. Once a context is established, the therapist can listen empathetically to the patient and family stories of the illness.

Patients expect to tell their illness story, and it is therapeutic to tell their stories to others (Kleinman, 1988; McDaniel, Hepworth, & Doherty, 1997). Family members, however, are not generally asked about their stories of illness, and it is frequently enlightening for the patient and the other family members to hear each other's experience. Doing so can also lead to significant emotion, because family members often have traumatic associations. Therapists must be prepared to hear the difficult stories and respond with respect for and recognition of the family strengths. Exhibit 2.2 lists questions that can help elicit each person's perception of the illness.

The illness stories give clues for a shared language for treatment with the family (Anderson & Goolishian, 1988; Weingarten, 2010). Physical complaints may have both biomedical and metaphorical meanings. Family members use powerful descriptions that when used in therapy, allow the therapist to enter the patient's and the family's world. Understanding the meanings is one of the first steps in facilitating change.

Wynne, Shields, and Sirkin (1992) described the construction of meaning about illness as a transactional relationship. It is a process requiring a continuing series of negotiations about what constitutes illness and responses. Family meaning is influenced by illness interpretations that reflect culture and personal experience and may have developed across generations. These family responses and beliefs become intricately woven into the fabric of family life, and each generation has new opportunities to replicate or alter the significant historical patterns (Boszormenyi-Nagy & Spark, 1973).

Beliefs about illness should be a significant part of therapeutic conversations (Wright, Watson, & Bell, 1996). McDaniel, Campbell, Hepworth, and Lorenz (2005) suggested that beliefs and expectations about illness can be obtained with an illness-oriented genogram in which families describe their experiences with previous illness: who was ill, what diseases run in the family, and how caregiving was provided. This is frequently new information. Just as partners differ in how their families celebrated holidays, a wife may not have noticed that her family expected stoicism around illness, whereas in her husband's family, the health concerns of relatives were a common dinner table topic. Discussion of these differences about history and unacknowledged assumptions enables families to separate previous assumptions from how they wish to respond together.

Carol Ellman was aware of the frightening similarities between her mother's care of her father and her own support for her husband. At the time of Carol's father's illness, Carol's mother was also a middle-aged woman with adolescent and emerging young adult children. Carol's father, like Bill, had a progressive chronic illness, with variable function but eventual decline. Both women needed to provide significant physical and emotional care, and both experienced losses in their ability to engage in social activities with others and increasing social isolation.

Carol's awareness helped her try to do things differently than her mother had done—continuing with her work outside of the home, for example. In therapy, however, she realized that her conscious attempts to maintain a full life did not fully protect her from the same feelings of disappointment and resentment that she had observed with her mother. As an adolescent, Carol had resented how much she had to help with her father's physical care, so she tried

For the patient:
1. What do you think caused your problem?
2. Why do you think it started when it did?
3. What do you think your sickness does to you? How does it work?
4. How severe is your sickness? Will it have a long or short course?
5. What are the chief problems your sickness has caused for you?
6. What do you fear most about your sickness?
7. What kind of treatment do you think you should receive?
8. What are the most important results you hope to receive from this treatment?
9. Should we expect complications?
10. What has been your extended family's experience with illness?
11. Has anyone else in your family faced an illness similar to the one you have now? If so, what was its course?
12. What is your and your family's past history of recuperation?
13. What might make healing now a struggle for you?
14. Do you see yourself as having much to live for?

For family members:
15. What changes in family responsibilities do you think will be needed because of the patient's sickness?
16. If the patient needs care or special help, which family members are going to be responsible for providing it?
17. If the illness is already chronic or appears likely to become chronic, what are the patient's and family members' plans for taking care of the problem over the long term?

Note. The first eight questions are from Kleinman, Eisenberg, and Good (1978); questions 9 and 10 are adapted from Seaburn, Lorenz, Campbell, and Winfield (1996); questions 11 through 14 are adapted from Friedman (1991); and questions 15 through 17 are from Shields, Wynne, and Sirkin (1992).

to protect her daughter, Tara, from assuming a strong caregiving function with Tara's father. Then, when Tara did not provide the same support to her mother that Carol remembered providing to her own mother, Carol felt critical of Tara, saying she was selfish. Over time, Carol and Tara were able to discuss how the balance between caregiving and support was handled in the previous and present generations, and each was able to more clearly state her desires. Discussion also let them accept the complicated nature of caregiving and that ambivalent feelings could still occur with whatever choice they made.

3. Respect Defenses, Remove Blame, and Accept Unacceptable Feelings

Medical family therapy requires a healthy respect for the coping styles that evolve among patients and families to deal with threats to their physical functioning or even survival. Patients and families frequently have to shift their daily schedules, stretch their emotional and financial resources, and push themselves physically and mentally to meet the challenge of serious illness. With these stressors, it is not surprising that maladaptive coping styles sometimes develop. It is important not to intervene too quickly in trying to change these coping styles but to focus first on the strengths the family exhibits. Families can be supported, for example, by a therapist who recognizes first how much they all care for one another. Only later can the therapist begin to help them sort out how they can take turns caring for the ill person, for example, so that other work and social responsibilities don't suffer. Families facing illness need a large dose of support for the difficulties they have experienced.

Denial

Denial is not always maladaptive—often it is useful in helping patients and families manage stress, anxiety, and early adaptation to illness (Livneh, 2009). Sometimes patients deny their illness or their need to change the way they are living to accommodate an illness (e.g., the patient who returns to a stressful job 3 weeks after having a serious heart attack). Sometimes it is the family members who deny illness (e.g., the wife who insists her husband continue to drive her to work after his physician documented that his vision was seriously impaired). The resistance to acknowledging changes may be particularly strong when the change signals aging or death. Families then may not adapt to an illness or disability in ways that appear healthy to the professional observer. Accepting the denial, then providing support and positive reframing, can help the family move to a more realistic view of the illness and the patient's future (see Chapter 4). This requires a balance of acceptance of decreasing resistance but care that therapists do not encourage false expectations. A patient who returned to work prematurely, for example, participated in a family session in which the therapist emphasized the patient's dedication to his work, then wondered aloud about how he might maintain this dedication and still take good care of his physical health. The patient and family negotiated a plan in which the man worked mornings and attended a cardiac rehabilitation program in the afternoons. Without the initial support and positive connotation of his resistance to the medical treatment plan, the patient seemed likely to fight any alternative plan proposed by professionals or family members.

Blame and Guilt

Most people harbor some personal theories about how or why an illness or disability occurs. When we hear that an older person has lung cancer, for example, some of us quickly wonder whether he or she was a smoker. It is common to try to determine why the illness happened, how it could be prevented, and even how we could avoid it ourselves. Personal habits certainly can influence illness and health, and current Western culture emphasizes individual responsibility for health. Popular books imply that with the correct diet, exercise, and attitude, heart disease, cancer, and other dangerous diseases might even be avoided. Although this approach is important to encourage positive health behaviors that can prevent or postpone some illnesses, it is easy to move from this position to one in which some behavior is to blame for an illness or a death.

The other side of blame is guilt. If people think they did something to "cause the illness," they may feel guilty that they did this to themselves and brought the difficulty to their families. Family members without illness often experience guilt about being healthy as well as conflict about feelings of resentment toward the ill person. These underlying concerns are not easily discussed within families.

By the time families see therapists, they have spent much time trying to understand what has occurred and often have privately or loudly blamed each other, bad genes, environmental events, or the medical system. Some families are fatalistic about illness; they believe that illness is part of God's larger plan, for example, and out of their control. Others feel responsible for their health and believe that illness is a result of not eating the right foods and generally "not taking care of themselves." Often these themes can be traced through several generations.

Therapists can inadvertently enhance blame by the nature of therapeutic conversation. Because families are concerned about guilt, they are often highly sensitive to concerns that their clinicians are blaming them. Blaming and shaming communication from health providers, even slight comments, is associated with higher levels of depression and anxiety, whereas positive communication is associated with enhanced participation in care (Bennett, Compas, Beckjord, & Glinder, 2005). Thus, therapists need to be careful about asking questions that imply blame, such as "Why didn't you seek care earlier?" Instead, medical family therapists can find ways to reassure families that they were trying to do their best. "It sounds like you thought this was like previous symptoms and would go away. Wouldn't it be great if we had crystal balls to know how things would work out?" Even when family dynamics clearly are contributing to unhealthy responses, change is most likely to occur when the patient and the family do not feel blamed.

In one family, the adult children and husband continued to hover over the mother long after she was in no medical danger from her stroke. Instead of resuming her daily activities, she and the family seemed to accept her decline, and she did less as the rest of her family did more. If a therapist focused on how the family members were "enabling" the patient to remain inactive, the family members could feel blamed and become resistant to change. A medical family therapist approach would instead focus on how all family members were frightened by the stroke and worried that more damage could occur if they were not careful. The medical family therapist could describe how early in recovery periods, it is helpful for families to pick up extra responsibilities and let the patient rest. As recovery continues or as a condition becomes chronic, however, the family should help the person with the stroke increase her functioning within any limitations. Focusing on the developmental phases of an illness and the tasks for that phase helps limit blame and increases the likelihood of helpful family responses.

Normalize Negative Feelings

Many feelings that occur routinely in families (e.g., anger, resentment, sadness, guilt) seem unacceptable when illness occurs. Such restraint is often constructive because serious illness can remind people that petty grievances are just that. Other times patients or family members feel they should protect the ill person from their true feelings. If they find the feelings unacceptable, they may not acknowledge them at all, resulting in misplaced anger or unexplained sadness. Medical family therapists help family members acknowledge their feelings, even when they seem inappropriate, and help them realize that they are expectable responses to this undesirable situation.

In an individual session, Carol Ellman described how she observed other couples in a restaurant and believed that they had freedoms that she and Bill did not. The therapist responded, "Other people I have talked with in your situation sometimes find themselves angry and resentful at strangers, since they seem to have an easier time. Does that ever happen to you?"

Carol seemed startled by the question but began to discuss how she sometimes felt resentful toward other couples who were able to live an active life. She expressed how unfair she felt her life was, and although it wasn't his fault, how she held anger toward her husband. She also knew that he would want a different kind of life for them, so she did not need to express her anger to him directly. The therapist initiating the discussion with the statement that others feel similarly gave Carol permission to release some of her concerns.

Families look to therapists for validation about how they are coping. They wonder if we think they are "crazy," and they are attuned to signs of judgment. When we initiate conversations that encourage them to express their unacceptable feelings, we provide opportunities for people to accept that the negative feelings are reasonable and common, and therefore acceptable. With recognition of the reality of unacceptable and mixed feelings, clients can determine how to respond and limit the unintentional "leakage" of unacceptable feelings that can be so hurtful.

4. Facilitate Communication

Facilitating communication is the art of any therapy, but in medical family therapy, several systems are considered. Communication generally needs to be enhanced between the patient and family members and between the patient, family, and treatment team.

Communication Among Family Members

There is never only one illness story. Each family member has a unique story of the illness, the meaning of the symptoms, and the impact on the family. There are multiple benefits when family members hear the perceptions of others. When an adolescent quietly mumbles that his father's stroke was caused by an argument he and his father had just before the event, family members can reassure one another and diminish blame. Listening to each other promotes empathy within the family. With different views elicited, the therapist can reinforce that many responses are acceptable and that it is expected that family members will feel and act differently from one another.

Some family members want to talk more about their concerns, whereas others believe that talking doesn't help. Still others differ according to when they want to talk about the illness. Lisa Baker (1987) described how this "rhythm of adaptation" can be considered an asset: If different family members respond at different times, the patient and other members are allowed necessary respite. When the family expects individual differences, members are not misunderstood as withdrawing or inconsiderate.

Clear communication assists families throughout the inevitable periods of uncertainty. Anticipatory discussions can help families plan or make accommodations before the crisis occurs. Communication can occur around emotionally charged topics, such as living wills, as well as around predictable aspects of chronic illness management.

A family session was held with Michael, a 25-year-old with Crohn's disease, and his visiting parents, after an emergency hospitalization and surgery. The family understood that Crohn's disease affects the digestive and excretory systems and how exacerbations can be related to diet and other life changes. The parents were respectful of their son's autonomy, pleased that he had moved to a new city and found an interesting job, and yet worried that the stress of living alone contributed to his unstable condition. Respect among family members was apparent, but so too was caution in their interactions. Once the therapist conveyed appreciation of the parents' respect for their son's autonomy, she also noted that they seemed to walk on eggshells around one another. The therapist suggested that sometimes the parents probably wanted to ask their son "parent" sorts of things, such as whether he ate well or drank alcohol too often, but worried about whether it was developmentally appropriate.

The parents and son discussed how they could more effectively raise their concerns with one another. They agreed that the parents could raise their concerns and that the son could say when he was not comfortable talking about an issue. The therapist noted how the usual life cycle stress of launching adult children was complicated by illness, an explanation that was both comforting and freeing for the family.

The desire to protect others is often cited as a communication barrier. Patients may appear secretive about their diagnoses because they do not want to "burden" other family members or destabilize the family structure. All patients and families deserve time to react and respond to new diagnoses, but some patients need support and encouragement to discuss the facts about their illness with others in the family. Often the avoidance of discussion or maintenance of a secret is more stressful than clearer acknowledgment (Imber-Black, Roberts, & Whiting, 2003).

Communication Among Patients, Families, and Medical Providers

Most patients with a chronic illness can describe some negative experiences of communication with someone in the medical system. This occurs because both family and medical provider are likely to be stressed during difficult phases of an illness and because many physicians and patients view disease from different perspectives.

Direct communication from the medical team about prognosis, disease course, and treatment plans provides patients with critical information. Medical teams vary, however, in what they tell patients about the biomedical aspects of their disease: some medical providers emphasize the positive aspects of a prognosis; some divulge extensive information about potential side effects or negative results; still others try to balance the amount of information based on what the patient and family seem to want. Individual preference is confounded when the medical team is uncertain about the illness course and finds it difficult to discuss the ambiguity.

To complicate the communication process further, patients or family members often do not hear everything when news is bad or unexpected. Frequently, the medical team will have to communicate the facts about the illness on several occasions before they are understood. Misperceptions are likely, given the differences between medical and lay language and culture and the high levels of fear and denial.

R. M. Epstein and Peters (2009) highlighted the difficulties of easily accessing patients' preferences, particularly in situations that are unfamiliar and emotionally charged and with outcomes that cannot be imagined. They described how clinicians may be unaware of how they help patients "construct" preferences by how they present information and possible benefits and side effects, as well as through nonverbal cues. They reminded clinicians that shared deliberation is a clinical skill that goes beyond information provision.

A medical family therapist can facilitate this important communication, both directly and indirectly. Direct involvement occurs with clear communication and collaboration between the therapist and the rest of the medical team. Indirect methods for facilitating communication include helping families identify what information they want, perhaps creating a list of questions that they can pose to their medical providers. This often requires some careful discussion of what information they may be reluctant to receive. For example, Ruth, a 63-year-old woman, was on a heart transplant list when she began to have significant electrical abnormalities of the heart that were perplexing to multiple cardiologists. As she tried different medications without significant change, she was told that unless her symptoms diminished, she might no longer be a candidate for a transplant. In a lengthy therapy session, she described her mixed feelings about wanting to know what further steps would be available to her and what her likely prognosis was if her electrical activity did not change. She realized that these mixed feelings had kept her from pushing for an answer from her physicians. In discussion with her husband, they both agreed that there were things they wanted to do together, particularly travel, and that if in fact her life was to be shortened, she would like to know so that they could proceed with some plans. After Ruth and her husband became clearer about their goals, it was easier for her to initiate the difficult discussions with her physicians.

5. Attend to Developmental Issues

Even though families would prefer never to deal with illness and loss, most recognize that there are seasons of family life in which illness and disability occur. It is sad but not surprising when severe illnesses occur among aging family members. It is not expected, however, that young children or young adults will develop chronic or life-threatening illnesses. This means that family support systems experience more disruption when illness occurs during these "unexpected" periods.

Combrinck-Graham (1985) described how families oscillate between periods of relative closeness and separation. Combrinck-Graham's spiral models how centripetal forces from communities and families pull generations in toward one another during times such as marriage, birth of children, or end-of-life care of aging members. For the developmental stages of separation, such as adolescence and early adulthood, the model demonstrates centrifugal forces that pull the members and generations farther apart from one another. Certainly this model varies for different families and cultures, but it predicts how it is easier for families to respond to chronic illness during the centripetal periods than during the periods of separation. A classic example is the difficulty of a new diagnosis of diabetes, for example, for a previously healthy adolescent. It is not surprising that the adolescent may not want his mother intimately involved with his diet, his finger sticks, or other activities related to disease management.

An example from another family developmental period is the impact of a 50-year-old woman's diagnosis of early Alzheimer's disease. The impact is different for her daughters if they have young children of their own (centripetal period) or if those daughters are just leaving home themselves (centrifugal period). Although young parents have additional stresses and are pressed for time, they have a more scheduled and predictable life and, paradoxically, may be more available to help with caregiving than young adults who are attempting to leave home.

Families find it helpful to discuss examples of how illness affects families at different developmental periods. Examples from other families, or thinking about how things might be different for them if it were a different developmental period, helps them understand why they may feel so burdened by illness or stressed by responsibilities at this particular time. Such examples also help to normalize their experiences. Developmental concerns are further discussed in Chapter 10.

Returning to the Ellman family, Bill's disability increased just when the couple's children were leaving home for college. The parents tried to encourage the children to move on with their own lives, but all family members had mixed feelings. Bill and Carol saw how their friends were enjoying their new freedom as "empty nesters." Just as their friends felt freer to travel or add more spontaneity to their lives, Bill and Carol felt more constrained. Had Bill been older, there would have been other friends with health limitations. Instead, Bill and Carol worried that they were burdening their friends and responded by avoiding some social situations and becoming more isolated.

Although the parents did not expect their children to come home for every hospitalization, they sometimes found themselves feeling abandoned and resentful. Similarly, the young adult children wanted to show their support for both of their parents but sometimes resented that they could not enjoy their own lives without worry or guilt. Conversation about the fit between their lives and the "life of the illness" helped members understand that their mixed emotions were quite expected.

6. Reinforce the Family's Nonillness Identity

Chronic or severe illness is an out-of-control experience for most patients and their families, and becomes an intrusive and demanding part of family life. Gonzalez, Steinglass, and Reiss (1987) described a vivid image in which a family is ready to start on a long car trip: "The illness comes along crowding the family with extra baggage, demanding to stop every five miles for snacks or to use the bathroom, and threatening to need emergency treatment at any moment" (p. 20). Families laugh when we use this metaphor, but it also rings true. It helps explain why families begin to feel that they become defined more by an illness than by other family goals or markers of identity.

As families feel that the "illness is taking over their lives," they become discouraged and begin to curtail other activities, creating a cycle in which the illness becomes the predominant identifying factor. A useful strategy is to ask family members to rate on a scale of 1 to 10 how much the illness takes over their lives. If we then ask what ranking they would prefer, they often wish for a low number. We can discuss how the reality of the illness requires significant family attention, but would it be possible for them to move the impact from an 8, for example, to a 6?

This concrete framing allows families to consider life goals apart from the illness and intentionally negotiate ways to "put illness in its place" (Gonzalez et al., 1987). This means that the family attends to the illness demands but does not allow the illness to dominate the family's schedule or organize their emotional life. Medical family therapists help families creatively think about how illness is unnecessarily limiting or isolating, and what relationships and activities could be renewed or begun.

This process may not be easy because family routines, activities, and priorities often have been put aside. Just as a couples therapist might ask a squabbling couple about the activities they enjoyed together in the beginning of their relationship, a medical family therapist can help families access how they defined themselves before the illness and how they want to define themselves now. Families genuinely enjoy conversations that focus on what they would like to do and how they might make adaptations.

A related strategy is the concept of "externalizing the illness" (M. White & Epston, 1990; Wynne, Shields, & Sirkin, 1992) in which one separates the illness from the person who is ill. This can be enhanced by asking the patient to anthropomorphize the illness—to describe the illness as if it were another person or an animal. What does it look like? How does it behave? What does it do to the patient? What does it do to other family members? What makes it act up? Does anything work to calm it? This "illness creature" can often be distinguished from the person who is the patient, and families can consider how they might "tame the illness" and find ways to not be defined by it.

7. Provide Psychoeducation and Support

Psychoeducation is a valuable component of therapy. Therapists can share information or strategies and find ways to demonstrate that the patient and family are not the only ones who are experiencing their concerns. Families may find it easier to discuss their unacceptable feelings when therapists provide stories about other anonymous families.

The availability of family support has increased since the previous edition of this text was published. We barely mentioned the Internet and could not envision the online communities that are available for people with every kind of chronic illness or condition. People have immediate access to information about course of illness, testing options, medical procedures, and ranges of treatment options. More significantly, they talk with others who have similar conditions and experiences.

There is the possibility of unlimited resources and support, but also the challenge of how to sift through it all because much available information is unfiltered. Families may learn things that are either not true or that make them concerned about the course of an illness. Therapists should ask families about how they are obtaining information and support, particularly whether they are using online resources, and what questions they have.

Many large cities or hospitals offer traditional support groups for patients and families with specific diseases. Cardiac illness, breast cancer, childhood cancers, and HIV are common examples. Many illnesses also have family associations for information, support, and advocacy. As with any support group, some patients and families can become discouraged by a particular group's focus on disability or a group whose members are in more advanced stages of an illness, and therapists should monitor a family's experiences.

A second significant change since the first edition of *Medical Family Therapy* is the development within primary care practices of group visits for disease management of chronic conditions such as diabetes, asthma, and heart disease, and for prenatal visits (Noffsinger, 2009; Wagner et al., 2001). Group visits are scheduled to provide some individual assessment of patients, education about the disease, management possibilities, and opportunities for patients and families to share information and support one another. Groups often are led by multidisciplinary teams, including physicians, nurses, care managers, and mental health specialists, and create new opportunities for medical family therapists.

Some patients and families become supports for others through blogs or by leading Internet support groups. This may be helpful for some phases of chronic illness, but it can also lead to an extensive focus on illness that limits nonillness activities. A former teacher had a rare, painful neuromuscular disease that required periods of hospitalization with significant anesthesia to attempt to reset neural pathways. Given her positive response and upbeat personal style, specialists referred other patients to her for support. After she had told her story too many times to other patients, she decided to keep an online journal about her treatments and experiences. In therapy, she discussed how she felt responsible to the strangers with similar symptoms and felt pressure to write about her experiences, even when she wished to distract herself from the illness. Therapy helped her realize how her support of others was in fact hindering her. She changed her online postings, stating that she wanted to be able to focus on nonillness activities and that she would only post infrequent comments. She hoped that others understood and that they too would work to limit the intrusion of the illness in their lives. She received multiple electronic messages of support.

8. Increase Family's Sense of Agency

Illness is an out-of-control experience. Many experience illness as a trap from which they must fight to escape. They search for mastery or control, but illness generally challenges that sense of control. Agency is enhanced when people decrease their attempts to fight or control the illness, become actively involved in treatment plans, and make intentional choices of how to construct their lives within the realities of illness.

When family members do not feel completely entrapped by illness, they have greater enthusiasm for constructing more enriching lives. Helping families see alternative ways of coping is a spark that draws us to family therapy. This is an area of expertise for family therapists, so this section briefly identifies some of the clinical considerations that are useful for helping patients and families expand options and increase agency. Attention to agency includes increasing participation in negotiation of treatment plans, continuing or substituting life activities, and underlining ways that families are coping well.

Negotiate a Treatment Plan

Therapists can communicate their confidence in the family's ability to make good decisions. This includes supporting them in gathering as much medical information as possible, helping them discuss the possible options, and perhaps facilitating communication with medical providers, as discussed earlier.

Conflict between patients and medical clinicians can occur when the recommendations conflict with their own sense of themselves ("I don't need help, and I certainly don't need medication"), with strongly held family values ("We eat as our grandparents ate; this is part of our tradition"), or with the patient's worldview ("If it's my time to go, then I'm ready; I don't need surgery or medications or any doctors making money off me"). Therapy discussions can help patients and families identify these often hidden views and determine whether they are truly incompatible with some of the medical recommendations. Sometimes it is useful to place a time frame around the negotiation or decision.

A man healing after a mild heart attack refused to change his diet, stating that he loved his wife's cooking just as it was. His wife was willing to cook differently, but he seemed adamant. The therapist suggested they consider trying the modified diet for a month and then reconsider. On the basis of the clear expectation that the reconsideration would be honored, the man agreed that it could be worth a try.

With any serious illness, patients' feelings about their illness and the required sacrifices often change over time. By bracketing the decision with a date for review, the therapist recognizes the patient's right to decide. This allows the patient and family time to digest information about the illness and to know that they can change their responses over time.

Although many areas of illness and care cannot be changed, therapists can help families identify the areas that can be adjusted and make mutually acceptable decisions. Therapists can also help families feel good about their decisions, particularly when families feel competing pressures from others. For instance, families can determine how much they will be responsible for physical care, both in the hospital or at home.

After much deliberation, Bill and Carol Ellman decided to have visiting nurses provide most of the care for the long healing of a wound after amputation. They agreed that Carol should return to work, a decision criticized by both of their mothers. In therapy together, Carol was clear that she wanted to be a spouse, not a nurse, to her husband. He agreed and was able to tell both his mother and mother-in-law that this was something they both wanted and was not up for debate. An unanticipated benefit of this discussion was that Bill was no longer only a man who needed much care but a husband who could stand up for his wife with their parents.

Adapt Activities to Illness Realities

Once families find ways to continue valued activities, they generally enjoy the intentional process of choosing how to live their lives more fully. Agency is enhanced when therapists help families determine what was or is important to them and find ways to incorporate that back into their lives. This requires a balance between acknowledging losses and disappointments and encouraging creative coping. One couple described how they continued their daily walks with the wife's arthritis by walking at the mall, where he could walk longer while she enjoyed window-shopping or having her coffee on a bench.

For Carol Ellman, there was discouragement that Bill's dialysis needs prohibited them from taking vacations. When they discussed what they missed from vacations, they identified a change of scenery and socializing with others. Their compromise was to join a country club, which enabled Carol to take afternoon swims and socialize and allowed the couple to dine occasionally and participate in organized social activities. Bill was concerned about the membership expense but balanced this with the lack of vacation expense and the benefits for them as a couple.

Emphasize Positive Family Responses

A medical family therapist can remind the family of how well, in fact, they are functioning. Families are not usually told that they are doing well— that they are meeting the ill person's needs; that they are adjusting to the social, economic, and physical changes; and that other family responsibilities are being accomplished. With support for the work that is going well, families will have renewed enthusiasm for attempting additional change. Sometimes, as in the following case, humor can be used effectively to demonstrate competence.

A wife felt that she could no longer tolerate her husband's depression after his cancer surgery and radiation. She felt out of control and described how she "lost it totally" in a fight: She took her husband's shirts out of the closet and threw them out of the window. The therapist asked if she had taken scissors to them or ripped them up before she threw them out. The wife look horrified and then laughed, realizing that even when she felt that she had no control, she had arranged her outburst so that the couple could easily retrieve the undamaged clothing.

Share Information With Others

Friends and neighbors show their concern by asking about the ill person's health. Although this is often appreciated, it sometimes is perceived as an intrusion. Community members may hear about someone's illness and want to show concern, but their questions may not be appreciated during a chance meeting at the post office. At the same time, the ill person and family know that others are generally being thoughtful, and they sometimes end up sharing more information than they would prefer. Therapy can address what people want to share and with whom. Therapists can remind families that it is not rude to want to limit discussion of illness. It can be helpful to create some stock answers that allow families to not feel rude but to have a choice in how and with whom they disclose information.

Carol and Bill Ellman had fun practicing responses so that they would be ready when they were surprised by requests for information about Bill's increasing disability. They laughed about rude responses, but settled on "Thank you for asking, but I'd rather focus on other things right now. How is it going for you?" At their session 2 weeks later, they described how frequently they had used similar statements and how people had responded well. Most important, they described how freeing it was to not have to always be responsive to the questions or interests of others.

9. Enhance the Family's Sense of Communion

Communion is enhanced when people move from isolation to allowing and inviting others to be part of their lives. It sometimes feels risky for the patient and family, and there is always the possibility that if others are asked, they may not agree. But our experience holds that when families realize how they have begun to inadvertently exclude others, the others are appreciative about being invited in again.

Bill and Carol increasingly turned down future social engagements with friends. They felt that they had to cancel too many plans because Bill didn't feel well. Carol found herself limiting her calls to friends because she felt that she was always saying the same thing and worried that she was boring to others. When the therapist asked them how they would feel if their best friends made plans with them and had to cancel, they quickly responded that of course they wouldn't mind. The discussion allowed them to realize that if their friends trusted them enough to make contingent plans, they would in fact be honored.

The Ellman's experience demonstrates how emotional connections with others are often frayed by illness. Many of our clients worry about being a burden to others. But uniformly, when asked what they would want if their sibling was sick, they always say that they would want to help the other. As therapists, we can frame this universal interest in being helpful to others as a recognition that a person with illness is in fact providing a gift when they let others assist.

Once Bill and Carol considered their role in limiting their connections with others, they found easy ways to ask small favors of others, most of which were readily granted. One of their favorite statements was one they practiced in a therapy session: "We would love to come with you that evening. There is a small possibility that Bill won't be able to that night. Is it OK if we make the plans, with the possibility that we might have to change them?"

10. Maintain an Empathic Presence With the Family

Like patients and families with chronic illness, medical family therapists must learn to tolerate uncertainty and situations not easily controlled. Therapists may feel most comfortable in the beginning stages of therapy when visible changes occur in family communication and interaction patterns. Some families are satisfied with these changes and soon cease therapy.

Other families elect to continue, perhaps less frequently, with the therapist continuing to be a significant source of emotional support.

Medical family therapy often includes a soft termination, in which the door is left open for future issues or problems. The family members have a sense of accomplishment about the changes they have made and confidence in their ability to continue without therapy; they also know that the therapist is available for further consultation if desired. A common example is therapy with a couple at an early period of an illness who wish to discuss their experiences accepting a diagnosis or explaining the illness to their children. It is not uncommon for some of these couples to return 2 or 3 years later to discuss the changes in their sexual relationship or communication conflicts.

It is essential that therapists not withdraw from families when cure or change is unlikely, but being with patients and families in this empathic way is emotional hard work. Therapists become attached to their clients, cheering during the times of better health and sharing disappointment during the times of crisis. We discuss the role of therapist self-care in Chapter 5, but we recognize that self-care is a learned skill and a required strategy for good medical family therapy. There is a growing literature about how clinicians can maintain empathy over time with the use of self-reflection, narrative work (Charon, 2001), and other creative work (Lorenz, 2011). One of us uses the following metaphor to teach physicians about self-care and awareness at times of crisis: "Before entering an emergency room or a time of crisis, the first pulse that should be taken is our own. If we are nervous, distracted, or concerned about ourselves, we will not be effective healers for our patients." This metaphor is equally useful for therapists.

We meet with families during periods of emergencies and crises. Therapists must avoid distractions or biases based on their own family health experiences. Yet the universality of illness crises means that sometimes we will be concerned about our own or a loved one's health. Separating our own illness concerns from those of our clients is an important skill, which we discuss extensively in Chapter 4. Creating our lives to recognize balance, to ensure a full life apart from our work as therapists, is not a luxury. It is required for good therapy.

LEARNING FROM CHRONIC ILLNESS

Coping with chronic illness is taxing work—for patients, families, and therapists. Families can become isolated, and patients and caregivers can become exhausted by daily care, the burden of responsibility, and feelings of disappointment and loss. Yet there are rewards and benefits for those who persist.

Patients with chronic illness often appreciate aspects of life that healthy people take for granted. When someone can walk without pain only intermittently, the days of painless walking become special days. Participating in new or favorite activities, even with physical disabilities, can be exciting and significant events. Families also share this recognition and may develop a thoughtful perspective about what is important in life. As clinicians, we benefit from learning from those who live with chronic illness.

We do not imply that learning to appreciate health and life in some way offsets the suffering of those with chronic illness. The disappointment and loss experienced by patients and their families are significant. Yet when families and providers support each other, the emotional and physical needs are shared by more people, and each part of the system is less likely to become overwhelmed. With more participants available as problem solvers, it may be easier to find meaning, to define new dreams, and to consider new possibilities for action and relating.

3

COLLABORATION WITH OTHER HEALTH PROFESSIONALS

In the first edition of this book, collaboration with other health professionals was conceptualized as a dyadic relationship between a medical family therapist and a physician, nurse practitioner, or physician's assistant. This is no longer so. Collaboration now is more expansive. In the 21st century, health care is delivered by teams of professionals, and so collaboration is conceptualized as being between the medical family therapist and the professionals on the health care team relevant for that particular patient and his or her particular problem. When a patient is struggling with a medical illness and the therapist does not communicate or collaborate with the relevant medical providers, the therapy is likely to be incomplete or even destructive. Doing medical family therapy without collaborating with relevant health professionals is risky; it is analogous to doing marital therapy with only one spouse.

Like collaboration with the patient and family, collaboration with other health professionals is an essential ingredient in the practice of medical

http://dx.doi.org/10.1037/14256-003
Medical Family Therapy and Integrated Care, Second Edition, by S. H. McDaniel, W. J. Doherty, and J. Hepworth

family therapy. Collaboration is not a relationship in which the medical family therapist is hierarchically superior to the medical provider or the medical provider is hierarchically superior to the therapist. It is a partnership of two or more practitioners who respect each other's skills and communicate in a way that enhances the care of our patients, a partnership that is increasingly important as health care integrates its physical and mental health services. Partnership occurs across a health care team—with physicians, nurses, nutritionists, pharmacists, and physical and occupational therapists, along with medical family therapists and other psychosocial providers. Collaborative partnerships are an integrated response to the inseparable biological and psychosocial processes with which our patients and their families struggle.

The extent of collaboration is dependent, in part, on the nature of the patient and family's problem. Realistically, in everyday health care with uncomplicated problems, it is possible to provide decent patient care when professionals simply tolerate each other, meaning that they communicate basic information about their respective treatments. Cooperation implies adapting to each other's care, and full collaboration involves dialogue and a coordinated, shared treatment plan (also known as *collaborative* or *integrated care*). See Figure 3.1. The more complex and difficult the problem, the more important that health professionals move along the continuum from tolerating each other, to cooperating, to collaborating.

As shared care has developed over recent decades, so has the terminology. C. J. Peek (2011) usefully organized the relevant terminology. *Colocation* refers to behavioral health (and medical providers (e.g., physicians, nurse practitioners) delivering care in the same practice but without a common framework or practice to integrate that care. *Collaborative care* is an overarching term describing ongoing communication between clinicians (e.g., behavioral health and health professionals) over time that results in a shared treatment plan for patients. The term implies collaboration with patients and their families as well as collaboration among the treatment team. *Integrated care* refers to on-site teamwork with a unified care plan. It sometimes refers to integration at the level of the program, funding, or other systemic infrastructure as well; this kind of integrated care is quickly developing and now normative in the U.S. Department of Defense and the U.S. Department of Veterans Affairs primary care clinics, for instance.

Figure 3.1. A continuum of working together.

Achieving a collaborative partnership with other health professionals requires medical family therapists to develop skills in joining, networking, consulting, and providing larger systems assessment and intervention. Exercising these skills provides the medical family therapist with opportunities to learn more about the physical and biological aspects of problems and to prevent the rigidity, burnout, or "psychosocial fixation" (McDaniel, Campbell, & Seaburn, 1989) that can come from working in isolation. Therapists and physicians or other health professionals can draw on their different perspectives and areas of expertise to share the care and responsibility for challenging, multifaceted cases.

Although medical providers and family therapists have much to offer each other, it was not until the 1980s that close collaboration between physicians and therapists became common. Doherty and Baird's (1983) description of their early collaboration inspired family therapists to explore new relationships with medical providers working in hospitals, offices, and agencies. This early enthusiasm also uncovered differences between family therapists and medical professionals in their approaches to problems—differences that, if allowed to go unrecognized or unacknowledged, can inhibit successful collaboration.

With time, distinct clinical roles evolved for the medical family therapist working collaboratively. These include provider and team consultation as well as systemic behavioral health consultation, brief systemic therapy, and intensive medical family therapy. The team consultation is particularly important as clinical teams develop in primary care and specialty clinics. Medical family therapists may also find themselves seeing physicians, other health professionals, and their families as patients.[1]

THE EVIDENCE FOR COLLABORATIVE CARE

In the first edition of *Medical Family Therapy*, collaborative care was conceptualized as a cornerstone of the approach because it is the natural extension of a family and larger systems approach. Since that time, a program of research has developed to test this idea. Which kind of collaboration works for which kind of patients with which kind of problems? Although definitive answers to that question await future research, we have started down the path of discovery (M. Butler et al., 2008).

Most studies are based on individually oriented behavioral or psychiatric interventions; few include systemic conceptualization or treatment.

---

[1]Physicians and other health professionals often see their friends as patients and so may need education about not seeing close colleagues (e.g., people who work closely together on-site) for psychotherapy.

Even so, these large-scale studies point to important elements that contribute to effective collaborative care. An early large-scale study in Hawaii of collaboration between primary care and mental health professionals working at different sites from each other ("off-site") showed impressive reductions in health care utilization and costs (Cummings, Dorken, Pallak, & Henke, 1990). Although clinicians did not work in the same physical space, the island of Hawaii afforded economic and geographic support for significant communication and collaboration.

Later meta-analyses of interactive communication between primary care physicians and mental health specialists[2] (joint initial sessions, team meetings, phone contact, and electronic notes) suggest that collaboration is associated with improved patient outcomes (Foy et al., 2010). Many collaborative care studies include stepped-care interventions, allowing patient preference for medication versus psychotherapy. If the initial treatment is not successful, the patient is "stepped up" to the other form of treatment.

Patients with chronic, persistent symptoms receive a combined approach from the beginning. Many of these studies include case managers to ensure strong links between the patient and providers, adherence to medication and appointments with primary care providers and therapists. Large-scale trials demonstrate the effectiveness of this model of collaborative care for mental health problems such as depression (Katon, 2009; Katon et al., 1995), postpartum depression (Gjerdingen, Crow, McGovern, Miner, & Center, 2009), and anxiety in primary care (Roy-Byrne et al., 2005). It has also been shown to be effective with common comorbidities, such as when depression co-occurs with chronic illnesses, such as diabetes (Ell et al., 2010) and arthritis (Lin et al., 2003), and in diverse populations (Vera et al., 2010). On-site collaborative care has also been shown to provide greater patient access to mental and behavioral health care services and yield higher physician satisfaction, reduced treatment time, fewer appointments, and hence lower costs than traditional referral to off-site mental health centers (Blount et al., 2007; Katon & Unutzer, 2006; van Orden, Hoffman, Haffmans, Spinhoven, & Hoencamp, 2009).

In a case study demonstrating the many advantages of a medical family therapist implementing collaborative care, Larry Mauksch completed an assessment of the Marillac Clinic in Colorado that provides primary care to a rural, poor population (Cameron & Mauksch, 2002). The Marillac population had a high prevalence of one or more mental health disorders (51% compared with 28% in the general population). On the basis of that assessment, Mauksch completed training for the Marillac staff on patient- and

---

[2]This study was primarily psychiatrists.

family-centered care. The clinic instituted screening for common problems such as depression, provided some mental and behavioral health services, developed an interagency consortium to strengthen linkages among related services for these patients, and conducted research to study outcomes. With Executive Director Janet Cameron, Mauksch and colleagues succeeded at transforming the culture of the clinic and the health care community, reconfigured its operations, and improved communication patterns among providers. In addition, they found that 90% of their patients preferred this kind of collaborative care (vs. traditional referral care for mental health problems).

The variables studied in research to date reflect the existing nature of collaborative care. These variables vary by the geography of the work, the model that is implemented, and the kinds of communication among providers. The studies also reveal the many challenges to large-scale implementation of collaborative care approaches to health care, which require attention to clinical, operational, and financial worlds (Peek, 2008). The rest of this chapter focuses on these variables and challenges from a practical, clinical perspective.

LEVELS OF SYSTEMIC AND ORGANIZATIONAL COLLABORATION

The degree of collaboration possible in the care of any particular patient is determined by the medical family therapist's skill at collaborating, the receptivity of the other health professionals involved, and also the orientation and infrastructure offered by the health system or agencies involved. Table 3.1 describes the degree of involvement possible in any collaborative case (Doherty, McDaniel, & Baird, 1996). It shows the extent to which collaboration occurs and indicates the capacity for increased collaboration in the health care setting as a whole.

Level 1, or *minimal collaboration*, assumes that mental and health professionals tolerate each other. They work at separate sites (as with private practices or mental health centers), rarely communicate, and have little appreciation for each other's work. Level 1 adequately handles patients with straightforward, uncomplicated problems.

Level 2, or *basic collaboration from a distance*, describes mental and health professionals who work at separate sites but have active referral linkages across facilities. It adequately handles cases with mild-moderate biopsychosocial interplay.

Level 3, or *basic collaboration on-site*, assumes that mental health and health professionals have separate systems but share the same facility (such as with some HMOs, rehabilitation centers, or hospitals) and have some regular

TABLE 3.1

Levels of Systemic Collaboration Between Therapists and Other Health Professionals

Level	Description	Location	Handles adequately	Handles inadequately
1. Minimal collaboration	Separate facilities and systems Rarely communicate	Private practice, most agencies	Routine medical or psychosocial problems	Refractory problems or those with biopsychosocial interplay
2. Basic collaboration, off-site	Separate facilities and systems Periodic communication about patients, linkages, treatment planning	Setting with active referral linkages	Patients with moderate biopsychosocial interplay (e.g., diabetes, depression)	Problems with significant biopsychosocial interplay
3. Basic collaboration, on-site	Separate mental health and other health care systems in the same facility Regular communication and appreciation of each other's work Ill-defined teams, no common language Physicians have more power and influence than other providers, who may resent this	Some HMOs, rehabilitation settings, medical clinics, without systemic approaches to collaboration, mutual consultation, and team building	Patients with moderate biopsychosocial interplay who require occasional face-to-face interactions among providers and coordinated treatment plans	Problems with significant biopsychosocial interplay and ongoing, challenging management problems

4. Close collaboration in a partly integrated system	Shared site and systems Regular interaction, mutual consultations Shared systemic and biopsychosocial paradigm Routines difficult, some attention to team building Unresolved tensions over physicians' greater power and influence on the team	Some HMOs, CHCs, rehabilitation settings, hospice, family medicine, and other clinical settings that systematically build teams	Problems with significant biopsychosocial interplay and management problems (e.g., chronic illness, somatization)	Complex patients with multiple providers and multiple systems, especially with conflicting agendas among providers or triangulation by patients or families
5. Close collaboration in a fully integrated system	Shared site, systems and biopsychosocial vision Shared expectations for team-based prevention and treatment Regular team meetings Conscious effort to balance power and influence among providers, according to patient need and provider expertise	Some large, closed health systems, primary care clinics, hospice, etc.	The most difficult and complex biopsychosocial problems with challenging management issues	Patients with insufficient team resources or breakdowns in collaboration with larger systems

Note. Data from Doherty (1995).
CHC = community health center.

communication but without significant knowledge of each other's roles. They do not have a shared language or paradigm or way to manage power inequities. It adequately handles cases with moderate biopsychosocial interplay that benefit from interaction and coordination between providers.

Level 4, or *close collaboration in a partly integrated system*, describes mental health and other health professionals who share the same site, systems, and biopsychosocial paradigm (some HMOs, rehabilitation centers, family practice clinics, and hospices that build teamwork). They have regular face-to-face interaction about patients, mutual consultation, and coordinated treatment plans for complicated patients. Attention to team-building is infrequent; tensions about power inequities are unresolved but manageable. Level 4 adequately handles cases with significant biopsychosocial interplay and management complications.

Level 5, or *close collaboration in a fully integrated system*, assumes mental health and other health professionals with the same site, systems, and biopsychosocial systemic paradigm (e.g., the Veterans Affairs and U.S. Department of Defense, Group Health Cooperative in Seattle, the Mayo Clinic, Tennessee Cherokee Health and Tenn-Care [Tennessee's Medicaid system]; M. Butler et al., 2008; National Academy for State Health Policy, 2010).

Within these highly integrated teams, there is a strong commitment to team-based care in which providers have an in-depth understanding of each other's roles and cultures and a shared language. Regular team meetings are held, along with conscious efforts to balance power and influence based on patient problem and provider expertise. Level 5 handles the most complex, biopsychosocial cases with multiple problems and providers. Of course, because our medical system is not integrated with other care systems such as social services, schools, and housing, breakdowns can still occur when patients must interact with multiple community systems. Specific issues and implications based on the level of collaboration are detailed in the following sections.

ON- AND OFF-SITE COLLABORATION

Most research about on-site collaboration has focused on a particular disease entity. In practice, collaboration can occur across illnesses and between professionals at more traditional practices in different locations (Ruddy, Borresen, & Gunn, 2008) as well at settings that provide on-site integrated care (Seaburn et al., 1996). Toolkits are beginning to emerge to help with Memos of Understanding and other aspects of the pragmatics of collaboration (Integrated Behavioral Health Project, 2009). Whether off- or on-site, accessibility to the treatment team is a prerequisite to effective collaboration.

In 1990, the Task Force on Family Therapy and Family Medicine, composed of representatives of the American Association for Marriage and Family Therapy and the Society for Teachers of Family Medicine, conducted an informal survey of 60 family therapists and physicians involved in collaborative relationships (Campbell & Williamson, 1990). The major themes that emerged from these questionnaires were that therapists wanted respect from their medical colleagues and that physicians wanted therapists to be accessible when needed. Physicians also wanted therapists to respect their time constraints and skills as physicians and support the physician–patient relationship during psychotherapy. Not much has changed in this regard.

What has changed is that although still not the dominant paradigm, integrating family therapists into medical care in primary and specialty care settings is now not unusual. Team-based care is an important part of the *patient-centered health care home* or *advanced primary care*, with many arguing that behavioral and mental health care professionals are essential members of the team (Council of Academic Family Medicine, 2012; McDaniel & Fogarty, 2009). Collaborative care also occurs in specialty centers such as cancer centers, cardiac rehabilitation, epilepsy centers, fertility centers, transplant units, and many other medical contexts. Although not all the mental health providers in these systems are medical family therapists, the move toward integrated care provides important opportunities for medical family therapists to participate in improving health care for patients and their families. Many health systems are focusing on improving their relationships with patients and families (B. Johnson, Ford, & Abraham, 2010) and, once educated, appreciate the knowledge and expertise of medical family therapists.

Practicing at the same location can occur by sharing office space with a physician or nurse practitioner group or by working at a community health center or managed care organization, at a hospital, or in a residency practice. All these arrangements allow therapists easy access to referrals, physicians and other health professionals easy access to consultation, and patients easy access to behavioral health consultation or mental health treatment. Whether medical family therapists work in the same building or across town (Driscoll & McCabe, 2004), being accessible means having an assistant, an answering service, or a pager; promptly returning calls; responding promptly to e-mail or electronic notes generated in the chart; or arranging to be available on the hour or at a particular time of day, so that other providers can communicate as needed. It also means attending team meetings when it benefits the patient's care.

Whether working on-site or off-site, even in this electronic age, nothing substitutes for knowing a referral source personally; it can be as essential to the overall success of medical family therapy as is joining with the patient and his or her family. Macaran Baird, a family physician, described how he developed a personal network when he began his practice by meeting with physicians, therapists, police, and social service workers in his community (Doherty & Baird, 1983). Once he had invested this relatively small amount of time joining with the professional members of his community, he was able to pick up the phone and collaborate, refer, or request help from many of these people efficiently and effectively.

Medical family therapists, especially when establishing a practice, should do the same. Therapists are often reluctant to ask for time from physicians and may find it helpful to secure an introduction from a respected medical colleague. Even without this, it is often possible to find a forum to introduce oneself to physicians and staff at a team meeting or lunchtime. Many physicians and nurse practitioners are acutely aware of the behavioral and mental health care needs of their patients and are frustrated by the lack of access to reliable services. The clinicians appreciate a request to discuss common interests because they need therapists who are competent and who communicate and support the treatment or their relationship with the patient. At these meetings, it is often useful to ask about their most challenging patients and problems because these often turn out to be situations well suited to medical family therapy skills. In addition, physicians and therapists can discuss treatment philosophies, common treatment strategies, and preferences for how to communicate once a referral is made. These interactions, whether the therapist works on- or off-site, articulate a blueprint for subsequent collaboration.

Colocation increases the rate at which referrals turn into actual consultation or therapy, but working in close proximity does not guarantee effective collaboration. Crane (1986) detailed her expectations and experiences working in a health maintenance organization with health professionals. She described how limited time for discussion and lack of role clarification led to adversarial and conflictual relationships among providers and frustration with patients. To be successful, one's model of collaboration must include effective communication and role clarification.

SYSTEMIC CONSULTATION AND COLLABORATIVE TREATMENT

Primary care professionals consult with specialists about their patients. Etiquette about this consultation includes an understanding that the consultant will deal only with patient concerns in his or her own area of expertise and the importance of maintaining support for the relationship between the patient and the referring provider. Many physicians make behavioral or mental health referrals just as they do referrals for oncology or ophthalmology, and they expect therapists to conform to this traditional medical etiquette. A systems consultation model (Wynne, 1986) allows family therapists to merge systems theory and techniques with a consultative role that conforms to medical etiquette. Three common forms of collaborative relationships are behavioral health consultation, joint sessions, and referral (Hepworth & Jackson, 1985; McDaniel, Campbell, Hepworth, & Lorenz, 2005).

Systemic Behavioral Health Consultation

A large body of literature is developing about behavioral health consultation, referring primarily to targeted intervention to promote health behavior change from an individually oriented, behavioral, health psychology perspective (Hunter, Hunter, Goodie, Oordt, & Dobmeyer, 2009; Robinson & Reiter, 2007; Strosahl, 1994). A systemic behavioral health consultant can incorporate these skills within a broader systemic treatment framework that takes into account other needed interventions with the patient, the patient's relevant family, as well as the treatment team. Family therapists as consultants are responsible for clarifying the nature of consultation and negotiating appropriate boundaries and roles (Wynne, 1986)—whether provider and team consultation, patient and family consultation, brief treatment, or intensive medical family therapy.

The medical family therapist as systemic behavioral health consultant includes many potential roles (see Exhibit 3.1):

- *Track patient medical and mental health outcomes.* For example, the therapist can have a patient with diabetes and depression fill out the Patient Health Questionnaire (PHQ9) at intake, track his or her depression scores with this scale with each visit, and report them to the patient and the referring provider to inform treatment, in addition to paying attention to this patient's hemoglobin A1C through the electronic health record (EHR). (Treating their depression in patients with diabetes has been shown to improve diabetes outcomes; Ell et al., 2010.)
- *Track medication and treatment adherence, including any adverse effects.* For example, patients who start on antidepressant medication often discontinue its use when typical side effects occur. Close collaboration with the patient and the medical provider can sustain the patient until the effects subside or the patient signals a need to try a different medication.
- *Support patients' relationship with their primary care provider and other relevant health professionals.* Patients will often give feedback about their physician to their medical family therapist and about their therapist to their physician. With the former, it can be useful to coach the patient on how to give feedback to the

EXHIBIT 3.1
Systemic Behavioral Health Consultant Roles

- Track patient medical and mental health outcomes.
- Track medication and treatment adherence, including any adverse effects.
- Support patients' relationship with their primary care provider and other relevant health professionals.
- Provide psychoeducation to patients and families about the diagnoses.
- Encourage patient activation and self-management.
- Use motivational interviewing techniques to clarify patients' motivation for change and treatment.
- Negotiate a mutually agreeable treatment plan among patient, family, and providers.
- Facilitate family support.
- Encourage medication or psychiatric consultation if mental health problems do not improve.

referring provider directly. With the latter, ask the other health professional to encourage the patient or family to speak frankly about the therapy, saying the professional knows the therapist is always interested in hearing feedback.

- *Provide psychoeducation to the patient and family about the diagnoses.* The medical family therapist may direct the patient and family to National Institute of Health websites that provide state-of-the-art education about various diseases. He or she can also provide information about the inevitable vacillating emotions that come with serious illness (see Chapter 4).

- *Encourage patient activation and self-management.* Increasing patient and family agency is a central tenet of medical family therapy. Any plan that helps patients take charge of their health behavior change such as exercise or diet, medication, or emotional response to the illness (e.g., keeping a diary about the experience; Bodenheimer, Wagner, & Grumbach, 2002) is useful.

- *Use motivational interviewing techniques to clarify patient's motivation for change and treatment* (W. Miller & Rollnick, 2002). It is important to determine whether the patient is not yet contemplating a change, is thinking about it, or is ready to take action. A plan that assumes action when the patient is in an earlier stage of contemplation is doomed to fail. It also is important to assess family members' readiness to change and ensure that they are supporting rather than blocking or pushing the patient to do what is best.

- *Negotiate a mutually agreeable treatment plan among patient, family, and providers* (McDaniel, Campbell, Hepworth, & Lorenz,

2005). This process can be brief or prolonged, depending on how close each person's view of the plan is to the rest of the treatment team. The first step is to elicit the medical provider's recommended treatment plan and determine the patient and family's response to it. If the patient or family does not agree with the plan for any reason (e.g., cost, religious beliefs, non-medical health beliefs), a joint meeting can be useful to openly discuss the difficulties and renegotiate a plan that everyone can agree to, or at least accept.

■ *Facilitate family support.* Some families immediately rise to the occasion when a medical crisis occurs. Some help too much, preventing the patient from making decisions or doing tasks he or she is fully capable of doing. Others hold back, fearing that their presence will signal disaster. The medical family therapist can facilitate a discussion with the patient about how he or she would like to be supported while ill.

■ Encourage medication or psychiatric consultation if mental health problems do not improve. A psychiatric consultation may be in order, for example, when a patient scores high on the PHQ9 or does not improve.

In many integrated settings, a medical family therapy consult involves a "warm handoff" in which the physician, physician's assistant, or nurse practitioner brings the medical family therapist into an office visit, introduces him or her, and provides justification and support for the patient or family's work with the therapist. This process jump-starts the therapeutic encounter and increases the chances of future therapy visits. Apostoleris (2000) found that if the primary care clinician introduced them, most of these patients kept the first behavioral health appointment. Without a "warm handoff," only 44% kept the first appointment.

Behavioral health consults can be as brief as 10 to 15 minutes or as long as any traditional psychotherapy session. The "informal hallway" consultation (Hepworth & Jackson, 1985) is available to practitioners whose paths cross because of geographic proximity or because the providers have easy telephone or computer access. A physician may call a therapist before a follow-up visit with an adolescent and her mother because the physician wants to know how to screen for anorexia. A therapist may stop a physician in the hall to ask whether a medical evaluation is appropriate for a particular symptom. Such discussions may or may not result in follow-up discussions, formal consultations, or referral. They reflect an ongoing, mutually supportive, and respectful relationship between colleagues. Typically, these collaborations that do not include the patient are not directly reimbursable in fee-for-service, noncapitated[3] environments in the United States. Some insurers are beginning to consider reimbursement for collaboration because it so clearly improves safety and quality; until then, it must be seen as part of the billing, just like documentation.

Formal consultations may occur between the therapist and physician or among therapist, physician, and family. They can occur much like a referral, but with a focused question to be answered over a brief period of time. Some approaches to integrated care provide only brief behavioral health consultation, referring out all behavioral or mental health needs that cannot be managed in one to three sessions. (Other settings provide behavioral health as well as psychiatric consultation and ongoing treatment. Those settings then refer out patients who need a higher level of mental health care, such as partial hospitalization, intensive substance abuse treatment, or hospitalization.)

At Salud Community Health Center in Denver, the goal is for all patients to see a behavioral health consultant at least once a year. If the behavioral health provider is not busy with a scheduled patient, he or she goes into any patient's room to check on the person's psychosocial well-being and then communicates directly with the primary care medical provider. Similarly, at Rochester General Hospital, medical family therapists often see a parent and child who come for a well-child check ahead of the pediatrician, communicating with that person through the EHR or in person about developmental and psychosocial issues before the medical visit. In both these settings, neither referral nor pathology is required for attention from the medical family therapist. As more systems focus on prevention and therapists become a salaried part of an integrated payment system, these practices are likely to become more common.

Andersen (1984), a family psychiatrist in Norway, described his practice in which he did not have his own office but traveled some distance across northern Norway to offices of general practitioners to consult with physicians and see their patients. Coons, Morgenstern, Hoffman, Striepe, and Buch (2004) described a similar, more geographically contained practice in Philadelphia focused on women's health and working in offices of obstetrician-gynecologists. The Internet and videoconferencing offer other opportunities for consultation between therapists and other health professionals.

---

[3]*Capitation* refers to lump-sum payment for health services for a population of people. This kind of financing, which was expected to become common in the 1980s, never took hold, other than in large HMOs such as Kaiser and large organizations such as the U.S. Department of Defense and the U.S. Department of Veterans Affairs. Unlike fee-for-service, which encourages providers to do more of what secures the fee (i.e., face-to-face contact with the patients who have problems), capitated plans allow providers to promote health, collaborate, and do whatever is necessary to improve the health of the largest number of people. Without other controls, the danger of fee-for-service plans is overtreatment; the danger of capitated plans is undertreatment.

Joint Sessions

Joint sessions may be arranged in advance, or the need may arise during the time of the medical visit, requiring flexibility (and sometimes interruption) in the medical family therapist's schedule. This degree of flexibility and juggling regarding patient care is different from that of a traditional mental health agency or practice. It can be experienced as exciting or chaotic and is an important part of training as a medical family therapist. Joint sessions require that the two professionals negotiate roles, hold frank discussions of the relationship between the collaborators, and continue evaluating the process and content of sessions.

An initial network session with the professional care providers, the patient, and family members is the most powerful way to begin a difficult medical family therapy case. It allows all parties to discuss the reasons for the referral, the goals for treatment, and the interaction between the medical and the therapy treatment plans. Professional roles can be clarified immediately. Compatibility between the medical and the psychotherapy goals can be ensured. This visible collaborative effort demonstrates to the family that the physician or other health professional and the therapist will work together to help them reach their goals. It helps mitigate any feeling on the part of the patient that the referral represents the physician's criticism or abandonment. A network session begins the process of openly clarifying and negotiating what Wynne, Shields, and Sirkin (1992) described as the differing perspectives of illness that are inevitably represented by patients, family members, and health care professionals.

In one case, for example, a cardiologist and a marital therapist needed to coordinate their treatment plan with a couple who had experienced sexual and marital dysfunction after the husband's heart attack. It was helpful to have both clinicians meeting with the couple together because the case involved significant medical and psychological-interpersonal issues. Some physicians are interested in close collaboration with a medical family therapist out of intellectual curiosity, dedication to their patients, or conflicting personal issues that are impeding treatment. Other health professionals may decline the invitation because of the time demands of their practice or their belief that the meeting is not necessary or their presence not important.

Joint sessions are effective with families in which there is considerable doubt or disagreement about the diagnosis ("illness ambiguity"; Wynne et al., 1992), with a patient who utilizes many health care services, in a problematic doctor–patient relationship, or when medical problems are chronic and variable or families are inappropriately focused on somatic problems (Frey & Wendorf, 1984; McDaniel et al., 2005; Sargent, 1985). For these concerns, the simultaneous involvement of medical and family therapy providers allows for a closely integrated biopsychosocial approach in which biological and psychosocial processes can be discussed together, information can be shared, and triangulation[4] can be minimized.

Most joint sessions, even for off-site therapists, will occur at the physician's office or hospital during a patient's admission. Sometimes it is not necessary for the physician to attend the entire interview. The physician may join the therapist at the beginning or the end of a session to describe a diagnosis or procedure, answer questions, and emphasize the collaborative nature of the treatment. When the therapist and the physician are unable to be in the same place at the same time, technology can help. By scheduling a phone call using a speakerphone or Internet conferencing, the referring provider can speak to the therapist and the family during the first part of an initial session to relate the reasons for the referral and discuss any issues of mutual concern.

Joint sessions are an excellent educational tool and easily available in residency programs in which family therapists are involved in teaching and clinical care. Campbell and McDaniel (1987), for example, described family systems treatment with joint sessions for chronic illnesses and somatization disorder. These joint sessions occur less frequently in private practice, but some fascinating experiments were conducted by pioneers in the private practice setting. Dym and Berman (1986) described a joint health care team of a family physician and a family therapist who together held initial meetings with all patients. After evaluating the symptoms and stressors from a systemic perspective, the two practitioners worked separately but with frequent, brief joint meetings. On the basis of his own practice experience as a family physician, Glenn (1987) proposed a similar collaborative model in which the family physician and the family therapist form the core of a primary health care team that involves other health personnel as needed.

A more recent version of care provided by medical and behavioral health providers together is the medical group visit now common in primary care (Noffsinger, 2009). These groups combine individual medical examinations, psychoeducation, and group support for a variety of issues such as prenatal care, diabetes, and depression.

Seeing two professionals at once can be difficult to fund in a fee-for-service environment in which two professionals cannot bill for the same service. McDaniel, at times, alternates billing with a physician for a patient

---

[4]*Triangulation* is when one person has a conflict or issue with another and tries to manage the problem by talking to a third person rather than directly to the person involved. With collaboration, this could happen, for example, when a patient complains about a therapist to the primary care physician. The result can be that the physician develops a distorted view of the therapy or the therapist, and the patient does not resolve the issue with the therapist. Ideally, the physician encourages the patient to talk directly to the therapist about any concerns, and the physician may make the therapist aware of the situation. This would be *detriangulation*.

service that clearly benefits from cotherapy. In capitated or socialized medicine environments in which professionals are salaried, these services are more easily funded for rare and complex patients who clearly benefit from this intensely collaborative approach.

Referrals

Many collaborative relationships between family therapists and physicians are based on referrals, whether for brief or intensive medical family therapy. With referrals, the family therapist and the referring health professional provide different kinds of care simultaneously, whether working at the same or separate sites. All providers are responsible for their respective treatments, and role clarification is essential.

In hospital settings, family therapists, as members of the health care team, generally accept referrals and are in close contact with other members of the health care team (McCall & Storm, 1985). Charts are shared, patients and families are discussed, and treatment plans are coordinated. Family therapists in residency training settings (Hepworth, Gavazzi, Adlin, & Miller, 1988; Seaburn et al., 1996) also often work as referral sources with separate sessions but with frequent contact between physician and therapist providers. Independent practice family therapists may receive referrals from physicians or nurses but not yet think of themselves as collaborative partners. Although they work in different physical locations, providers inform families how they communicate and function as a team (Driscoll & McCabe, 2004). It is the communication between providers, from the referral question to prognosis and treatment outcomes, that characterizes the success of the collaboration and often the outcome of the case.

COMMUNICATING WITH OTHER HEALTH PROFESSIONALS

Regardless of the structure or geography of the collaborative relationship, communication about shared patients is at the center of collaboration and begins when either the therapist or the medical provider requests help.

Exploring the Consultation or Referral Question

One of McDaniel's first medical referrals was from an obstetrician who requested a "psychological evaluation" of a 39-year-old single woman who was requesting a donor insemination procedure to have her first child. The obstetrician said he always asked any single obstetrics patients to see a therapist, both for his own protection and for the patient and her family to have the opportunity to discuss the request and its likely consequences. McDaniel thought this request sounded straightforward and scheduled a session with the patient, her mother, and her sister to discuss the procedure. During the session, it became clear that the patient was ambivalent about the procedure and more interested in proving to her family that she was an "adult" than she was in actually raising a child. The session ended with the woman realizing she did not want to proceed with the insemination and the family agreeing to communicate better.

When this outcome was reported back to the referring physician, he became angry and implied that the therapist had "talked this woman out of her last chance to have a baby." McDaniel then realized that she had not explored the physician's view of the problem when he made the referral. It was several years before this physician made another referral to her. As a consequence, McDaniel learned to spend time in the early phase of the referral soliciting the physician's view and discussing the possible outcomes of a consultation.

The timing of a referral can be critical. When a referral is premature, the referring provider may be more motivated for the treatment than either the patient or the family, and the patient or family is likely not to appear for their therapy appointment. In these cases, the medical family therapist will want to consult informally with the referring provider to gauge the patient's motivation for change. The therapist may suggest how the physician can better manage the patient in his or her practice and slowly seed the idea of a therapy referral (Seaburn et al., 1996). With many patients, the referral process requires the medical provider to cultivate a complex set of assessment and interviewing skills while being supported by the medical family therapist.

Sometimes the referral occurs from the patient or the physician when considerable stress accompanies the diagnosis and treatment of a serious illness. Most physicians are trained to cure diseases but not to treat the experience of illness (Kleinman, 1988; Wynne, Shields, & Sirkin, 1992). The patient or family may diagnose the problem one way and the physician another, leading to conflict and eventual referral. Sometimes family therapists are consulted when the patient's experience of illness may not be recognized or validated by the medical team.

When a health professional makes a referral to a medical family therapist, the therapist needs to solicit or retrieve information about the patient and family. Information may be available in a shared EHR, with the referral made to the therapist through an electronic note attached to the chart. Medical family therapists must learn to use these computer-based documentation systems, including negotiating the chart to find relevant information, reading medical notes, and asking questions about the patient's health status as relevant to their care.

Clarifying Roles

Role confusion results in ambiguities in the therapeutic relationship (Wynne, 1986). Patients may bring biomedical complaints to therapy and psychosocial complaints to their physician. Thus, clarification of the nature of the relationships and a coordinated management plan are important requirements of effective collaboration. For a patient with chronic headaches, for example, the physician may wish to order tests and prescribe medications, leaving the stress reduction and counseling to the family therapist. Then, when the patient's husband questions the therapist about the medication being given to his wife, it is relatively easy to refer him back to the physician. Similarly, therapists must communicate to physicians the particular areas they wish to handle. It may be helpful to suggest that patients or families who raise a particular emotional issue with the physician be encouraged to raise their concerns in their next therapy session. Such role clarity limits destructive patterns of triangulation.

Medical family therapy sometimes includes collaboration with other mental health providers. Many avenues are available for the psychosocial treatment of patients with physical illness. A depressed patient may require a medication evaluation from a psychiatrist or a primary care physician. A patient with chronic pain may benefit from acupuncture or biofeedback. Patients with chronic illness may benefit from psychoeducational multifamily groups (Gonzalez, Steinglass, & Reiss, 1987). The ideal behavioral health team for a medical setting may include a medical family therapist, a psychiatrist, a case manager, and others.

When multiple health and mental health providers participate in one case, the possibility of role confusion, triangulation, and lack of communication multiplies. The medical family therapist needs to help negotiate clear expectations regarding who is to do what and to maintain close communication with other providers. With complicated or recalcitrant problems, a network session with the mental health providers, the family, and the health professionals can be useful in achieving these goals (Speck & Attneave, 1972).

Referral Etiquette

Many physicians report that they receive no communication from off-site therapists to whom they refer (Ruddy, Borresen, & Gunn, 2008). Therapists, of course, complain that physicians are busy and difficult to reach, but most physicians will respond to a persistent attempt to communicate. Treatment without communication is like two blindfolded drivers on a racetrack; not colliding is a matter of luck. Communication is the foundation of successful collaboration.

Most physicians send letters or electronic notes to therapists describing the patient and the reasons for referral, as is the custom with referrals to any specialist. In return, the physician typically expects pragmatic communication from the therapist regarding assessment, treatment, and recommendations for the physician. These communications may provide information valued by the traditional medical model (e.g., a mental status evaluation) as well as brief information about systems dynamics that might be useful in the medical care of a patient. Phone calls are also sometimes necessary but should be brief during physicians' patient hours when time is already pressured. Therapists and medical providers may differ in both their beliefs about confidentiality and their style of communicating.

Confidentiality

The need to share information arises because nursing and medicine, and the therapy disciplines, socialize their trainees differently about maintaining patient confidentiality. Most therapists are trained not to share the details of therapy with others, including other health professionals. Generally, therapists are taught that the therapy relationship is unlike the patient's relationships with other professionals and that patient confidentiality in psychotherapy is sacred. To encourage the patient and family to safely discuss embarrassing or personal material that might help them improve their lives, therapists do not communicate with others about the patient or family without a signed release from the relevant parties.

Health professionals, on the other hand, are trained to work within teams that share relevant information to coordinate and facilitate patient care. Many health professionals, such as primary care physicians, also attend to the psychosocial needs and information of their patients and so resent the practice of therapists not encouraging patient consent and sharing of information. Fragmentation of care may occur, and it is considered a major safety and quality problem when one provider is unaware of the treatment plan of another provider for the same patient. EHRs have improved this communication but provide new challenges for confidentiality. With law related to HIPAA (the U.S. Health Insurance Portability and Accountability Act of 1996), confidentiality is viewed as critical for all health professionals and staff, with breaches considered serious misconduct with grave consequences. With EHRs, viewing can be tracked, and a professional or staff member who views someone's chart but is not part of the team's patient panel typically loses his or her job.

The privilege of confidentiality is the patient's, not the provider's.[5] Therapists may wish to obtain signed releases from patients agreeing to this collaboration, and some EHRs require extra steps or passcodes to read mental

---

[5]Health systems are rapidly moving toward patient portals and other mechanisms for patients to access part or all of their own medical records.

health notes to ensure that only those providers working with the patient have access. The vast majority of times, patients are pleased to have their providers communicate with each other and coordinate their treatment plans. When this is not the case, the therapist needs to determine whether maintaining confidentiality about a particular topic is reasonable because it does not affect the patient's medical care or whether the issue represents triangulation, is part of the patient's interactional problems, and needs to be handled like any other destructive secret in family therapy (Imber-Black, 1993).

Sometimes systems organize themselves and manage confidentiality in ways that make collaboration unlikely. For example, professionals working at a health center wished to have a closer, integrated relationship with the group providing mental health services to these patients. The two services were geographically separated and used separate charting systems; providers at both services bemoaned the lack of collaboration. Because of a lack of communication, physicians and nurse practitioners felt that the mental health services group was of little practical help in general. Therapists felt that the health professionals were not interested in the mental health of their patients and wondered why they received so few referrals.

When the director of the mental health unit and the director of the medical unit discussed this problem with a medical family therapy consultant, issues about confidentiality were identified as a major barrier to collaboration between the two units. If a patient self-referred to a therapist, the policy was that the patient would decide whether to inform the medical provider that he or she was in therapy. This was rarely encouraged, and therapists never negotiated with patients about collaborating with a medical provider. The health professionals, for their part, referred only those patients who requested therapy or who were in the process of decompensating.

Discussion with these competent and well-meaning directors heated up when the consultant asked about psychotherapy patients who had medical problems. For example, did the units collaborate when a patient needed to have an HIV test? The director of the mental health unit said that patients were occasionally referred to the medical unit but that AIDS raised such important confidentiality issues that they recommended patients be tested by the Health Department to ensure privacy. The director of the medical unit became enraged at this and said that the therapists' actions were unethical because this medical issue was directly related to these patients' medical care. This policy meant that unknowingly some of his staff could be treating patients who were HIV-positive, resulting in inappropriate care for these patients. Clearly a nerve had been struck.

The directors eventually calmed down, and the consultant praised both leaders for their strong commitment to caring for patients. Over several sessions, they examined practices on both sides that undermined collaboration, then developed policies such as those described earlier that protected patient and family confidentiality while allowing for collaboration around joint medical and mental health issues. These policies helped to increase trust and understanding between the professionals. The eventual introduction of EHRs, required for both units, forced the mental health services to chart more carefully and supported fuller collaboration between these services.

Style of Communicating

Physicians are taught to use a straightforward, concise style of communicating about patient care that highlights important issues and saves time. More lengthy descriptions of patient and family dynamics and possible treatment strategies are typically experienced as unnecessarily time-consuming. For example, the medical family therapist might send the referring physician a note in the EHR saying,

> Mr. and Mrs. Brown came for two 30-minute visits over the past 3 weeks. They discussed the effect of Mr. Brown's recent myocardial infarction on their relationship. Mrs. Brown agreed to cook a heart-healthy diet and to start walking daily with her husband. Mr. Brown is concerned about when it is safe for them to resume sexual activity. He will discuss this with you at his appointment next week.

In addition, charts are becoming more available to patients so that the reader (whether referring provider or patient and family) must be considered. Some medical family therapists, like their medical counterparts, now do their chart notes with the patient and family, providing them with a copy (the After Visit Summary) at the end of the session. This is an intervention in and of itself.

For patients who have been difficult for the physician to manage, sometimes more communication and consultation are important. Jeffrey Harp (1989), a family physician with medical family therapy training, described three categories of patients referred to a therapist and the expectations that a referring physician is likely to have regarding communication from the therapist (see Table 3.2). For most patients, as described earlier, appropriate communication includes a brief note following the initial contact.

Some physicians, well versed in a patient's psychosocial problems, may have attempted some counseling themselves and reached an impasse. Typically they desire greater involvement, such as being consulted about their assessment of the patient and family or describing their treatment to date. These providers are likely to want more communication regarding treatment, in addition to the initial report and end-of-treatment summary. Harp described a third category as an intense doctor–patient relationship in which the patient may have stimulated the physician's own personal issues so that

TABLE 3.2
Physicians' Expectations Regarding Communication
after a Mental Health Referral

Physician closeness to patient	Who initiates referral	Expectations of own role	Expectations of therapist
Distant	Physician or patient	Minimal	Intake and end of treatment letters
Midrange	Physician	Assess patient, remain involved	Support previous work, monthly feedback
Intense	Physician	Treat patient as coauthor of treatment plan	Frequent feedback, consult on treatment, "cure"

Note. This table was constructed from ideas presented at a talk by Harp (1989).

the physician is angry with the patient (e.g., the patient who, like the physician's brother, refuses to stop excessive drinking) or is more motivated for the patient to begin therapy than is the patient or family (e.g., the physician who insists that her morbidly obese patient try to lose weight even though the patient is not yet ready to commit to doing so). The physician in these situations is likely to be stressed by his or her interactions with the patient or family and have high hopes for the medical family therapist to "fix this patient." Close communication and support for the physician as well as the patient and family are key. Joint sessions, in fact, may be important to the success of the treatment.

CHALLENGES TO EFFECTIVE COLLABORATION

Even with the tremendous growth of collaboration since 1992 due the expansion of on-site integrated care and increased recognitions of the mind–body connection, significant barriers remain. These barriers include differing paradigms, discipline bias, inadequate interprofessional training, and practical problems such as billing, space, and regulatory barriers (Kathol, Butler, McAlpine, & Kane, 2010). Even though physicians and therapists treat patients with similar problems, both parties report that clear communication and positive relationships between the two groups are not routine when providers do not work together on-site in a medical setting. These problems have a long history.

Psychotherapy in general, and family therapy in particular, in its early history, often mistrusted or disapproved of medical approaches to problems. In the early 1980s, when family therapists began to apply systems theory beyond the family to the treatment system and the larger systems relevant to the family, medical professionals were often viewed as part of the problem. An article published in 1980 by Palazzoli, Boscolo, Cecchin, and Prata drew attention to the importance of attending to the referring person in the treatment system. However, the article's title, "The Problem of the Referring Person," indicated that the referring professional was seen as a part of the patient's difficulties and, as such, a target for intervention by the family therapist. Instead of promoting collaboration, this approach perpetuated the underlying fear by physicians that therapists will blame them for patients' problems and "shrink" anybody who dares approach them. This is not to say that physicians and other health professionals (or therapists, for that matter) do not become embroiled in their patients' problems; this can and does happen. In fact, part of the value of collaboration lies in the opportunity for collaborators of all kinds to provide alternative points of view that can help other professionals recognize their biases and become more comprehensive in their approach to promoting patients' health and well-being.

Team care is based on task interdependence; it is essential to understand the functioning of different members of the team (Cooke, Salas, Kiekel, & Bell, 2004). Differences in training, language, theoretical model, and culture have traditionally made it difficult for mental health professionals and health professionals to build successful collaborative relationships (Hepworth, 1985; McDaniel & Campbell, 1986). Table 3.3 lists some of the marked differences

TABLE 3.3
Differences in the Cultures of Primary Care and
Behavioral Health Professionals

	Primary care clinicians	Behavioral health clinicians
Language or traditional paradigm	Medical Biomedical	Humanistic, psychoanalytic, systemic
New paradigm	Biopsychosocial	Cognitive-behavioral, psycho-dynamic Family systems
Professional style	Action-oriented, advice-giving	Process-oriented, avoids advice
	M.D. takes initiative	Patient takes initiative
Treatment orientation	Fix-it	Facilitate
Standard session time	10–15 minutes	45–50 minutes
Demand for services	Around the lock	Scheduled sessions (except emergencies)
Use of medications	Frequent	Infrequent
Use of individual and family history	Basic	Extensive
At risk for	Somatic fixation	Psychosocial fixation

Note. From *Family-Oriented Primary Care* (2nd ed.; p. 436), by S. H. McDaniel, T. L. Campbell, J. Hepworth, and A. Lorenz, 2005, New York, NY: Springer-Verlag. Copyright 2005 by Springer Science+Business Media. Reprinted with permission.

in working styles that lead to tensions between the two groups of profession-als (McDaniel et al., 2005). These differences, if not acknowledged, impede collaborative work. In a book for health professionals on family-oriented care, McDaniel et al. (2005) used the following extreme, stereotypic scenario to illustrate how these differences in style, language, theoretical paradigm, and expectations can interfere with collaboration[6]:

Dr. P: Hello, this is Dr. Psycho.

Dr. M: Hi, Sue? This is Dr. Medic at the Family Medicine Center. I have this patient I'd like you to see, but I just have a minute to tell you about her as I'm already 45 minutes behind in my appointments. She's a 16-year-old primigravida at 34 weeks gestation complicated by some intrauterine growth retardation and mild preeclampsia. The problem is that this lady just won't come in for her prenatal visits or any of the tests she needs. I've tried everything to get her in. She's really impossible! I keep telling her that the baby is going to die if she doesn't do what I tell her. Can you see her? Maybe you can convince her she's got to come in for these appointments.

Dr. P: Well, Dr. Medic, I can hear you're really upset. What do you think is going on? Could she be depressed?

Dr. M: I don't know; that's your department. She doesn't seem very happy, but who would in her situation? Say, if you want to put her on an antidepressant, let me know so I can be sure it's a safe one for pregnancy.

Dr. P: Seems like you're jumping to medications rather quickly, Dr. Medic. I feel I need to know something about the patient— her history and her family—before we rush into pharmacother-apy. What do you know about her family?

Dr. M: I don't have time for that stuff. It's hard enough dealing with all her medical problems. All I know is that I've seen her boy-friend and I'm sure he's on drugs. I've checked the lady for AIDS and she's okay so far, but she's not cooperating with me.

Dr. P: Boy, sounds like this case is really getting to you. You're pretty angry at her, you know.

Dr. M: I am not the patient here. Will you see this patient or not? Just convince her to come back for her tests.

[6]From *Family-Oriented Primary Care* (2nd ed.; pp. 435–437), by S. H. McDaniel, T. L. Campbell, J. Hepworth, and A. Lorenz, 2005, New York, NY: Springer-Verlag. Copyright 2005 by Springer Science+Business Media. Reprinted with permission.

Dr. P: Calm down, Dr. Medic. I'm going to need some time to do a complete evaluation on this patient. I've got an opening in two weeks.

Dr. M: Two weeks—she'll have a dead baby by then! Besides she probably won't show up. I'm calling now to get an appointment for her, which I'll give to her social worker so I can be sure she'll get there.

Dr. P: That's being too directive. We need to use her ability to secure an appointment and get to my office as a measure of her motivation for change. I can't badger her to come. That's her decision.

Dr. M: Look, I don't have time for this. Forget about seeing the patient. I'll just call Child Protective. They'll do something about this.

Dr. P: I'm sorry, Dr. Medic. I'm trying to be helpful to you. I have to tell you I'm concerned you're falling back on strong-arm tactics instead of demonstrating the caring and sensitivity that's supposed to be part of being a health professional.

Dr. M: Big help. Thanks a lot.

Dr. P: Good-bye.

Implicit in this satire on physicians' and therapists' styles are differing assumptions about the theory and practice of these two helping professions. Misunderstandings can arise because of differences in the working styles of medical providers and therapists. Professional competition and turf issues can also impede the development of a successful collaborative relationship.

Negotiating Language Barriers

The language used by a professional discipline reflects the worldview of its members. It is useful to remember that some of the language used by family therapists and other mental health professionals is as incomprehensible to physicians as medical language is to non–medically trained therapists. In addition, different professions use the same words with different meanings, creating still further opportunities for miscommunications to multiply. An example is the inconsistent use of the terms *illness* and *disease*. Kleinman, Eisenberg, and Good (1978) distinguished illness, which is the patient's experience, from disease, which is the biomedical understanding of the patient's illness. It may be simplistic, but accurate, to generalize that many physicians attend to disease and therapists attend to illness.

With regard to medical language, the medical family therapist should err on the side of ignorance and freely ask the medical provider to explain medical terms or procedures ("Excuse me, I'm not sure I understand that term"). Not only is this important information for the therapist to be an engaged learner, but it may also model asking for information for the patient and family. With regard to psychological or systemic language, it is important to use simple lay language or shared diagnostic information rather than behavioral health jargon when communicating with other health professionals.

Recognizing Theoretical Models

When a physician and a therapist have both been trained in bio-psychosocial, "relationship-centered health care" (Frankel & Inui, 2006; Frankel, Quill, & McDaniel, 2003), collaboration is relatively easy. However, most physicians are trained in a biomedical model that empha-sizes identifying pathology and eliminating or halting pathological pro-cesses. Although this mechanistic orientation has wide utility, it does not fit the complexity of human behavior. In this case, the different models used by physicians and therapists result in predictably different assess-ments of a patient and family.

For example, a physician referred a family with a son who had asthma to a family therapist because he felt frustrated that, although the parents obvi-ously cared for their son, they seemed unmotivated to move out of a housing project with flaking concrete and large amounts of dust into a safer environ-ment for their son. He attributed their inaction to laziness. The therapist saw the parents' concern but felt that a great sense of helplessness precluded their changing any aspect of their surroundings.

Differing assessments usually result in differing treatments. In this case, the physician focused on educating the parents about how their living con-ditions affected their child's breathing. The therapist, on the other hand, focused on how the parents might make changes in other aspects of their lives so they could gain the confidence to make changes in their living situa-tion. This physician and therapist needed to communicate about their views of the disease and the illness and their goals for treatment to support one another, clarify their roles, and then negotiate a joint treatment plan with the family.

Given their different models and expectations, health professionals often educate and give direct advice, whereas therapists traditionally are taught to help the patient or family find their own solutions. The physician visit is often seen by patients as a brief encounter with an expert, with advice giving being part of the medical ritual. Patients also seek advice from mental health professionals, but both by dint of training and time availability, thera-pists are more able to help patients and families arrive at their own solutions without frustrating their need to feel that an expert is advising and caring about them.

Working With Different Time Constraints

Perhaps the most obvious difference in working styles is the use of time: medical family therapists traditionally see patients for somewhere between 15 and 50 minutes, whereas physicians or nurse practitioners typically spend 5 to 15 minutes with most of their patients. Time management is a major challenge for physicians and other health providers; there is a constant drive toward maintaining both efficiency and quality while treating as many patients as possible per day and meeting standards for appropriate documentation. The time allowed for any single medical patient or family is determined by the goal of the interaction, which naturally affects the quality of psychosocial information gathered.

Medical family therapists, especially those working on-site, have their own time pressures. When working as a salaried behavioral health consultant, the medical family therapist may see 10 to 15 patients in a day for brief 10- to 15-minute visits focused on behavioral health change. Or these brief visits may be interspersed with more typical 30- to 50-minute therapy visits, with time-consuming requirements for documentation. In any case, most therapists have somewhat more time with patients and families than do their medical colleagues. Understanding the time pressures experienced by each discipline makes it that much more important to conform to the conventions for efficient communication among health professionals.

Health professionals and therapists may also differ in their expectations regarding length of treatment: Family therapists generally anticipate gradual improvement over time rather than a quick cure, whereas many patients and physicians hope for a cure to come when a patient interacts with a health professional—the sooner the better. Some of this difference in expectations has been modified in recent decades; successes in medical science allow us to live longer with chronic conditions that cannot be cured but are often managed by healthy behavior and lifestyles. Chronic disease management puts therapists and other health professionals in the same boat, working to enhance health behavior change over the long term of a patient's life. Patients may see the medical family therapist periodically, as they do their physician, when their chronic illness flares or they are having difficulty with a treatment regime. In any case, at the time of referral, the family therapist should communicate with the medical provider about expectations regarding length of treatment to prevent misunderstandings among the treatment team or with the family.

Dealing With Power Struggles

Physicians and therapists can be drawn into competitive struggles about who best understands or who most cares for patients. These struggles are rooted in the identified differences in training, language, and theory, as well as the economics of health care and the cultural hierarchies that affect each profession (McDaniel, 1995). Medical family therapists may at times resent the financial and social power that some physicians typically have. Physicians perform necessary and valued work, and other people often make allowances so that work can be done. When one of us was detained in a hospital elevator by two physicians who held open the door while conversing about a particular procedure, another physician asked them to complete their conversation outside the elevator. He then explained to the passengers that the physicians appeared inconsiderate but that "doctors who are involved with the care of a patient are not aware of anything else." The physicians' conversation could have been about gardening, but their bad manners were to be excused by their medical responsibilities.

Stories of physician abuse of power abound, but the stories may also reflect intimidation or perhaps envy of the privileged status of physicians in some settings. Without open acknowledgment of differences in cultural prestige, associated power, and salary, these inequities may remain barriers to effective collaboration and cooperative care for families.

Therapists also have been known to behave badly. Some therapists avoid their concerns about power inequities by not working in medical settings or not communicating with other health professionals about their patients. Other therapists may respond to financial or power differentials with physicians either by acting deferential and eventually passive aggressive or by acting competitive and actively aggressive. Both of these defensive patterns can lead to undesired physician behavior and initiate a sequence of competitive rather than collaborative interactions. Unresolved disagreements based on actual interaction or general resentment toward other health professionals can result in fewer referrals and less successful treatment. It can also result in triangulation—for example, when a therapist agrees with a patient's complaints about her medical care rather than encouraging her to speak with her provider and suspending judgment without direct data.

Inequities do exist in the way health care is reimbursed in the United States, but large-scale financial issues are best addressed by political advocacy and active participation in our professional organizations. One-to-one interactions between physicians and therapists about patients and families work best when founded on mutual support and respect. Pediatrician and child-family psychiatrist John Sargent (1985) emphasized the importance of the therapist valuing his or her own work, performing as a professional who exercises a set of skills and not as an adjunctive provider following the physician's lead. Clarifying roles and responsibilities helps the family therapist support the physician or other health professional in providing successful medical care for the patient and helps the physician support the family therapy. Respecting another's professional territory without giving up one's own space provides the foundation for healthy collaboration among professionals.

CONCLUSION

Among mental health professionals, systemic family therapists are uniquely equipped to overcome barriers to collaboration with other health professionals—barriers created by training, working styles, and professional rivalries. (See the Appendix for illustrations of multiple real-life collaborations in varying contexts.) Family therapists understand systems and the multiple perspectives that occur in any one context and therefore can position themselves to understand the experiences of patients, families, and members of the health care team. Medical family therapists who collaborate with health professionals require persistence and creativity. Family therapists must find common interests with their medical colleagues, gain the trust of these health professionals, and show that medical family therapy can be helpful to them and their patients. Collaborators who overcome these barriers can enjoy the professional stimulation and enthusiasm that results from working together to deliver high-quality care to families. This collaborative relationship between medical family therapists and other health professionals forms a foundation, often augmented by community engagement, for supporting healthy lifestyles and, when necessary, for the successful treatment of a patient and family.

4

THE SHARED EMOTIONAL
THEMES OF ILLNESS

In the narrative of every human life and every family, illness is a prominent character. Even if we have avoided serious illness or injury ourselves, we
cannot escape its reach into our family lives and our friendship circles. Illness
brings us closer to one another in caregiving, and it separates us through
disability and death. It moves us to make sense of our lives, and it creates
confusion and doubt. It inspires courage and fear, anger and acceptance, hope
and despair, serenity and anxiety. From childhood onward, our personal and
family experiences of illness shape us as surely as the food we eat and the love
or rejection we experience.

Yet in the first edition of *Medical Family Therapy: A Biopsychosocial
Approach to Families with Health Problems*, we commented little on these emotions so commonly associated with illness. They sprang up in the section on
medical family therapy techniques as something to be assessed and normal-
ized, and again by implication in our use of such terms as *communion*, a more

http://dx.doi.org/10.1037/14256-004
Medical Family Therapy and Integrated Care, Second Edition, by S. H. McDaniel, W. J. Doherty,
and J. Hepworth

affective laden term than *communication* or *connection*. Yet given the universal association of illness with emotion, we commented on it very little. Why? Like many family therapists at the time, we focused first on the relationships and communication affected by the illness and less on the inevitable emotions associated with the experience for patients and families.

It was in the experience of reading illustrations of medical family therapy and therapist stories of illness for our casebook *The Shared Experience of Illness* (McDaniel, Hepworth, & Doherty, 1997) that the importance of emotion surfaced. As a result, we examined the stories more systematically, looking for the experience of emotion through a biopsychosocial lens. Since that time, we also have become sensitized to how challenging it is for a health care system organized around a purely biomedical approach to health and illness to deal with emotion. Emotion is not part of the dominant biomedical model, although it is a dominant part of the patient and family experience. Not recognizing and validating emotional experience can exacerbate the suffering for patients and families.

Recent studies support the importance of emotion in influencing health communications and decision making. Affect can cause undue anxiety, and fear can result in overestimating risk (e.g., of a particular treatment or recurrence in breast cancer patients). It can also result in avoiding treatment and distract from important educational information (Peters, Lipkus, & Diefenbach, 2006). Studies have also shifted to identifying factors that help patients and families achieve that healthy adjustment. In particular, de Ridder, Geenen, Kuijer, and van Middendorp's (2008) review of this topic suggests that psychological adjustment is facilitated by expressing emotions:

> Patients should remain as active as is reasonably possible, acknowledge and express their emotions in a way that allows them to take control of their lives, engage in self-management, and try to focus on potential positive outcomes of their illness. (p. 246)

Note the importance of emotion, and of agency and communion, in these findings. Family therapists, such as Susan Johnson, have developed approaches that focus on emotion in couples and families and applied them to illness (Kowal, Johnson, & Lee, 2003). Kaethe Weingarten (2012) movingly described the therapeutic importance of "compassionate witnessing" of the chronic sorrow, self-loss, and narrative disruption that often accompany those with chronic illness or permanent disability. Along with our colleagues, we recognize the value of witnessing and normalizing the range of emotions as part of the therapist's function in integrated care, and we are pleased to move this aspect of caring to the front of medical family therapy.

Part of the present-day challenge for medical family therapy is to create effective systems that can be sustained. Reimbursement systems now recognize that many patients and families who benefit from the help of a medical family therapist have predictable emotional reactions to serious illness but do not wish to be labeled with a mental as well as a physical health diagnosis. Health and Behavior Codes,[1] developed by the American Psychological Association, are part of the effort to allow patients with illnesses to access medical family therapy services without being inappropriately diagnosed with a mental health disorder.

ILLNESS STORIES

A common message in illness stories is that coping with illness can be an intense experience, an emotional roller coaster ride that is both draining and empowering. Families' strengths and optimism exist alongside their tragic and sorrowful responses. These emotional themes coexist alongside the traditional foci of family therapy, family structure, and family beliefs. Once focused on illness as an emotional crucible, we saw many varying emotions that families experience while living with serious illness. This focus helped us see that families' emotional experiences are often draining and empowering at the same time. Families learn to live with emotions that seem on the surface to contradict one another but that on a deeper level create the full human experience of illness.

In this chapter, we describe eight emotional themes and three common emotion-based behaviors in response to illness or injury. These themes and behaviors are derived from an informal qualitative analysis of patient and therapist stories of illness contributed by medical family therapists working as part of integrated care in a medical setting or an outside practice. The emotional themes are as follows: denial versus acceptance, anger versus peace, despair versus hope, guilt versus forgiveness, burden versus relief, fear versus courage, loss versus renewal, and senselessness versus meaning. Behavioral reactions that frequently occur in families as they try to cope with these emotions include secrecy versus sharing, isolation versus connection, and passivity versus taking charge.

A quick reading of this chapter may lead one to believe that these emotions and behaviors are categorical (either an illness is denied or it is accepted; it is a secret or it is shared). However, they are more accurately described as

---

[1]Reimbursement systems now recognize that many patients and families have predictable emotional reactions to serious illness but do not wish to be labeled with a mental as well as a physical health diagnosis. Health and Behavior Codes, developed by the American Psychological Association (APA), are part of the effort to allow patients with illnesses to access medical family therapy services without being inappropriately diagnosed with a mental health disorder. See http://www.apapracticecenter.org/reimbursement/billing/index.aspx for an APA web page on Health and Behavior Codes and billing.

dialectic, with tension involved in complex and often contradictory emotions that represent both internal and interpersonal struggles. Patients and families can place themselves along continua with regard to each emotional descriptor, denying some aspects and accepting others. An individual may feel despairing at one moment and hopeful at another, or even experience both simultaneously as part of the complex experience of illness, known in one children's book as "double-dip feelings" (Cain & Patterson, 2001).

These emotional themes and responses cut across illnesses; they occur in acute as well as anticipated illness, in adolescents as well as older adults. They describe universal tensions that may be triggered by an illness, tensions that activate the most basic of human concerns about the meaning of life, relationships, and spirituality. Of course, not all families will struggle with all these emotional themes. Rather, each family, with its particular history, will find some illness challenges easily negotiated and others almost insurmountable. The emotional themes and responses that disable the family then become the focus of therapy.

EMOTIONAL THEMES

"We are all more human than otherwise," as Harry Stack Sullivan (2010, p. 7) said, and the prominent themes in family illness stories are universal human struggles. They do not necessarily or even typically represent psychopathology.[2] Although universal, each person's experience is unique and deserves a unique response. In addition, each theme is filtered through the history and cultural experience of the family. Let us consider each emotional theme in more detail.

Denial Versus Acceptance

Being told that one has a serious illness is like being doused with a bucket of cold water. Some of us respond by screaming and shaking until the initial shock subsides; then we dry off, warm up, readapt, and move on through life. Others freeze or shrivel up and withdraw, as if to deny that anything important has happened. Adjustment to a new reality always takes time. Every patient and family member, when told about a serious diagnosis, goes through a struggle to comprehend what the illness entails.

---

[2]Health and Behavior Codes (http://www.apapracticecentral.org/reimbursement/billing/index.aspx) allow therapists to help patients deal with normal emotional and behavioral responses to coping with serious illness, rather than requiring a *Diagnostic and Statistical Manual of Mental Disorders* diagnosis of psychopathology before reimbursing for this work.

Family members, and even professionals, often align themselves along a continuum from denial to acceptance. It is as if some in the family need to deny the illness and advocate for life to go on, and others need to help the family grapple with the hard realities. Of course, people may polarize and move into major conflict with each other. Medical family therapists can elicit and normalize each person's response to the challenge of illness, allowing the dust of the struggle to settle so as to bring the family's story into clearer focus. What often emerges as a result of the inevitable vacillations between denial and acceptance is a new understanding of the problem, one that moves the whole family along the continuum from denial to acceptance.

For example, Kate, a 60-year-old woman, waited 2 days after having severe pain in her chest before seeking medical treatment. She was hospitalized for a heart attack, and her eight adult children were furious over how she denied her symptoms. The more the children argued for her to acknowledge her cardiac condition, the more she refused medical intervention. The medical family therapist met with Kate, her children, and her primary care physician with the goal of respecting and validating their various viewpoints. The therapist made space for Kate to describe her thoughts and feelings relating to grief over her husband's death a year before. The children then talked about their desire for her to be available to her grandchildren. After a 35-minute meeting, Kate worked out a treatment plan with her physician that represented a compromise between her desire for limited medical intervention and her children's desire for her to accept all possible treatments.

Anger Versus Peace

Many people respond to a serious diagnosis for themselves or a family member with anger, either expressed at those who care the most (e.g., other family members) or at those who deliver the message of the diagnosis (e.g., health professionals). Anger versus peace depicts the most visible responses to illness, often easily recognized by others or by patients themselves. The full range of behaviors associated with anger can be present, from lashing out at others to simmering resentment or withdrawing. However, anger and peace can also be more subtle than overt. For example, a peaceful-looking person may have significant unrecognized anger that is keeping him or her from engaging more fully in other activities. Medical family therapists help patients and families recognize and accept the inevitable mix of feelings associated with illness.

In the example of Kate, some of the residents taking care of her in the hospital complained about how hostile she was and how she rejected all treatments in the first 24 hours. Several individual sessions following her hospitalization focused on the grief Kate had over the loss of her husband and how that grief was expressed through anger. Whereas Kate denied her illness, her children denied the profound effect of their father's death on their mother.

Despair Versus Hope

Adapting to illness or injury is a stormy journey, complete with dark clouds as well as surprisingly sunny spots. Like tumultuous weather patterns, the clouds of despair change without warning to bright skies of hope, and then just as quickly, turn stormy again. These oscillations of hope and despair seem unpredictable. Patients and their families generally feel discouraged during the early phases of an illness. Yet they also look eagerly for positive stories about anyone who ever had a similar condition. After the illness seems stabilized, health care professionals, patients, and families are often reassured and become hopeful. Even when illnesses run a stable course and rehabilitation moves forward, the inevitable waves of disappointment return as function is lost or improvement is delayed. Patients can feel either at the mercy of these oscillations of emotion or learn to anticipate and cope with them, discovering ways to modulate the stormy highs and lows. Medical family therapists normalize these feelings, emphasizing hope for the family and its future.

Between losing her husband and her own heart attack, Kate was despairing. She needed time in therapy to express her anger, grief, and fear. As she did so, expressions of hope began slowly to emerge. In the family therapy sessions, the therapist disrupted the cycle of Kate expressing her distress, followed by her children pointing out all she had to live for. The therapist insisted the children listen to their mother and accept her feelings. Gradually Kate began to acknowledge the aspects of life that were valuable to her, including those involving her children and grandchildren.

Guilt Versus Forgiveness

Illness engenders a sense of personal failure and even moral lapse for many people. "What did I do to deserve this?" is a common question when illness or injury strikes. In the West, where personal mastery is so highly valued, many people feel guilty for not taking better care of themselves physically or psychologically. Guilt is amplified for the parents of a seriously ill child, who ask, "Why didn't I protect my child?" Some regret may be understandable, as in the case of a smoker who develops lung cancer or a parent who ignored a child's early symptoms. However, excessive or unrealistic guilt cripples patients and families. Medical family therapy emphasizes that the antidote is to forgive ourselves, a process of accepting our mistakes and understanding the limits of what we can do to preserve our own health or that of our loved ones.

In the first few days after Kate's heart attack and before her hospitalization, none of her children visited or called. This happened partly out of frustration at their mother's negative attitude since their father died and partly because of their own busy lives. The guilt was palpable when the children talked about their absence. Kate was clearly upset. Over time, however, as she accepted her own feelings of grief and anger, she began to forgive her children, saying she knew they each had their own lives to manage without checking in on her. Once the feelings of guilt and forgiveness were expressed during the medical family therapy session, the children worked on a rotating schedule so that someone visited Kate each day.

Burden Versus Relief

Burden is nearly synonymous with caregiving. It is the heavy feeling of the invisible weight of chronic illness and disability on the family. The sense of burden is both physical (requiring the caregiver to take on second and third work shifts each day) and psychological (as the family realizes that certain health problems will never go away). Caregivers need regular doses of support to experience relief from their sense of burden—physical help for the workload and psychological help for the painful emotions and preoccupation. Sometimes real relief comes only when the ill person dies or moves to institutional care, in which case the caregiver may experience both relief and guilt in addition to loss.

The rotating schedule organized for Kate's care helped her children to feel that she was being cared for without it being an untoward burden on any one child. Individual therapy sessions with Kate focused on her lifelong role as caregiver for her husband and children. She acknowledged both a sense of loss of identity when her husband died and she herself became ill and a sense of relief at relinquishing the role.

Fear Versus Courage

Fear rides into a family alongside serious illness. What will become of me or my loved one? Can I cope with the pain or with the treatment? Can I sustain caregiving? Will my family fall apart? Will I die, or will my loved one die? Public figures can become heroes because of their courage in the face of terminal illness, as happened with Senator Edward Kennedy during his bout with brain cancer. When people find their courage in the face of illness, they do not banish fear, or even conquer it. Rather, they find the strength to live with fear and carry on. Family members often trade fear and courage back and forth during the course of an illness; they may need help in seeing how necessary and interdependent these two experiences are.

To everyone's surprise, the medical family therapy sessions made clear that Kate's biggest fear was about being disabled and in pain from arthritis, like the older women in her family. She felt that her husband's heart attack and rapid demise was a far better way to go than what she had witnessed in her family. The therapist emphasized Kate's courage in committing to her rehabilitation plan and creating a new life without her husband.

Loss Versus Renewal

Illness events are milestones that remind us of our mortality. Most chronic illnesses bring losses of some kind, such as the loss of abilities or dreams. They point to larger losses that we all face: the inevitable, permanent losses through death. For some, a focus on loss is a paralyzing, demoralizing process; others claim that only by experiencing loss can they truly recognize all of life's pleasures. It is common for those who closely escape death to feel a new appreciation of their loved ones and the significant aspects of life. Thus, the pain of loss is frequently associated with the joy of appreciation and with a renewed commitment to life goals and values.

Much of the medical family therapy sessions with Kate and her children focused on the ongoing grief they all felt from the death of Kate's husband and the threatened loss for the children of losing a second parent so soon after the first. The therapist was able to teach the family basic listening skills so that each person could express their deepest feelings without interruption and feel understood.

Senselessness Versus Meaning

The search for meaning occupies many of our patients in psychotherapy. When a serious illness or disability strikes us or our loved one, it challenges our capacity to make sense of life and death. Some who face illness fall into deep despair, questioning the senselessness of, say, a cancer diagnosis in a young child. Eventually Kate and her children came to feel that her heart attack gave them each a new perspective on life and increased the emotional intimacy in the family relationships that had been strained after the death of her husband. In addition, two of Kate's children began raising money as volunteers for the American Heart Association. Two others returned to active participation in their Catholic parishes. In this way, they exercised agency and worked to shape the meaning of their experiences with both their mother and their father.

Although any illness is certainly unwelcome, the heightened awareness of life's gifts is often an outgrowth of the search for meaning. For many, this search can take the form of a spiritual quest and can be an opportunity for invaluable family discussion. Medical family therapists do not offer answers to life's most important questions. Rather, medical family therapy offers a forum for patients and families and therapists to share their anger, values, hopes, and fears as together they construct a story that brings meaning to biological experience.

Secrecy Versus Sharing

The emotions associated with serious illness or disability often stimulate predictable coping behaviors related to agency and communion. One of the first decisions a patient or family must make is about disclosure: whom to tell and whom not to tell. Each person may respond in characteristically passive or active ways in terms of caring for the self, the illness, and loved ones. Illness stimulates existential issues that can result in loneliness or meaning making, disconnection or increased intimacy.

Such a need for secrecy about illness may extend from a learned privacy about our bodies, or it may be a way to be brave and not burden loved ones. For many Americans, illness, like sex and money, should be kept private, as was true for the Addison's disease of President John F. Kennedy or the extent of Franklin Roosevelt's disability because of polio. For some, keeping illness secret reflects a belief that illness is a personal failing or an indication of guilt.

At the other extreme, the popularity of talk shows and the criticism by some of their vulgarity reflect both our fascination with and aversion to stories about illness and injury. A cornerstone of medical family therapy is the idea that illness journeys are eased when shared with others. The therapeutic task is to balance a family's preference for privacy with its desire to be helped and comforted by others.

For example, Catherine, a woman with advanced breast cancer, had six siblings and a large community of friends. When she developed a serious infection postsurgery and was in the intensive care unit, the family grappled with who would be told of the seriousness of her condition and who would be permitted to visit. At a family meeting with their medical family therapist, her husband and children decided to allow the three siblings closest to the patient to visit and participate in family meetings with the physicians and health care team. The other three siblings, with whom she had had significant conflict over the years, and her friends were told they would receive daily updates by e-mail but that she was too ill to receive a large number of visitors.

Passivity Versus Taking Charge

Illness is the ultimate out-of-control experience. Some unknown foreign body invades a previously healthy person, often changing them permanently.

Even when lifestyle factors such as nutrition or smoking contribute to the onset, illness is experienced as an unanticipated and unwelcome guest. In a hospital or nursing home, people are too often stripped of their identities and treated as a bundle of organ systems. Family members are often relegated to the margins, visiting only at specified times and participating too little in the care and decision making required during treatment. It is easy for the patient, and sometimes the family, to succumb to a passive-dependent approach to an illness.

Our health care system is organized in large part for the convenience of health care professionals and the efficiency of their work. As such, it plays a powerful role in inviting (some say, demanding) a passive, "good patient" role from those who have the misfortune to fall ill (note the passivity inherent in the phrase "to fall ill"). According to the stereotype, a "good patient" asks few questions and does exactly what the physician tells him or her to do. This role is a prescription for the helplessness and hopelessness of depression. Medical family therapists work to increase a sense of agency for patients and families by helping them to accept what they must and to work to change what they can. This therapy supports the patient and family in their bid to maximize the outcome, improve their quality of life, and cope with the process.

When Catherine finally was alert and able to interact in the hospital, she was shocked at what had transpired. Her fear made her uncharacteristically passive with regard to any decisions that needed to be made. "Whatever you think, doctor" became her mantra. However, some decisions had no clear answers. In several medical family therapy sessions, Catherine expressed her fears. Gradually, with support from the therapist and her husband, she began to ask more questions about her options and participate more in the decision making that was necessary in dealing with her cancer.

Isolation Versus Connection

Because illness befalls individuals, it is necessarily a lonely and self-defining experience. Some patients begin this experience embedded in a tightly knit family and community. As with Kate's, their families may respond to the existential challenge by hovering, protecting, and caregiving. In extreme situations, they may smother the patient emotionally in a futile attempt to prevent dissolution of the family as they know it, running the risk of incapacitating the patient and burning out the caregiver. Other families, frightened by the threat and faced with the reality that death comes to us all, respond by distancing themselves from the patient. Their fears override their feelings of love and loyalty. (This happened with Catherine's son. Only her daughter was able, eventually, to persuade him to come to the hospital with her.) Medical family therapy offers an opportunity for communion, for friends and families to recognize the singular experience of the patient and the complicated emotions of family members, creating new opportunities for intimacy and understanding.

CONCLUSION

The richness of these emotional themes and responses help to describe the full range of experience involved in coping with illness in the family. These experiences are normative for families. The task of the medical family therapist is to validate the complexity of each person's experience and to avoid polarizing conversations. In doing so, medical family therapy becomes a crucible for the family that can ultimately increase intimacy, heal long-standing interpersonal wounds, and provide support during the stresses and strains of ill health.

5

THE SELF OF THE MEDICAL
FAMILY THERAPIST

Everyone who is born holds dual citizenship, in the kingdom of the well
and in the kingdom of the sick. Although we all prefer to use only the
good passport, sooner or later each of us is obliged, at least for a spell, to
identify ourselves as a citizen of that other place.

—Susan Sontag, *Illness as Metaphor*

We are so fond of one another, because our ailments are the same.

—Jonathan Swift, *The Journal to Stella*

Literature, whether modern or ancient, is replete with reminders of
our own mortality. Illness is both a threat to agency and communion and a
"call to consciousness" to deepen these domains of life (Williamson, 1991,
p. 229) for the patient, family, therapist, and other members of the health
care team. As medical sociologist Arthur Frank (2004) stated, "Ill people
may hear the call first, but the call is for everyone" (p. 69). Empathy and
compassion, central features of medical family therapy, are derived from this
identification with the patient; acceptance of our own mortality prevents
distancing that can be alienating. Working with ill people stimulates these
existential issues, so that healthy adjustment to this work requires attention
to the self of the therapist.

The casebook that is the companion to the first edition of this book
is called *The Shared Experience of Illness* (McDaniel, Hepworth, & Doherty,

http://dx.doi.org/10.1037/14256-005
Medical Family Therapy and Integrated Care, Second Edition, by S. H. McDaniel, W. J. Doherty,
and J. Hepworth
Copyright © 2014 by the American Psychological Association. All rights reserved.

1997). In that book, well-known medical family therapists illustrate their work through case illustrations, tell a story about illness in their own family, and relate that personal experience to their approach to therapy. The riveting stories reveal much about the motivation behind a particular therapist's approach to medical family therapy. In this chapter, we invite you to discover your own story of illness and meaning. We begin with general comments about the importance of the illness experience of the medical family therapist, explore related personal development concerns, and attend to self-awareness issues related to collaboration with other health professionals. We conclude with suggestions about self-care that can lead to a sustainable and rewarding career in medical family therapy.

The training of most nonmedical psychotherapists recapitulates the mind–body split of Western culture, with therapists focusing on the psychosocial realm and leaving the biological realm to physicians and nurses. For many therapists, biology begins and ends with the brain; for most family therapists, the family is a social group, not a nexus where the biological, psychological, and social domains converge. Exceptions to this generalization include health psychology (which often does not teach a systemic or family-oriented approach) and programs with a course, an emphasis, or even a degree in medical family therapy.

Because traditional psychotherapy programs focus almost exclusively on the psychosocial world, most therapists are not trained to examine how their own experiences with biologically based illness shape their lives and their relationships with patients and families. Processing countertransference examines psyche, not soma. Personal and family experiences of emotional cutoffs or conflict are mined for developmental and countertransferential implications, but family experiences with cancer or diabetes or Alzheimer's disease are barely noted. Attitudes toward parents or teachers are explored, but attitudes toward physicians as authority figures in illness experiences are neglected. The management of emotional pain is examined, but the management of physical pain is not. In medical family therapy, all this information is important grist for the mill.

Therapists' personal experiences with illness can be a healing resource in therapy if it increases their empathy and range of options. When George Engel (1977) proposed the biopsychosocial model as an alternative to the traditional biomedical model of medicine, he emphasized the human side of medicine and the importance of the patient's experience of illness and the physician's experience of the patient. Medical family therapists see a seamless web of connections among body, mind, family, and community, as well as connections between their own experiences with illness and the experiences of their patients.

PERSONAL DEVELOPMENT ISSUES SPECIFIC TO ILLNESS

The typical personal development issues for therapists related to self-awareness and family-of-origin work may not be sufficient when working with a patient and family facing serious illness. In medical family therapy, therapists must maintain their capacity for empathy and manage their own reactions to death and threatened loss. Additional attention should be paid to tolerance for uncertainty and loss, family-of-origin health beliefs, illness experiences, and personal and current family illness experiences.

Tolerance for Uncertainty and Loss

The most important challenge facing medical family therapists is tolerance for dealing with uncertainty, loss, and death, which permeate the experience of families facing illness in its members. Families and health professionals wrestle with the uncertainty that accompanies illness diagnosis and treatment. Much of medical education emphasizes what is known rather than what is unknown. Most patients and families want their medical providers to cure their ills and not apologize for what science does not yet know. The medical family therapist who remains relatively nonanxious while facing these difficult issues of uncertainty can provide useful consultation for medical colleagues and serve as a model for patients and families who struggle with prognosis, treatment, and questions about "why me?" and "why now?" (For an excellent discussion of the importance of uncertainty in medicine, see Bursztajn, Feinbloom, Hamm, & Brodsky, 1981.)

When working with illness, loss, and death, a spiritual dimension to medical family therapy becomes unavoidably poignant and rewarding (Walsh, 2009). Medical family therapy deals directly with death anxiety in reality, not just in the abstract. Therapists face their personal mortality as well as that of their patients. As Donald Williamson (1991) wrote, "Any person who is dying is simply dying a little bit ahead of the observer" (p. 234). Facing these issues allows therapists and families to reflect on the meaning of their lives—what it means to be human, to live, to love, and to die. As with a midlife crisis (which also deals with issues of mortality), the medical family therapist may help the patient and family evaluate their priorities and whether they are living their lives in the most meaningful ways.

Just as the therapist provides a safe, supportive environment for patients and families to explore these issues, he or she too can benefit from a safe, supportive environment in which to share and consult with colleagues about the stresses, strains, and uncertainties, as well as the rewards, of working with families with a sick member. Some physicians have participated in "Balint groups" in which the physician shares personal experiences generated from working with patients. Based on the work of Michael Balint (1957), a British physician influenced by psychoanalytic and Tavistock training, the groups are popular in primary care training programs in the United States and Europe. Although Balint groups are traditionally for physicians, many include therapists and other health professionals. McDaniel, Bank, Campbell, Mancini, and Shore (1986) reported on a group of physicians and family therapists who provide a family-systems-oriented adaptation of the Balint group for each other.

Family-of-Origin Illness Issues

Dealing with uncertainty, loss, and death in the course of medical family therapy inevitably stimulates family-of-origin medical issues for the therapist. Broadly speaking, these issues relate to the therapist's family experience of illnesses, loss, health behaviors, health beliefs, and interactions with physicians and other health professionals. In an obvious example, the therapist whose father or mother is a physician will have a clear connection between medical and generic family of origin issues, but every family—health professional or not—has a health history loaded with feeling and meaning. Our assumption is that it is important for medical family therapists to sort out and come to peace with these issues. As we mentioned in Chapter 1, a useful training technique is to have trainees do a "health and illness" genogram focusing on how their families define health and illness, and how they respond to health problems and crises. Susan H. McDaniel's history illustrates some of these concepts.

McDaniel is a medical family therapist who grew up with an obstetrician-gynecologist father. Her father was a sensitive man who rarely expressed his feelings. He was an excellent surgeon with little psychosocial training who said he chose obstetrics so as not to have to deal with dying people on a daily basis. McDaniel dedicated her career to training physicians to be skillful in dealing with the psychosocial issues of their patients. To her, the link between family and professional focus was not subtle, and early in her career McDaniel made several mistakes by trying to push this psychosocial approach too hard with physicians (McDaniel et al., 1986). In presenting her "health and illness" genogram to colleagues, she recognized that she was trying to convert the medical profession as a way of trying to resolve issues with her father.

Recognizing this dynamic allowed McDaniel to relate her concerns directly to her father and move more slowly in teaching physicians who were struggling with psychosocial concepts or skills. She also recognized her father's concerns about avoiding death through choosing obstetrics and worked to desensitize herself to become less anxious around dying patients and issues of her own and others' mortality.

Each medical family therapist also has a family health and illness history, complete with critical incidents, difficult and painful moments, and loss. These experiences can contribute positively to the empathy and skill of the medical family therapist. They also, like other countertransference issues, need examination and monitoring in order not to interfere in our patients' experiences.

In *The Shared Experience of Illness* (McDaniel et al., 1997), Hepworth described how her personal experience with her father's diagnosis and death from AIDS in 1995 both positively and negatively affected her ability to work with patients and couples dealing with AIDS. She described how she became aware of AIDS early in 1985, when she visited with her father and his friends at Fire Island, New York, a popular gay summer community and one of the earliest communities to begin to experience quick and frightening deaths.

As she recollected her feelings during that time, she realized that in some ways she had made a pact with herself that if she could learn about AIDS, work with other families and patients, perhaps she could keep her father safe. Thus, for many years she participated in AIDS education efforts and saw many patients and couples coping with HIV in her practice. But when her pact didn't work, and her father became ill, she realized that she had become a member of a family who was coping with AIDS and could not objectively work clinically with other families in similar crises.

Our professional work, like life, does not always go as expected. Although she no longer accepted new patients with AIDS into her practice, Hepworth found herself treating a gay couple, who noted almost accidentally that one member, Michael, had AIDS. They stated however, that it wasn't a big issue in their lives, and in fact Michael had not disclosed his illness to many, including his family of origin. Hepworth's chapter in *The Shared Experience of Illness* describes in detail her struggles as a therapist about how much to push the couple to "accept" and address his illness (Hepworth, 1997). She had been fortunate to have good colleagues for consultation, who helped her try to separate her own family's experiences about disclosure and acceptance from the needs of this couple. There are and were no right answers, as evidenced with the analysis of the therapy. Yet it is clear that attention to Hepworth's own feelings was a necessary part of her being able to work with the couple over time.

Personal Health Issues

A third area for personal development work is the therapist's own history with illness, health behavior, and health care professionals. Therapists are more attuned to some emotional themes than others, in part because of their personal journeys with illness and loss. A therapist who is ashamed of his or her own stress-related physical problems will not work effectively with patients who have similar problems. However, a therapist with diabetes may have particular skill in dealing with the challenges of self-care and the denial that can sometimes accompany serious chronic illness. A therapist who survives cancer may have both special empathy and possible bias when dealing with cancer patients and their families. A therapist who struggles with being overweight or who has a history of smoking cigarettes must sort through the meaning of these issues when working with health behavior problems of patients.

Good therapy emerges from what Mony Elkaim (1990) called the *resonance* of the therapist with the strengths and the struggles of the patient and family. Therapists naturally compare their own experiences of health and illness with those of the patient family, using the common ground as a springboard for generating questions that help patients and families discover novel responses to the new challenges posed by the illness. A therapist who is proud of how her family found courage in the face of death may be particularly helpful to a family frightened by a patient's terminal illness. In contrast, the therapist must beware of a mismatch. A primary focus on courage in the face of terminal illness for a family bogged down by guilt may in fact keep the family from discussing their unspoken and irrational fears about blame and serve the therapist's needs more than the family's.

When dealing with patients who cannot see how life stress is affecting their health, Bill Doherty keeps in mind the time his own doctor, when trying to sort out the sources of abdominal pain, inquired about whether this was a particularly stressful time. The therapist–patient immediately answered in the negative and returned the discussion to biomedical issues. While driving home, he allowed himself to realize that in fact there were loads of stressors going: a recent move, an ill relative, and a deadline for a big grant proposal. He marveled about how easily he had failed to apply the biopsychosocial model to himself, an experience that helps him identify with others who have the same difficulty.

The issue of whether to disclose to patients one's own health issues is complicated and the subject of some research and much debate among health professionals. Morse, McDaniel, Candib, and Beach (2008) reported that some physicians feel that self-disclosure can strengthen the doctor–patient relationship, increase empathy, or model coping. An example would be: "I know how hard it is to quit smoking; I did it myself." This kind of *empathetic validation* can occur when clinician and patient share a difficult experience; it may offer patients reassurance, commiseration, or an understanding of the challenges involved. Morse and colleagues concluded that physician self-disclosure is only likely to result in positive effects for the patient if it is related to the patient's concern, is brief, and returns directly to the patient's issues. A study using undetected standardized patients visiting primary care physicians showed that this type of restrained physician self-disclosure is rare. Although one in three visits included a physician self-disclosure (McDaniel et al., 2007), 100% of these did not appear to benefit the patient. Most were innocuous distractions. For example:

Patient: I was concerned when I saw your "For Rent" sign here. I thought you might be moving. Are you going to stay here?

Physician: Oh yeah. There are two different offices upstairs. They are both rented right now, but one of the people will be moving out in September. It's very hard to rent sometimes. Sometimes you're lucky and somebody just comes along, and other times you're just not so lucky. Why, do you want to rent?

Patient: Nope.

Physician: Give you a good price.

Patient: No, I just wanted to find out what's going on, really. (McDaniel et al., 2007, p. 1324)

Eleven percent were rated to be disruptive to the patient. For example:

Patient: I'm six feet, and she just told me I was 204.

Physician: Is that up a little bit for you weight-wise?

Patient: It might be up a few pounds . . . I used to jog and . . . I just haven't lately.

Physician: See, 'cause I'm weighing more like 172, 173, and I'm six foot . . . and I'm still running . . . I'm still doing the 5 and 10 and 15Ks. The half-marathons and . . .

Patient: So . . . I'm 30 pounds heavier than you?

Physician: Right now, yeah. (McDaniel et al., 2007, p. 1324)

This kind of study, with high validity, using recordings of undetected standardized patients, has not been done with psychotherapists. Of the few well-designed studies of self-disclosure among therapists, results are mixed. Several demonstrated increased patient satisfaction (Barrett & Berman, 2001; Hill et al., 1988), but most did not associate therapist self-disclosure with improved patient outcomes (Hill & Knox, 2001; Kushner, Bordin, & Ryan, 1979). There may be circumstances in which therapist self-disclosure about some illness experience that is similar to the patient's helps the family feel deeply understood. Revealing, for example, that the therapist has diabetes like the patient or also lost a spouse to cancer could result in relationship-building and enhanced understanding. However, the McDaniel and colleagues (1997) study sounds a strong note of caution in this regard. This kind of sharing can distract from the patient's and family's exploration, raise unrealistic hope or infuse pessimism about a particular outcome, or result in a role reversal in which the patient and family focuses on the therapist's health rather than their own. Regardless of whether the medical family therapist's experience is shared openly or only subliminally, it can be useful in shaping the interview and promoting empathy for the experience of the patient and family. It is the therapist's responsibility, in training and ongoing consultation, to develop and maintain an awareness of the emotional themes that guide and challenge his or her own life. The art of medical family therapy is to maintain a personal connection with a patient's experience without imposing one's own struggles onto an already burdened family.

PROFESSIONAL DEVELOPMENT ISSUES IN PRACTICE

Working as a medical family therapist requires attention to our physical selves, including illness, physical trauma, and other biological aspects of the human condition. Usually the domain of physicians and nurses, dealing with challenging personal issues can stimulate issues for which many therapists are not trained. These include concerns about professional identity, feelings of isolation from mental health colleagues, role confusion, challenges regarding power and status, and teamwork function.

Anxiety About Illness

As noted earlier in this book, medical family therapists often have anxiety about the physical aspects of illness and treatment. To provide effective medical family therapy, these therapists must become desensitized to the physical processes of disability, illness, and treatment. Most physicians will allow therapists to accompany them on rounds or observe them during an afternoon of standard patient care. These experiences can help the education and desensitization process, as illustrated by Mr. T.

Mr. T found himself working as a therapist in a medical context despite his lifelong anxiety about medical procedures, blood, and injections. His mother died of cancer when he was an adolescent, and before her death, he was never told of the seriousness of her illness or allowed to visit her in the hospital. Her death was a shock that eroded his trust in physicians and their procedures. In the first 6 months of his job, he rounded at the hospital with several medical colleagues and also observed outpatient sessions on a weekly basis. These experiences allowed him to build trust in his medical colleagues as he watched them share information with patients and families. After this period of time, he retained his skittishness about blood, injections, and procedures but no longer turned white when they were described or discussed with colleagues or families. As part of his annual review, he and his supervisor developed an ongoing plan to continue this desensitization. He also consulted with a medical family therapist for several sessions to work on the unresolved grief stimulated by his new job. Active attention and engagement with this issue resulted in personal healing as well as skill development for this new medical family therapist.

Potential Isolation From Mental Health Colleagues

It is both rewarding and exciting for medical family therapists to participate on the front lines of health care. With identities as health professionals rather than solely as mental health professionals, medical family therapists may experience potential isolation from family therapy and other mental health colleagues. A biopsychosocial framework may distance them from the "psychosocialism" of their mental health colleagues. Yet culture and training differences between therapists and physicians (detailed in Chapter 3) can leave therapists feeling isolated and unappreciated when among physicians, especially when medical family therapists are new to medical settings.

Medical family therapists, particularly those working in a medical setting, can feel both valued and extraneous to the medical system. Role clarification is essential, as are supportive colleagues who are familiar with medical settings. Medical family therapists may benefit from continued involvement with family therapy and other mental health colleagues in more traditional positions through peer supervision groups or educational experiences. For example, Hepworth, Gavazzi, Adlin, and Miller (1988) described how training family therapy interns within a medical setting can provide the supervisor with a generative role and a means to remain rooted in traditional family therapy. The same may be true for psychologists or physicians providing training in integrated care.

Isolated therapists who are not physicians or nurses can feel overwhelmed by the medical knowledge, the complexity, or the difficult situations brought to medical family therapy. Cole-Kelly and Hepworth (1991) identified ways in which the severity of problems and time demands in medical situations can lead therapists to neglect their self-care strategies and respond in defensive or inappropriately authoritarian ways. As they try to demonstrate their utility, for example, they may find themselves lecturing more than listening. When unconsciously reacting to pressure to prove oneself to colleagues, therapists compromise their strengths as contributors to the medical system.

Power and Status in Medical Settings

Collaboration, the foundation of medical family therapy, is based on the concept of shared power with patients and families, and within the health care team (McDaniel & Hepworth, 2003). It is an alternative approach to the traditional, hierarchical use of power in health care relationships. Medical family therapists need to monitor their own sense of agency, and of power and status issues, in their relations with physicians and other health professionals. It is not uncommon to hear therapists express resentment and even hostility toward physicians as a group. Working with physicians triggers whatever personal ambivalence therapists have about their own status and power as professionals and as persons. The twin temptations are to treat physicians as intimidating authority figures instead of collaborators or as figures of contempt or avoidance. Differences in cultural prestige, associated power, and salary are difficult to acknowledge and discuss. Without open acknowledgment, however, these differences can remain barriers to effective collaboration and more cooperative care for families.

A piece of the therapist's personal work may have to do with what Donald Williamson (1991) labeled *intergenerational intimidation*. By this, he meant that professionals who have not resolved issues with parents may have fear of control and difficulty claiming personal authority in interactions with colleagues perceived to be powerful. Williamson applied this problem to young primary care physicians who must interact with subspecialists, but it also applies to therapists who interact with any physicians. To paraphrase Williamson, as medical family therapists resolve intergenerational intimidation within their personal families of origin, they are increasingly better prepared psychologically to handle issues of professional intimidation as well.

Negative attitudes toward physicians compromise the therapist's ability to do medical family therapy. Collaboration requires straightforward assessment about one's personal feelings and conscious attempts to recognize bias and engage in honest and respectful relationships. Close collaboration allows for sharing the rewards and frustrations of caring for patients and demonstrates all that medical family therapists and medical colleagues have to offer one another. *Positive relationships can trump stereotypes and previous experience.*

Gender issues and hierarchy are other aspects of power and status. Historically, medicine has been a male-dominated, command-and-control profession. The hierarchical approach may be appropriate in the operating room, whether the surgeon is male or female. Even so, clear roles and teamwork are the goal in today's operating rooms, where team members are trained in safety and quality, such that anyone is responsible to raise a concern. This team approach to surgery, using checklists to ensure that each professional completes the procedures for which that person is responsible, has been shown to increase successful outcomes and decrease medical errors (Haynes et al., 2009). Other parts of medicine, such as primary care, are focusing on collaborative teamwork among health professionals. These changing practices may be helped along by the fact that women now predominate in health professions (U.S. Department of Health and Human Services, 2008). Whatever the gender of the medical family therapist, it is useful to be able to be curious, collaborative, and directly address issues that may be associated with the gender of the patient or the gender mix and authority structure of the health care team. Like race, age, or disability status, gender and role has the potential to bias our perceptions of patients and colleagues. The medical family therapist can help the team become more self-aware and address these issues on a routine basis, when potentially relevant (McDaniel & Hepworth, 2003; Prouty Lyness, 2004).

Role Clarity and Scope of Practice

Exhibit 5.1 describes the skills that are part of the toolbox of the medical family therapist and that define the therapist's role and scope of practice. They include skills in patient care, self-care, and promoting healthy team functioning. For patient care, most fundamental are skills to involve family and significant others in the diagnosis and treatment of the patient's health problems. The medical family therapist should acquire basic information about the most common chronic illnesses such as diabetes, cardiac disease, and cancer. The therapist should be well acquainted with evidence-based practice, including identification and early intervention for the most common mental health disorders such as depression, panic, and other forms of anxiety (Patterson, Peek, Heinrich, Bischoff, & Scherger, 2002). The medical family therapist

EXHIBIT 5.1
Medical Family Therapist Self- and Team-Care Skills

Self-care
- Stay tuned in to one's own health issues, including diet, exercise, sleep, and healthy relationships.
- Develop preventive strategies for chronic illnesses that run in one's own family.
- Explore one's own family history with uncertainty, loss, death, and dying.
- Clarify one's role as a medical family therapist.
- Stay cognizant of one's scope of practice.
- Have a consultation group.

Team care
- Facilitate healthy team functioning.
- Facilitate other clinician self-care.
- Check in on how clinicians and staff are handling work stress.

should also be informed about prevention and intervention strategies for maintaining healthy lifestyles (see Chapter 7), as well as with the professions and roles of other members of the health care team, to facilitate collaboration (see Chapter 3).

Medical family therapists are responsible for being informed about these areas of expertise and being willing to acknowledge their limitations. They should ask medical colleagues about medical and psychosocial complications for particular patients and their illnesses. Physicians and families may wrongly assume that the therapist already has pertinent medical information, and the therapist needs to identify areas of experience and limitations. For example, a medical family therapist working with people dealing with diabetes would have competence in the challenges of maintaining a healthy diet and regular insulin injections, including helping people use effective coping strategies when their blood glucose level plummets and they start behaving irrationally (e.g., after a spouse's directive to immediately drink orange juice).

In other words, a competent medical family therapist would be able to work on the intricacies of living with the biological and psychosocial aspects of diabetes. However, if the patient were to bring up a strictly medical question, such as whether a newly prescribed medication for another illness could limit the effectiveness of the insulin, the therapist would refer the patient back to their medical or nursing provider for an answer. In other words, information and advice that are strictly biological must be referred back to medical professionals.

Role clarity is essential for patients and colleagues. Medical family therapists who are not trained as physicians or nurses should resist any temptation to give medical advice. Families who ask their therapists to validate their treatment or medication regimens can be referred back to their medical provider. Therapists can help families clarify their questions or facilitate a joint session when confusion or conflict persists. Case discussions with medical colleagues are opportunities for therapists to ask and learn about new terms and procedures. Far from indicating ignorance, such questions can clarify roles, show respect for the medical provider, and demonstrate the therapist's own skills.

Teamwork and the Patient-Centered Medical Home

Role clarity is also important to the patient-centered medical home model that dominates primary care (McDaniel & Fogarty, 2009). Pediatrics, family medicine, and general internal medicine have embraced a model based on patient-centered care, continuity, coordination, and team-based care. For medical family therapists, this means learning to be a contributing team member with a focus on behavioral health, promoting healthy team functioning, helping include patients into team decisions, and actively work-ing on relationships among team members. Because the team is to the health professional as a family is to a patient, the medical family therapist can apply many family systems skills to enhance individual and team functioning as well as patient and family relationships.

Sarah, a medical family therapist, was known on her team for her interest in treating patients with diabetes. She herself had juvenile diabetes and so understood the various stages in which self-care is challenging for most patients (e.g., adolescence). Team C had one diabetic teenage patient, Marne, who was persistently difficult—not taking her insulin appropriately and not monitoring her diet. This behavior earned her a trip to the hospital several times per year. Sarah became involved with Marne when she had an episode that her parents and her health care team thought was preventable. Her physician in particular was frustrated because he had worked hard to educate Marne about her diet. The nurse practitioner who shared Marne's care identified with this patient, remembering her own teen years, and argued with the physician about being hard on her. Sarah validated both perspec-tives and suggested that she spend some months trying to help Marne become more responsible about her own health care. Just having Sarah work with this patient and family and maintain close communication with them helped the physician and nurse practitioner to feel more comfortable and not struggle with Marne.

Marne's parents, naturally worried about their daughter's disease, also struggled with her, monitoring and advising her about food intake. Marne's reaction to any advice was to resist it; she needed to prove to herself that she could not eat junk food and sweets like some of her friends did. Sarah had both individual and family sessions with Marne. She told Marne that she would help her take charge of her disease as long as she was responsible about her diet. In a family session, they negotiated that her parents would earn the right to advise her for a month if she had an episode related to irresponsible eating. They worked together on and off for a year, with Sarah supporting Marne's parents and working closely with the rest of the health care team through some difficult incidents, until Marne became increasingly capable of managing her disease.

As clinical teams are learning how best to work together and care for patients, the roles for medical family therapists are evolving and growing. Medical family therapists can work with teams to improve their functioning in a variety of ways, for example, by

- having members examine their own family histories of health and illness, and use of health care (McDaniel, Campbell, Hepworth & Lorenz, 2005);

- helping to organize effective meetings that encourage all team members to actively participate (Pigeon & Khan, 2012);
- providing exercises that enhance communication skills;
- role-playing difficult patients;
- role-playing with team members playing each other's roles;
- having the team assess its own functioning (Lurie, Schultz, & Lamanna, 2011); and
- developing quality improvement plans to focus on areas needed for growth or doing regular social network analyses of the team (Metzer et al., 2010).

SELF-CARE AND SUSTAINABILITY

Managing patients' serious illnesses means dealing with our own difficult emotions as well as those of the patient, family members, and other health professionals (McDaniel et al., 1997). In addition to one's own mortality, the medical family therapist is faced with the limits of the team's ability to cure disease or change patient behavior. Burnout can be a major problem for both mental health practitioners (Paris & Hogue, 2010; Rosenberg & Pace, 2006) and other health professionals (Leiter, Frank, & Matheson, 2009). A supportive team helps to share the responsibility and the many challenging moments involved in working with patients and families facing significant health problems.

As we have noted, the medical family therapist needs to have a self-care plan that will reduce the risk of burnout and allow for sustainability over time. Having case consultations or a Balint-like group with other health professional colleagues to examine one's own reactions to patients can be an invaluable resource (McDaniel et al., 1986). Mindfulness training can also help diminish stress, improve focus and attentiveness, and increase personal awareness (Didonna, 2009; Krasner et al., 2009; Ludwig & Kabat-Zinn, 2008). Calming one's mind through meditation, writing, exercise, or spiritual practice can be helpful in sustaining ourselves through a profession that is both rewarding and stressful. Tending to one's own health behaviors and engaging in one's own psychotherapy or medical family therapy when needed, will support the therapist's own growth and health. As we counsel family caretakers, "We can't take care of others if we don't first take care of ourselves."

6

COMMUNITY ENGAGEMENT

The empowerment of patients and families as informed agents of their own health care has been an important trend during the past two decades. The movement away from the traditional "doctor knows best" approach had been advancing in the prior decades, but the Internet has been a game changer in the balance of clinician–patient relationships (Forkner-Dunn, 2003; Griffiths, Lindenmeyer, Powell, Lowe, & Thorogood, 2006). Consider what patients now have access to at the click of a mouse:

- reliable medical information on websites of prominent medical institutions,
- medical journal articles,
- important components of their own medical record,
- quality ratings of medical providers and hospitals, and
- support and information from the experience of many people with similar health problems.

http://dx.doi.org/10.1037/14256-006
Medical Family Therapy and Integrated Care, Second Edition, by S. H. McDaniel, W. J. Doherty, and J. Hepworth
Copyright © 2014 by the American Psychological Association. All rights reserved.

At the clinical level, physicians and nurse practitioners now deal with far more patients who arrive at the clinic with printouts of medical information and advice, as well as questions generated by people they know only through the Internet. Although not universally available because a digital divide still exists along generational and social-class lines, the World Wide Web has become an additional player in many health care encounters (Baker, Wagner, Singer, & Bundorf, 2003).

A related trend is occurring at the community level. There is increasing public and professional awareness that the most important opportunities to prevent disease and manage illness lie not in the clinic but in the larger community. Of course, the field of public health has focused on the community for generations, but now there is more wind in the sails of a community approach to health care. Research on health and social contagion, discussed in Chapter 1, has provided new empirical support for the idea that we influence one another in small and large social clusters to engage in healthy or unhealthy practices. The Centers for Disease Control and Prevention's (2010) Healthy Communities initiative has stimulated a large number of innovations in community health across the United States. Importantly, this new approach to community work emphasizes the development of local lay leaders rather than relying only on traditional public health messaging.

ROLE OF MEDICAL FAMILY THERAPISTS IN COMMUNITY ENGAGEMENT

Collaboration with patients and families in treatment has always been a cornerstone of medical family therapy. The difference now is that medical family therapists are riding a major cultural wave, brought on by the Internet and other forces that have empowered patients, when we promote deeper, reciprocal collaboration in medical encounters. In other words, more and more patients and families are insisting on being treated as partners in health care. In this chapter, we focus on an area that is beginning to take more prominence in medical family therapy: engagement with patients and families as members of communities.

Although all helping professionals can learn to do community work, systems-trained therapists have something distinctive to offer. Because they are accustomed to working with groups of family members, they know how to connect with multiple people who come with different needs and agendas. They have skills in forging a common purpose across diverging interests. They know how to create processes in which everyone has a voice and powerful individuals do not dominate the dialogue. They know how to ask key questions of a group of people and let the interaction flow to surprising places not anticipated in advance. They know how to be central to the process when necessary to keep it productive and how to be peripheral to avoid getting in the way. In other words, there is continuity between the knowledge and skills set of medical family therapists and the community and citizen work we describe next.

For the purposes of this chapter, *community* means a set of interconnected social relationships that can be located in a neighborhood or a larger geographic unit or that can be defined by a common challenge (e.g., diabetes), or even more specifically by a common ethnicity facing a challenge. *Community engagement* means working with communities in a nonhierarchical fashion to solve problems together.

We begin by distinguishing among hierarchical, collaborative, and citizen models of health care (see Table 6.1). Then we describe the theory and practice of *citizen health care* as a way to use systems principles in community work.[1]

HIERARCHICAL, COLLABORATIVE, AND CITIZEN MODELS

The hierarchical model of professional authority has characterized much of our contemporary thinking about professional roles and ways of practice. The collaborative model of professional partnership, which emerged in the last third of the 20th century, represents an effort by professionals to deconstruct traditional notions of hierarchy in clinical interactions. The goal is to engage people as active participants and agenda setters in the services they receive. The citizen model embraces the collaborative model and goes a step further by emphasizing democratic partnerships between professionals and families to tackle problems and coproduce solutions at the community level.

We distinguish these models on four dimensions: (a) domain of practice, (b) processes of leadership, (c) location and duration of the work, and (d) the orienting ideal of the model. This typology should be seen as being primarily descriptive and comparative, rather than evaluative and critical in nature. We recognize that each model in the typology has areas of intervention for which it is particularly suited and that each contributes to the well-being of patients and families. Likewise, we acknowledge that professionals work within a variety of settings that constrain the scope and nature of the professional services offered to families. In particular, we fully embrace the collaborative model for clinical practice. It's just that the collaborative model alone will not equip a professional to do citizen health care work in communities. The

---

[1]This discussion is derived from work originally presented in Doherty and Mendenhall (2006); Doherty and Carroll (2002); and Doherty, Mendenhall, and Berge (2010). The Citizen Health Care Project is led by William Doherty, Tai Mendenhall, and Jerica Berge.

TABLE 6.1
Partnership Models for Professionals

Dimension of practice	Hierarchical	Collaborative	Citizen
Domain of practice			
• What is the scope of practice?	Individuals and families	Individual, families, and groups	Communities
Process leadership			
• What is the patient and family role?	Passive consumer, patient, client	Active, engaged but still a consumer, patient, client	Cocreator, coproducer
• Who leads the process?	Professional	Professional leads but shares decision making / Professional always has primary responsibility for the process	May begin with collaborative professional leadership but becomes family led
• Who defines the problems?	Professional, after assessing needs	Professional assesses, consults with patents and families, then codefines the problems	Communities of patients and families are the main definers, with professional input
• Who develops the intervention or curriculum?	Professional	Professional proposes, consults, shares decisions on how to proceed	Jointly generated from the outset
Location and duration			
• Where does the work occur?	Professionally determined site	Professionally determined site; may be tailored to family's needs	Jointly determined sites and locations
• What is the time frame for the work?	Tightly bounded appointments / Duration determined by professional	Schedule and duration generally set by professionals, with consideration of patient family needs and preferences	Jointly decided meeting times, duration of initiatives often open-ended

reason is that collaborative care assumes a clinical relationship with a patient, whereas in citizen health care, no one occupies provider and patient roles when groups meet to work on community problems.

Domain of Practice

Domain of practice means who is seen as the unit or system of intervention. Hierarchical models of partnership work almost exclusively with individual patients and families. In fact, most hierarchical systems make a strong distinction between the private and public domains of life and engage with individuals and their families around private dimensions of their life. Collaborative models also tend to work mostly with individual and families but may also work with groups of individuals and families—for example, in medical group visits in which patients support one another but are still consumers of a service created and run by professionals. A distinctive feature of the citizen model is that the practice is with groups of community members. These community members might also be patients in the clinic initiating the project, but they are not involved mainly as consumers of health care services. In other words, in the citizen model, professional efforts are aimed at facilitating change at the community level in partnership with patients and families in their role as citizens.

Processes of Leadership

Hierarchical and collaborative models are fundamentally expert led, but with a difference. In the former, professionals tend to define the problems and challenges people are experiencing and administer professionally developed interventions and curriculums. In collaborative models, practitioners generally see themselves as responsible for bringing a treatment model and leading the partnership process—asking the questions, preventing sessions from going awry, protecting vulnerable family members—but not as unilaterally responsible for the content of sessions and the outcomes. They see themselves as sharing the work with their patients at every stage until the patients are able to function well without the professional. Within a citizen model, the professional is the leader in the early stages (e.g., brings the model, facilitates the meetings) but looks to develop new leaders in the group who will take over after a time. The goal is for the work to become community-led and directed, with the professional serving as a resource. To repeat, the fundamental shift in paradigm with the citizen model is that of interacting with families as cocreators and coproducers of visible, public work as opposed to being passive consumers as patients, clients, or students (hierarchical model) or active partners in their individual or group treatment or education (collaborative model).

Location and Duration of the Work

Traditional paradigms of partnership have tended to define the elements of space (location) and time (duration) in limited, predetermined ways. Most work occurs in professionals' offices, clinics, and agencies according to professionally determined schedules. In citizen work, a working group of health professionals and community members jointly decides where to meet, whether in the clinic, school buildings, religious institutions, places of employment, homes, or community centers. Thus, a defining characteristic of the citizen model is that the location of the work is democratically determined rather than predetermined. Often political considerations go into this decision, such as what kind of message the group wants to send to the larger community by where it meets. For example, a group of American Indian people and medical family therapists might decide to meet at a Department of Indian Works building (see the Family Education & Diabetes Series [FEDS] Project described later in the chapter) rather than a medical clinic. In other cases, where the goal is to build linkages to a clinic (see the Citizen Health Care Home Project described later), the working group may decide to meet only at the clinic.

Even more challenging than location is the citizen model's concept of the duration of the work. In hierarchical and collaborative models, the duration of the intervention (or at least the outside limits) is often known from the beginning and is more determined by professionals or insurance companies than by patients. Community-based, citizenship work is more fluid in its approach to the duration of the work. Because patients and families are directly involved in defining problems and developing actions, the duration and end point are not known from the beginning, and indeed there may not be an end if the project becomes permanent or mutates into something else. This open-ended process is necessary to citizen work.

Orienting Ideal

At their core, all models of professional work are guided by an orienting ideal that inspires their practitioners. This ideal captures what the work is about, what its practitioners are trying to accomplish for the well-being of families. A model's orienting ideal defines good professional practice and suggests the criteria for professional success and competence. The orienting ideal of hierarchical partnership can be framed as taking good care of patients by giving them the best help that professional expertise can offer. For collaborative models of partnership, the orienting ideal is creative partnership to enhance patient and family well-being. For the citizen model, the orienting ideal is to develop creative partnerships with communities that activate individuals and families as builders of their world. The citizen model aims to promote enduring agency and communion in a community. To do this, citizen professionals strive to develop an ongoing process of community leadership development and action that will continue to influence families long after their own personal involvement in an initiative has diminished or ended.

Medical family therapists are well positioned to increase their effectiveness outside the office or clinic by engaging communities. In addition to a systems orientation and collaborative skills set, many medical family therapists have earned the trust of their communities, which allows them to call people together to address a community health need. What they require is the development of their "public skills" as citizen professionals working in groups with flattened hierarchies—that is, where community members and professionals work with a disciplined, democratic process to pool their distinctive knowledge areas and skills, and where professional expertise is "on tap," not "on top." We now describe an approach to this kind of work called *citizen health care*.

THE CITIZEN HEALTH CARE PROJECT

Citizen health care is a structured way to engage patients, families, and communities as coproducers of health and health care. It goes beyond the activated patient to the activated community, with professionals acquiring community organizing skills for working with individuals and families who see themselves as citizens of health care—builders of health in the clinic and community—rather than just as consumers of medical services. Citizen health care emerged from work across a variety of disciplines. First is family therapy with its systems orientation to viewing the individual within the contexts of his or her larger relationship, family, and social systems (Imber-Black, 1989; Minuchin, 1974). Second are medical family therapy and collaborative family health care, which add biopsychosocial dimensions to family systems theory and view the therapist as part of a larger, integrated treatment team. The third key influence came from outside of health care in the realm of political theory. The public work model of the Center for Democracy and Citizenship at the University of Minnesota was developed by Harry Boyte, Nancy Kari, Nancy Shelton, and their colleagues (Boyte, 2004; Boyte & Kari, 1996).

Exhibit 6.1 outlines the main principles of the model. Citizen health care aims to engage a resource that is largely untapped in our strained health care system: the knowledge, wisdom, and energy of individuals, families, and communities who face challenging health issues in their everyday lives. The idea of *citizen* refers to people becoming activated along with their neighbors and others facing similar health challenges to make a difference for a community. Ordinary citizens become assets in health care, coproducers of health for themselves and their communities. They are no longer simply consumers of services who look out for their own health and that of their immediate loved ones.

EXHIBIT 6.1
Principles of Citizen Health Care

1. See all personal problems as public ones too.
2. Look to family and community resources first.
3. See families and communities as producers, not just clients or consumers.
4. See professionals as citizens and partners, not just providers.
5. Let citizens drive programs rather than programs service citizens.
6. Make sure every initiative reflects the local culture.
7. Grow leaders, then more leaders.
8. Make all decisions democratically.
9. Go deep before taking action.
10. Think big, act practically, and let your light shine.

This combination of leadership and flattened hierarchy is a distinctive feature of citizen health care. Although the goal is to develop citizen leaders, at the outset the health professional must bring a vision and set of democratic public skills to the process of identifying key issues of concern to the community and to mobilizing citizen groups to work on these concerns. The professional brings a disciplined process to the citizen initiative so that it is genuinely democratic and is not hijacked by a dominant group member or lapses into the conventional provider–consumer dynamics that both patients and professionals are so accustomed to. However, the professional does not control the outcome of the group process by bringing in an action plan for others to react to. A principle of citizen health care is that if you begin with an established plan or program, you will not end up with an initiative that is "owned and operated" by its citizens.

A key decision point in implementing citizen health care is the delineation of the community to be involved in a project. Here the model reflects the influence of the community organizing tradition and its emphasis on mobilizing relatively small communities where people can have face-to-face relationships. We have found that a clinic population often serves as a good community boundary for citizen health care initiatives. No matter what community, each citizen health care initiative should have its unique flavor instead of simply adopting what another project did (although projects are encouraged to learn from other groups' successes). Local communities must retrieve their own historical, cultural, and religious traditions of health and healing and bring these into dialogue with contemporary medical systems. This is different from standard dissemination models in which professionals start with an established program and recruit community members to embrace it and help it run.

A key to all of these community conversations in citizen health care is the blending of the "I" and the "We"—how the health issue challenges not just each individual in the group but the whole community as well, and how ordinary people can organize to address problems facing the larger community. Local leadership among community members helps to guarantee that the project is suited to local needs and resources.

There have been more than 15 citizen health care projects since 1999. Although the core elements of these projects apply consistently across a diversity of socioeconomic and ethnic groups, their implementation has differed across communities and problem areas. A summary of key implementation strategies can be found in Exhibit 6.2. In the following two sections, we describe two mature applications of the citizen health care model. The third application is a newly emerging one. Each illustrates the guiding principles and strategies of citizen health care.

EXAMPLES OF CITIZEN HEALTH CARE PROJECTS

Department of Indian Work and FEDS

American Indian (AI) community leaders and tribal elders in the Minneapolis–St. Paul area were worried about the ever-increasing prevalence of diabetes and its impact on their people. Its pervasiveness was made even more alarming by the acquiescent sense of defeat that many AIs communicated—that diabetes is expected and not preventable. Providers working with members of the AI community shared similar concerns and were frustrated with the failure of conventional care and educational programs.

Medical family therapist Tai Mendenhall and leaders in the St. Paul Area Council of Churches' Department of Indian Work (DIW; Nan LittleWalker, Betty GreenCrow, Sheila WhiteEagle, and Steve BrownOwl) approached this challenge with a community-based participatory research approach, using the citizen health care model as a guide. Considerable effort was spent in designing a partnership with providers that was different from conventional top-down models of care. AI community members succeeded in sensitizing clinical researchers regarding the process, pace, and importance of building trust within AI circles. As the team engaged in a series of meetings, discussions, and AI community events, this trust evolved. Researchers learned about AI culture, the diversity of cultures and tribes within this larger frame (e.g., Dakota, Ojibwe, Hocak), spiritual and belief systems regarding health and "living in balance," and interpersonal propriety and manners—all because they were allowed into the AI community. In turn, community members gained more understanding regarding how Western medicine is oriented and thus gained insights into providers' habitudes and perspectives in care delivery.

EXHIBIT 6.2
Action Strategies for Citizen Health Care

1. **Get buy-in from key professional leaders and administrators.** These are the gatekeepers who must support the initiation of a project based on its potential to meet one of the goals of the health care setting. However, we have found it best to request little or no budget, aside from a small amount of staff time to allow the project enough incubation time before being expected to justify its outcomes.

2. **Identify a health issue that is of great concern to both professionals and members of a specific community** (e.g., clinic, neighborhood, cultural group in a geographic location). Stated differently, the issue must be one that a community of citizens actually cares about, not just something that we think they should care about. The professionals initiating the project must also have enough passion for the issue to sustain their efforts over time.

3. **Identify and meet with potential community leaders who have personal experience with the health issue and who have relationships with the professional team.** These leaders should generally be ordinary members of the community who in some way have mastered the health issue in their own lives and who have a desire to give back to their community. "Positional" leaders who head community agencies are generally not the best group to engage at this stage because they bring institutional priorities and constraints.

4. **Establish an initial consultation group.** This is a group of three or four community members who meet several times with the professional team to explore the issue and see if there is a consensus to proceed with a larger community project. These are preliminary discussions to determine whether a citizen health care project is feasible and to begin creating a professional–citizen leadership group. This group decides on how to invite a larger group of community leaders (10–15) to begin the process of generating the project. A major task of the small initial consultation group is to decide on the criteria for expanding its membership—for example, just within the clinic community or beyond its walls, people known to group members who are connected to a cultural community, or soliciting nominations from health professionals. One necessary criterion is that those invited should have leadership potential.

5. **Recruit and begin work with the citizen action group (about 12 members) that will plan and implement the initiative.** The professional facilitates the meetings. During this planning phase, most of the professional's time is spent in planning and facilitating biweekly meetings, and keeping in touch as needed with other stakeholders who want to be kept informed of the group's progress. Over the next 9 to 12 months of meetings, the group works through the following steps:
   - exploring the community and citizen dimensions of the issue in depth;
   - doing one-to-one interviews with a range of stakeholders, as appropriate;
   - deciding on a name and mission;
   - generating potential action initiatives, processing them in terms of the citizen health care model and their feasibility with existing community resources; and
   - deciding on a specific action initiative and implementing it.

6. **During this process, use professional expertise selectively—"on tap," not "on top."** In this way of working, all knowledge is public knowledge, democratically held and shared when it can be useful. Professionals bring a unique font of knowledge and experience—and access to current research—to citizen health care initiatives. However, everyone else around the table also brings unique knowledge and expertise. Because of the powerful draw of the provider–consumer way of operating, professionals must learn to share their unique expertise when it fits the moment and to be quiet when someone else can just as readily speak to the issue. A community organizing axiom applies here: Never say what someone in the community could say, and never do what someone else in the community could do.

7. **Keep articulating a larger purpose beyond the immediate problem and the local community.** Hold out a vision of how this work can contribute to the transformation of health care and show what democratically engaged people can do.

The DIW's FEDS program was designed and implemented as a supplement to standard care for members of the AI community touched by diabetes. Patients, their families (spouses, parents, children), and providers (physicians, nurses, dieticians, mental health personnel) come together every other week for an evening of fellowship, education, and support. Generally six to seven providers, four to five tribal elders, and 40 to 50 community members attend. Meetings begin with members checking and recording each other's blood sugar, weight, body mass index, blood pressure, and conducting foot checks. Participants cook meals together that are consistent with AI cultures and traditions, and a great deal of discussion is put forth regarding the meal's ingredients, portion sizes, and relevance to diabetes. Educational programs follow (which are designed according to participants' interests and wants), take place in talking circles, and involve a variety of lively activities (e.g., traditional and modern music, chair dancing and aerobics, drumming and singing, impromptu theater and role-plays). Instructional topics are similarly diverse (e.g., basic diabetes education, obesity, foot care, stress management, exercise, family relationships, retinopathy, dental care, resources to facilitate access to medical services and supplies). FEDS evenings conclude with devoted time for informal sharing and support. These biweekly series are scheduled to last for 3 hours, but most participants arrive early and stay late.

Quantitative evaluations of the FEDS have found significant improvement across key objective diabetes-related measures (e.g., weight, metabolic control). Qualitative evaluations (conducted within the culturally consistent contexts of talking circles) have found that the community-owned nature of the program—as well as the social support and interpersonal accountability that this encompasses—is perceived as the principal driver of said improvements and change.

It is clear that clinical and lay participants in FEDS worked collaboratively throughout every stage of the initiative's development—from early efforts in relationship building and establishing mutual respect and trust, to brainstorming the program's design, educational foci and format, public visibility, implementation, and ongoing modifications. The DIW and its clinical collaborators are now considering extending their efforts to create new programs in other areas of the AI community that are not readily reached by state- or reservation-sponsored care systems (e.g., inner city, low-income AIs). They are also working to partner with local AI-serving elementary and secondary magnet schools to create and implement culturally engaging and developmentally appropriate coeducation and community and interpersonal support for youth, alongside new programs designed in partnership with and for adult AI men and fathers (who have historically not been well reached by conventional or community-based participatory research [CBPR] initiatives in care).

Students Against Nicotine and Tobacco Addiction

The Hubert H. Humphrey Job Corps Center in St. Paul, Minnesota, is a federal vocational training program for at-risk youth ages 16 to 24. Site administrators, teachers, health care providers, and student groups had long recognized smoking to be problem on-site. Campus-wide surveys conducted in 2006 in response to this anecdotal evidence confirmed students' smoking prevalence to be twice that of the national average (> 61%). A follow-up survey found that almost 70% of smokers wanted to quit, most had tried to quit (several times), and few had been successful.

Job Corps personnel (one administrator, three teachers, and one counselor), students (eight smokers and eight nonsmokers), and University of Minnesota faculty (one medical family therapist and one family practice physician) approached this problem with a CBPR approach, using the citizen health care model as a guide. Considerable effort was spent in designing a partnership between students and professionals that was different from conventional top-down models of smoking cessation services and on-campus care. Students worked to sensitize Job Corps personnel and clinical providers regarding the social culture(s) and stressors of campus life, who in turn gained more insight into broader pressures from the federal government to lower students' smoking prevalence (to increase employability) and providers' struggles with facilitating behavior change.

The Students Against Nicotine and Tobacco Addiction (SANTA) project has encompassed a 5-year (and counting) collaboration in which all involved participants have worked together in identifying goals and developing action steps and solutions together, implementing interventions, evaluating outcomes, and refining interventions in response to said outcomes. After first surveying the entire campus regarding major antecedents to smoking, SANTA confirmed that it needed to target students' stress and boredom more than it needed to offer conventional smoking cessation literature and assist with "quit plans." It then went to work in changing several facets of the campus environment, for example, creating and facilitating a combination of social and exercise activities (yoga, dancing, arts and crafts, volleyball, basketball, weights, drama, and rapping contests), move the campus's designated smoking area to a less desirable location, change the color (to bright red) of underage students' identification cards so that they are easily recognized as being younger than 18 years, and change policy for employees who smoke (specifically, that all who wish to smoke during breaks do so in their cars instead of with students at the campus's designated smoking location). SANTA continues to work with the evolving nature of Job Corps and its students, sustaining efforts that are well received and designing and implementing new efforts as indicated. Ongoing campus-wide data collection efforts confirm reductions in students' smoking with continued exposure to project interventions.

As SANTA moves into the next phases of its work, the project will build on its early and preliminary findings that citizen health care is a promising way to intervene within high-risk populations to reduce smoking. Locally, SANTA is striving to meet federal mandates to convert the Jobs Corps to a smoke-free facility within the next few years. The group is also beginning to target other health-related behaviors recognized and identified by students and administrators as problematic (e.g., alcohol and drug use) and is considering the formal revision of one of its name's original "A"s from "Addiction" to "Abuse" and the addition of another "A" for "Alcohol." This would then translate SANTA's new name to "SANTAA": Students Against Nicotine, Tobacco, and Alcohol Abuse. Nationally, project members plan to implement a nonrandomized controlled trial to compare smoking, smoking-related outcomes, and potentially other health behaviors and outcomes across the Minnesota-based intervention site with demographically similar comparison sites. These efforts will help to inform the work of others whose missions encompass the improvement of their students' health.

The Citizen Health Care Home Project

Here we describe a project in its developmental stage. As mentioned in the Preface to this volume, the patient-centered medical home (or health care home) is a promising innovation in the organization of primary care in the United States. The federal Agency for Health Care Research and Quality (AHRQ) characterizes the health care home as a delivery mode involving five characteristics of care: comprehensive, patient centered, coordinated, accessible, and high quality, and safe (AHRQ, 2012). In its ideal form, the health care home offers a wide range of clinicians working in collaborative teams with patients and families to improve health outcomes and quality of life for people living with chronic health conditions and disabilities. If payment systems encourage its further development, the health care home model can create a path for the kind of integrative, collaborative care we advocate in this book.

A weak area in current health care homes is how to engage patients both individually in their own health care and collectively in the mission of the health care home—what is typically called *consumer engagement* (Nutting et al., 2009). Most of the work on the health care home thus far has focused on building provider systems and reaching out to patients, but not on actively engaging patient in their own health care. Health care clinics traditionally have had no patient leaders and no pathways for people to become involved in the broader mission beyond their own personal health care. There is no equivalent of the PTA in schools. There is no "we." This is no small gap because there is general consensus that unless patients and families become more responsible for their own health promotion and health care, the economics of health care will become unsustainable. To address this key pressure point in health care change, the citizen health care project has begun working with HealthPartners' Como Clinic in St. Paul, Minnesota, a large primary care clinic to create the citizen health care home.

The goal of the citizen health care home is to create a new way to involve patients deeply in the mission of the clinic in promoting health and to create a collective sense of responsibility for the health of the clinic community. The core idea is to create pathways for consumers to become citizens of a health care home community. This citizenship has two levels: personal and family responsibility for one's own health care in relationship with the professional team, and opportunities for leadership within the health care home community. The work started in 2010, when a medical family therapist approached the medical director of Como Clinic in St. Paul. Como is a primary care clinic affiliated with HealthPartners, a large health care organization that is moving toward the health care home system. The medical director recruited two other providers who met with the medical family therapist to get oriented to the citizen health care model. These three providers then invited a number of "leader patients" from their practice panels to form a working group with the providers. This group of 10 patients and three providers has developed and piloted the Active Member Project.

With the medical family therapist guiding the process, the citizen action group worked through the following sequence of questions over a year of biweekly meetings:

1. What challenges do we face in staying healthy and managing illness well, even when we have good access and quality professional care?
2. What are the traditional health care approaches to helping people with these challenges, and what are the limitations of these approaches?
3. How do we manage our health together in our everyday lives?
4. What action projects could we create to address these challenges that would follow from the citizen health care approach?

The first action initiative to emerge was the Active Member Project. An *active member* is defined as someone who sees oneself as the primary agent of his or her own health care, works in partnership with health professionals, and views personal and family health care as connected to the broader community. The key innovation is the creation of a formal status or role as an active member of the clinic, with mutual expectations between patients and providers, and membership in a community of active members. The key elements in the Active Member Project thus far involve the following:

1. orientation meetings for potential active members led by citizen patient leaders and providers;
2. baseline self-assessment of health goals, challenges, resources, and priorities for taking action for personal or family health;
3. meeting with one's provider to decide on health goals for the next year and preferred sources of support for achieving those goals (there is also a planned follow-up with the provider); and
4. following up gatherings and the formation of health goal groups around the goals and interests of active members.

Thus far, two groups have formed: one on active living and one on healthy eating. The groups are citizen-patient led, with process suggestions and consultation from the medical family therapist, and the participants set their own agendas and activities. The healthy eating group, for example, has focused its early work on cooking healthy meals together in the clinic kitchen, sharing recipes, and encouraging one another in a variety of healthy eating practices (it is not a weight loss group). The active living group has begun meeting around joint walks, with e-mail connection for accountability and encouragement.

What makes this project different from regular health promotion programs is the patient leadership in partnership with providers. The leadership group continually tunes the project, growing it slowly, learning from what is working and what is not working, and deciding when to start additional initiatives. After launching the pilot of the Active Member Project, the group decided to begin developmental work on a second project, the Experienced Patient Project, which aims to pair veteran patients with those who could benefit from the lived wisdom of someone who has "been there." The emphasis on leader development is exemplified by one of the citizen patient members deciding to nominate herself for the Board of Health Partners, the large parent organization, and then lobbying other patients to vote for her. She was elected to this board as the first self-nominated member in many decades. (Most health care organizational boards nominate their own future members, and the rare self-nominated person is infrequently elected.) In this way, she has become a citizen patient leader on a larger scale than the local clinic project.

In spring 2012, the Citizen Patient Project formulated the following statements as its mission, focus, and guiding principle:

Our Mission: to engage patients as active agents of their own health care and as citizens of the Como Clinic community.

Our Current Focus: to make the Active Member Project available to all patients at Como Clinic and to develop a second project that connects experienced patients with others who could benefit from that experience.

Our Central Premise: The greatest untapped resource for improving health and health care is the knowledge, wisdom, and energy of individuals, families, and communities who face challenging health issues in their everyday lives.

CONCLUSION

For systems-oriented therapists, engaging at the level of community can lead to an expanded sense of professional contribution and enjoyment of a closer relationship to their local world, whether in a formal citizen health care project or in less formal ways. There is usually little funding available for these projects in their early stages. Generally, professionals donate their time in the same way that community members do. (On average, launching a citizen health care project takes 6 to 8 hours per month from each professional involved.) Usually infrastructure support is provided by a clinic or agency in the form of meeting spaces, website development, and general communication tools. As projects mature and develop positive evaluations and a good reputation in the community, there are often sources of funding that offset some project expenses, including professionals' time. When a project is truly owned by a community, however, community members find ways to keep going through the ups and downs of funding cycles.

Exhibit 6.3 lists other "lessons learned" from implementing citizen health care projects. An important point to keep in mind is that citizen

EXHIBIT 6.3
The Citizen Health Care Project: Key Lessons Learned

1. This work is about identity transformation as a citizen professional, not just about learning a new set of skills.
2. It is about identifying and developing leaders in the community more than about a specific issue or action.
3. It is about sustained initiatives, not one-time events.
4. Citizen initiatives are often slow and messy in the gestation period.
5. You need a champion with influence in the institution.
6. Until grounded in an institution's culture and practices, these initiatives are vulnerable to shifts in the organizational context.
7. A professional who is putting too much time into a project is overfunctioning and not using the model. We have found the average time commitment to be on the order of 6 to 8 hours per month, but over a number of years.
8. External funding at the outset can be a trap because of timelines and deliverables, but funding can be useful for capacity building to learn the model and for expanding the scope of citizen projects once they are developed.
9. The pull of the traditional provider–consumer model is strong on all sides; democratic decision making requires eternal vigilance.
10. You cannot learn this approach without mentoring, and it takes 2 years to get good at it.

health care is not just about people helping people; it is about social change toward more activated citizens in the health care system and larger culture. This understanding inspires members of the Citizen Health Project about the larger significance of their work. It also attracts media and other prominent community members to seek to understand, publicize, and disseminate citizen health care projects.

At a larger level, if the current health care system is to be transformed in the United States, it will take more than new clinical strategies for the clinic and hospital, fairer reimbursement systems, or even universal health care access (as important as these changes would be). Quality and cost challenges will continue to overwhelm our care systems if we rely only on front-line professionals delivering services to people who are not empowered to take responsibility for their own health and that of their communities. While we continue to move medical family therapy more deeply into the care system, medical family therapists must also work to engage with our fellow citizens in community practice.

II

MEDICAL FAMILY THERAPY ACROSS THE LIFE CYCLE

7

HEALTH BEHAVIORS THAT HARM

We have become enemies of our own health. The alarm was sounded as early as 1979 when the *Surgeon General's Report on Health Promotion and Disease Prevention* attested, "Of the ten leading causes of death in the United States, at least seven could be substantially reduced if persons at risk improved just five habits: diet, smoking, lack of exercise, alcohol abuse, and use of antihypertensive medication" (U.S. Department of Health, Education and Welfare, 1979, p. 14). Throughout much of human history, the great debilitators and killers were infectious diseases transmitted through air, water, and incidental bodily contact: A stray skin puncture could easily end in premature death from bacterial infection; water- and airborne diseases killed millions of people as Europe became densely populated.

Not so now. In the 21st century, the greatest health scourges in economically developed countries are chronic diseases, which now constitute 63% of deaths in the world, and even more in developed countries (World Health

http://dx.doi.org/10.1037/14256-007
Medical Family Therapy and Integrated Care, Second Edition, by S. H. McDaniel, W. J. Doherty, and J. Hepworth

Organization, 2012). Most of these chronic conditions are strongly connected to personal behavior, particularly smoking, diet, alcohol and drug use, sleep disturbance, and sexual behavior leading to AIDS. Yet with the exception of a decline in cigarette smoking, progress has been scanty in recent decades, and in the area of obesity prevention, things are getting worse (Kumanyika & Brownson, 2007).

Any discussion about health-related behavior is a discussion about families, because it is in families that we first learn health habits that we then practice throughout our lives. This is why medical family therapists have an important role in helping both families and medical professionals deal with the complex issue of how to modify long-standing health behaviors. As family therapists, we have been trained to work with families to help change inter-action patterns that lead to psychosocial distress. As medical family therapists, we learn to work with families around health behavior issues that therapists don't normally deal with. In this chapter, we discuss two of the major behavior problems encountered in health care: obesity and smoking.

Medical family therapists generally encounter these problems in patients whose lifestyles are complicated by medical problems such as hypertension, diabetes, cardiac disease, and lung disease. The referral to the medical family therapist may be made by a frustrated physician or family member who asks for help in changing a recalcitrant family member's behavior. Other times a patient approaches the therapist because of feelings of helplessness and shame about being unable to "control" his or her own behavior. Thus, the therapist's work with smoking and obesity is likely to be part of a larger set of assessment and treatment issues; few medical family therapists work in specialized smoking cessation or obesity treatment programs.

This chapter complements the other discussions in this book on treat-ment issues such as chronic illness, depression, and marital problems. The medical family therapist addresses health behaviors as they come up in therapy, focusing on them for a time, defocusing at other times, and then returning at timely moments to deal with them again, always avoiding the trap of turning the therapy into yet another effort to force the patient to adopt different health behaviors. An attractive body weight in particular has become such a cultural obsession that working with obesity issues is fraught with the potential for psychological and social complications.

In this chapter, we highlight work on health behavior change that has become prominent since the first edition of this book appeared, and we then focus on the clinical aspects of obesity in a medical family therapy context that involves other team members who are interacting with the patient and family. We emphasize one of the hallmarks of medical family therapy: embracing a family-centered approach that enhances some of the best of the prevailing patient-centered approaches reviewed in the chapter.

SELF OF THE MEDICAL FAMILY THERAPIST

Therapists may have strong feelings and beliefs about weight, dieting, smoking, and sedentary lifestyles; indeed, it's almost impossible not to be influenced by our own histories and by American cultural norms about these problems. One of the authors overheard two female therapists in heated argument over whether a shared female patient was "just overweight" or "disgustingly fat." This was not just a clinical discussion. As smoking becomes more and more a lower social class phenomenon, negative social stereotypes about low-income people can creep into therapists' consciousness. Unless they carefully examine their family- and culture-based ideas about weight and smoking, therapists may attempt to work out their own issues by vigorously trying to "help" patients and end up forming coalitions with family members and other health professionals to force a client into self-control—a dubious enterprise, to say the least.

The medical family therapist should also be aware that sometimes the treatment for a cultural obsession can be worse than the "disease," with the most obvious example being anorexia nervosa. Sometimes the best we can do is to help the patient, family, or health professional accept the likelihood that no change may be possible at present. Other times, by carefully sifting out our needs, the cultural issues, and the issues of the patient, family and professionals, we can work with health behaviors in a way that leads to meaningful behavior change and improved physical and emotional health for all involved.

MEDICAL FAMILY THERAPISTS AND SMOKING CESSATION

The statistics on the effects of smoking are staggering. Here are some figures from the Centers for Disease Control and Prevention (2010c):

- Worldwide tobacco use causes more than five million deaths per year.
- Current trends indicate that tobacco use will cause more than eight million deaths annually by 2030.
- On average, smokers die 13 to 14 years earlier than nonsmokers.
- In the United States, cigarette smoking is the leading preventable cause of death, responsible for about one in five deaths annually, or about 443,000 deaths per year, including an estimated 49,000 deaths from secondhand smoke exposure.

Deaths from smoking occur mainly from lung cancer, other cancers such as mouth and pancreatic, cardiovascular diseases such as heart and arterial diseases, and respiratory diseases such as bronchitis and emphysema. Two of the great pioneers of family therapy, Nathan Ackerman and Murray Bowen, died prematurely, probably from the results of cigarette smoking. The human cost is enormous.

Outside of public health approaches, the focus of smoking cessation research and interventions has been on the individual smoker, despite growing evidence for the familial factors in the onset and maintenance of this problem. We now know, for example, that parental use and attitudes toward smoking influence whether children will become smokers (Chassin et al., 2005) and that family practices such as regular meals decrease the likelihood that adolescents will smoke (Franko, Thompson, Affenito, Barton, & Striegel-Moore, 2008). Smokers tend to be married to other smokers (Sutton, 1980) and to influence one another's smoking patterns of initiation and cessation (Homish & Leonard, 2005). There is good research evidence that support from a spouse or partner improves smoking cessation success (Mermelstein, Lichtenstein, & McIntrye, 1983; Ockene, Nuttall, & Benfari, 1981; Park, Tudiver, Schultz, & Campbell, 2004). A fascinating observational study by Shoham, Butler, Rohrbaugh, and Trost (2007) found that couples in which both partners smoke reported more positive affect when they lit up, whereas couples with one smoker and one nonsmoker reported negative affect when one lit up. These findings were consistent with Whitehead and Doherty's (1989) observation that smoking can become caught up in the dynamics of couple relationships. Overall, there is good evidence for the social and familial nature of smoking.

One other social factor in smoking has come to the fore in recent years. Environmental tobacco smoke (ETS; "secondhand smoking") has become a major health concern prompting changes in laws and social practices. It is also a family issue because the home and car are important sources of children's exposure to ETS, a situation that is particularly dangerous for children with asthma. Thus, a priority for tobacco researchers is how families of smokers can create smoke-free homes. One study of an inner-city population found that only 40% of current smokers had smoke-free homes (i.e., have family norms in which smokers go outside to smoke), whereas 61% of never smokers and 77.8% of former smokers from the same sample reported having a smoke-free home (Hymowitz et al., 2003). Pyle, Haddock, Hymowitz, Schwab, and Meshberg (2005) studied how families connected to a pediatric clinic created rules for smoke-free homes and called for more emphasis on this problem among clinicians. Clearly there are stakeholders in smoking other than smokers themselves.

In everyday practice outside of smoking cessation programs, medical family therapists are more often in a consulting or coaching role to patients, families, and providers on the issue of smoking cessation rather than dealing with smoking as an integral part of therapy. (This is different from obesity, which tends to be more powerfully caught up in power, control, and intimacy issues in families, as is discussed later in the chapter.) Two models from the field of health psychology are useful to medical family therapists as coaches and consultants on smoking cessation: (a) Prochaska's transtheoretical model of stages of change and (b) motivational interviewing. We summarize each model briefly and then mention how a systemically oriented medical family therapist can address a weakness of these models.

Prochaska's Transtheoretical Model

Originally developed in the 1970s, James Prochaska's transtheoretical model has been widely incorporated into research and practice on helping people make behavioral changes. The core insight is that individuals are at different psychological points on a continuum of interest and willingness to change and that providers need to know how open and ready someone is to change before giving input into how to make a change. Otherwise, providers fall into a one-size-fits-all approach to educating or motivating people. In the Prochaska model (see Exhibit 7.1), change is a process involving progress through a series of six stages (Prochaska & Velicer, 1997).

Although the research evidence tailoring specific interventions to specific stages has been inconsistent (Aveyard, Massey, Parsons, Manaseki, & Griffin, 2009; Prochaska et al., 2008), this stages of change model can help therapists avoid the common trap of getting too far ahead of patients in their process of considering when to stop smoking (or when to make another difficult health behavior change). When a physician complained to the medical family therapist consultant that a 60-year-old woman in the early stages of chronic heart disease was unwilling to seriously consider giving up cigarettes, the therapist asked what else was going in the patient's life. The physician noted that the woman had mentioned her daughter's upcoming wedding. The therapist suggested that the physician acknowledge that this was probably a hard time to think of giving up a stress-releasing behavior like cigarette smoking and ask the patient if she was willing to return to the smoking conversation

EXHIBIT 7.1
Prochaska's Transtheoretical Model: Stages of Change

Precontemplation: The person is not interested in making a change in the near future.
Contemplation: The person intends to change in the near future (e.g., 6 months).
Preparation: The person intends to take action in the immediate future (e.g., 1 month).
Action: The person has begun to make changes in the health behavior.
Maintenance: The person is working to prevent relapse (this stage can last for years).
Termination: The person has successfully changed the behavior and has high confidence in maintaining the change.

---

after the wedding. The patient readily agreed. In Prochaska's model, the patient was in the contemplation stage and not the preparation for action stage, but she might be later.

A limitation of Prochaska's model is that it is individualistic in orientation. Medical family therapists can also determine where family members are in their interest in their loved one's smoking cessation. If a spouse or partner is still smoking, for example, his or her investment in the patient's change might be quite limited, or he or she may sabotage the change (Whitehead & Doherty, 1989). (See the case at the end of this smoking cessation section.)

Motivational Interviewing

First developed by W. Miller and Rollnick (2002) as an early step to encourage treatment in alcoholism and other problems, motivational interviewing is now used as a stand-alone, brief treatment in areas such as smoking cessation, diet, exercise, HIV treatment, and drug treatment. It is a focused method for enhancing motivation to change by exploring and resolving ambivalence. The main insight is the importance of drawing out, supporting, and accentuating the side of the patient that wants change, rather than getting out in front of the patient by urging change that he or she will resist with "yes, but" or "you don't understand." Motivational interviewing is more structured and focused than nondirective counseling, and it is different from the persuasive methods most often practiced in health care. The general principles are as follows:

- *Express empathy.* People need to know that we understand how hard it is to quit smoking or make any other major lifestyle change. This is a step that clinicians are tempted to skip in smoking cessation because the "evidence" for the value of quitting smoking is so strong—and perhaps because few clinicians themselves smoke.
- *Develop the discrepancy between present behavior and broader goals and values.* Most people want to quit smoking to be healthier. Asking about their goals gives the patient the opportunity to say for himself or herself why it's important to make this change. The patient gets to say that the short-term pleasure of lighting up is outweighed by long-term health damage and goals, such as living to see one's grandchildren grow up.
- *Roll with resistance.* When the patient returns to the other side of the ambivalence ("it's too hard to change," "I've failed so often before"), the provider goes back to empathy rather than saying "yes, but." Ambivalence is normal, a part of the process of change.

- *Support self-efficacy*. When the patient affirms an intention to change, the provider emphasizes that this is the patient's decision to make and that if the patient decides to quit, he or she has the ability to make it work. Supporting the patient's agency also means accepting his or her decision not to make the change at this point in time.

In terms of research, there is strong evidence for the efficacy of this approach in alcohol or drug treatment and some evidence (but less strong) in health behaviors such as smoking, diet, and exercise (W. Miller & Rolnick, 2002). An advantage of motivational interviewing, which along with the stages of change model is familiar to many primary care physicians, is that it can be taught to a variety of providers and does not require therapy skills, although it does require a shift in orientation toward a more patient-centered approach. Motivational interviewing principles and practices can give medical family therapists and medical providers a common language to discuss challenging patients. The medical family therapist can also model a sophisticated use of motivational interviewing during joint visits, which helps the medical provider appreciate what the medical family therapist can offer patients.

However, like Prochaska's stages of change model, motivational interviewing suffers from an individualistic orientation, which a medical family therapist can overcome by viewing the ambivalent patient as involved in a complex web of relationships with people who themselves may be ambivalent or who may be pressuring or undermining the patient. For example, the therapist can inquire about what others in the patient's life are saying about the smoking and whether he or she should try to quit. Here is an example of where a systemic orientation helped a patient who was ready for change to actually make the shift.

A family physician asked a medical family therapist to help him work with a couple who were in conflict over the husband's repeated failures to stop smoking cigarettes. He would abstain for a few weeks and then relapse. She wanted to become pregnant and did not want herself or the baby exposed to his "dirty" smoke. Exploring the context of the smoking revealed that the husband was not "allowed" to smoke in the house, so he went to the coffee shop located near the couple's house to smoke after dinner, and there visited with his friends. (This was in the era of smoke-filled coffee shops.) He did want to quit for health reasons, but at the times when he quit smoking, he also quit visiting with his friends, leading him to feel "boxed in" by the marriage. The medical family therapist elicited his goal of change, listened to his wife's concerns while supporting the husband's autonomy in making this decision, pointed out that smoking served as a way for him to gain privacy, and then helped the couple negotiate new ways to obtain privacy without the presence of smoking.

The medical family therapist and the physician then coached the couple to negotiate a more collaborative way of handling the husband's challenge with smoking. This consisted of the husband promising to be straightforward and honest if he had a cigarette, and the wife resigning from the monitoring and criticizing role. (The husband also realized that he knew ex-smokers at the coffee shop who managed to socialize without smoking themselves.) They agreed that if the husband had a major relapse (i.e., returned to regular smoking), then the couple would come back to the doctor's office for a discussion about what to do next. The couple was able to use their smoking issue as a way to learn to deal with boundary and control processes in their young marriage.

MEDICAL FAMILY THERAPY AND OBESITY

With adults, obesity is usually not part of the original reason for therapy but is part of a larger set of problems related to a chronic illness such as diabetes. With children, a weight problem may be the primary impetus for the consultation or referral because the child is seen somewhere along the continuum between being psychosocially impaired to medically threatened by overweight. For this reason, after the overview of the obesity problem in the whole population, we focus on clinical treatment issues with children and their families. For adults, much of the earlier discussion of handling consultations on smoking would apply to obesity: stages of change, motivational interviewing, awareness of boundary and control issues, and sensitivity to the family context.

First, let's consider some definitions. Obesity in adults is generally defined as a body mass index (BMI) of 30 or higher. (BMI, which is calculated from a person's weight and height, provides body fat and weight categories that may lead to health problems.) Obesity is associated with increased health care costs, reduced quality of life, and increased risk for premature death. Common medical conditions associated with obesity include coronary heart disease, hypertension and stroke, Type 2 diabetes, and certain types of cancer. Overweight tends to begin in childhood, proceeds to become a lifelong problem for many people, and runs in families. For overviews of the extensive epidemiological literature on obesity, see Hu (2008) and Bagchi and Preuss (2012).

The challenge of obesity in the United States is clear. There was a dramatic increase in adult obesity from 1990 to 2010. In 2009–2010, the prevalence of adult obesity in the United States was 35.5% among men and 35.8% among women (Flegal, Carroll, Kit, & Ogden, 2012). Rates were highest for African Americans. In terms of states, no states had an obesity rate under

20% in 2011; the range was Colorado with 20.7% to Mississippi with 34.0% (see http://www.cdc.gov/obesity/data/trends.html).

Obesity in children and adolescents is an especially ominous trend. Rates have tripled since 1980. Approximately 17% (or 12.5 million) children and adolescents ages 2 to 19 years were obese in 2011. Health disparities persist, especially for Hispanic boys and African American girls, whose rates of obesity are much higher than those of White children. One in seven low-income preschool children is obese (see http://www.cdc.gov/obesity/data/childhood.html).

The consequences of childhood and adolescent obesity used to be considered long-term risks for adult problems, particularly cardiovascular disease and morality. But in recent years, overweight children and adolescents are facing current serious risks. There has been a dramatic increase in the prevalence of Type 2 diabetes among overweight children and adolescents, in addition to an increase in metabolic syndrome, a condition defined by a combination of high blood pressure, alterations in cholesterol and lipid levels, and elevated blood sugar (Centers for Disease Control and Prevention, 2010b; Gold, 2008).

The causes of obesity are assumed to include genetic factors and family, social, and environmental factors; in a smaller subset of individuals, it is influenced by metabolic and endocrinological disorders (Hu, 2008). Both adults and children consume too many high-calorie foods, especially fast food with appealing combinations of fat, sugar, and salt, and there are powerful food industry contributions to this excess (Kessler, 2009).

Dieting has been the principal means that individuals use to lose their excessive weight. However, relapse rates from diets are high, and many scholars are concluding that biological and psychological mechanisms make it likely that dieters, even those in high-quality treatment studies, eventually regain at least as much weight as they had lost (Butryn & Lowe, 2008). The failure of diets and weight-loss programs has led to an increased emphasis on prevention to get the public to eat healthier foods and participate in more exercise. So far, however, small-scale preventive measures such as higher taxes on soft drinks and limiting access in schools have not been effective in curbing soft drink consumption or improving children's weight (Fletcher, Frisvold, & Tefft, 2010). Perhaps a more substantial national commitment like the one proposed by Michelle Obama in 2010 will be necessary to change the culture and practices that lead to childhood obesity.

At the same time, there is increased concern that public health efforts could backfire by feeding the cultural obsession with being thin, leading to increased stigma toward obese people and more problems with low self-esteem, depression, and eating disorders. For this reason, the public health focus has begun shifting from weight loss as the central goal to an emphasis on healthy eating and active lifestyles (Bacon, & Aphramor, 2008).

OBESITY AND FAMILIES

It has long been known that obesity is passed down in families, but after Hilde Bruch's pioneering analysis of obesity and the family (Bruch & Touraine, 1940), nearly 40 years passed until family systems and obesity issues were taken up again in the 1980s. Behavioral psychologists' interest in spouse and parent support for weight loss led to a series of studies that suggested family involvement could be helpful (Brownell, Kelman, & Stunkard, 1983; L. H. Epstein, Valoski, Wing, & McCurley, 1990), and by the mid-1980s, family therapists were showing interest in obesity (Ganley, 1986; Harkaway, 1983, 1986; Hecker, Martin, & Martin, 1986; Stuart & Jacobson, 1987).

However, as managed health care in the 1990s drove the field toward focusing on diagnosable illness, there was little reimbursement (medical or psychosocial) for treatment of obesity among children or adults. Even medically oriented treatment centers for pediatric obesity could only be reimbursed if the patient had a separate medical disorder. In the 21st century, however, there has been increased interest in multimodal obesity treatment, as the country realizes the importance of obesity as a health care and economic problem. In some pediatric obesity centers family therapists have begun to be included in clinical multidisciplinary obesity treatment programs for children (Pratt & Lamson, 2009).

In the research domain, Berge (2009) identified a parallel development to what has occurred among clinicians in recent decades. It was not until around 2000 that researchers began to include family systems constructs in research on childhood obesity. In her review of 80 studies published since 2000, Berge found substantial evidence that an authoritative parenting style (i.e., love and limits) is associated with child and adolescent lower BMI, healthy dietary intake, and more physical activity. She also reported that research on family meals has consistently shown an association between the frequency of family meals and lower BMI and healthy dietary intake in children and adolescents. In fact, emphasizing the importance of home-prepared family meals (as opposed to fast food) may be the most useful and practical prevention strategy that family therapists can use for families facing the risk of obesity.

Along with research on family factors in obesity, the intervention research evidence has grown that family-informed treatment (mostly involving spouses and parents) can be effective for treating obesity in children and adults (McLean, Griffin, Toney, & Hardeman, 2003). Much of the contemporary research has focused on serious childhood obesity treated in specialized, multidisciplinary settings. A meta-analysis documented that interventions with a family treatment component are more effective than those without this family component (Young, Northern, Lister, Drummond, & O'Brien, 2007). In fact, there is now widespread consensus that it is essential to involve parents in the treatment of childhood obesity, although there is much uncertainty among obesity intervention researchers, most of whom are not trained in family therapy modalities, about how to skillfully engage parents and the overall family system (Latzer, Edmunds, Fenig, Golan, et al., 2009). The good news is that researchers are coming to understand that parents and other family members cannot be relegated to the role of implementing a child-focused treatment plan on behalf of the researchers. Furthermore, a new generation of medical family therapists (e.g., Keeley Pratt, Angela Lamson) are bringing family systems and ecological perspectives to a field that had been limited by an individual behavioral focus (Pratt et al., 2009).

A final fascinating line of research from social network analysis has contributed to our understanding of how obesity spreads through social networks. Christakis and Fowler (2007), using decades of data from the famous Framingham Study of predictors of heart disease, have shown how weight gain occurs through social influence in family and friendship circles. The strongest effects are for people who are closely connected in reciprocal relationships, but even third parties not known to an individual have an influence. For example, when a sibling's friend gains weight, it is more likely that another sibling (who does not know the friend) will also gain weight. The same effect has been found for smoking cessation; it occurs in social clusters via a positive "contagion" (Christakis & Fowler, 2008). This line of research is consistent with a family systems approach to health—we think in terms of multiple, reciprocal social influences. It also helps explain why spouses who are not involved in weight loss projects tend to lose weight themselves through a "ripple effect" (Gorin et al., 2008).

A FAMILY SYSTEMS APPROACH TO OBESITY

The following discussion is based on the collaboration of Doherty and Harkaway, the latter of whom is a family therapist with expertise in working with families of children with chronic, serious obesity. Doherty and Harkaway (1990) organized the assessment and treatment of obesity around the family FIRO (fundamental interpersonal orientations) model. It can complement the behavioral methods most commonly used in the family treatment of obesity (Keeley & Lamson, 2009).

Family FIRO Model

Mentioned earlier in this book, the family FIRO model, developed by William Doherty and Nicholas Colangelo (1984) and adapted from Will Schutz's (1958) FIRO model, has been used to provide a family systems perspective on obesity, smoking, and chronic illness (Doherty & Campbell, 1988; Doherty & Harkaway, 1990; Doherty & Whitehead, 1986; Whitehead & Doherty, 1989). Here we briefly describe the model and then apply it to obesity in families. The model's conceptual framework is described most fully in Doherty, Colangelo, and Hovander (1991).

The family FIRO model offers three core dimensions of family relationships: inclusion, control, and intimacy. *Inclusion* refers to interactions that relate to bonding and organization and shared meaning in the family. Inclusion represents the "glue" of the family—how it is structured, how members are emotionally connected, and how the family creates shared meanings about itself and its environment. *Control* refers to interactions that relate to influence and power in the presence of conflict. In other words, the control dimension of family interactions represents how family members deal with overt or covert conflict or disagreement. *Intimacy* refers to interactions that relate to open self-disclosure and close personal exchange. It represents the in-depth dimension of open and vulnerable conversations between family members. In this model, intimacy interactions are distinguished from inclusion-connectedness interactions by the depth of self-disclosure; thus, a relationship can be highly bonded and committed but still have few emotionally intimate interactions as defined here.

The core insight of the family FIRO model for health behaviors is that inclusion, control, and intimacy constitute a developmental sequence for managing major family change, with inclusion coming before control and control coming before intimacy. Thus, intimacy problems in families are difficult to resolve in the presence of major control struggles, and unresolved conflict pollutes the waters of intimacy. Furthermore, control problems are difficult to resolve in the presence of inclusion problems such as lack of commitment to the relationship, confused boundaries, or patterns of overinvolvement. These inclusion issues, which seed control struggles in the family, need to be addressed before the likelihood of meaningful progress on the control problems. For example, marital conflict over the patient's lack of compliance with a diet or medication regimen may flow from overinvolvement by the spouse in the health behaviors of the patient coupled with the patient's underresponsibility for self. According to the family FIRO model, these inclusion issues related to roles and boundaries should be the initial focus of the therapist's effort to help the couple create positive change. Doherty and Colangelo (1984) believe that the family FIRO model's priority sequence is used implicitly by many experienced family therapists who know which issues to focus on in the early stages of therapy and which to postpone addressing.

The primary therapeutic implications of the family FIRO model for medical family therapy lie in the areas of assessment and priority setting in treatment. For assessment, the model suggests that the therapist pay particular attention to inclusion issues, such as how a medical problem or health behavior issue has become incorporated into the structure of the family (e.g., in role patterns or alliances), how it has become a vehicle for bonding or disengagement, and how the family manifests beliefs around the problem; control issues, such as how the medical issue has become a battleground for power and influence; and intimacy issues, such as how the medical issue either bars open dialogue or sometimes provides the starting place for open dialogue.

We want to reemphasize that the major clinical implication here is for priority setting in the face of multiple family problems. The family FIRO model suggests that it is usually a mistake to focus on increasing emotional intimacy (as defined earlier) before treating coercive or passive-aggressive control patterns (because these problems will foul the waters of intimacy). Similarly, it is usually a mistake to focus on modifying control or conflict styles before systematically addressing inclusion issues that are feeding the conflict (e.g., a sense of abandonment by the partner, a lack of agreement about the roles family members should play in relation to an illness). *Focus* is emphasized here to indicate that in particular sessions, the therapist should not feel compelled by the model to ignore nonpriority issues that emerge. Sometimes in order to connect with the family, the therapist must work on their presenting issue first, even if that order does not seem logical. For example, if parents insist on viewing their child's failure to take medication as a control problem, the therapist may have to initially accept this frame to engage the family in treatment. Skilled therapists, however, know how to work on presenting issues at the overt level and underlying issues at a less overt level.

Finally, the family FIRO model applies beyond the family group to the therapeutic system created by the therapist, the family, and the other health professionals. These clinical systems have their own evolving patterns of inclusion, control, and sometimes intimacy. The model offers a language and procedure for analyzing and intervening with these clinical systems. When a physician is behaving coercively and a patient reactively, for example, the therapist can look for underlying inclusion issues, such as boundary problems and lack of shared meaning about the diagnosis or treatment plan.

It is important to note that we do not assume that obesity in children and adults invariably serves functions in the family system. In some cases, the genetic load or personal eating and exercise habits make obesity highly likely, and the individual's weight becomes incorporated in nonproblematic ways into the family's interaction patterns. When these individuals try to lose weight, the family is supportive, does not feel threatened, and stays out of control struggles over food, eating, and weight. The medical family therapist's role with these families is to help the patient and family cope as best they can with the possible negative effects of the overweight on the patient's health and to minimize the negative self-image the patient might have developed because of social stigmatization. These are situations in which straightforward behavioral techniques can be effective.

There are other situations, however, in which the therapist believes that the family has been organized around the obesity in a dysfunctional way, as generally shown in serious psychological problems in the obese member; inability to master life transitions such as leaving home; obsession with food or weight, or continual conflict in the family over food or weight; and problematic interactions with health care professionals. This analysis presented here pertains to those difficult family situations.

Obesity and Inclusion Patterns

Obesity can serve the following inclusion functions in some families.

Loyalty to the Family

In some families, obesity is a multigenerational theme that provides a sense of self-definition. In such families, obesity may demonstrate loyalty to the family, and losing weight can be perceived as an affront to the others, who continue their struggle alone. Loyalty can better be managed by trying to lose weight but failing. Doherty and Harkaway (1990) illustrated this dynamic with a family in which the highly obese adolescent boy was following the model of his uncle, who had held a world record for weight. All members of the family were overweight, and the uncle was the family star.

Coalitions in the Family

When one parent is overweight and the other thin, the child may be making a political statement by his or her weight. The child does not consciously choose a weight to correspond with one parent, but similarities in body shape and weight problems can indicate coalitions in the family. Pay particular attention to whether the thin parent criticizes the fat child for the same behaviors in which the obese parent engages.

Delaying Entry Into the Adult World

Because of the stigmatization of obese children in social groups, they often hold tight to the family for emotional support. For some families, this situation is considered acceptable and even encouraged. By delaying a child's entry into the adult world, obesity can protect the family's boundary. In fact, by staying out of the mating "market," the obese child never has to leave home.

Protecting the Marriage

A plaque one of us saw on the Ohio Turnpike read as follows: "A plump wife and a full barn never did a man any harm." This bit of sexist folk wisdom communicates the protective value of obesity in some marriages. Some couples admit that they feel that there is a protective value to obesity and that if one or both partners lost weight, they would worry more about extramarital affairs and the stability of their marriage.

Obesity and Control Patterns

Obesity tends to be viewed culturally as a problem of self-control. Obese people are thought to overindulge in food, although no evidence shows that obese people in general eat more than nonobese people. Because obese people are thought to be unable or unwilling to control their appetites, family members may try to perform the control task for the obese member, in which case weight control serves as a metaphor for relationship control. The following specific sequences of control interactions were observed clinically by Doherty and Harkaway (1990).

Maintaining Control by Losing Control

A paradoxical power struggle can occur in families dealing with obesity. The partner tries to control the obese person, who agrees to "be good"—that is, to lose the unwelcome weight. Over time, however, the partner's helpfulness begins to feel coercive, and the obese person resists or rebels, prompting further efforts at control by the partner. Eventually, the obese person abandons the diet, and the partner gives up in disgust. The obese person has won the control struggle by making the partner back away but has lost the weight struggle one more time. This incongruous hierarchy (Haley, 1976) can also be played out with health professionals, weight loss program staff, and therapists— to everyone's frustration.

A Rebellion That Backfires

This form of paradoxical power struggle can occur with parents and children: the child's weight is too high; the parents tell the child to reduce sweets intake and not to eat between meals; the child rebels by both refusing to eat less and perhaps even eating more; the more the parent tries to control the child's weight, the more weight the child gains. Although perhaps resembling a successful rebellion, this is a pseudo-rebellion: Although the child is trying to maintain autonomy from an intrusive parent, the child actually becomes more closely tied to parents through both the preoccupying power struggle and the isolating social stigma that can come with obesity.

The Obese Child With Too Much Power

Sometimes the child's weight does not have a strong inclusion function in the family. It is not tied to loyalty, connecting, or alliance issues but indicates a child with too much power. The battleground over control happens to be played out around food, with the child's tantrums being successful (often with one parent) in obtaining snacks. The parents are too divided to resist effectively, but they are not invested in the child's obesity. These cases are more easily treated than ones in which family inclusion issues are paramount.

Obesity and Sexual Patterns

Sexuality is closely tied to body weight and body image. In the family FIRO model, although sexual interactions can be understood in terms of inclusion (e.g., fidelity) and control (e.g., power struggles), here we deal with emotionally intimate sexual encounters and obesity. Weight can be used to manage sexual closeness and distance. For someone who is having trouble managing emotional closeness in the relationship, gaining weight (if thinness is seen as a barometer of attractiveness) can send a message that sexual intimacy is not desired. Conversely, the thinner partner may use the other's weight gain as an excuse to have fewer sexual interactions. In their research study of weight and marriage in a cross-section of American couples, Stuart and Jacobson (1987) found that wives who were mildly discontented with their marriages were most likely to use their weight to foster emotional and sexual distance from their husbands. Contented wives did not want sexual distance, and strongly discontented wives did not need any excuses for sexual distance.

TECHNIQUES FOR WORKING WITH OBESITY IN FAMILIES

Here we emphasize some special aspects of treating obesity in a family systems context (see Exhibit 7.2). Many of the techniques apply more generally to other health behavior changes as well.

Attend to Personal Weight Issues

Therapists who fear personal identification with obesity, based on past experience, present assessment of their own weight or family members' weight, or concern about becoming obese in the future, are particularly prone to excessive enthusiasm about helping obese individuals or excessive pessimism about the possibility of change. For the unaware therapist, the therapy becomes a

EXHIBIT 7.2
Techniques for Working With Obesity and Families

1. Pay attention to your own biases about weight.
2. Focus initially on the patient's decision-making process about losing weight.
3. Distinguish between weight that creates medical problems versus culturally defined weight goals.
4. Accept weight loss failure gracefully.
5. Help the family stay supportive but not overinvolved in the weight loss efforts.
6. For individuals involved in major control dynamics, encourage attendance at community programs.

way to work on personal or family issues around weight, self-indulgence, and self-control—and be paid for it! However, when the patient begins to regain any weight lost (many patients oblige the doctor and the therapist by losing a few pounds at the outset of treatment), the therapist may be prone to becoming coercive or giving up. As with any therapy issue in which we may become personally hooked, the therapist should get consultation or supervision on these cases. The main signal that a consultation is needed is a high level of personal frustration.

Focus on the Patient's Decision

By using motivational interviewing techniques focusing initially on the patient's decision-making process and even being strategically neutral about whether the patient loses weight, the medical family therapist is in a position to help the patient analyze the reasons for trying to lose weight and thus avoid attempting the drastic changes that often accompany dieting. Obese people and their families tend to have magical beliefs about how wonderful life will be if the weight is lost. Sometimes the obese individual is basing the decision on self-loathing or pressure from others, neither of which is likely to lead to a desirable outcome. By taking a "go slow" approach, the therapist can work effectively with the inclusion issues surrounding obesity: Who will the patient be disloyal to if he or she loses weight? What relationship might be disturbed? With whom will the patient stop having meals? How will he or she handle new sexual possibilities?

Separate Medical and Cultural Issues

The therapist needs to distinguish between weight that creates medical problems and culturally defined weight goals that might lead to eventual frustration. A patient's diabetes might be controllable with a 15-pound weight loss, but the patient may want to lose 40 pounds to reattain the weight she had as a 19-year-old. The therapist can identify with the health goal—if the patient genuinely embraces the goal of controlling the diabetes—while being neutral on the patient's choice to lose a larger amount of weight. Patients who have encountered health professionals who pressure them to calibrate themselves to the idealized norms of the weight charts sometimes find it liberating when a pragmatic therapist concentrates on losing only enough to get out of medical danger.

Accept Failure Gracefully

The therapist can discuss these weight loss failures in terms of timing in the patient's life, always emphasizing the patient's sense of agency. People have multiple priorities in their lives, and controlling a chronic illness may not necessarily be near the top of the list. The medical family therapist, preferably in conjunction with the patient's physician and nurse, can help the patient and family become clear about these priorities, even if that means that everyone accepts the likelihood that the patient's weight will remain higher than is medically indicated, say, for safe blood sugar levels. In these cases, the patient might be encouraged to set a more realistic goal of not gaining more weight.

Help Families Stay Supportive but Not Overinvolved

One of the best ways for spouses to support weight loss in obese partners is to be quietly supportive and to stay out of the way. Talking about food, dieting, and weight can create inclusion and control dynamics that complicate matters for the obese person. Faricy (1990), in her qualitative study of 25 couples in which one partner had successfully lost more than 25 pounds in a weight loss program, found that in most cases the partner was supportive from a distance and not involved in the process. In Epstein et al.'s (1990) study of obese children, parents were taught ways to deal with their own weight and were taught, along with their child, certain behavior modification approaches. This program helped parents and children achieve a moderate level of involvement during the weight loss process, with parents concentrating on themselves as well as on the child.

Encourage a Decision to Try a Community Program

For chronically overweight people who struggle with major psychological and family control issues over eating and weight, Overeaters Anonymous offers a potentially helpful approach to eating and weight. The program's use of Alcoholics Anonymous principles helps individuals short-circuit control issues around eating by emphasizing the "powerlessness" of the individual over food. This reframe sometimes reduces the sense of struggle, and the group cohesion helps reduce social isolation. Unlike most commercial weight loss programs such as Weight Watchers, the goal of Overeaters Anonymous is more about personal growth than weight loss. For patients who are interested in the commercial weight loss programs, the therapist can support their personal choices about joining but also their choices about quitting a program that is not helpful without guilt.

The following two cases of medical family therapy with obesity are taken from the work of Harkaway, as described in Doherty and Harkaway (1990).

Joan was a 12-year-old girl referred for obesity and compulsive overeating. She had become symptomatic with a rapid weight gain after her parents divorced and her father remarried. The family believed that the father was the only one who could understand and manage her behavior because he himself was obsessive and a compulsive overeater. The apparent loss of control over her eating and subsequent rapid weight gain led to the father's continued involvement with Joan and her mother. Every day after work, he stopped at their house for dinner, rather than going home to his new wife, to ensure that Joan was not bingeing and was eating a proper diet meal. He called daily and spent time on weekends with Joan and her mother. Thus, the father, who would otherwise be drawing a clearer boundary and aligning himself with his new wife, remained a member of the "old" family because of the child's problem.

The therapist's goal was to help the family manage its inclusion issues around the formation of a new set of boundaries that would allow the family transition to be completed. In this case, the therapist credited the father's dedication to his daughter and leveraged the father's frustration with his current efforts to help him (and his ex-wife) understand that the daughter was using binge eating as a way to grieve the parents' divorce, keep connected to her father, and make sure her parents saw each other every day. The outcome was that the family allowed the father to give up his old role and find a different way to connect with his daughter without her having to compulsively overeat.

In the second case, Linda, age 35, sought treatment for lifelong severe obesity. She was involved with a man who loved her but wanted her to lose weight. She agreed with him that she was too heavy and promised to lose weight for him. They had become locked in an unfortunate sequence: The more he tried to help her lose weight, the more weight she gained. She said she desperately wanted to lose weight, not only for him but for herself as well.

The therapist learned during the second interview that the couple had been discussing marriage for some time but that their concerns about weight and its meaning in their relationship had become a source of pain and confusion for them both. The confused messages were, "If she loved me, she'd lose weight" and "If he loved me, he wouldn't care what I weighed." The conflict over the weight kept them at once overinvolved and emotionally disconnected.

Although the struggle over weight was the couple's "ticket" to therapy and weight was a major battleground for control, the therapist saw the primary issue as one of boundaries and commitment (inclusion) and focused treatment accordingly. When these issues were handled successfully, Linda was free to handle her weight as a personal issue concerning health and self-image and not as a metaphor for marital commitment. In cases such as this, the "success" of medical family therapy is not in the pounds lost but in reducing emotional trauma and salvaging a relationship.

SPECIAL ISSUES IN COLLABORATION ON HEALTH BEHAVIOR ISSUES

Working with health behavior issues can bring forth striking differences between the culture of the traditional hierarchical medical approach and more patient- and family-centered approaches. It's easier for a medical family therapist to collaborate with a biomedically oriented physician on managing psychosocial stresses from heart disease or cancer than it is with cases in which seemingly deliberate behavior choices (overeating, smoking, not exercising) are directly undermining the patient's health—and the doctor's ability to manage the patient's illness. In the emerging health care culture of physician accountability for patient outcomes, physicians are even more tempted to "double down" on ineffective methods of behavior change such as reciting the information, using scare tactics that haven't worked before, or even antagonizing the patient enough so that he or she leaves the practice. Unprocessed provider frustration is a hidden threat to good health care.

In collaborating with providers, medical family therapists can bring a systems understanding to these understandable struggles. The first thing to avoid is the isomorphic process of being critical of the doctor for being critical of the patient. Like patients and families, providers deserve empathy and contextual understanding for their frustration and difficulties in making changes. Medical family therapists can model in their own words and actions the kind of healthy boundaries necessary in working with health behavior issues: appropriate concern for the consequences of the patient's and family's behavior; appreciation that real control lies in the patient and family as opposed to the professionals; and use of effective, noncoercive strategies to help patients and families make the changes that they are capable of at this time. Ultimately, the medical family therapist tries to promote agency and communion for all involved: the patient, the family, the provider and provider team, and oneself. *Agency* here means taking responsibility for what one can change and not change. *Community* means maintaining human bonds in the face of successes and failures. As Pratt et al. (2011) argued with regard to childhood obesity, effective collaborative practice will require the three-world view described earlier in this book: the integration of clinical, operational, and financial procedures in multidisciplinary teams.

CONCLUSION

The systems orientation to health behavior problems that are typically defined as individual is a strikingly new approach for both patients and professionals. It offers not only a new technology for behavior change but also a broad and complex view of health behaviors and the goals of treatment. Health behavior change is a team sport. From a family therapy perspective, an effective therapeutic intervention can be defined as one in which any member of the system (the patient or a family member) or any relationship in the system (a marriage relationship; a parent–child relationship; or a relationship involving the physician, a nurse, or therapist) changes in a healthy direction. Sometimes the overweight diabetic patient keeps the weight on and the blood sugar high, but the family and physician learn a lesson about who is ultimately responsible for the patient's health. Sometimes the smoker, freed from the burden of family or provider inclusion and control dynamics, feels free for the first time to choose to quit smoking cigarettes. The victory here is not merely in the abstention or the improved lung or heart functioning but also in the promotion of agency and communion in patients and those who care for them.

POST MAMMOGRAPHY INSTRUCTIONS

You have done something wonderful for yourself – having a mammogram is one very important phase in total breast examination.

You may have experienced some temporary discomfort from the breast compressions applied during the mammographic examination. You should not be alarmed if, as a result of the compression, there is some temporary skin discoloration involving one or both breasts. Occasionally there will be a mild aching as a result of the compression. If this discomfort is bothersome, you might try the medicine you usually use for pain or soreness.

It may be helpful for you to know that because of the compression, the images of your breasts were much clearer and were obtained with less radiation than would have been possible without the temporary discomfort you experienced. It is important, therefore, for you to understand that:

1.   The compression is not dangerous, it does not damage breast tissue; and

WellSpan Health Screening Mammography Services at ECH

Thank you for choosing WellSpan Ephrata Community Hospital's mammography services for your screening mammogram.

Screening mammography is for women who have no signs or symptoms of a breast cancer. If you feel a mass, ball, knot or lump, have pain or nipple discharge, you should call your doctor. You will need a diagnostic mammogram to specifically study the concern.

A registered technologist specializing in mammography will perform your screening mammogram. The radiologist interprets your mammogram within the next business day. Within 2 business days, you will receive a phone call from our technologists with your results. If there is a change in your breast tissues, or the study is inconclusive, we will offer an appointment to schedule additional images as recommended by the radiologist.

About 10 – 15% of our screening mammography patients need to come back for additional images and/or breast ultrasounds. *This does not mean that you have cancer.* In the majority of cases, these additional images or ultrasound examinations will be all that is required to completely evaluate the health of your breasts. The additional images and/or ultrasound will

longer appointment.   hen you return for these images, the radiologist will in_ _p. .. ....
while you are here and you will receive those results before you leave.

We like to be sure our patients are aware that there are additional charges for this/these exams which may apply to your deductible. If you have a co-pay or deductible with your insurance plan, you will receive a bill after your insurance has been billed. You will receive two (2) bills; one for the exam and one for the interpretation of the exam by the radiologist. Please direct any questions about your bills to Customer Service (717- 738-6261.

Finding breast cancer early significantly reduces the mortality rates associated with breast cancer, however, mammography alone cannot detect all breast cancers. For complete breast health, you should have your breast examined yearly by a trained professional as well as performing breast self-exam monthly.

Your health care provider will receive the mammogram report.

You will receive a letter in the mail notifying you of the results – even though we told you over the phone and you will receive a separate explanation of your breast density.

possible image of the inside of your breast with the least amount of radiation.

While the mammogram is the single best method of detecting breast cancer, it does not find all breast cancers. Please continue getting periodic mammography examinations, see your doctor for a clinical exam and continue monthly breast self-examinations.

Your mammogram was performed by _____ *Tina*

Please call Tina Stewart, R.T. (R)(M), chief mammographer, Women's Imaging Center at 717-721-5777 if you have any questions or comments about mammography.

8

COUPLES AND ILLNESS

"In sickness and in health," a common Western marriage vow, is often cited by couples who pay little attention to the words. For most long-term couples—gay or straight, legally married or not—a committed relationship often includes a belief that they will cope with any life crisis. This optimism also makes it easy to distance oneself from the reality that health crises will actually occur. Couples therapists may unwittingly participate in this cultural denial and comfortably address communication and sexual problems, money issues, work and family stresses, without exploring a couple's medical history.

Illness can stress a relationship just as much as infidelity, addiction, or abuse. Stressful developmental periods for couples, for example, when having a baby or during a child's adolescence, or when coping with chronic illness, are all periods of high vulnerability. However, with vulnerability comes the opportunity for strengthening the relationship and improving health (Staton, 2009). Almost always one member of a couple will outlive the other,

http://dx.doi.org/10.1037/14256-008
Medical Family Therapy and Integrated Care, Second Edition, by S. H. McDaniel, W. J. Doherty, and J. Hepworth

and the time before the loss generally includes significant illness or disability. This chapter describes the multiple ways in which couples are affected by illness crises and identifies clinical strategies that are particularly useful during these universal life experiences. Research findings and themes are included for the clinical strategies that have empirical support. This chapter is for medical family therapists as well as all couples therapists because couples may not recognize illness as a stressor or seek help for health concerns. They may attend couples therapy complaining of something other than illness, as exemplified by the following case.

At their first marital therapy session, Margaret said, "Paul, you talk. I'm tired of doing it all." So began what appeared to be a standard session in which each described disappointment and ascribed blame. Paul felt that Margaret didn't appreciate his hard work, and Margaret felt that Paul dismissed her work as a school nurse and took for granted her management of the home and family. In their time-pressured family with active children in junior high school, they didn't spend much time together as a couple. Indeed, like a surprising number of couples, they reluctantly admitted that they'd "just ended up in separate bedrooms."

When asked about the arrangement, both agreed that it happened for "practical reasons" and didn't reflect their mutual commitment. Seven years earlier, Paul had suddenly been diagnosed with a nonmalignant brain tumor. His diagnosis was followed by surgery, infection, and complications for several months, during which time he was in the hospital, a rehabilitation facility, or at home with nursing care requiring sterile surroundings. It was practical for Paul to have a separate room during his recovery.

Although Paul had fully recovered nearly 5 years earlier, the couple had not moved back into the same bedroom. They didn't consider this a significant issue and were eager to return to describing the ways each felt misunderstood. The couples therapist, who was also a medical family therapist, gently noted that significant health crises often have long-term impacts on relationships and suggested that it might be useful to consider how Paul's illness had affected their relationship.

Without a formal decision, Margaret and Paul's temporary sleeping plan had become a permanent arrangement, like a scar in the relationship that remains long after the illness. It is possible that the illness provided some justification for the new sleeping arrangement, which might have been preferred for other reasons, but there are observable and less visible ways that couple relationships can be forever transformed by illness. Some couples will seek assistance during or closely following their health crises. Many will be like Paul and Margaret, who come much later for "communication" or other problems, not seeing the connection to an illness or accident. They think they should be able to cope with illness crises, especially when there is a positive outcome.

HOW HEALTH CONCERNS AFFECT COUPLES

Couples are touched by health crises throughout their life span and throughout the life span of their families. We consider three distinct time periods when illness can have an impact on couples: caring for aging or ill parents, coping with illness of a child, or responding when illness strikes a partner. The clinical cases described in this chapter provide examples of couple concerns for each of these situations.

The Expected: Illness in a Couple's Parents

Most couples will experience the aging, illness, and loss of one or more parents. Each member of the couple comes from a unique family, with differing expectations and resources for care of the elders. Often these expectations are assumed and not discussed, and the unacknowledged differences between members of a couple can lead to smoldering or overt conflict. Even when couples are able to discuss these issues and agree about responsibilities, the increased tasks and the emotional strain take a toll.

Rose Miano and Ed Kern (see Figure 8.1 for genogram) sought couples therapy to address their increasing conflict and sense of emotional separation. Ed, a minister, and Rose, a social worker, felt they had always had a strong and caring relationship and were happy with the growth of their daughter, Marnie, age 11. Ed's parents lived several states away, and his father had been diagnosed with Alzheimer's disease for 2 years. Ed visited his parents for 2 days each month and provided much support to his mother with almost daily telephone contact.

Rose was proud of Ed's commitment to his family and understood that Ed's brother was not particularly helpful to his parents. At the same time, she

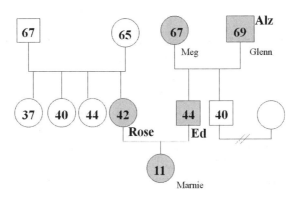

Figure 8.1. Miano genogram.

found herself angry and hurt that Ed was away and distracted so much. Her ambivalence was confounded by his multiple caregiving responsibilities with members of his congregation. As a social worker, she fully understood and admired his position. As a spouse, she felt neglected, and then felt guilty for those feelings.

Caring for aging parents often becomes a couple crisis or conflict that is a prime target for medical family therapy support and intervention. Role strain, conflicted loyalties, and reactivation of earlier parent–child difficulties emerge when adults change roles and care for their parents. When a partner is visiting and caring for an elderly parent, he or she is not participating in activities with the spouse or their children. The buildup of other responsibilities adds stress, and couples may find themselves arguing more frequently. More complex than arguments are the often unacknowledged feelings of resentment. A spouse like Ed can feel betrayed that his spouse does not understand that he would prefer to be with her, but he also needs to provide caregiving to his parents.

The necessity of caring for elderly parents frequently occurs at the time when couples have raised their children and hope for renewed couple time. Instead, caregiving can reactivate earlier couple developmental issues such as whether the spouse was fully accepted by the parent or which set of parents should be visited for holidays. Couples note in therapy how dismayed they are that these loyalty issues arise again, when they thought they had been negotiated long ago.

Not all couples who care for parents have a long history with one another. If a couple marries later in life, one spouse may not have known the aging parent and may not have the attachment that makes difficult caregiving duties easier. A second wife may feel that she is not welcome to help care for her new mother-in-law because her husband's first wife of 20 years remained close with her. Or conversely, a newer partner may view the elderly parent as a pleasant distraction and not understand why his partner complains about how hard it is to care for his father now when he felt his father was not emotionally available for him when he was a child. The crisis of caregiving, discussed more fully in Chapter 13, brings these issues to the forefront, and provides important material for therapy.

The Unexpected: Illness in a Child

Tonya and Manuel Hunter (see Figure 8.2 for genogram) were referred to a medical family therapist by Tonya's primary care physician, after Tonya confided that she and Manuel often argued about how to handle Tonya's son, Mike. Tonya and Manuel had married 4 years earlier and lived with Tonya's two children from her previous marriage. As a stepfather, Manuel tried to refrain from parenting conflicts with Tonya and her children. In the past few

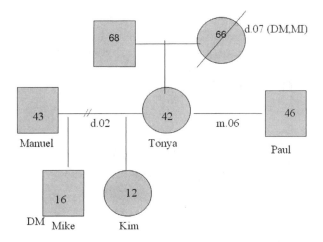

Figure 8.2. Hunter genogram.

months, however, he had become increasingly frustrated with the fighting between Tonya and Mike.

Mike, now 16, had been diagnosed at age 10 with diabetes. Like many school-age children, he initially was a "model patient." He kept charts about his blood sugar levels, learned to handle his own injections, and kept his mother informed as needed. According to his mother, Mike had become much less responsible about his illness in the past year or two. When she tried to talk with him about it, he became angry and withdrew. In the last semester, he had passed out at a track meet after not eating before the event. Tonya understood that adolescents often ignore healthy eating, experiment with alcohol, and want independence about their decisions, but her mother had died of complications from diabetes only a few years earlier. Tonya felt that Mike could not afford to be cavalier about managing his illness.

When Manuel suggested that the arguments were not helping Mike become more responsible, Tonya became angry and responded that Manuel couldn't understand her position because they weren't his children. Conflict about illness management then frequently escalated to couple conflict about other issues, including those about inclusion and acceptance, so significant in second marriages.

Couples often differ in their views about how to handle illness in a child or experience such individual distress that they are unable to support one another. Either or both of these patterns can be addressed with medical family therapy. (The impact of childhood illness is discussed more thoroughly in Chapter 10.) Here we emphasize that couples may present for therapy and not recognize how the stress of their child's illness affects their conflict and sense of decreased intimacy. Therapists have an opportunity to work with couples to help them see their experiences as normal responses to the health crises instead of as significant breaches in their relationship.

The Constant Companion: Illness in a Partner

The caseloads of medical family therapists are full of couples in which one member has a chronic or progressing disease. When one spouse is severely incapacitated by illness, the impact of the illness is what brings the couple to therapy or more readily becomes a focus of discussion and intervention. With other couples such as Margaret and Paul, introduced early in this chapter, therapists may not learn of a significant health crisis unless they ask about illness history.

Couples may have residual concerns from illness crises, which may be unaddressed but have a significant impact on the nature of their relationship. In fact, couples often describe how they jointly pull together to respond to the illness at the time of the crisis. Only later, especially when the threat has dissipated, do they begin to allow themselves to experience their disappointments, resentments, or conflict about how they handled the crisis. This reaction is similar to how individuals respond immediately to an automobile accident with clarity and efficiency but then later find themselves shaking and crying. For this reason, couples can benefit from medical family therapy both during and after a health crisis.

CLINICAL STRATEGIES AND THEMES

Many of the general clinical strategies identified in Chapter 2 are useful for medical family therapy with couples, particularly facilitating agency and communion and "putting the illness in its place." The primary case discussed in that chapter is a couples case in which Bill and Carol Ellman coped with his increasingly debilitating diabetes and end-stage renal disease. In this chapter, we highlight clinical strategies (see Exhibit 8.1) that address the differences in expectations and coping styles of each member, and the impact on their relationship. The case example of Margaret and Paul exemplifies use of these strategies, with the exception of the first clinical strategy, in which Rose and Ed's story is helpful.

Explore Family Histories and Expectations

Just as families can disagree about how to spend holidays or money, they can disagree about how they expect to care for ill or elderly family members.

In some families, adult children hear of their elderly father's hospitalization only after their stepmother has brought him home. In other families, the son schedules and attends all medical appointments for his relatively healthy mother. Sometimes these patterns occur because families are either overly or insufficiently attentive to one another. More frequently, the differing patterns reflect family preferences, pride, historical patterns, or assumptions.

Each spouse or partner comes from a family in which expectations are more or less discussed and therefore more explicit or implicit. The clinical skills for comparative histories include helping people understand their own and their partner's history in order to help them separate their covert presumptions and consider how the differences influence their present choices and relationship.

Rose and Ed, the social worker and minister, had talked often of the differences in their families of origin but had not really considered how those differences affected their response to illness and caregiving for their parents. Rose came from a large Italian American family in which three of the four daughters and their families lived within an hour of their parents and visited frequently. Rose's parents were in relatively good health, and she and her sisters had not been faced with caregiving challenges. Although they hadn't discussed it much, she thought they all assumed that they would respond as their parents had. Her grandmother had lived with her parents for several years before her death, and Rose assumed that when it was time, her parents would live with one of her sisters or herself.

In contrast, Ed's parents had always been proudly independent. They indicated to their sons that they would not burden them. They had recently moved into a retirement community where they had friends and activities, and they did not need to drive often. Ed's brother lived many states away from their parents and did not have the financial flexibility for frequent visits. Their mother frequently said she did not want her sons to worry about them, but she also appreciated and began to count on the frequent calls and visits from her attentive son. Ed felt that she needed help and that he was it in terms of available help.

The differences in family history and expectations provided content for Ed and Rose's arguments. By acknowledging the different family expectations in the couples therapy, Rose was able to see how she felt that Ed's mother was claiming to be independent but putting too much pressure on them by subtly telling Ed that he wasn't with her enough. Rose understood that Ed's brother wasn't a resource, but she suggested that it would be easier if they could move Ed's parents to their community. Ed described how his mother was losing so much of her sense of independence, and he was reluctant to push her to "give up more." Therapy allowed Rose and Ed to stop arguing and consider their different preferences to find a solution that might be more effective for all.

Once Ed realized how he was trying to preserve his mother's independence in the face of her losses, he realized that talking honestly with her was a way to enhance her dignity. He and Rose considered multiple options, and Ed visited his mother to discuss them with her and ask for her help. As he included her in his decision making about how to make his own life more manageable, his mother determined that a move to a new community near Ed and Rose would be helpful. Not all family differences can be negotiated so easily, but therapy can help couples identify and acknowledge the core beliefs, values, and assumptions behind their different views. They then can be freer to look for solutions instead of fighting to have their values respected.

Elicit the Divergent Illness Stories

Long after a medical trauma, both partners can describe the events and their experiences in exquisite detail. As with most couple issues, each sees his or her journey differently, and each partner may never have heard the other's detailed view. It can be revealing for both partners in a couple to describe their unique view and consider the meanings that each ascribed to their experience. It is important to take the time to not only elicit the stories but affirm each partner's experience.

Paul's recollection confirmed that he had wanted to have as much control as possible of his medical situation. He readily ticked off dates when he first knew his symptoms were serious, as well as when he visited his family physician, the neurologist, and the surgeon. He could chronicle the details of his initial surgery and the second postinfection surgery like a medical student and had an excellent grasp of his diagnosis, treatment, and prognosis. He described having good relationships with his physicians and felt that he'd been well informed throughout—almost a member of the medical team.

In contrast to her husband's memories of personal agency, active involvement, and a realistically positive attitude at the time of his illness, Margaret mostly remembered her fear. She shuddered as she recalled the day she first learned Paul was scheduled to see a neurosurgeon and how nervous she'd been as they waited in the doctor's reception room. She talked about how tiring it was to spend hours each evening on the phone, updating family members and friends about Paul's condition. She tried to maintain a positive attitude but described how, as a nurse, she'd had to fight off her nursing school memories of people with shaved heads, loss of cognitive functioning, and terrible prognoses, fearing that future for Paul.

Paul claimed to understand her fears, but even as Margaret described her fears from the early days, he tried to assure her that his tumor was gone and there was no reason to fear a recurrence. Margaret felt no such security. She said she envied Paul's certainty, and although she hoped that he was clear of danger, she still found herself worrying when he was late from work or unavailable on his cell phone. After more discussion, Margaret began to sob. She said that Paul didn't understand how hard it had been for her and the children, because he'd been unconscious much of the time. It became clear that Paul and Margaret had never talked directly about her experiences during the height of his crises.

It had not occurred to Paul and Margaret that their trauma several years ago could have much to do with their present troubles. They responded well to a metaphor: A serious illness like Paul's tumor and surgery resembles a large tree falling on the house. It suddenly comes crashing down as if from nowhere, does a lot of damage, and leaves much debris, requiring repair and cleanup. It can be dangerous, even fatal. Although it may be tempting to try to assign blame for the falling tree or obsess about ways the illness could have been avoided, most agree that this is just an unfortunate, random event that nobody could predict or prevent. Afterward, however, those involved continue to relive the event, discuss it, and may become wary about walking near trees (or minimizing physical symptoms). Years later, they still remember that first terrifying crash of the tree—or the first time they heard the diagnosis— and are reminded that crises can occur at any time.

Attend to Affect

Paul and Margaret's conversations identified differences both in their affect and how they responded to the illness events and to each other. In these conversations, it appeared that Paul had a sense of competence and closure about the illness. Margaret, even years later, still showed physical signs of distress, to which Paul responded with attempts to comfort and reassure her. There was a gentleness between them that had not been present when they were focusing on their grievances.

As therapists, we can jump at opportunities to reinforce any glimpses of tenderness in feuding couples. Even the most estranged couples can often appreciate the warm support they have received from each other during past times of family loss or illness. In fact, partners who are highly critical of each other may make exceptions when asked what it was like between them when a parent was seriously ill or when a close cousin died. Discussing couples' recollections of how they supported one another during illness can result in the same kind of positive feelings that emerge from descriptions of their first meeting or engagement.

Not all couples, however, respond in the positive ways that Paul and Margaret recalled. People who feel that their partner did not provide sufficient support during past crises generally identify that time as a significant breach in trust or in their relationship. A therapist's response requires the subtle couples therapy skills used to address similar breaches of trust, such as marital infidelity. This includes attention to grief, trust, reparation, forgiveness, and future plans.

One of us worked with a couple who came in stating that they had "nothing left in their marriage, now that their kids were grown." Only after obtaining an extensive history was it revealed that the husband had undergone radical prostatectomy for prostate cancer and that both members of the couple were determined not to let this make a big difference in their lives. As a couple, they had focused on keeping their lives stable, but in retrospect, the husband felt that his wife did not understand the difficulty of the diagnosis, treatment, and impact on sexual functioning. The couple coped by avoiding sexual intimacy and stating that it was not important to them. Only during arguments did they complain to one another that their sexual relationship had dwindled, and each blamed it on the other.

It took some time for the couple to be willing to discuss their disappointments and sexual relationship with the therapist. Only after the husband's disappointment was explored could the couple discuss next steps. When the therapist asked about the sexual impact of the surgery, the husband spoke about the variability of his erection, the possibility of urination during excitement, and how he had found it easier to avoid sexual activity. The wife, too, described how she did not want to embarrass her husband and so also avoided sexual activity. In addition, she missed their previous easy sexual activity. Several sessions were needed for them to discuss their disappointments and mourn their previous ease of sexual intercourse. Only then could they become more comfortable with one another as they explored alternative sexual activity. As they noted in one later session, "In our early life we had to deal with diaphragms; now we deal with towels."

Attention to affect includes creating opportunities for couples to express the range of strong feelings that inevitably accompany illness crises. Anger, resentment, and guilt all often present as important themes. Most confusing for people is that feelings don't exist in isolation but occur simultaneously and can seem inconsistent. A man may feel guilty about being healthy at the same time that he feels resentment about being held back by his partner. In the family in which the son had diabetes, Tonya experienced guilt about her perceived genetic link between her mother and son's diabetes. At the same time, she felt angry that she should experience guilt for something that wasn't her "fault."

Ill partners can experience frustration about their limitations and may project blame upon their partner for pushing them or not understanding their incapacities. Couples may mourn the loss of their previous relationship or grieve the potential death of the other. Couples often do not have ways of carefully sifting these complicated feelings, and the opportunity of couples therapy can unleash powerful emotions and strong statements.

Emotionally focused therapy (S. M. Johnson, 1996; S. M. Johnson & Whiffen, 2005) helps couples process, validate, and normalize their emotional experiences and find comfort with one another. The empirically supported therapy helps clients experience the difficult emotions, make sense of them, and then manage the emotions with a new perspective that includes the positive attachment of the spouse and therapy. The founders of emotionally focused therapy described how the model's attention to attachment is particularly consistent with goals of medical family therapy because the loss and attachment issues are so significant with severe illness (Kowal, Johnson, & Lee, 2003).

Identify Preferred Coping and Support Styles

No single communication strategy serves all couples. For couples in which one spouse had cancer, those couples with matching communication styles reported the least amount of conflict and stress (Dakof & Liddle, 1990). Couples in which both partners wanted to talk about their feelings did well, as did couples who both preferred to not discuss the illness. The couples with divergent styles were more likely to report conflict and distress about the illness and their relationship, such that concordance in communication styles was more important than candor about the illness. Rolland (1994) described how differences in communication preferences is one of the relationship skews that can separate rather than enhance intimacy of couples dealing with illness. Other common relationship skews include differences in when each member accepts a diagnosis or whether the illness is something that the couple describes as a shared concern or that belongs solely to the ill partner.

An extensive review of research about couple responses to a range of chronic illnesses (Berg & Upchurch, 2007) focused on shared couple responses rather than individual coping styles. A shared appraisal, in which the couple views the crisis as happening to both partners, allows couples and therapists to consider how they can pull together as "we against the illness," allowing them to externalize the illness. Couples who seem to share their experience, exemplified by the use of the words *we* and *us* to describe their experience with the illness, have less psychological distress (Scott, Halford, & Ward, 2004). The review concluded that couples reported better adjustment when they had a shared appraisal of the illness crisis and when the spouse was supportive and collaborative, rather than controlling, overprotective, or underinvolved.

Margaret and Paul discussed how they had each coped with Paul's brain tumor. Both noted that Margaret's fears had not been a topic of conversation between them. This common pattern, in which healthy spouses hide their own concerns and worries and give in to the ill partner to avoid conflict, is considered *protective buffering* (Coyne & Smith, 1994). The other two coping styles identified by Coyne and Smith (1994) are *overprotection* of the ill partner and *active engagement,* which includes involving the patient in discussion about plans and problem solving. Several studies support the clinical intuition that protective buffering strategies are generally viewed as unhelpful (Manne et al., 2007) and are related to lower marital satisfaction (Hagedoorn et al., 2000). Although the patterns may exist alone, protective buffering is commonly used with overprotection of the ill partner (Kuijer et al., 2000). This pattern, perhaps useful during a new crisis, can over time lead to decreased competence of the ill partner, as well as overfunctioning and resulting resentment of the well partner.

Wives' active engagement strategies have been reported as beneficial in helping to change the health behaviors of their husbands following myocardial infarctions (Vilchinsky et al., 2011). This means that wives positively support their husbands' changes and avoid criticism of undesired behaviors. Interestingly, the wife's positive responses were more influential when the man also perceived the partner as supportive. Clinicians can assess how couples provide and receive support and help couples consider joint support and problem solving.

As Margaret and Paul recognized how they each maintained these protective buffering and overprotective patterns, they felt disappointed that they had not responded better. As with any other therapy, when couples examine some of their past patterns, they can feel discouraged. A medical family therapist needs to limit the self-blame that can accompany a retrospective analysis. Illness is a traumatic and isolating experience, and couples have few guideposts with which to chart their reactions.

Therapists can normalize a couple's responses and underscore how different responses may be adaptive at times. For example, Paul's focus on health, the future, and being cured may have been his best option, and may even have been helpful for Margaret at that time. The therapist reassured them that their earlier responses seemed to have worked years before, but circumstances had changed and they were no longer facing an illness crisis. It might be helpful to consider different styles of coping at this time.

They discussed how ambivalence about an illness is often expressed within the couple. One may take the role of the worrier while the other voices certainty of good health. It is a way of "sharing" their ambivalence, but it can lead to polarization when each adheres to one position. Paul's statement that he didn't dwell on fear allowed Margaret to see that although he did not discuss it, he had also experienced some uncertainty. It was freeing for her to realize that she did not need to hold all of the uncertainty for them. In medical family therapy sessions, couples can experiment with "sharing the concern."

As Margaret and Paul recognized that their experiences, although different, were both valid, they also took more risks in therapy. They explored the common patterns that evolve when one partner provides long-term care for the other. Although Margaret's occupation as a nurse may have exacerbated the polarization of their roles, it is common for a caregiver–patient relationship to emerge, which frequently upsets the balance of a partnership. Discussing this pattern helped Margaret and Paul notice how they had generally maintained an equal partnership throughout this time, a recognition that added to their sense of competence as a couple.

Describe the Dance of Illness Control

A spouse of a husband who was not attentive to his diabetic diet described how tired she was of "being the only one who cared." It is common for a partner to feel that her spouse accepts his disease too readily and does not "fight" against it enough. When this happens, the spouse with the illness frequently retorts that he is managing the illness as well as possible and that he is tired of the spouse "hounding" him to take his medications and watch his diet.

This "dance of control" is seen in many subsets in families. Adolescents with illness and their parents frequently engage in unproductive struggles about illness control and management. Couples, too, commonly exhibit this pattern, which can frustrate those around them and can be the issue that brings them to therapy. The pattern may have begun rather innocuously as a partner asked about the illness-required activities of the other. It is not uncommon for one person's "care" to be perceived by the partner as criticism or control. Then, if the partner chooses to not acknowledge the "care" of the other, and chooses his or her own behaviors, the caring spouse feels ignored, disregarded, and excluded. The pattern easily escalates so that both feel ignored, not respected, and frustrated.

Rohrbaugh et al. (2001) described *ironic processes*, in which attempts to change others may perpetuate the behavior that the partner wishes to change. Even when partners know the behavior is not helpful, the processes continue because people repeatedly attempt to solve the problem with the same unsuccessful methods. Attempts by spouses to regulate or constrain a spouse's drinking or smoking behaviors, for example, often appear to increase those behaviors (Lewis & Rook, 1999). Rohrbaugh and colleagues described a family consultation model in which they helped couples identify the ironic processes and then determine how at least one of them could participate less to deescalate the process.

For some couples, fine lines exist among helping, controlling, and criticizing. Criticism and hostility are recognized as significant factors in the *expressed emotion* (EE) research regarding families and mental illnesses, particularly schizophrenia (Leff & Vaughn, 1985). The link between criticism and other medical illnesses is less clear. A review of expressed emotion research in health care identified how criticism and hostility may negatively influence health outcomes related to behavior or stress, such as obesity management (Weardon, Tarrier, Barrowclough, Zastowny, & Rahill, 2000). Similarly, wives with rheumatoid arthritis had less adaptive coping behaviors and poorer psychological outcomes when their spouses were more critical (Manne & Zautra, 1989). Although EE may have an impact on health behaviors, there is no evidence that EE or criticism is associated with illness course (Weardon et al., 2000) or survival (Benazon, Foster, & Coyne, 2006). Therapists then should focus less on identifying critical behaviors that may not influence illness outcome and instead try to amplify positive couple behaviors that may promote behavior change and adaptation to the illness.

The challenge for medical family therapists is to recognize how difficult it is for partners who wish to help. It is easy to slip from reminding behaviors to those that seem controlling, or even critical and hostile. For spouses, the stakes are high, and they frequently feel that there is so little they can do. For the person coping with illness, perceived intrusion by a spouse complicates decision making and behavior choices. The push–pull or "dance" of illness control can be hard to stop, but couples can learn to dance better together— to place the illness outside of them both and consider how they can work together to manage its challenges most effectively.

Initiate Discussion of Sexuality

It is generally up to the therapist to initiate any discussion of sexuality because couples frequently have decreased and often halted sexual activity during illness. Limiting sexual activity sometimes, although not always, correlates with a sense of decreased intimacy between the couples. Some research suggests that couples who maintain physical intimacy may be able to buffer the effects of disabling illness on their psychosocial adjustment (Druley, Stephens, & Coyne, 1997).

It is not always easy, however, to maintain physical intimacy. Research with men following radical prostatectomy surgery has reported moderate levels of difficulty with sexual and urinary functioning (Perez, Skinner, & Meyerowitz, 2002) with more than 80% of participants reporting sexual dysfunction (Badr & Taylor, 2009). Partners reported decreased sexual satisfaction (Badr & Taylor, 2009; Neese, Schover, Klein, Zippe, & Kupelian, 2003; Shindel, Quayle, Yan, Husain, & Naughton, 2005). Spouses who reported high degrees of mutually constructive communication reported higher levels of marital adjustment, regardless of their own level of satisfaction. Partners who reported greater mutual avoidance of discussing problems reported greater distress.

Breast cancer for women, like testicular or prostate cancer for men, has physical implications that affect sexual interest and satisfaction. Body image concerns related to sexuality are amplified for women who have mastectomies and other cancer treatments (Hopwood et al., 2000), and women's perceptions of their partners' responses, particularly negative responses, affect their psychological and sexual adaptation (Manne & Badr, 2008). A woman's perceptions of her partner's positive acceptance of her, particularly his initial reaction to any scar or to a mastectomy, were related to her sexual interest and general satisfaction (Wimberly, Carver, Laurenceau, Harris, & Antoni, 2005).

This sensitivity to initial reaction is worth highlighting because the conflict can continue long after the surgery. It is common for a woman to say that she knows her husband loves her, that he was present for her throughout her breast cancer treatment but that she also believes he is put off by her scar or mastectomy. A husband responding to this concern tried to tell his wife that he was so disturbed by the initial sight postsurgery not because he was unattracted to her, but because he was so distraught that she had undergone a large cut in any part of her body. Even when a husband had been initially nervous or distressed, therapy can help couples understand that initial reactions do not need to become permanent.

The take-home message from this research is not about the impact of erectile dysfunction or changed self-image but about the significance of couple communication and relationships following health crises. Sexuality, intimacy, conflict management, communication, and physical adjustments are all related. There are clear opportunities for sensitive medical family therapists to help couples recognize these complex interactions. With estimates that nearly 5,000 gay or bisexual men are diagnosed with prostate cancer each year (Blank, 2005), we know little about the sexual functioning and relationship issues that gay or bisexual, as well as heterosexual single men, experience.

Therapists must be curious about each couple's unique experience and concerns. Therapists can initiate conversations by stating that many couples avoid or limit sexual interactions during health crises and then find it difficult or awkward to resume sexual intimacy. By normalizing the experience and then asking couples if this has been a concern for them, the therapist provides an invitation for couples to discuss these issues more freely.

It took several sessions before Paul and Margaret were willing to discuss the impact of the illness on their sexual relationship. Even when Paul felt physically healthier and they wanted to resume their sexual activities, there was some reticence. There is often awkwardness about reinitiating sexual relationships after interruptions for any reason, but there are unique illness concerns. A partner may fear causing the other pain after surgery or disability or, as in Paul's case, be nervous about exerting pressure on his wife, who was already exhausted by her increased responsibilities. Sometimes the disruption reflects a change in roles—from romantic partners to caregiver and patient. The change in roles is a pattern that slowly enters the relationship and may require overt discussion and attention to alter. Discussion of this process helped the couple recognize that other couples had experienced this interruption in their lives and that they could stop blaming themselves and each other; it provided hope that they could return to a "normal marriage."

Margaret and Paul were relieved to recognize that their basic bonds of trust and intimacy had been broken not by neglect, loss of love, lack of commitment, or personal failure but by the illness that had shaken their core sense of well-being. Experiencing a life-threatening illness or event is frequently an existential crisis that can alter a person and a couple's basic sense of security, and yet intimacy is best maintained when a basic trust and sense of identity are present. Couples often require intentional work to rekindle intimacy and trust, including attention to creatively exploring their sexual relationship. Therapists can be crucial and creative allies through this process.

Focus on Resilience

This chapter has identified some of the significant stressors and therapeutic responses for couples coping with illness. Given these difficulties, it is noteworthy that there does not seem to be an increase in divorce rates when one member of the couple is diagnosed with life-threatening illness. A group of oncologists (Glantz et al., 2009) prospectively collected data from 515 consecutive referrals to three clinics: neuro-oncology, general oncology, and multiple sclerosis. Over 5 years, the average rate of divorce was 11%, consistent with previous studies and consistent with divorce rates for healthy couples.

There is some indication in this study, however, of gender differences in the likelihood of divorce following illness onset. In 88% of the separations, the ill partner was the woman. Separation occurred in 20% of the couples when the wife became severely ill, and in only 2.9% of the couples when the husband was ill. Although gender was the most significant variable, length of marriage also factored into this study, in that couples who separated had been married for a mean of 14.4 years and couples who remained married through illness had been married a mean of 27.4 years at onset of illness.

For a variety of reasons, longer marriages and more traditional gender role expectations for caregiving may have an impact on whether couples remain married in the face of difficult illness situations. Therapists, however, are most likely to see the couples who are trying to cope with the difficulties and find ways to balance multiple responsibilities and role changes.

The couples described in this chapter came to therapy because they felt they were not coping well with the stresses of illness, whether in their parents, their children, or in one of the partners. They had feelings of failure—that they weren't able to cope with what should be normal life events and transitions. Tonya and Manuel were disappointed because they intentionally had many premarital discussions about how they would manage conflict in a blended family, particularly around managing Tonya's children. They had not factored in the emotional strength of Tonya's feelings about her son's diabetes management. Rose and Ed were angry with themselves because they both knew that Ed's support of his mother was a priority for them but still resulted in Ed's feeling burdened and Rose's feeling neglected. Both felt misunderstood. Through examination of what previously had not been discussed, Margaret and Paul were disappointed that they had let their initial responses to Paul's cancer become a permanent pattern that left them with decreases in their intimacy and honest communication.

Therapists can attend to these feelings of failure, disappointment, and self-blame and clarify the specific successful ways that the couple has responded. Identification of a couple's strengths helps them create a new narrative that recognizes the positive ways that they have responded to the crisis. *Resilience*, described extensively by Walsh (1998), is the "capacity to rebound from adversity strengthened and more resourceful." Through their therapy, each of these couples learned that they had in fact been resilient. It is also likely that the therapy helped them to become more resilient for future stresses. Each couple had opportunities to express their concerns, disappointments, and fears and acknowledge the impact of the medical trauma on their relationship. Yet they also had the opportunity to recognize how they had handled multiple crises and responsibilities, how they appreciated new qualities in the other, and how they could continue to demonstrate their commitment and love. They also received recognition and validation for their efforts, something that may not have occurred in any other setting.

HEALTH CONCERNS AS HISTORY FOR ALL COUPLES THERAPY

We suggest that medical family therapy considerations are not just an addition but should be an integral part of all therapy with couples. All long-term couples have or will cope with the illness and loss of parents and likely with some significant illness for one of the partners. As we have described, health crises exacerbate some of the significant issues that couples must negotiate: relationship to each partner's family of origin, ways that each partner feels supported, communication differences, sexuality, and attachment and loss. These are the core issues that bring couples to therapy. Couples therapists who do not ask about history of illness and loss miss an opportunity to help couples access these core concerns. In an extensive review of couple and family interventions in health problems, Shields, Finley, and Chawla (2012) noted how most interventions are not couples therapy but are family psychoeducational programs. Yet they also noted that the literature shows the potential for family interventions to reduce spousal distress, promote greater adherence to medication, and strengthen couple relationships.

Therapists can easily include illness, loss, and caregiving responsibilities as part of a couple's history. How couples cared for aging parents or how they responded to a partner's illness event is a stage on which other simmering couple issues become visible. Therapists can use this content to help partners realize how they have supported each other in the past. If one of the members of the couple did not or does not feel supported, the therapist can normalize how families care for their family members in different ways and begin to promote healing. Most significantly, therapists can help couples talk about their past experiences, make their unacknowledged concerns more overt, and help them negotiate how they can care for others while caring for one another.

9

PREGNANCY LOSS, INFERTILITY, AND REPRODUCTIVE TECHNOLOGY

When we were young, we were taught again and again that we shouldn't get pregnant. Now we can't get pregnant.
　　　　　　　—Holly Finn, *The Baby Chase: An Adventure in Infertility*

Pregnancy loss, infertility, and reproductive technology encompass some of the most common problems and the most cutting edge technology addressed in medical family therapy. At least one in five pregnancies ends in a miscarriage (Covington, 2006). For those who desire children but for whom pregnancy and delivery do not come easily, 21st century science has produced an astounding range of possible interventions while also posing ethical and psychosocial dilemmas that often accompany scientific advances. Because these reproductive issues are both common and illustrative of the challenges involved in medical family therapy, we examine them in this chapter in some depth.

Having children is a much-anticipated goal for most women and men. Many religions (e.g., Hinduism; ancient Greek, Celtic, and Navajo religions) have fertility gods or fertility symbols that speak to the role of faith and hope in conception. According to the Pew Center, 74% of 18- to 29-year-olds who are not currently married and have no children say they want to have children (Wang & Taylor, 2011).

http://dx.doi.org/10.1037/14256-009
Medical Family Therapy and Integrated Care, Second Edition, by S. H. McDaniel, W. J. Doherty, and J. Hepworth

Currently, there is a range of reproductive possibilities. People who consider these options run from those who voluntarily become parents through successful pregnancies with their partners, reproductive technologies, surrogacy, or adoption to those who do not wish to become parents but find themselves pregnant and choose to raise their children, to involuntary parents who surrender their children for adoption, to the involuntary childless who wish to have children but experience pregnancy loss or infertility, to the voluntarily childless who choose either to abort their pregnancies or never to become pregnant.

Many professionals and grandparents-in-waiting view the reproductive stage of the life cycle as a prominent marker of adulthood. It is an extended family event that immediately changes the new parents' relationships with their parents, offering opportunities for reparation or reconciliation after what can be turbulent times during adolescent separation and emerging adulthood. Many psychological and family studies texts from the 20th century focused on traditional, biological reproduction as the centerpiece of family continuity. For example, Boszormenyi-Nagy and Spark (1984) wrote, "Familial loyalty is characteristically based on biological, hereditary kinship" (p. 42). Whatever the process of making a family, whether with genetic or nongenetic ties, it is the adult attachment to the children, from generation to generation, that forms family identity, family legacy, and family myths.

Women often anticipate becoming mothers for years. Little girls are taught from as early as they can hold a doll to value caregiving and raising the next generation. Socialization and biology combine to make women acutely aware that they do the childbearing, that they often assume the largest share of child-rearing obligations, and that their options are time-limited as their reproductive potential ends sometime in their 40s. Men also are taught to place great value on having children. In ancient Jewish law, a man who is not a father is incomplete. Often, men are expected to carry on the family line, and, traditionally, children signal a man's virility (Edelman, Humphrey, & Owens, 1994).

However, the reality is that about one in 10 couples worldwide have some infertility problem that prevents them from having biological children. In the developing world, the cause is most likely related to a sexually transmitted disease, malnutrition, or some other untreated health condition (Butler, 2003).

Global rates of infertility vary widely. In the United States, approximately 12% of women ages 15 to 44 have trouble getting pregnant or staying pregnant, and 7.3 million women have used infertility services at some point in their lives (Centers for Disease Control and Prevention [CDC], 2011). Among women ages 40 to 44, the rate of impaired ability to have children is close to 18% (Chandra, Martinez, Mosher, Abma, & Jones, 2005). The CDC also estimated that between 3.3 million and 4.7 million men have sought help related to conceiving a child. Although about 20% of women in the United States have their first child after age 35, one third of couples in which the woman is over 35 have fertility difficulties (CDC, 2011).

About one third of infertility cases can be attributed to factors relating to the man, and about one third can be attributed to factors relating to the woman. In the remaining one third, infertility is due to a combination of problems in both partners or is unexplained (American Society for Reproductive Medicine, 2008). Assisted reproductive technology has a success rate of 41% in women ages 35 and under, and this rate declines as a woman gets older (CDC, 2011).

For these individuals, couples, and their families, the biology of reproduction is not a straightforward process involving selection of a partner, sexual expression, pregnancy, and delivery. Instead, it can involve identity confusion, traumatic loss and grief, feelings of inadequacy and envy, and a potentially long period of interaction with health professionals who become intimately involved in the couple's life. In addition, issues around sexuality, control, and loss may either be shared or divisive for any couple experiencing the stress of pregnancy loss or infertility.

Psychological evaluation and counseling is now the standard of care in most fertility clinics (Domar, 2011). Sometimes couples do not realize the impact of infertility treatment on their emotional lives. One couple came for a consultation because they were embroiled in the wife's brother's attempt to gain access to his young daughter, whose mother would not allow him contact. They felt their own loss, as an aunt and uncle of this girl, and they empathized strongly with the loss of the brother in his role as father. However, they were perplexed about why this situation so immobilized them, as they saw themselves as typically competent people. Toward the end of the consultation, the therapist asked this couple, who were in their late 30s, why they did not themselves have children. They revealed a stressful 7-year history of infertility treatment but had not related this experience to why they might be so emotionally involved in the brother's loss.

Behavioral health consultations or psychotherapy referrals may come at any stage of the process—from the initial diagnosis of a problem, through stressful treatment procedures, to seemingly unrelated problems that stem from unresolved issues around infertility or pregnancy loss. Some clinics have medical family therapists integrated into their women's health or fertility clinics in which physicians, midwives, or nurse practitioners routinely refer patients with reproductive problems for counseling. Other obstetricians and fertility specialists refer patients who exhibit acute emotional reactions to a diagnostic workup or a loss. Some patients will self-refer either for professional support during a stressful period or for help in considering treatment options. Collaboration between psychotherapists and other health professionals can help patients negotiate the medical system and can provide reciprocal support to the reproductive clinicians and therapists who do this difficult work.

An evidence base for psychosocial interventions with infertility is beginning to develop. A review of this literature reveals that infertility counseling is more successful at reducing negative affect than improving relational functioning. Pregnancy rates are historically considered unlikely to be affected by psychosocial interventions. However, women undergoing in vitro fertilization (IVF) were found to have significantly higher rates of pregnancy after receiving a 10-session group mind–body intervention (e.g., changing negative thinking, reducing stress, relaxation) compared with women assigned to a control group (Domar et al., 2011). Groups that emphasize psychoeducation and skills training (increasing agency and decreasing stress) are more likely to be effective than those that emphasize emotional expression and support (Boivin, Griffiths, & Venetis, 2011). Relaxation training, eliciting social support, and modifying expectations of oneself and others can all be helpful approaches to managing the difficulties associated with infertility. Well-controlled, scientifically rigorous studies are needed regarding psychosocial interventions with infertility and the reproductive technologies—their effect on patients, their partners, their children, and extended families.

As discussed later in the chapter, medical family therapy is often confronted with ethical issues in reproductive medicine that require thought and, sometimes, consultation from institutional ethics teams (Horowitz, Galst, & Elder, 2010). Couples who experience difficulties with reproduction present complex and challenging personal, interpersonal, and ethical dilemmas that strike at the core of family life. The technology for treating infertility, especially, is constantly changing, and the psychosocial impact of infertility, loss, and reproductive technology is only beginning to be fully understood. Medical family therapists can help couples, families, and medical providers develop an approach to these problems that maximizes the couple's communication and sense of control over the decisions they face.

Patients with reproductive problems can stimulate strong reactions in the therapist related to gender, reproduction, and loss. Female therapists may see more of these cases than male therapists because of the biological and cultural biases that make reproduction more the responsibility of women than men and because of the belief of many patients that female therapists may be more empathic and supportive about these issues. However, as society recognizes the importance of both women and men in childbearing and child rearing, more male therapists may indicate their interest in these areas, and more systems-oriented therapists are needed to help with these problems.

Many therapists specialize in pregnancy loss and infertility, but because of the numbers of couples who experience these concerns, most therapists are likely to treat couples who experience pregnancy loss or infertility regardless of their specialization. The couples may present with a primary interest in coping with the loss, or are in therapy for another issue, and the pregnancy loss or infertility is an unresolved or reactivated concern. This chapter therefore includes a description of the kinds of concerns medical family therapists will see in couples. We first identify specific concerns, beginning with pregnancy loss—including miscarriage, fetal death in utero, and elective termination. We then describe the experience of infertility for men, women, couples, and therapists. This is followed by discussion of the types, prevalence, and assisted reproductive technologies for male and female infertility—including insemination, IVF, and surrogacy. Discussion of medical family therapy skills for assessment and intervention is interwoven throughout these sections.

PREGNANCY LOSS

Our society has only recently begun to recognize the importance of miscarriage and other pregnancy losses. Sometimes even now, denial of the importance of this loss results in isolation for the woman, her partner, and those who care about them. In many cases, parents experience powerful grief over pregnancy loss that takes months to years to resolve. DeFrain (1991) found the average recovery time for families after a miscarriage to be 9 to 15 months and 3 years for stillbirth or a SIDS death. Blackmore et al. (2011), in a study of more than 13,000 women in England, found that women who experience miscarriage or stillbirth experience significantly higher levels of anxiety and depression in a subsequent pregnancy and that these symptoms do not resolve with the birth of a healthy child. Another study of 7,770 U.S. women found a 22% increased risk for divorce after miscarriage or pregnancy loss before 20 weeks, compared with couples with a successful pregnancy (Gold, 2010). This makes early psychosocial support and intervention by a medical family therapist and other members of the health care team important in facilitating a healthy grieving response. Pregnancy loss peer support groups also can be helpful (Leff, 1987; Leppert & Pahlka, 1984).

Grief over a pregnancy loss is complicated by how much the pregnancy was desired, the length of the pregnancy, the amount of medical and social support available for the couple, the ability of the couple to offer each other support, and the couple's ages and fertility histories. If the loss occurs to an older couple whose pregnancy was a result of lengthy infertility treatment, it may have a different meaning than to a relatively young, healthy couple.

Medical family therapy can normalize the experience of the loss and facilitate rituals, like tree planting, that help couples honor their loss. As with any crisis, it can be an opportunity for the individual and the couple to increase their sense of agency and communion by pulling together, examining their life goals, and working through the experience. Family therapists may see couples just after a pregnancy loss, perhaps in professional groups, or as a result of a complicated grief reaction. Because of the historical lack of social support for pregnancy loss, even today this forgotten grief can result in a range of individual and interactional problems that may or may not be recognized by patients as related to the loss. Consequently, therapists taking a genogram and family history should always ask specifically about dates and information regarding miscarriages, stillbirths, and other reproductive problems, to assess the impact of pregnancy loss and any delayed grief.

Miscarriage

Miscarriages (defined as pregnancy loss up to 20 weeks), or spontaneous abortions, are especially common events, with estimates that between 20% and 50% of all conceptions end in miscarriage (Covington, 2006). Some occur so early that they go unrecognized by the woman or her partner. Assisted reproductive technologies have introduced new categories of pregnancy loss—failed IVF cycles, loss of one fetus in a multiple pregnancy, and elective reduction in multifetal pregnancies. In both traditional and assisted pregnancy loss, symptoms of shock, intense sadness, and grief are typical, lasting as long as a year.

For some couples, early loss is painful and made more so by the lack of support extended them by family and friends who either did not know about the pregnancy or do not appreciate the significance of the loss. This sort of grief is *disenfranchised;* that is, it is neither evident nor recognized socially (Harvey, 2002). Some women and some partners experience the due date for the lost pregnancy as a time of great sadness. Family therapy can normalize the experience of the loss and facilitate rituals that may further the grieving process. As with any crisis, therapy can be an opportunity for the individual and the couple to increase their sense of agency and communion by pulling together, examining their life goals, and working through the experience.

One couple presented for marital therapy soon after Tracy, age 28, experienced a miscarriage of their first child. Tracy was distraught, not sleeping at night, and had experienced considerable weight loss in the 6 weeks since the miscarriage. Bob, age 49, focused on his wife's distress. This was his second marriage, a relationship that began as an affair during his first marriage. Bob had two teenage children from his first marriage and had agreed to have one child with Tracy only because she wanted so badly to be pregnant and be a mother. After an initial negative reaction to the news of the pregnancy, Bob bought several baby items, began to build a cradle, and had been speaking positively about the baby just before the miscarriage. However, after the loss, he worried out loud that his ambivalence had "caused them to lose the baby."

During treatment, the couple decided to hold a private memorial service. Both Bob and Tracy wrote messages to the child they lost. Close family and friends came with food to share for dinner. Tracy's serious symptoms remitted soon thereafter, but both members of the couple experienced intermittent sadness in the year after the miscarriage. Therapy moved to dealing with trust issues that were unresolved from early in the relationship.

Fetal Death in Utero

Fetal death in utero (FDIU) resulting in stillbirth is a loss that occurs late in a pregnancy, when much time has elapsed for the woman and her partner to bond to the fetus and develop hopes and dreams for their unborn child. FDIU is a particularly devastating experience because in some cases the woman must continue to carry the pregnancy after she is aware that the fetus is dead. She must then endure labor and delivery without the end reward of a living baby. For those unaware of an FDIU, a stillbirth comes as a shock at the end of labor and delivery. It can be an acute and unexpected loss accompanied by predictable feelings of shock, anger, depression, and guilt. Many times the cause of fetal demise or stillbirth is unknown, contributing to the couple's sense of despair.

Most hospitals have *bereavement teams* to provide crisis intervention and support with this loss (L. Cohen, Zilkha, Middleton, & O'Donnahue, 1978; Leff, 1987). Medical family therapists can be important members of these teams. Many couples find it useful to view their stillborn baby after delivery and, along with their community of support, conduct a ritual such as a memorial service to honor the baby and the loss.

Elective Termination

Medical family therapists can help facilitate decision making about a potential pregnancy termination with a woman, her partner, or her family, as desired. For most women, the planned termination of a pregnancy, an abortion, has few long-lasting behavioral health consequences (Munk-Olsen et al., 2011). In one study of teenagers who presented to a clinic for a pregnancy test, the group who elected to abort scored higher 2 years later on social and psychological functioning than did either the group who had babies or the group whose pregnancy test was negative (Zabin, Hirsch, & Emerson, 1989). The women at greatest risk for problems following an abortion have a prior history of depression, anxiety, or other mental illness (Munk-Olsen, Laursen, Pedersen, Lidegaard, & Mortensen, 2011). Another source of difficulty can be disagreement about the procedure between a woman and her partner or within families.

A particular group of women and their partners who may struggle about a decision to terminate the pregnancy are those who test positive for genetic anomalies that reveal a significant problem with the fetus. For those who decide to maintain the pregnancy, medical family therapy offers a safe place to discuss how having a child with an illness or disability may change the life trajectory of the family. For all these women and their families, medical family therapy offers a place to recognize the complex and sometimes contradictory feelings associated with the loss, address any past trauma or loss experiences triggered by the abortion, and provide support for grieving.

Medical family therapists may see individuals or couples either before or after the procedure. Because most abortions are performed in the first trimester of the pregnancy, and the sooner the better from a medical standpoint, family members feel intense pressure to resolve the issue quickly. This time pressure can increase anxiety and the potential for miscommunication among family members, making these cases challenging for any therapist. Therapists whose personal beliefs allow them to do this work can function as facilitators to clarify communication without taking sides, so that women and their partners can make the best decisions possible. Sometimes conflict in families about this issue is unresolvable, as the following example shows.

Mr. and Mrs. Musica presented for couples therapy in the midst of an argument about Mrs. Musica's pregnancy. The couple had three children under 6 years old, and Mrs. Musica wanted to continue this fourth pregnancy. Mr. Musica felt that their marriage was already unstable and that this pregnancy should be terminated. Both agreed that the timing of the pregnancy was stressful. However, they were polarized around the issue of whether to abort the pregnancy. Mrs. Musica was enraged at her husband and saw his position as a symbol of his wanting to dominate and control her. Mr. Musica felt shut out of the decision-making process about the pregnancy and saw his wife's position as a symbol of her refusal to incorporate his needs into her decisions. After two sessions in close succession, Mrs. Musica refused to discuss the issue further and asserted her right to make the decision about her pregnancy independently. She had the baby, and the marriage ended within 2 years. After the divorce, therapy was helpful in maintaining a positive parenting relationship between the couple and all four children.

In addition to seeing couples about an abortion decision, family therapists may also see patients and their partners who experience distress or unresolved grief following an abortion. Because abortion involves a choice, some women carry tremendous guilt. Sometimes referrals to clergy can be helpful. Other times the medical family therapist can help the couple develop informal rituals to work through past regrets and promote healing. One woman, married with two children, was plagued by guilt over five abortions she'd had before meeting her husband. She was Catholic and had a strong desire to have children, even when her male relationships were unsatisfactory. Her nightmares about the abortions stopped after she was able to go to a lengthy confessional with a trusted priest and then, with her husband's help, plant five small trees in her backyard in recognition of the pregnancies she had felt she could not continue.

Part of the challenge of working with patients and families who are struggling with these issues lies in clarifying the therapist's own position about abortion and communicating that clearly to patients, while emphasizing that each woman and her partner have to make the unique decision that will be the best for them. For example:

> I myself am not opposed to abortion, but I do feel this is an important and personal decision for each couple. I would like to help you discuss the issue so that you can make the decision that is going to be best for you and your family.

Some therapists may not want to work with cases involving decision making about abortion because they believe abortion is wrong and do not wish to participate in treatment that could result in such a decision. These therapists may be useful to women and couples who share their belief system and need to find alternatives to abortion. In any case, value judgments by the therapist about these situations cannot be ignored and must become part of the treatment process. Acknowledging this fact openly can help prevent the therapist from covertly influencing patients' decision making at a time when they can be vulnerable and conflicted.

INFERTILITY

Women and their partners facing decisions about abortion often agonize about the inappropriate timing of a pregnancy. Couples struggling with infertility have a different agony, one over which they have much less control. Infertility is a medical, psychological, and social experience requiring a redefinition by the couple of each of their identities as individuals and as partners, moving from expecting to become pregnant to recognizing that they may be unable to have biological children. Ready to have children, they discover that reproduction will be complicated or impossible. Most infertility specialists define infertility as the failure to conceive after 1 year of trying; women who are over the age of 35 are advised to consult with a doctor if they are unable to get pregnant within 6 months of trying (American Society for Reproductive Medicine Practice Committee, 2008). However, Cook (1990) suggested a more experiential definition of infertility, as the failure of an individual to achieve a pregnancy within his or her own elective time frame.

The prerequisites for a successful pregnancy are biologically complex, involving the interrelationship of various organs and hormones. (For a concise description of the medical aspects of infertility evaluation and treatment written for psychotherapists, see Keye, 2006.)

The most common causes of infertility are complex and varied. Medications, cancer treatment, and other illness can cause fertility problems in men and women (Mayo Clinic Staff, 2012). Psychological factors, such as anxiety and stress, may interfere with fertility in ways that are not fully understood and difficult to study because the infertility itself results in considerable stress for the patient and the family. In the first half of the 20th century, studies showed a strong relationship between infertility and negative attitudes of women toward pregnancy. These have long been refuted (Noyes & Chapnick, 1964). Most current psychosocial research and treatment for infertility avoids blaming the victim and focuses on the psychological consequences rather than antecedents of infertility.

The Experience of Infertility

The psychosocial experience of infertility seems similar in some ways to coping with the death of a loved one and in other ways to coping with the diagnosis of a chronic illness. As with a death, patients may go through stages of mourning after the diagnosis: denial, shock, anger, bargaining, depression, and acceptance (Kübler-Ross, 1969; Myers, 1990). During treatment, they endure a chronic hope–loss cycle every 28 days. As with a chronic illness, adjustments in lifestyle must be made to accommodate the diagnostic and treatment procedures. Diagnostic procedures can be invasive, embarrassing, and stressful (e.g., men may have to masturbate into a bottle to produce sperm for a sperm count, women may have to go to their physician's office for a postcoital examination several hours after intercourse).

A sense of failure and loss of control is prominent. Many patients ask, "Why me?" Evaluation and treatment can reinforce sexual insecurities and doubts. Some believe their infertility is a punishment from God for some sexual or other misdeed (Menning, 1977). In addition to searching for a cause or explanation, many couples experience infertility as stressful boundary ambiguity, in that they experience the child they wish to have as psychologically present but physically absent (Burns, 1987). The cause of all this stress is invisible and so can lead to secrecy and social isolation for the couple.

Men and women report different experiences with infertility. The evaluation for an infertility diagnosis is much easier and less invasive for men than for women. These technical and biological factors, as well as sex role socialization, influence the differences in men's and women's experiences of infertility.

Infertility in Women

Especially since the availability of new and better birth control devices, many women around the world have come to feel they have much greater control over their reproductive abilities. A larger number of women now delay childbearing for education and careers, and they and their families are anxious for them to have children quickly when they decide to do so. Other women remarry in middle age and then wish to have a child. However, female fertility is finite; women hear their biological clocks "ticking." Ovulation is a function of a woman's age, so fertility decreases with a woman's age, dropping sharply at 35. An estimated one third of women who delay a first pregnancy until after age 35 will have problems with conception. After age 40, 50% will have difficulty achieving a successful pregnancy (Petok, 2006).

Women may experience reproductive failure as a personal inadequacy. They can develop worries about sexual desirability, lack of sexual desire, or other sexual dysfunction or experience general withdrawal from their primary relationship. Infertile women have greater levels of psychological distress, including higher rates of depression, than control groups (Chen, Chang, Tsai, & Juang, 2004; Greil, 1997). Stress related to the trauma of infertility has been well documented (Benyamini, Gozlan, & Kokia, 2005); counseling has been shown to decrease this distress (Smeenk et al., 2001). Women typically express more distress than their partners (McCartney & Wada, 1990) and are generally the first to suggest seeking medical advice when an infertility problem is suspected (Matthews & Matthews, 1986). Because psychological factors can be improved with intervention, counseling is recommended.

Infertility in Men

Studies across cultures find that many men report being largely unaffected by infertility (E. W. Freeman, Boxer, Rickels, Tureck, & Mastroianni, 1985; Lee & Sun, 2000), whereas women report being devastated. In a study by Kraft et al. (1980), one man said of his infertility, "It only upset me for about 20 minutes" (p. 625). Men often say that the hardest part of infertility for them is their wives' pain. Many men feel they must be strong for their wives. However, as Myers (1990) stated, "there is danger in equating men's silence about reproduction with acceptance and cooperation" (p. 34). For some men, denial and silence may reflect strong feelings that infertility is unacceptable to them as a man and as a husband. Indeed, there is evidence to support more stigma associated with male factor than female factor infertility (Miall, 1994). Cella and Najavits (1986) reported a study of men treated for Hodgkin's disease with radiation and chemotherapy who were told that their treatment leaves 80% to 90% of men infertile. Almost 40% of the men failed to bank sperm before treatment even though they were advised to do so. The overwhelming majority (93%) of those who failed to bank sperm said they believed they would remain fertile. Perhaps related to the fact that some men do not acknowledge distress about infertility, infertile men have a higher incidence than fertile men of somaticizing disorders (Covington, 2006).

Because society often does not support men expressing their emotions or claiming ownership of their role in reproduction, some men may be out of touch or secretive about infertility, and their distress may be missed. Meanwhile, women often "take care" of the infertility, regardless of who carries the medical diagnosis and may be the partner who expresses the pain for the couple. Some women with infertile partners report lying to friends and family, saying that they themselves have the problem to protect the man and his sense of potency (Czyba & Chevret, 1979).

Although some men deny or avoid their feelings about an infertility diagnosis, others experience decreased self-esteem and a sense of personal failure, and obsess about their adequacy as a man. Some studies show that men with an infertility diagnosis are at risk for erectile dysfunction (Zolbrod & Covington, 1999) and other sexual problems. Given the complexity of the problem of infertility and men's reactions to it, medical family therapists may acknowledge men's legitimate emotional stress and pain even if it is not spoken.

Mike was a 29-year-old man with a history of having trouble keeping a job. He was playful, affectionate, and rather passive, especially next to his outgoing, aggressive, and well-organized wife, Linda. In the course of marital therapy, initiated by Linda because she was frustrated with Mike's history of not finishing school and not completing tasks at home, the couple began an infertility workup.

Characteristically, Linda pursued her diagnostic tests energetically and Mike kept forgetting to schedule the time for his appointments. Within 8 months and multiple appointments, all Linda's tests came back negative, including one procedure that required outpatient surgery. Mike had one appointment that uncovered a questionable sperm count. His physician asked him to give two more samples to verify the problem. Mike never did so, despite Linda's anger. He forgot appointments, and when he remembered them, he forgot his sperm samples. His therapist spoke to Mike and recognized his unspoken distress. She treated him with respect and discussed how his sense of pain about being sickly as a child and not being treated as a man by his father and his wife made it difficult for him to endure the infertility testing. Mike seemed to feel that the tests would confirm biologically what he had feared emotionally for so long: a lack of potency as a man.

Eventually, in their therapy Linda accepted the fact that her husband did not want to continue with the infertility workup. The couple applied for adoption and adopted a beautiful baby girl. Mike seemed fulfilled and became the parent who spent the most time with their daughter, taking care of her, playing with her, and looking out for her well-being. He was happy and proud of his abilities as a father.

Infertility for Couples

Like any crisis, infertility can bring a couple closer or result in significant problems. Sexual, financial, and emotional strains are all common challenges for the infertile couple. Diagnosis and treatment of infertility result in major invasions of privacy in the most intimate area of a couple's relationship: their sex life.

Several studies have documented the potential for infertility and fertility treatments to damage a couple's sexual intimacy (Boxer, 1996; Saleh, Ranga, Raina, Nelson, & Agarwal, 2003). Sabatelli, Meth, and Gavazzi (1988) found that close to 60% of women and men in an infertility support group sample reported decreased frequency of sexual intercourse and decreased sexual satisfaction after diagnosis.

Other relationship problems can occur after the diagnosis of infertility. For some couples, parenting is so basic a component of the marriage contract that infertility threatens the very concept of marriage (Kraft et al., 1980). For these people, renegotiating the contract after this diagnosis can be difficult or even impossible. Some couples implicitly or explicitly rely on childbearing to help them "become a family." For many young couples, childbearing forces them to shift their loyalties from their families of origin to each other.

Some couples have complementary styles that allow them to increase their bond during this crisis. McEwan, Costello, and Taylor (1987) found that a woman's adjustment to infertility is significantly better if she has a confiding relationship with her spouse. Other couples find their coping styles clash. These women want to talk about the stress, whereas their husbands want to "try and forget it."

In general, couples who perceive equivalent levels of infertility stress report higher levels of marital adjustment, compared with those who perceive different levels. Women in couples who report a similar need for parenthood report less depressive symptoms than women in discordant couples (Peterson, Newton, & Rosen, 2003). Discordance about parenthood or fertility stress can add to the burden of the problem. This underlines the importance of medical family therapy in helping couples better understand and empathize with each person's experience and desired coping style.

Matthews and Matthews (1986) found that the person carrying the diagnosis may feel guilty and doubt the affection of the other partner. That person may fantasize that if the spouse had another partner, he or she would be able to conceive. Occasionally, partners do have an affair or develop substance abuse or eating problems. These symptoms are understood as disorders of control in a situation in which the couple feels out of control.

Infertility for the Therapist

Infertility can be a potent topic for therapists, especially those in their reproductive years who are trying to get pregnant or whose spouses are trying to get pregnant. Pregnant therapists may choose not to begin seeing couples with infertility problems because of how negatively stimulating the pregnancy may be to patients. Long-term patients may choose to stay with a pregnant therapist if the relationship has already proven itself beneficial.

Therapists' reproductive issues can be problematic for patients, and the reverse is also true. McDaniel worked with a couple experiencing secondary infertility[1] who went through 3 years of diagnostic testing and treatment before conceiving again. Throughout this period, McDaniel knew she wanted to have a second child, so the couple's struggles were especially poignant for her. This reality was acknowledged in therapy. Regular peer consultation was useful in helping the therapist to express her own concerns with colleagues and then attend to the patients' goals in therapy. Fortunately, the therapist and the couple both delivered their second children within months of each other.

Therapists who themselves have had infertility problems can offer special empathy as well as valuable information to couples with this problem. Again, the issue is to stay focused on the patients' experiences of infertility and their needs, rather than the therapist's own experience. Therapists' self-disclosure is dependent on the specifics of each particular case. Therapists who have experienced infertility and moved beyond this crisis may use their own difficult experience to develop expertise informed by both medical and emotional knowledge.

REPRODUCTIVE TECHNOLOGIES IN THE 21ST CENTURY

Reproductive technologies have transformed the possible ways for an individual or couple to become parents. Consider the February 2, 2011, *Newsweek* article titled "Meet My Real Modern Family." The genogram in Figure 9.1 shows a family that used IVF technology and surrogacy to build a large extended family.

---

[1]*Secondary infertility* is infertility that occurs after a couple has successfully conceived, carried, and delivered a child (or children) without difficulty and then experiences problems when trying to conceive or carry an additional child.

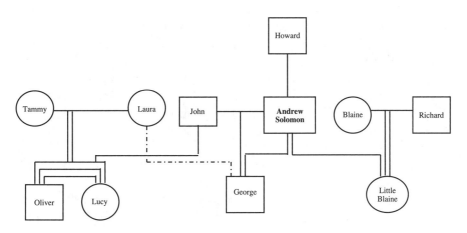

Figure 9.1. A genogram of a 21st century modern family. Clockwise from upper left: *Tammy* (she and Laura are mothers to Oliver and Lucy; Andrew's partner, John, is the biological father of both children); *Laura* (she was also the surrogate for Andrew and John's son George); *Andrew* (married to John, he is the biological father of Little Blaine and George); *Little Blaine* (the daughter of Andrew and his college friend Blaine, who conceived through IVF); *Blaine* (Andrew's college friend and the mother of Little Blaine); *Oliver* (Laura and Tammy's son; John's biological child); *Richard* (Blaine's partner); *Howard* (Andrew's father); *George* (Andrew and John's son, whom Laura carried using donor egg; Andrew is the biological father); *John* (Andrew's partner, George's dad, and the biological father of Oliver and Lucy); *Lucy* (daughter of Tammy and Laura; John's biological child).

Early in 2010 (January 2), the *New York Times Magazine* published an article titled "Meet the Twiblings," by Melanie Thernstrom. Melanie, 41, and Michael, 36, married late. They did not conceive and quickly moved to hormone treatments, then IVF. After six failed IVF rounds, they turned to surrogacy. They decided they'd like to have two children about the same age, so they negotiated with two surrogates who became their gestational carriers. The carriers used another woman's eggs and Michael's sperm. Their family photo includes the two gestational carriers, Fie and Melissa; Melanie and Michael; and their babies, Violet and Kieran, born 5 days apart. The egg donor is the one member of this reproductive picture who is not an ongoing part of the family.

How did we get from a couple struggling with infertility to these two examples of 21st century family life? It is a long journey from childlessness to parenting. This section describes the most common reproductive technologies, the associated psychological and interpersonal issues, and the role of the medical family therapist in negotiating some of these tricky boundary issues. Couples who want biological children and have financial resources have many noncoital options, including artificial insemination with the partner's sperm, artificial insemination by a donor, IVF, embryo freezing for future transfer, embryo transfer from one woman to another, donor eggs, and, where legal, surrogacy.

In the United States in 2006, 44% of assisted reproductive technology transfer procedures resulted in pregnancy, with 36% resulting in live births (Sunderam et al., 2009). Precise success-rate predictions vary with the diagnosis. As a couple moves up the ladder of technological interventions to achieve a pregnancy, each new procedure represents an increased amount of physical invasiveness, increased expense, and decreased success rate. The process can take from months to years.

Although low-income couples are more likely to be infertile, biotechnical intervention to achieve pregnancy is an expensive, middle-to-upper-income phenomenon (U.S. Office of Technology Assessment, 1988). One in vitro procedure with a success rate of about 30%, costs about $12,400. Laws governing insurance coverage of infertility treatments vary widely by state (American Society for Reproductive Medicine, n.d.). Some medical insurance policies cover medications; many do not. The procedures are rarely covered.

The new reproductive technologies also introduce new ethical and emotional issues into the process of procuring a baby. Some patients struggle with their religious beliefs when facing decisions about these procedures. The Catholic Church opposes all alternative means of reproduction, Jewish law permits insemination and IVF with the couple's own gametes but not donor insemination, whereas most nonfundamentalist Protestant religions allow these procedures (Schwartz, 1991). To many couples facing treatment for infertility, there are no right or wrong answers, only difficult choices. Medical family therapy can provide a place for families to raise and discuss these options and their foreseeable consequences.

Within-family gamete donations offer couples genetic continuity, but it can introduce a host of other complex dynamics amongst family members. Evaluation and counseling are important to ensure that no coercion occurs and that all involved are crystal clear about their functional roles with any future child. Intragenerational gamete donation (e.g., sister-to-sister oocyte donation, brother-to-brother sperm donation) is generally considered less psychologically and ethically complicated than intergenerational gamete donation (e.g., daughter-to-mother oocyte donation, son-to-father or father-to-son sperm donation).

Medical family therapy with couples beginning to undergo infertility treatment includes helping them to carefully examine their options and explore both parties' motivations for proceeding with treatment. Sadler and Syrop (1987) pointed out that not all couples seeking infertility treatment desire children. Some couples' motives may include pressures from extended family, marital discord, replacement of a loss, or desire to do what is "normal" at their stage in life. Medical family therapy helps the couple decide whether they wish to pursue having a child or whether their problem requires other treatment. When they are motivated to pursue fertility treatment, medical family therapy then moves to a process of negotiation and renegotiation between the partners about their current status, what should be done next, and when to end treatment. It includes acknowledging the stresses inherent in the procedures, the ethical conflicts that emerge, and the risks that may accompany these treatments. In keeping with the evidence base, medical family therapy coaches the individuals and couple to reduce negative affect and anxiety, promote healthy behaviors, use relaxation exercises, and provide psychoeducation. Inevitably, some technologies are so new that little is known about people's experiences, especially how children and parents adjust in the long term.

An important dynamic involves the couple's relationship with their fertility team—the physician, nurse, genetic counselor, and laboratory and administrative personnel. In the best situations, the couple and the health care team have common goals and a common "enemy" (Covington, 2006). However, the physician treating an infertile couple is especially imbued with the power to impregnate. The physician, and sometimes the team, becomes the receptacle for lifelong gratitude if the procedures are successful or may be the object of rage if they are not. At times, frustration with the physician or team may serve a latent function of unifying a disappointed couple. The cycle of idealization early in treatment followed by anger if a successful pregnancy is not achieved can be stressful for the physician and clinical team. Collaboration between the medical family therapist and the staff can provide mutual support and information.

The medical family therapist works with the couple to smooth out what can be an emotional roller-coaster of treatments, hopes, and disappointments. Strategies include focused communication skills so that each member of the couple understands the other's way of coping with the uncertainty of the treatment, focusing on rewarding aspects of their life outside of fertility treatments, and choosing to take vacations from treatment.

TREATMENTS FOR MALE FERTILITY

Insemination

The most common treatment for male infertility is insemination, either with a partner's sperm (which may have been "washed" or "pooled" to increase the chances of success) or with a donor's sperm. The most important recent advance in the treatment of male factor infertility is intracytoplasmic sperm injection, in which a single sperm is injected into a single oocyte to create a fertilized oocyte. This advance is important because it allows men with low sperm counts to father a child. There are many other arduous and uncertain treatments for men, including medication, surgery, and repeated sperm counts (Keye, 2006).

Insemination With Donor Sperm

Insemination with donor sperm poses complex issues for patients, both psychologically and interpersonally. Several controversies exist about donor insemination (DI). It may be done by couples themselves, producing so-called turkey baster babies, or with medical assistance. In the latter case, physicians and sperm banks are in a powerful position in choosing the pool of donors. Most sperm banks have catalogs so that prospective parents can pick their donors on physical characteristics, blood type, special interests, skills, and so on. Donors give sperm for humanitarian and financial reasons. Except for being screened for AIDS and other illnesses (the sperm is typically frozen and quarantined for 6 months to ensure they do not carry any sexually transmitted diseases), traditional sperm banks expect little from the donors; donating sperm is generally assumed to be a psychologically uncomplicated issue for men, and their identity remains anonymous. However, with a growing outcry about "genetic ambiguity" from adults who are anonymous DI babies, some sperm banks are now *open*, that is, allowing future children access to the names and contact information of the person who donated the sperm.

Some religious traditions (e.g., Roman Catholic, Orthodox Judaism, fundamentalist Christian, Muslim) hold that pregnancies should be achieved only from the eggs and sperm of married men and women, and so oppose DI (Christian Apologetics and Research Ministry, 2012; Dietzen, 2010; Shirazi & Subhani, n.d.; U.S. Office of Technology Assessment, 1988).

Couples are sometimes hesitant about DI and may present for counseling to consider carefully the issues involved. In choosing DI, the woman grieves the loss of having her partner's biological child, whereas the man feels the direct loss of his capacity to reproduce and may envy both his wife and the donor. Typically, the emotionally problematic issues in DI fade when the baby is born and the mother and father begin a relationship with their new child. In an early study (Levie, 1967), after 11 years, couples who underwent DI reported a high degree of satisfaction. More than 96% said they would select this approach again. These couples also rated their marriages as consolidated and improved.

DI allows some heterosexual couples with infertility problems to have children; it also allows single women and lesbian couples to have children.

Medical family therapists may be asked to evaluate or counsel single women or lesbians who request DI. Single women who request DI tend to be well educated, financially stable, in their late 30s, and want a child before their biological clock runs out. Many of these women may view marriage or a committed relationship as more complex, difficult, or undesirable than parenthood. Counseling may help these women make realistic decisions about whether they wish to continue with DI. Counseling with lesbian couples can involve discussion of issues such as which partner is best suited to carry a pregnancy (European Society of Human Reproduction and Embryology, 2001).

The issue of secrecy about DI remains controversial. DI allows couples privacy about their infertility problems. DI children may appear to family and friends as if the parents jointly produced a biological child. In earlier times, some physicians and mental health professionals recommended that DI children not be told of their origins (Waltzer, 1982). More recently, groups of adult DI children have organized and argued for transparency of donor records, much like in adoption (Noble, 1987). Mental health professionals have long argued that children have a right to know and that family secrets can be emotionally destructive (Shapiro, 1988). Devastating scenarios can occur, such as a divorcing father revealing the DI to his child in a moment of anger. In 2004, the American Society for Reproductive Medicine began recommending that couples be honest from early on about their children's biological origins and birth story (American Society for Reproductive Medicine Ethics Committee, 2004). Although these recommendations are based on sound theory and practice, research to date is limited and has not shown that disclosure results in an emotionally healthier outcome for children. Results of a study of 184 San Francisco couples showed no difference in parental bonding or quality of relationships in groups of children with disclosure and those without (Nachtigall, Tschann, Quiroga, Pitcher, & Becker, 1997). A longitudinal study of 30 families in the United Kingdom found that disclosure does not create significant difficulties for family functioning or child adjustment (T. Freeman & Golombok, 2012).

Medical family therapists may help couples develop a narrative for their child, filled with love, support, and information about his or her background. These narratives may start with the story of the child's conception, recorded in a baby book and shared from early in the child's life to show how much this child is wanted and loved, as part of what is special about him or her.

TREATMENTS FOR FEMALE INFERTILITY

Treatments for female infertility include medications, surgery, IVF, and surrogacy. Choice of treatment depends on the diagnosis, although many treatments occur in the absence of a firm diagnosis. Biotechnical interventions to achieve pregnancy can be physically and emotionally taxing (Stotland, 1990). Many require some time off work for employed women.

Medication

Some women without a clear diagnosis are given medication, such as an ovulation-inducing hormone like clomiphene or tamoxifen. Sixty to 70% of women will ovulate on these medications, and 30% to 40% will conceive within 6 months (Keye, 2006). Women diagnosed with adhesions and tubal occlusions after pelvic infection may be treated with microsurgical reconstructions of their fallopian tubes. Pregnancy rates following these procedures can be up to 50% (Keye, 2006). For those who do not achieve a successful pregnancy, medical family therapy can be useful in negotiating discordant couples issues, decreasing self-blame, discussing ways to protect the spontaneity and intimacy of their sex life while still adhering to any needed schedule to maximize the chance of pregnancy, and facilitating grieving.

In Vitro Fertilization

IVF is a procedure in which a sperm fertilizes an egg in a test tube and then is reimplanted. It is a complicated, expensive, and stressful procedure involving blood tests, ultrasound, fertility drugs, and surgery. Couples may see more than one specialist, hoping to increase their chances of success with a different doctor. The medical family therapist should work to help the couple connect with a specialist whom they like and trust, understanding and accepting the uncertainty associated with IVF. The general success rate is about one in four—higher for younger women, lower for older women (Lalwani et al., 2004; WebMD, n.d.), with significant expense and distress for the majority of individuals or couples who are not helped by this process.

Psychological evaluations are typically required for couples who use donor (rather than their own) gametes, to ensure that patients can provide informed consent and have thought through the relevant physical, psychological, and interpersonal issues (Verhaak, Lintsen, Evers, & Braat, 2010). These evaluations typically include psychological tests such as the Personality Assessment Inventory (Blais, Balty, & Hopwood, 2010) and individual interviews of the woman (donor and recipient), the couple (donor and recipient), and for known donors, both women and any partners. Individual interviews include exploring the donor's motivation (beyond financial) and willingness to view the gametes as a gift to which she will no longer have any claim once transferred. Couple interviews included exploring each member of the couple's motivation to pursue IVF. Family interviews emphasize open communication because it is difficult to fully predict one's response to a future pregnancy and baby. Issues such as discipline (what if the donor disapproves of the recipients' discipline tactics?), godparents (who will raise the child should something happen to the parents?), and disclosure to any children of the donor and other extended family members (McDaniel, 1994; McDaniel & Speice, 2001). Once proceeding with IVF, medical family therapy can be useful in supporting the couple through this stressful process and facilitating what are often difficult decisions about proceeding or stopping cycles when they do not result in a successful pregnancy.

Two new developments since 2000 have expanded reproductive technologies, with implications for IVF: the means to freeze oocytes and preimplantation diagnosis. Freezing oocytes enables women to use their own gametes when they have age-related factors, ovarian failure, or illness-related concerns such as cancer treatment. Although a distinct advantage in terms of preserving a woman's opportunity to use her own eggs, freezing also introduces the possibility of having "leftover" frozen embryos. Some couples have difficulty destroying these embryos, especially if their sibling embryos resulted in babies. McDaniel saw one couple who wished to give their frozen embryos to another couple who were long-term close friends, although one couple was Black and the other White. Both couples were committed to the process and to their connection to each other. (Interestingly, the White couple had grown up in a Black neighborhood, and the Black couple had grown up in a White neighborhood.) Medical family therapy consisted of separate and joint couples therapy to examine the possible difficulties with this situation.

Preimplantation genetic diagnosis makes it possible to select embryos that are not likely to produce a child with a genetic predisposition to a serious inheritable disease. Like other forms of termination, some religions and some couples do not support this process. However, regardless of religion, many couples in which one member has experienced debilitating chronic illnesses are anxious to have their child protected against this possibility. (For more about genetic conditions, see Chapter 12.) This is controversial, and not all fertility centers do this. Even more controversial is the process some call *family balancing*, that is, selecting an embryo for the gender of the child. Some centers allow for this if the family already has a child of one gender and wishes to add the other. These difficult ethical issues benefit from family discussion with a medical family therapist as well as the other medical professionals.

The relationship between stress and infertility has been a matter of controversy for many years; some studies have shown a relationship between distress and poor IVF outcomes (Ebbesen et al., 2009; Klonoff-Cohen, Chu, Natarajan, & Sieber, 2001), whereas a meta-analysis showed no relationship (Boivin et al., 2011). Distress is by far the most common reason given by women who voluntarily terminate treatment (Domar, Smith, Conboy, Iannone, & Alper, 2010).

The evidence is mixed about whether psychological interventions increase the rate of pregnancy with IVF (Hämmerli, Znoj, & Barth, 2009). A review of the individual and group literature (Domar & Prince, 2011) stated that educational and cognitive interventions are more effective than emotionally oriented, supportive interventions. Most effective interventions were at least five sessions in duration. Domar and colleagues (2011) designed a 10-week mind–body stress management group intervention for women who were about to undergo their first IVF cycle. The intervention included cognitive behavior interventions, health behavior change, relaxation training, and social support. In a randomized, controlled trial of 143 women, Domar et al. (2011) found that those in the intervention group had significantly increased pregnancy rates for cycle two. Whether or not future studies support this finding, medical family therapy can provide a systemic metaframework for these evidence-based therapies.

Surrogacy

As shown in Figure 9.1, surrogacy as a treatment for female infertility, or as a way to provide gay male couples with a child, has received much media attention. Surrogacy is not legal everywhere. Where it is legal, family members, such as a sister, may volunteer to carry a child out of love and concern (using her sister's egg fertilized by her brother-in-law's sperm, or using her own egg fertilized by her brother-in-law's sperm). With someone outside of one's family, without emotional connections, it is typically expensive. Whether within or outside one's family, it can be complicated psychologically and interpersonally, with the most important concern being whether the surrogate will be able to turn the baby over to the recipient couple after the pregnancy. Most appear to be able to do so without regret (Jadva, 2003). Collaboration with the physician and the attorneys involved is important (Hanafin, 2006). These cases benefit from careful evaluation and medical family therapy before pregnancy and after delivery.

WITHIN-FAMILY FERTILITY SOLUTIONS

Although it can be expensive and complicated, within-family gamete donation or surrogacy can offer a couple genetic continuity from at least one member of the couple. McDaniel has followed cases from evaluation to many years after delivery in which brothers donate sperm to their infertile brothers, and several in which sisters or sisters-in-law carried babies for their infertile sisters, all quite successfully (McDaniel, 1994).

Family Donors

In DI cases, much of therapy involves careful consideration of whether to use an anonymous or a family donor. In some cases, a family donor is chosen so that the child can have the genetic heritage of the father's family. Therapy typically occurs over 4 to 6 months and includes such issues as who to ask to be a donor, who to reveal the plan to, and how to tell the child. In one case, a male patient with infertility secondary to testicular cancer and his wife held meetings with extended family members to discuss the issues involved. As with the IVF cases mentioned earlier, the couple was careful to frame their request as a gift and to reinforce that the donor's functional relationship with the child would be that of uncle. Potential donors were ruled out if they or their family expressed any significant hesitation. Most family members reacted in a supportive and poignant way to the possibility of helping their brother have a child. The extended families became supportive of the plan over time, and the families and children have done well. One family has had multiple children through DI with a family member as donor.

Sibling Surrogate Mothering

Although the examples mentioned early in this chapter were successful, surrogate mothering within families can be complicated physically and emotionally, and some decide not to go through with the procedure after meeting for several family therapy sessions. In our practices, concerns have arisen about such things as how to handle the pregnancy with the surrogate mother's own children as well as her friends. Another couple abandoned the process after their house burned down. Somehow, for these families the surrogacy seemed like a better idea in theory than in practice. Medical family therapy allowed these families the opportunity to explore the many issues involved and decide against the procedure or continue with their eyes open.

The families who completed a surrogate pregnancy all involved sisters who were quite close, and the surrogate had a stable marriage and already had children herself. Some worry about long-term outcomes for children born of surrogacy. Early studies of children evaluated at ages 3, 7, and 10 did not reveal any psychological difficulties (Golombok, Blake, Casey, Roman, & Jadva, 2012). One illustration of success appeared when a national newspaper magazine asked people to write in about their nontraditional families (White, 1990). Debra White wrote a letter describing her experience with her sister as surrogate. Rise, her sister, was inseminated with Debra's husband's sperm and carried the pregnancy for her sister. The family was open and discussed the process. Debra was Rise's pregnancy coach: "Sometimes I honestly forgot I wasn't pregnant. That's how much she let me get involved."

Since Judson's birth, Rise has continued her close relationship as Judson's aunt, and the extended family remains accepting. By age 9, Judson had run into a few unusual reactions from outsiders. He once came home with a note from his Sunday school teacher:

> Mrs. White, when the children were asked to share a love story, your son said your tummy was broken, he grew in your sister's tummy and she gave birth to him. He sounds confused. Perhaps you'd better talk to him.

As with the issue of disclosure with children, medical family therapy offers patients the opportunity to plan their own responses and coach their children about how to react to outsiders' reactions to information about surrogacy or other assistive reproductive technologies.

Throughout our discussion of pregnancy loss, infertility, and fertility treatments, we have identified issues that can be addressed with couples to demonstrate compassion, allow them to tell their stories, and help them negotiate the often-bewildering options and decisions. Exhibit 9.1 identifies how the techniques of medical family therapy can be particularly helpful to couples coping with these issues.

EXHIBIT 9.1
Clinical Strategies for Individuals and Couples Experiencing
Problems with Reproduction

Acknowledge stress and loss.
   Actively acknowledge what are often invisible losses.
   Mark loss with rituals or memorial services.
   If possible, wait a year before trying to conceive another child after a pregnancy
      loss, especially if the woman experienced postpartum depression or anxiety
      (Hughes, Turton, & Evans, 1999).

Normalize the experience.
   Consider previous family and personal losses.
   Normalize "incongruent mourning" between the couple.
   Discuss difficult ethical or religious issues.
   Discuss the "secret" of infertility or pregnancy loss. Coach the individual or couple
      to tell people what would feel most supportive.
   Discuss how to respond to family pressures.
   Listen carefully to the couple's stories to understand the specific meaning the
      infertility has for each person and for the relationship.
   Normalize differences between the couple.

Encourage education.
   Encourage the individual or couple to ask for details about their condition
      from their fertility team.
   Seek information from National Institutes of Health websites.
   Attend support groups such as RESOLVE (a national organization with
      local chapters for people with infertility, http://www.resolve.org) or PEND
      (Parents Experiencing Neonatal Death).
   Encourage the couple to develop a realistic financial plan.

Monitor physical and emotional health.
   Intense grief may mimic or cloak other illnesses.
   Screen for extreme and persistent grief reactions, such as delusions, suicidality,
      flashbacks, and disproportionate responses to subsequent crises.

Externalize the problem of infertility.
   Discourage the individual's infertility from dominating all other roles and
      reinforcing other feelings of inadequacy.
   Encourage the couple to continue with hobbies and other activities they have
      always enjoyed rather than adapting to infertility as a way of life.
   Separate fertility from potency, in sexuality and other aspects of life.

Explore motivation for fertility treatment.
   Explore each partner's motivation to endure the stresses of fertility treatment
      or the pressures of adoption procedures, as opposed to choosing childlessness
      and shifting their needs for generativity to work or other arenas.

Set limits.
   Encourage the couple to take periodic breaks from the active pursuit of pregnancy.
   In conjunction with the medical team, help the couple decide when to stop trying.

Collaborate with the fertility team.

Develop a loving story.
   Help couples who are successful to develop a loving story to tell their child about
      how he or she came to be born, starting with a baby book.

Monitor the therapist's personal reactions.

CONCLUSION

What was once science fiction is fact today. Medical family therapists
have much to offer individuals, couples, and families who experience difficulty
in achieving the transition to parenthood. Working with individuals and
couples using reproductive technology involves managing the many ethical,
psychological, and interpersonal challenges involved in using cutting-edge
21st century scientific advances. Medical family therapists have the opportunity, even the responsibility, to participate in these astounding advances—
helping patients, families, physicians, and health care teams understand the
psychological, interpersonal, and ethical implications of reproductive technologies and helping to increase the sense of agency and communion for
those who wish to become parents.

10

MEDICAL FAMILY THERAPY WITH CHILDREN

Severe childhood chronic illness can be emotionally challenging for therapists. Working with these families triggers personal fears for our own children or child relatives, our desire to protect children, our sense of unfairness that young ones should suffer and die, and our anger at parents, physicians, and other adults whom we may see as not providing the best care for sick children. Immediate compassion and identification provide therapists with a strong incentive to help these children, but they also bring a tendency toward over-involvement and scapegoating parents or other health professionals. This chapter describes some of the unique features of therapy with families who have a chronically ill child and builds on this book's previous chapters on treatment, collaboration, and chronic illness in adults.

Although most children are healthy, chronic illness is a strikingly common feature of childhood. An estimated 7.3% of children have limitations of activity due to chronic health conditions (Centers for Disease Control and

http://dx.doi.org/10.1037/14256-010
Medical Family Therapy and Integrated Care, Second Edition, by S. H. McDaniel, W. J. Doherty, and J. Hepworth

Prevention [CDC], 2008a). Among diagnosed illnesses, asthma tops the list as most common chronic medical condition in children, affecting about 7 million children or 9.5% of the population (CDC, 2013). Whereas the majority of adult chronic illnesses come in the form of three disease categories—cardiovascular disease, diabetes, and cancer—childhood chronic illnesses are much more diverse in prevalence, making each illness much rarer than the "big three" adult illnesses. Examples are seizure disorders, cerebral palsy, juvenile arthritis, hemophilia, and cystic fibrosis, along with diabetes. One implication of this diversity of childhood chronic illnesses is that medical family therapists have to do additional research to learn about the medical aspects of the cases they treat.

LEVELS OF RISK FOR FAMILIES

With childhood chronic illness being so common, it is important to identify which families are in greatest need of medical family therapists' services. Indeed, many families cope well with childhood illness, and some have challenges they handle in their communities without the need for a therapist. Kazak and Noll (2004) offered a useful framework, adapted from the National Institute of Mental Health prevention framework, to categorize the level of psychosocial risk for families facing serious illness death of children. The three categories are *universal* risk, *selected* risk, and *targeted* risk. All families are stressed by the initial diagnosis and treatment of serious illness in a child. Many families, especially those without preexisting psychosocial problems, adapt over time and are not likely to see therapy. From studies of childhood cancer, Kazak and Noll estimated that 60% of families with a seriously ill child fall into this universal category. These families have adequate social supportive and realistic beliefs about the illness and generally were functioning well before the diagnosis.

Another group of families (about a third of participants in Kazak and Noll's, 2004, study) have preexisting risk factors that increase the probability of significant adjustment challenges. This is the selected risk group. Their coping skills are challenged, they may have problems adhering to the medical regimen, and they may have other life stressors that threaten to compromise their functioning. Depending on their previous experience with professionals, they may be open to medical family therapy services provided routinely in primary care settings, and they often appreciate close collaboration among their providers.

The smallest group of families (7%) is the targeted risk group with high stressors and low coping resources. These families were troubled before the diagnosis and are overwhelmed afterward. They have serious difficulty following through with treatment and may have relationship problems with health professionals. Some family members may have psychological impairment. Although this is the group in most need of medical family therapy, they can be difficult to engage in treatment, requiring high levels of collaboration between medical and psychosocial professionals.

This risk framework is useful for thinking about the roles of medical family therapists in health care settings. Universal risk families can benefit from educational and supportive offerings as they address the challenges of childhood illness, but they do not need intensive therapy resources. Selected risk families are the "voluntary" medical family therapy cases, often referred by medical and nursing professionals who see them struggling. Targeted risk families are apt to be "involuntary" medical family therapy cases that begin as consultations with frustrated medical providers who gradually bring the therapist and the family together. Targeted risk families may also be "veterans" of many mental health professionals who do not resist the referral to the medical family therapist but present challenges in triangulating among providers. They require the highest level of skills and the most trust on the professional team. However, their success can be the most satisfying for all who work with them.

SPECIAL ISSUES FOR FAMILIES WITH A CHRONICALLY ILL CHILD

Although all families are stressed by a chronic illness in any family member, several issues are especially pertinent in the case of childhood illnesses.

Parental Guilt

Because they see themselves as their children's protectors in life, parents often feel personally responsible in some way for their child's illness. This guilt may be demoralizing for parents and may show itself in anger against other family members or against health professionals for their failure to cure the child. One father realized that the rage he was feeling stemmed from his inability to forgive himself for "letting" his daughter contract leukemia.

Grief Over Losing "Normal" Childhood and Imagined Future

When family members realize that the illness or disability is chronic, which means it's here to stay, they mourn having to relinquish their dream of having a healthy child. When this grief begins at the child's birth, as in the cases of many genetic and birth trauma disorders, it can complicate the process of bonding with the child. When family members realize that the illness will limit the child's life expectancy or his or her quality of life as an adult, there is an additional grieving and anger over being cheated out of future hopes and plans. Although this reaction is common in adult illness as well, there is a particular poignancy to the loss of many decades of healthy living in the case of childhood illness or disability. One older mother of a child diagnosed with a fatal form of muscular dystrophy said that an unexpectedly profound grief came over her when she realized she would never have grandchildren.

Fear of "Contagion"

Because of fear and ignorance, other parents and even relatives may avoid the child and the family out of fear that the child's severe illness (e.g., cancer, seizure disorders, AIDS) will somehow contaminate their own child. The family of origin of one of the authors experienced a decades-long rift during the polio epidemic of the 1950s, when the aunt and uncle of a child with polio declined to visit the child in the hospital out of the fear, understandable but misguided, that they would bring the disease home to their own children.

Developmental Issues

Depending on the child's developmental position, the timing of the onset and exacerbations of a chronic illness can have serious long-term implications. The illness, or how it is handled by the family, can "freeze" a child developmentally. One of the authors worked with a young adult who never grew up psychosocially once her Crohn's disease began in her early adolescence. Just as for individual development, expected family transitions can be delayed or stopped by a childhood illness. Transitions that occur normally for other families, such as children leaving home, can become excruciating decisions for parents, say, of a child with Down syndrome.

Vulnerability to Health Professionals

Parents experience a unique vulnerability to perceived criticism or lack of support from health professionals who have the task of keeping the child alive and as healthy as possible. This vulnerability occurs particularly in chronic disorders such as cystic fibrosis and diabetes, in which parental actions and supervision frequently show measurable results in the child's condition. When parents are sometimes held accountable for poor outcomes, they feel as if they are being told they are bad parents.

An example of this dynamic occurred with family that had a child with serious asthma, an illness that is strongly connected to the emotional climate of the family (B. L. Wood et al., 2006). Seven-year-old Tanya and her older sisters, ages 11 and 13, were adopted by their parents 4 years earlier. Tanya took medication regularly for her asthma and used an inhaler for acute flare-ups. On a number of occasions, the parents took her to the emergency department with medical crises. Tanya's asthma episodes stemmed primarily from allergic reactions but could also be precipitated by stress, particularly when separating from her parents when going to school or being left with a babysitter. The parents explained to the therapist that Tanya had been found abandoned in China at age 2. Part of the parents' stress stemmed from a lack of support from their extended families, who viewed Tanya as "damaged goods" foisted on the family by the adoption agency. Because Tanya looked healthy most of the time, these family members believed that the parents were overprotective and too worried about her condition. Tanya's allergist and pulmonologist became involved mainly when there was an emergency, at which time the parents felt as if they had failed to do their job. The parents argued with each other about what risks were acceptable, such as allowing her to go to a birthday party at a good friend's house, where she might have an asthmatic reaction to the house cat.

Tanya's family illustrates several special issues for families with a chronically ill child. Because their daughter's asthma is environmentally induced—and they are supposed to control the environment—the parents feel guilty when she has an attack. They worry about her future when they are not there to protect her and also about whether she will be able to have an independent future. Although relatives do not fear contagion, they do not understand the child's problems and view the parents as overprotective. For their part, the parents are vulnerable to criticism from health professionals who are more concerned with asthma control than with whether Tanya is able to attend social events.

FAMILY DYNAMICS THAT INFLUENCE CHILDREN'S HEALTH

One of the most fascinating areas of research on childhood chronic illness is the growing body of work on how family interaction affects biological activity in children. Noting that many research studies have associated marital conflict with behavioral adjustment problems in children, Gottman and Katz (1989) decided to investigate the effect of marital discord on 4- to 5-year-old children's physiological health, physiological arousal, stress-related hormones, and peer relationships. Using complex laboratory procedures to assess marital and family interaction, along with a variety of physiological measures, the researchers found that children of maritally distressed couples have higher levels of chronic stress (as indexed by high levels of stressed-related hormones in their urine), higher levels of illness (as reported by mothers), and higher levels of physiological arousal (as measured during the laboratory interaction tasks). In other words, health-related physiological processes in children were shown to be linked to the quality of the parental relationship.

The "Psychosomatic Family"—Updated

In this study, which used updated assessment tools, Gottman and Katz (1989) continued a research tradition begun 11 years earlier by Minuchin, Rosman, and Baker (1978). Their book *Psychosomatic Families* proposed a family systems theory of psychosomatic illness, along with results of an experimental research study showing a linkage between triangulating behavior of the parents toward the diabetic child and the child's blood levels of free fatty acids, which are thought to be related to stress. The original psychosomatic family model proposed that the following patterns of family interaction influence, and are influenced by, childhood chronic illness:

- enmeshment, which means overinvolvement and hyper-responsivity;
- overprotection, which means excessive nurturing and restricted autonomy;
- rigidity, which means the tendency to maintain fixed patterns that are not working;
- poor conflict resolution or conflict avoidance; and
- triangulation, in which the focus on the child's illness detours marital or family conflict.

The psychosomatic family model, which stimulated considerable interest in the family dynamics of childhood chronic illness, has come under criticism for blaming parents for children's illnesses and having an insufficient empirical base (Coyne & Anderson, 1988; but see also the rejoinder by Rosman and Baker, 1988). Until medical family therapy was formulated as a subspecialty in the 1990s, some family therapists' only familiarity with the psychosocial aspects of childhood illness was the psychosomatic family model—and they generally had only a superficial understanding of this model. These therapists tended to misuse the model by taking a judgmental and blaming stance toward parents, neglecting the biological dimension of diseases such as diabetes and asthma, and taking a conceptually simplistic view that family dynamics "cause" certain childhood diseases. Worse still, some even took the clinical stance that the family's "need" for the child to be ill somehow creates the original illness. Without the biopsychosocial framework that Minuchin and colleagues (1978) intended, the psychosomatic family model can be dangerous.

Beatrice Wood and her colleagues have updated the original psychosomatic family model with greater theoretical sophistication and more accurate research methods (B. L. Wood et al., 2006, 2008). These researchers examined how family processes interacted with three childhood abdominal illnesses: Crohn's disease, ulcerative colitis, and functional recurrent abdominal pain syndrome. Families were rated during standard, videotaped family interaction tasks; lunch; and an interview. The authors used laboratory scores of disease activity as outcome measures (e.g., platelet counts, levels of hematocrit and albumin). Across studies, they found that disease activity is associated with triangulation, marital dysfunction, and a total psychosomatic family score. Two important findings have implications for the psychosomatic family model: that the three diseases differ in how family patterns related to disease activities, with Crohn's disease being associated with the highest psychosomatic family levels, and that marital dysfunction and triangulation are more powerful factors than enmeshment, overprotection, rigidity, conflict avoidance, and poor conflict resolution.

The effects of the combination of family problems and threatening childhood illness appear to continue after the child has recovered. Research used attachment theory as a way to study the long-term consequences of serious chronic illness (in this case, childhood cancer). Alderfer, Navsaria, and Kazak (2009) found a strong relationship between family functioning and adolescent posttraumatic stress disorder. The at-risk families were either overinvolved or underinvolved with their child, did not handle emotional communication well, and were less able to solve problems. The authors concluded that much more attention needs to be paid to how childhood cancer survivors grow up in family systems that have experienced traumatic effects of the disease and its treatment, with long-term implications for parents and children.

There is mounting evidence for a linkage between certain family interaction processes and children's physical as well as psychological well-being. The original psychosomatic family model stimulated much useful clinical work and some subsequent research and theoretical development in this area but has been surpassed by more sophisticated theoretical and empirical work. Scholars such as Gottman, Wood, and Katz have demonstrated complex levels of subtlety in the connections between family relationships and children's health.

Diabetes

In terms of specific illnesses, childhood diabetes has received the most attention in the families and health literature. In the United States, about 186,300 people younger than 20 years have diabetes; this represents 0.2% of all people in this age group (Centers for Disease Control and Prevention, 2010b). The majority of childhood and adolescent diabetes cases have historically been

Type I, which occurs when the pancreas no longer makes insulin because the body's immune system has destroyed the beta cells in the pancreas. Individuals with this condition can develop diabetic ketoacidosis, which can lead to diabetic coma and death if not aggressively treated. In recent decades, however, an increasing number of adolescent and preadolescents have been developing Type II diabetes (previously called *adult-onset diabetes*), which typically begins with insulin resistance in various organs and a progressive inability of the pancreas to make enough insulin to counteract the resistance. Eventually, the pancreas often loses its ability to secrete enough insulin in response to meals, and the individual experiences excessive blood glucose level and a variety of complications. Obesity is a common risk factor for Type II diabetes, and the recent increase in childhood and adolescent obesity has put many children at risk for this form of the disease (Kumanyika & Brownson, 2007; Sperry, 2009).

Research has shown that children and adolescents from families with high levels of conflict have more difficulty controlling their diabetes (Sander, Odell, & Hood, 2010). They experience recurrent episodes of severe hypoglycemia and ketoacidosis. Family conflict can also lead to the onset of eating disorders, which are more common in adolescent who have diabetes (Gonder-Frederick, Cox, & Ritterband, 2002). Observing family conflict, often accompanied by parental intrusiveness, can lead the therapist to blame parents and want to rescue the child. The clinically valuable concept of *miscarried helping*, introduced by Coyne, Wortman, and Lehman (1988) and amplified by Harris et al. (2008), can steer therapists away from this trap.

Miscarried helping comes from an investment by parents in being good caregivers and a belief that parent-directed help will lead to better health for the child. When the child's health does not improve (in the case of diabetes, when glycemic control is not achieved), the parent feels like a failure and communicates frustration and disappointment to the child. The child, who feels intruded on and blamed, becomes angry and resentful. The ensuing conflict exacerbates the illness by creating a stressful environment and stimulating the child to defy the parents and not adhere to the medical regimen. It's a classic family systems dynamic of good intentions gone awry, with sometimes devastating interpersonal and biological consequences (Harris et al., 2008).

HOW THE CHILD'S CHRONIC ILLNESS AFFECTS THE FAMILY

The following quote from Hobbs, Perrin, and Ireys's (1985) book *Chronically Ill Children and Their Families* summarizes the multiple, simultaneous challenges these families face:

> Families with a chronically ill child confront challenges and bear burdens unknown to other families. The shock of the initial diagnosis and the

urgent and compelling need for knowledge; the exhausting nature of constant care unpredictably punctuated by crises; the many and persistent financial concerns; the continued witnessing of a child's pain; tensions with one's spouse that can be aggravated by the fatiguing chronicity of care; the worries about the well being of other children; and the multitude of questions involving the fair distribution within the family of time, money, and concern—these are challenges that parents of chronically ill children must face. (p. 80)

The acute phase of an illness, after the diagnosis, can be one in which the family pulls together in mutual support and determination to manage the crisis (Alderfer & Kazak, 2006; Doherty & Campbell, 1988). But as treatment commences and the family has to reorganize itself, as the new family reality of workload and doctor appointment sinks in, stressors mount and the family's cohesion and flexibility are challenged. They are more apt to fall into the enmeshed or disengaged ends of the family functioning spectrum.

In two-parent families, the marital relationship undergoes strains during the marathon that is childhood chronic illness. For example, Berge and Patterson (2004), in their review of research on cystic fibrosis and family functioning, reported that

parents (especially mothers) of children with cystic fibrosis have increased psychological problems, role strain, and decreased marital satisfaction. Decreased marital satisfaction was related to having less time to spend together, decreased communication skills, decreased sexual intimacy, and role strain between parenting and caregiving. (p. 87)

Patterson (1988) organized this information on the effects of childhood chronic illness on the family under the heading of the family adaptation and adjustment response model (the FAAR model was developed by Patterson and Hamilton McCubbin, 1983). In this model, families are viewed as balancing their demands and capabilities within a set of beliefs or meanings. Childhood chronic illness can tip the balance toward the side of the demands—physical, emotional, social, financial—and leave the family's resource capabilities depleted and inadequate. The family then goes into crisis and must find a way to rebalance itself.

The medical family therapist is apt to become involved with the family at times when it is out of balance, and the therapy may be a factor in increasing the family's capabilities to manage both the illness and other life demands. Sometimes the family seeks therapy not because they are not handling the ill child well but because the marital relationship or siblings are suffering. Because childhood chronic illness can unbalance families in many areas, a therapist's working with subsystems in the family can be invaluable.

In the case of Tanya and her family, who were dealing with asthma, it became clear how the family dynamics and asthma mutually influenced each other. Vigilance was a central theme in the family: The parents were vigilant about Tanya's asthma symptoms and her anxiety, and she was vigilant about signs of separation from her parents. In addition, Tanya took on the stress of other family members when conflict arose, sometimes translating this stress into problems with her breathing. When this happened, her parents would drop what they were doing to give Tanya her medicine or sometimes take her to the emergency room. When a previous therapist suggested that the parents needed to go out on dates and take time for themselves for the good of their marriage, Tanya had an anxiety attack after they left, which led to an asthma attack. For the parents, separation from their daughter seemed like a life-and-death issue. They decided to engage in home-based schooling for her, with the mother doing the one-to-one teaching. This, in turn, compromised Tanya's ability to take social risks, make new friends, and engage with new adults. Thus, the child's predisposition to asthma, combined with her personal history of abandonment and the enmeshed, overprotective family dynamics, created a troublesome medical and psychosocial situation.

SPECIAL ASSESSMENT ISSUES IN CHILDHOOD CHRONIC ILLNESS

This discussion on assessment and the following one on treatment expand on the discussion of clinical strategies in Chapter 2. They highlight several important aspects of working with families when the chronically ill or disabled family member is a child (see Exhibit 10.1). The distinctive contribution of medical family therapists for this population comes from taking a systems perspective that sees the interlocking needs and contributions of the child, the parents, the siblings, the treatment team, and the social network that surrounds the family. To a medical family therapist, the family system in particular is not just a "context" in the child's life to be taken into account in treatment but the central matrix within which the drama of childhood illness plays out.

EXHIBIT 10.1
Special Assessment Issues in Childhood Chronic Illness

1. What beliefs and meanings do family members bring to the child's health problems?
2. Has the child's illness become part of dysfunctional triangles in the family?
3. How are other relationships being attended to?
4. How are the siblings functioning?
5. What part of the problem is developmental, and what part is illness-related?
6. How are the parents relating to health professionals?
7. How supportive is the family's social network?

Family Beliefs

Family members bring beliefs and meanings to the child's health problem (Wright, Watson, & Bell, 1996). Most important, children may not be developmentally able to understand their illness in the way that their parents and health professionals do. For example, children with cystic fibrosis may not believe the disease is present when they feel no discomfort or may see no connection between managing their illness and the back pounding (for drainage of fluid from the lungs) they resent receiving from their parents several times a day. The health beliefs of parents, grandparents, and other relatives and close friends may also be important factors for the family. Similarly, the splits and controversies in beliefs among family members are important to assess. When a child's health and survival are at stake, adults' convictions can run very strong.

Dysfunctional Triangles

Sometimes the child's illness becomes part of dysfunctional triangles in the family. Family therapists are generally well equipped to assess triangulation and detouring of parental conflict onto a child. A chronic illness or disability provides a fertile ground for these family dynamics to blossom. These triangles may take the form of *detouring*, in which parents retain their unity by focusing on the child, or *cross-generational coalitions*, in which one parent forms an alliance with the child against the other parent.

In Tanya's family, the parents played out their conflict through arguments about being "hard" or "soft" on Tanya's accommodations to her asthma. This conflict culminated in an argument about whether she should attend a friend's birthday party despite the risk that the friend's cat could trigger one of Tanya's asthma attacks. The father "won" the struggle over the mother's caution, and Tanya went to the party; the mother "won" the aftermath, however, because Tanya had an acute attack, the mother stayed up with her all night, and the doctor agreed with her opinion in the morning. These conflicts stemmed both from relational issues in the parents' marriage and from different health beliefs about how to manage the asthma in light of Tanya's other developmental needs—in this case, the importance of having normal peer activities and relationships. In other words, the parents differed on how big a place to make for the illness in Tanya's life and the family's life. The father wanted "business as usual" as much as possible within the bounds of acceptable risks, whereas the mother's focus was on preventing asthma flare-ups.

Other Relationships

The most common family interaction difficulties in childhood chronic illness begin when one parent (usually the mother) becomes the main caregiver for the child. As the father or other adults become more disengaged over time from the mother–child dyad, other relationships in the family—marital, father–child, parents to other child, extended family, friendship—begin to erode. Pressure builds on the mother–child relationship. Others begin to accuse her of being overprotective; she accuses them of not understanding and not supporting. Eventually, when the relationships are far enough out of balance, someone or some relationship breaks down.

Siblings

Siblings are often the neglected figures in families of chronically ill children. Milton Seligman (1988) described how siblings are often kept out of the information loop in the family, how they may assume caregiving responsibilities, how they fear "catching" the illness or disability, and how they often feel anger and guilt over their sibling's condition. If, as the saying goes, "the squeaky wheel gets the grease," healthy siblings may have trouble competing for parental attention. Sometimes they develop their own "squeak" in the form of behavioral problems as a way to persuade their parents to attend to their concerns. Parents, however, are apt to see this misbehavior as a betrayal by a child who has "no reason" to be uncooperative, given the already major strain the family is under. In these cases, the family may present to the therapist with the sibling as the identified patient, not the chronically ill child.

Developmental and Illness-Related Problems

A problem may have both developmental and illness-related components. A noncompliant adolescent diabetic may use the illness behavior to engage in typical adolescent resistance to parents. Children with chronic illnesses are naturally going to challenge their limitations and their medical regimen from time to time. Similarly, an ill child may experience a flare-up at a family developmental transition such as the birth of a new sibling. Therapists should not necessarily assume that the child's problematic behavior is stemming from problematic family dynamics related to the illness. Sometimes the illness is just the playing field for a normal, but irksome, family struggle.

Parents and Health Professionals

When a family has a member with a chronic illness, the family also has a "chronic relationship" with health professionals: Both are part of the family's life more or less forever. As mentioned before, parents feel particularly vulnerable to and may resent nonsupportive behavior from health professionals. Negative escalation is common in two scenarios, and each leads to frustrated staff and angry and resistive parents: when the diagnosis is uncertain or the treatment not working well, parents are apt to be angry with the health team for not helping enough; when the health team is showering the child with supportive and technically competent care, the parents may feel supplanted as nurturers and protectors of their child. The situation becomes even more difficult when parents triangulate staff into family conflicts. Helping families with these disabled relationships with professionals is one of the hallmarks of a competent medical family therapist.

The Family Social Network

Ultimately, children are raised not just by their parents but by an extended support network of family, friends, neighborhood, school, church, and community. Raising a chronically ill or disabled child is so difficult for most parents that their support network must be active and committed. Particularly important resources are other parents with ill or disabled children, because they really understand chronic illness. It is important to assess how well the family accesses their support network. How do they ask for help? How do they accept help? Can they relate to others outside of the illness context—that is, can they engage in mutual exchange of support with others when the child's illness is not a main focus?

Tanya's family illustrates many of the special assessment issues that arise in working with families coping with chronic childhood illness: As the parents' marriage increasingly centered on Tanya and their other two children, disagreements over health beliefs became even more troublesome because little else remained of their marital relationship. The oldest sister, age 13, was left with the caregiver role when both parents had to be absent from the home. She felt helpless whenever Tanya had a separation anxiety attack, and then she resented her parents for leaving her in charge. The 11-year-old sister resented the amount of attention Tanya received and engaged in numerous small rebellions against her parents. This sister formed an alliance with her father over the issue of how overprotective the mother was toward Tanya. The mother, in turn, felt she had lost control of her 11-year-old daughter. Health care professionals unwillingly became triangulated into this family's coalitions when they dealt only with the mother, who the father believed distorted what the doctors said about Tanya. Finally, Tanya's family was isolated from its families of origin, who were unsympathetic to the adoption in the first place, and from the major community institution for children (i.e., the school) because Tanya was taught by her mother at home.

The family did have some important strengths, however. Church provided the family with a sense of community, and the family showed a good deal of resilience in maintaining caring, committed relationships despite their problems. Although generally anxious-appearing, Tanya had an attractive personality and a great ability to empathize with other children.

SPECIAL TREATMENT ISSUES IN CHILDHOOD CHRONIC ILLNESS

Given our view that medical family therapy is a metaframework and not a specific clinical model, this chapter does not promote a single way of doing therapy when childhood chronic illness presents in the family. As long as they have a biopsychosocial systems perspective (the hallmark of medical family therapy), therapists can successfully use a wide range of clinical models and techniques, but they should keep in mind—and address in a manner that suits their mode of therapy—the following special issues.

Accepting the Child's Illness

Patterns of denial and unresolved grief often prevent families who adapt poorly to a child's illness or disability from adjusting to the new reality. They do not make a place for the illness in their life, and inevitably they do not accept the health professionals who also have entered their lives. The therapist has to work with these issues of denial and grief as a prelude to helping the family change its behavioral patterns. It is not uncommon for one parent to accept the illness and begin to make a place for it, while the other parent or grandparents experience such adjustments as a betrayal. Often health professionals see as underresponsible a family that has not been able to cognitively understand or emotionally accept the reality of the child's serious medical problem.

Accepting the realities and limitations of a progressive illness requires continual reevaluation, and each cycle of reevaluation carries its own possibilities for blocked grief, denial, and parental splits. When a single parent of a child with Duchenne's disease (a progressive, fatal form of muscular dystrophy) told her mother that it was time for a wheelchair for her son, the grandmother was appalled that her daughter was "giving up" on the child in this way. The therapist had to help the family make a place for the wheelchair as a metaphor for accepting the presence and power of the illness in their lives.

Putting the Child's Illness in Its Place

The next challenge for a family that has adjusted to a childhood chronic illness or disability is maintaining the integrity of its relationships, rituals, and worldview in the face of the demands of the illness (Gonzalez et al., 1989). Illness is inherently unbalancing for families, and the worse the illness or disability, the more unbalancing it is. Unbalancing can occur when the child is not given appropriate developmental responsibility and challenge; in such cases, the child has disappeared behind the illness. Unbalancing can occur in a two-parent family when the parents' relationship is subsumed by discussion and worry about the child, and in a one-parent family when the parent has too few outside enjoyments and interests. A sibling may be left out of the family emotional hearth or given responsibilities that curtail normal childhood experiences. Just as families who do not make a place for the child's illness develop underresponsible patterns, families who fail to put the illness in its place develop overresponsible patterns of handling their child's problems.

We have found it helpful to speak with families about protecting themselves from the illness, even using metaphors such as assigning a room in the house to the illness—an upstairs spare bedroom, perhaps, but not the kitchen or living room, where the family has its most intimate transactions. The therapist can then work concretely to help family members plan activities that are not based on caring for the illness. Another technique for putting the illness in its place is to emphasize the normal developmental aspects of a child's presenting problems, such as age-appropriate rebelliousness or nonresponsibility, and thereby treat the child as a child and not as an illness.

Promoting Open Communication

Open communication about the illness or disability is one of the first casualties of a child health problem. Parents are afraid to upset the ill child or the siblings. Children likewise are afraid to upset parents and each other. The child's condition becomes a taboo subject, spoken about only with code words such as "fine," "doing well," or "wait and see." One of the principal tasks of a medical family therapist is to facilitate communion in the form of an open discussion among family members about their beliefs, expectations, fears, and hopes about the illness. This can take the form of family sessions in which the therapist asks each family member in turn for his or her thoughts and feelings about the illness and the challenges it brings and then accepting and normalizing the almost inevitably wide range of responses. Sometimes these sessions will be with the whole family and sometimes with the parents alone or the child alone. In one case, the father, who had never openly expressed his deep worry for his disabled child because he was trying to be strong for his openly distressed wife, had a chance to tell his wife (through the therapist's gentle questions) that often when he was in the basement "working," he was really feeling sad and worried about the future. This revelation had a softening effect on the wife, who had been faulting him for not seeming to care. The medical family therapist's presence and support can help the family break down the walls of silence that distance and confuse family members. When there is a chance to involve a medical provider in one of these breakthrough moments, that professional is often better able to understand and support other families going through similar experiences.

Helping Families Negotiate With Health Professionals and Schools

For some parents, interactions with health professionals are one of the most painful aspects of a childhood chronic illness. The medical family therapist should carefully analyze the family's past and present interactions with professionals, looking especially for critical incidents that shaped the family's beliefs and expectations. For example, families with a child with muscular dystrophy have said that the callous way in which they felt that the physician told them about the diagnosis predisposed them to dislike the physician. One family was even asked for an autopsy permission by a resident who approached them immediately after the attending physician gave them the diagnosis. Parents with disabled or chronically ill children must grapple with the educational system as well as the health care system. They must conduct difficult negotiations with school personnel about whether to mainstream their child or provide out-of-classroom school services and in-home educational services. These discussions are often complicated by a lack of coordination and communication between school and health care professionals (Doherty & Peskay, 1993).

The challenge for the medical family therapist is to listen and support parents without scapegoating or triangulating against the health care team or the school team. The therapist needs to understand the workings of the health care system and the culture of medical care. Families can be coached to empower themselves without being disrespectful to health professionals: They can learn to ask questions, make legitimate demands, seek consultations and second opinions, check the accuracy of medications and medical communications, and, if necessary, terminate certain professional relationships and seek new ones. The same skills apply to dealing with school systems, although families may be more limited in their options to leave the public school system and go elsewhere.

A critical incident in Tanya's case illustrates how the medical family therapist worked with her family and their interactions with the health care system and the school system. Tanya was scheduled for surgery for a chronic knee problem, a congenital condition that sometimes led to injuries but otherwise did not affect family life as much as her asthma did. She and her parents were concerned about repeating the painful experience of her previous surgery, when medical students and surgery residents took 45 minutes to start an intravenous line in her arm. She felt like sliced meat, an experience that was worse for her than the surgery and the subsequent recovery. The parents felt helpless to do anything about the situation because they knew that her veins were difficult for the doctors to work with.

The medical family therapist pointed out that anesthesiology residents are generally expert IV starters; they do it routinely, sometimes in emergency situations, and commonly are called in by other physicians to start an IV line for difficult cases. The therapist coached the parents to request, and to insist if necessary, that the most senior anesthesiology resident start the IV. The surgeon made no objection, and the resident started the line on the first try. Tanya was thrilled, and the parents felt empowered to choose options within the health care system.

Working together as a couple with their daughter's surgery and its aftermath (when the parents prevented a medication mistake) proved to be a positive experience for the parents. As for the problem with their daughter's asthma, the therapist acknowledged the difficulty of balancing their need to protect Tanya with their desire to let her decide to take risks. Part of the parents' disagreement, the therapist noted, came from having different information because the mother and Tanya generally visited the pulmonologist alone. The parents agreed to both participate in key discussions with doctors and to make joint decisions only after they had both heard the medical information and advice directly from the physician.

The medical family therapist did other balancing moves with these parents, including holding Tanya responsible for taking her medication and encouraging her to attend public school. At the therapist's suggestion, the parents met with Tanya's teacher and principal to explain their daughter's medical condition and separation fears. The mother walked Tanya to and from school for several months until Tanya was ready to walk on her own. The therapist then turned to the sibling issues, helping to clarify the limits of the oldest sister's responsibilities, addressing openly her resentment of her younger sister for receiving more attention than the other siblings, and reestablishing the parental boundary with the 11-year-old.

After progress was made on these medically related and child-rearing issues, the couple wanted to work more strongly on the marital relationship and family-of-origin relationships, with periodic returns to medical issues as they reemerged. Both parents went on to make important strides in their strained relationships with their parents and siblings, which lessened the pressure of their isolated relationship.

SPECIAL ISSUES IN COLLABORATION

A special issue for therapists who collaborate with physicians and other health professionals around problems of childhood chronic illness is the exceptional level of vulnerability and protectiveness that professionals experience in the face of seriously ill children and their sometimes dysfunctional families.

When these cases are discussed, it is not uncommon for physicians and nurses to show emotional distress about the child's condition. Sometimes the most helpful collaborative activity is for the therapist to listen and offer emotional support (see Chapter 3 for a general discussion of collaboration). Of course, the therapist may also need support when children are sick and dying. These feelings of distress seem especially intense for professionals who are parents themselves.

Connected with the pain and grief are feelings of anger and resentment toward parents who do not "do right" by their children. When difficult medical and family cases are discussed, someone on the health care team may call for removal of the child from the home, a suggestion that can stem from emotional overinvolvement, burnout, frustration with the parents, and lack of understanding of complex human behavior and family dynamics. The challenge for the medical family therapist is to support the feelings and legitimate concerns of the health professionals while preventing the parents from being scapegoated and coerced. Systems-trained therapists can avoid replicating this problem by making sure they do not scapegoat the health care team on behalf of the family. As in the case of Tanya's family, the therapist also reaches out to schools and other systems that interact with the child and the family. Even in "disaster" cases in which the family–professional split is so wide that the family is not amenable to help, the therapist can help the health care team to learn from the case and try to work differently with similar cases in the future. Over time with these difficult cases, the health team can learn to ask the core question that denotes a systems perspective: "Are we helping to maintain this problem in some way?"

CONCLUSION

Working with chronically ill children and their families is central to the mission of medical family therapy in the health care system. It is where Salvador Minuchin and his colleagues started in the mid-1970s with their psychosomatic family model following an informal request for help from the head of diabetology at Children's Hospital in Philadelphia (Minuchin et al., 1978). What we have learned since the mid-1970s is that children's health is biologically as well as psychosocially part of their family relationships. Children's bodies, like all of ours, are tuned to the resonance of family rhythms, and when something goes wrong with their bodies, the reverberations penetrate deep into the consciousness of families and health professionals alike. We owe our children better than we are giving them in health care—better prenatal care, better access to preventive care and treatment, and a more healthful environment. We also owe them more help for the families who influence their lives so profoundly and who struggle, often without adequate support and guidance from professionals, to cope with the unanticipated shock and burden of a chronically ill child.

11

SOMATIZING PATIENTS AND THEIR FAMILIES

Mr. Brown:	My back hurts. My head is throbbing. And I can't eat because my throat is closed up. I think I may have cancer. Could there be a tumor in my throat?
Dr. M:	I understand that you are very uncomfortable today. Mr. Brown, I know your physician does not currently think you have cancer, but you should discuss any new symptoms with him. A few minutes ago, when we were drawing your genogram, you said that two of your babies died soon after birth. Can you tell me some more about this?
Mr. Brown:	They are gone. I had to be hospitalized soon after because my back was killing me. I had surgery on a disc in my back. It's never really been right ever since. I haven't been able to work, and my wife accuses me of being lazy. Do you think that new medicine that's in *Newsweek* might help me?

http://dx.doi.org/10.1037/14256-011
Medical Family Therapy and Integrated Care, Second Edition, by S. H. McDaniel, W. J. Doherty, and J. Hepworth

Somatizing, a process whereby people like Mr. Brown with difficult life situations present not with anxiety, depression, or relationship problems, but with numerous physical symptoms, is simultaneously one of the most vexing and most fascinating of human processes. Existing at the interface of mind and body, somatizing behavior is not fully understood. We can't predictably treat it. We can't even agree on what to call it. And it is a massive expense within our already burdened health care system, a problem that calls out for creativity, research, and collaborative care.

Somatizing patients do not differentiate between emotional and physical experience, nor do they use emotional language to express emotional distress. Instead, they use somatic language to describe all difficulties, whether physical or emotional. For some people, somatization is part of a lifelong coping style, functioning like a chronic illness that ebbs and flows depending on other physical and emotional stresses. Mr. Brown, in the vignette that opened this chapter, experienced a ruptured disc soon after the death of his second son. The emotional components of his problem played a significant role in his inability to recuperate fully.

Somatizing includes problems that the *Diagnostic and Statistical Manual of Mental Disorders* (*DSM*; American Psychiatric Association, 2000) labels *somatoform disorders*, such as hypochondriasis and somatization disorder,[1] but it also includes the broader spectrum of somatizing behavior that is frequently seen in physicians' offices. Some prefer to call these problems *medically unexplained symptoms* (R. M. Epstein et al., 2006), arguing that "somatizing" implies an artificial separation between bodily and psychological symptoms that patients do not experience and stating further that somatization is a "demeaning diagnosis" (S. K. Johnson, 2008). Others prefer *functional disorder, psychophysiological disorder,* or *contested illness*. Recognizing limitations with each of these labels (Creed, 2010), we use the terms *somatizing* and *somatic fixation* in this chapter because they imply an interactional process.

Medically unexplained symptoms constitute the most common disorders seen in primary care (Kroenke et al., 1997). They can occur with or without coexisting mental disorders or organic disorders and result in cycles of help seeking from physicians. Somatizing patients have strong organic disease convictions; they frequently seek medical attention, but they provide challenges for their medical providers. Their physical symptoms either do not make physiologic sense or are grossly in excess of what would be expected from physical findings. Some, but not all, somatizing patients vociferously deny any emotional component to their problems.

---

[1]See the most current *DSM* for the established criteria for these terms. For example, the fifth edition of the *DSM* has a very particular definition of somatization disorder that requires a history of many physician complaints beginning before age 30 and must include four pain symptoms, two gastrointestinal symptoms, one sexual symptom, and one pseudo-neurologic symptom over the period of several years.

```
   *              *             *            *            *
Somatic      Sensitive to     The "worried   Obsessed      Somatic
denial      bodily sensations    well"      by symptoms    delusion
```

Figure 11.1. The range of somatic fixation by patients. From *Family-Oriented Primary Care* (2nd ed.; p. 126), by S. H. McDaniel, T. L. Campbell, J. Hepworth, and A. Lorenz, 2005, New York, NY: Springer-Verlag. Copyright 2005 by Springer-Verlag. Adapted with permission.

Many of these patients are those referred to as the *worried well* (see Figure 11.1) and require some reassurance and time from medical providers. One study showed that some patients with unexplained symptoms provide opportunities to discuss psychosocial or stress-related concerns, but these patients have "voiced but unheard agendas" as their physicians generally disregarded these opportunities (Salmon, Dowrick, Ring, & Humphris, 2004). The technical skills of providers and the escalating costs of the medical system are most challenged by the small group of patients with serious somatizing disorders who rarely voice psychosocial concerns. DeGruy, Columbia, and Dickinson (1987) found that patients with the more serious diagnosis of somatization disorder[2] had a 50% higher rate of office visits, 50% higher charges, charts close to twice as thick as the average chart, and significantly more diagnoses than matched control subjects. These patients may have expensive, potentially dangerous, and unnecessary procedures and treatments. It is not unusual for patients with somatization disorder to have a history of numerous hospitalizations and surgical procedures. The overall cost of these patients to the health care system is staggering. Barsky, Orav, and Bates (2005) estimated that $256 billion per year in medical care costs could be attributed to somatizing patients alone.

CULTURAL SUPPORT FOR SOMATIZATION

The Cartesian mind–body dichotomy pervades the structures and the meanings we construct to describe our illness experiences. The notion that a physical symptom must have a primarily organic cause, or that an emotion is primarily determined by some psychological experience, is widely accepted in our society. The idea that mind and body are an integrated, related, communicating whole has only recently and tentatively been considered by mainstream Western society. The complex disorder of somatization symbolizes our

---

[2]Somatization disorder is a *DSM* diagnosis that includes a history of physical complaints before age 30 and eight symptoms that cannot be fully explained by a known medical condition. The symptoms are not intentionally feigned or produced.

culture's struggle to recognize the integration and interdependence of physical and emotional aspects of life. Medical anthropologist Arthur Kleinman (1986) described somatization as "culturally authorized, socially useful, and personally availing" (p. 151). Somatization varies in prevalence across cultures. Asian cultures, even less accepting of psychosocial explanations than Western cultures, appear to have a higher incidence of somatization than does the West (Bhatt, Tomenson, & Benjamin, 1989; Ryder et al., 2008). Latinos also tend to have a higher incidence of somatization than do Anglos (Willerton, Dankoski, & Martir, 2008).

Western culture also struggles with the relationship between individual responsibility and illness. Again we dichotomize. We tend to hold people responsible for their emotional problems while believing on the whole that they are not responsible for disease or illness. Framing a problem as "physical," as is true for somatizing patients, allows for a passive-dependent patient role that most people sanction.

The fields of medicine and psychotherapy struggle with the mind–body dichotomy, as does our culture as a whole. Medicine's increasing reliance on biotechnology seduces physicians and patients alike into becoming somatically fixated and concluding that biomedicine *is* medicine rather than only one important component of the diagnosis and treatment of a patient. As we demonstrate, exclusive application of the biomedical approach to somatizing behavior is likely to escalate the symptoms, frustrate the patient and physician, and increase medical visits and costs. In the psychotherapy field, likewise, exclusive focus on psychosocial issues often results in rejection of therapeutic treatment by the somatizing patient and rejection of the patient by the therapist.

A biopsychosocial approach to somatizing behavior counteracts the cultural support for the mind–body dichotomy. It allows both the physician and the therapist to assume that every physical symptom has some biological, some psychological, and often some social component to it. The biopsychosocial approach avoids the reductionism of trying to discover whether some symptom is "organic" or "all in your head." Somatizing behavior is most often a complex blend of physical, emotional, and interactional processes.

THE EXPERIENCE OF THE REFERRING PHYSICIAN

Somatization has been termed medicine's "blind spot" (Quill, 1985). If the problem of persistent physical symptoms is frustrating for the patient and the patient's family, the experience of the physician whose satisfaction comes from healing is also intensely frustrating. Consider the following poem, written by a physician who was moved to question his career choice after an afternoon encounter with a somatizing patient:

Second Thoughts

It's five o' five
Day's almost done.
All the patients seen
But one.

I stand outside
The exam room door.
Read the nurse's note
With horror.

"New patient says
Teeth itch at night,
Stomach aches when shoes
Too tight.

"Numbness starting
In the knee,
Dizziness
Since '63.

"Food goes up
Instead of down,
Always tired,
Lies around . . . "

Tears start to fall
I just can't hide 'em.
The note goes on
Ad infinitum.

" . . . climbing stairs
Causes gas,
no sense of smell
When driving fast.

"Left hand hurts
and right hand's weak,
sneeze sends pain
From hands to feet.

"Last week had
a pain in the chest . . . "
Stop! No more!
Can't read the rest!

I think business school
would have been wiser,
'cause they don't have
somaticizers.

—Tillman Farley, MD[3]

Some physicians are themselves somatically fixated in their approach to medicine—that is, they focus exclusively on the somatic aspects of a complex problem (van Eijk et al., 1983). They misunderstand the indirect communication conveyed by somatizing behavior and use a biomedical frame to understand and treat the complaint. When these physicians tell somatizing patients that they are healthy or give a relatively benign explanation for their symptoms, the patients feel misunderstood and respond with persistent complaints and demands. (In contrast, most other patients react with relief to this news.) Somatizing patients believe these doctors cannot find what is wrong and do not want to care for them. The biomedically oriented physician, feeling incompetent, may then react to the patient's demands with anger ("This is all in your head"), distancing (e.g., not returning phone calls), more

---

[3]Reprinted with kind permission from the author.

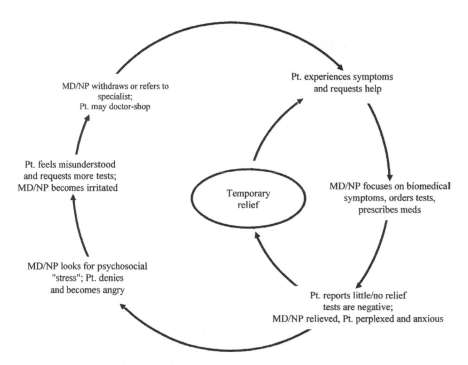

Figure 11.2. Somatically fixated physician–patient interaction. MD/NP = physician/nurse practitioner; Pt. = patient. From *Family-Oriented Primary Care* (2nd ed.; p. 133), by S. H. McDaniel, T. L. Campbell, J. Hepworth, and A. Lorenz, 2005, New York, NY: Springer-Verlag. Copyright 2005 by Springer-Verlag. Adapted with permission.

diagnostic tests, or referral to a specialist (see Figure 11.2). Family members who share somatically fixated health beliefs with the patient may express their own frustration at the health care system for not curing their loved one's symptoms. Some of these patients and families seek help from nontraditional health care providers such as homeopaths and *curanderos*.

The way out of this cycle for the physician or nurse practitioner is to take a biopsychosocial approach to patient care from the beginning (see Figure 11.3). In this approach, the physician does a comprehensive evaluation by conducting an interview that intersperses biomedical and psychosocial questions (Doherty & Baird, 1983). He or she establishes a collaborative, rather than authoritarian, relationship with the patient and the family, models tolerating uncertainty, legitimizes the patient's suffering, and may ask a medical family therapist to join the treatment team (McDaniel, Hepworth, & Doherty, 1995). Together, the physician and therapist set limited goals, and the health care team monitors patient functioning rather than symptoms. The therapist can help the physician stay cued to possible psychosocial factors (see Taplin, McDaniel, & Naumburg, 1987, for an example of this collaboration). Once

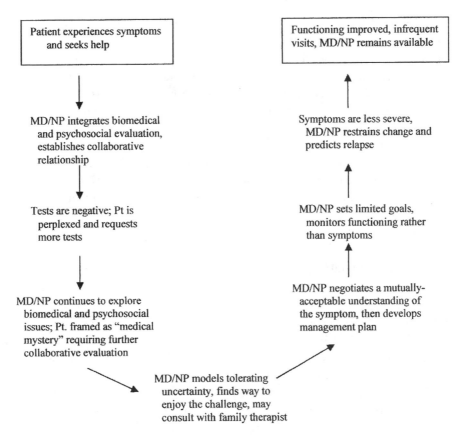

Figure 11.3. A biopsychosocial approach to somatic fixation. From *Family-Oriented Primary Care* (2nd ed.; p. 135), by S. H. McDaniel, T. L. Campbell, J. Hepworth, and A. Lorenz, 2005, New York, NY: Springer-Verlag. Copyright 2005 by Springer-Verlag. Adapted with permission.

collaborative relationships with the relevant health professionals and the family are established, the medical family therapist can help to develop an integrated approach that allows the medical team to understand the patient's symptoms and treat the somatic components of the problem, the family to support patient's health and well-being, and the patient to develop competence and confidence in monitoring and managing his or her physical and emotional needs. The physician and health care team continue to be available after the family has terminated with the therapist.

Traditional mental health approaches have failed these patients. Psychodynamic theory understands somatization as part of the patient's character structure—part of the way the patient defends against frightening emotional experiences. Because somatization is seen as deeply rooted and because these therapists recognize the difficulty in establishing a working alliance with somatizing patients, these patients were traditionally thought of as "poor candidates for psychotherapy" (Greenson, 1965). We each have received referrals from a primary care physician, desperate for help, and reports from psychiatrists saying that the same patient is basically untreatable. Somatization is a problem in which patient experience and functioning, as well as collaboration with the family and the medical team, can be more central than a diagnosis (Epstein, Quill, & McWhinney, 1999). Although a cognitive behavioral approach can be successful with some individuals (Allen & Woolfolk, 2010), too often treating these patients in individual therapy can become a losing battle between the patient's symptoms and the therapy. Dealing with the family context and interactional issues around the somatizing behavior can provide leverage and the necessary intensity for successful treatment.

UNDERSTANDING THE SOMATIZING PATIENT AND FAMILY

The somatizing patient is extremely sensitive to bodily cues (Barsky, 1979). Using a diary to record physical symptoms, Kellner and Sheffield (1973) found that 60% to 80% of healthy people experience some somatic symptoms in any given week. Of course, most of them do not label those symptoms as problems that require physician intervention. However, individuals' perceptions of a symptom are variable. Several studies have shown that the same amount of tissue pathology produces varying degrees of functional impairment and subjective distress in different individuals (Eisenberg, 1979). Those who are sensitive to bodily cues and experience greater impairment and distress are more likely to label their symptoms as problems in need of treatment. Figure 11.1 describes the spectrum of somatic fixation presented by patients, ranging from somatic denial at one end to somatic delusions at the other.

> Suzie presented as a 28-year-old separated woman with multiple somatic complaints. Her head and arms ached, and she had shooting pains in her head and her legs, frequent stomach distress, and early morning awakening. Suzie was convinced that she had a serious, potentially life-threatening illness that had not been discovered by her physician. She requested all the blood tests and diagnostic procedures she knew of (including an expensive magnetic resonance image) to discover the problem. Of great concern to her was her 5-year-old son, who she felt was manifesting many of the same symptoms she had. She worried that her "disease" was communicable and she had given it to him. On several occasions, Suzie wondered whether she should be quarantined to ensure that no one else got the disease.
> Most of the time Suzie functioned extremely well. She was a highly valued and productive employee at the large company where she worked.

She also worked out and went to a strenuous aerobics class 5 days a week. Frustrated with the difference between this patient's internal experience and her external appearance, her physician referred her to a medical family therapist.

It took several months in therapy to uncover Suzie's story. Her symptoms, she said, began around the time of her marital separation. Suzie left her husband partly out of dissatisfaction with the relationship and also because of a blossoming relationship with a man at work. After the separation, this man continued his sexual relationship with her but made it clear that he did not want a serious commitment. After hearing this, Suzie had a rapid succession of affairs, two with men who were casual acquaintances, but then she quickly felt distressed about these experiences. Soon after this, Suzie contracted a viral infection.

Suzie asked her doctor to check for any sexually transmitted diseases. Her tests were negative, but the viral symptoms persisted and developed into symptoms that she worried might be life-threatening. At first she was concerned her "disease" was something similar to AIDS, sexually transmitted and eventually fatal. After she experienced symptoms for about a year, articles on the symptoms of chronic fatigue syndrome began appearing in the media. Suzie then described herself as having "chronic fatigue syndrome without the fatigue." She denied any lingering stress or emotional difficulty with her separation or subsequent affairs. The "stress" was experienced, she said, because no one could diagnosis or treat her illness.

Suzie is typical of many somatizing patients in her experience of her illness and her frustrations in trying to obtain treatment for her problems. She was also typical in that she had many of the physical symptoms of depression and anxiety, even though she denied any mood disorder. (Suzie fervently believed that she never experienced any depression, "only relief," after her separation.) Somatic fixation can be part of an obsessive–compulsive disorder, or obsessive–compulsive tendencies (Okasha, Saad, Khalil, El Dawla, & Yehia, 1994). Somatizing patients may benefit from treatment that includes antidepressants with or without antianxiety components. Suzie eventually agreed to a trial of antidepressants because of the evidence that they are helpful with chronic fatigue syndrome. Although the medication did not cure her problems, she did report that it was helpful in diminishing her pain. Patients with physical symptoms may also benefit from cognitive behavioral techniques (Kroenke & Swindle, 2000; reinforced by family members), or a class in mindfulness-based stress reduction (Baslet & Hill, 2001; Bohlmeijer, Prenger, Taal, & Cuijpers, 2010; best attended by the patient and her partner or caregiver, rather than the patient alone).

Like Suzie, all somatizing patients should be screened for major depression and panic disorder. Both conditions are common in these patients, are often missed by referring physicians, and respond to antidepressant treatment (Katon & Russo, 1989). Family therapists who do not prescribe medication can collaborate with the patient's primary care physician or consulting psychiatrist to facilitate this aspect of the treatment plan.

How does somatizing behavior develop? Kellner (1986) described the cycle he believes occurs with many somatizing patients:

> a common sequence in a hypochondriacal reaction is the experience of new somatic symptoms at times of anxiety or depression followed by a selective perception of bodily sensations, motivated by fear of disease and subsequent increase in anxiety with more somatic symptoms; elements become linked in a vicious cycle, by frequent repetition overlearned, and the chain becomes predictable. (pp. 10–11)

It not difficult to imagine the interactions with both family members and physicians that might reinforce this behavior.

FAMILY FACTORS IN THE DEVELOPMENT AND MAINTENANCE OF SOMATIZATION

Many family factors can encourage or support somatizing behavior (Phillips, 2008). Some families lack any language for emotional experience: All family members may be alexithymic and allow only language about physical experience; children receive attention for physical pain but no attention for emotional pain. This approach conditions children to experience any need or problem as physical, and physical symptoms become their language for a range of experiences. Abuse is not uncommon in emotionally impoverished environments. Several studies have uncovered a relationship between severe somatizing behavior and early deprivation, physical or sexual abuse, or trauma (Fiddler, Jackson, Kapur, Wells, & Creed, 2004; Katon, 1985; E. A. Walker et al., 1999). For these patients, early emotional trauma has a significant physical component. A systematic review of studies on the development of somatoform disorders in children and adolescents found the following additional family risk factors: somatization of parents, organic disease of a significant other, psychopathology of close family members, and dysfunctional family climate (Schulte & Petermann, 2011).

Clinically, it seems that families with severely somatizing members share patterns of interaction that seek to avoid or anesthetize emotional pain. A significant number of somatizing adults are married to other somatizing adults. These couples share a language of bodily discomfort. Other somatizing adults marry caregiving partners. The caregivers may not themselves be ill, but they, too, privilege communication about physical events and deny most emotional experience. Somatization also occurs frequently in association with alcoholism or a family history of alcoholism.

> Suzie denied any history of physical or sexual abuse. However, her child-hood had been difficult. Her father was alcoholic and quite unpredictable. Her mother, she said, was "always sick." Suzie learned about somatizing behavior quite early. Then she married a man who also seemed to be always symptomatic. He requested frequent nurturing from Suzie because of his illnesses and the many accidents that occurred on his job as a line-man for an electric company. Suzie came to resent her role as caregiver, and the couple argued about whether she nurtured him enough when he was sick. After separating from her husband, her next boyfriend was physically healthy but "had a tendency to drink too much." In this relation-ship, she became the patient and her boyfriend the caregiver.

Including family members of somatizing patients is essential to interrupting communication patterns based solely on physical symptoms, to create space and obtain permission for additional communication based on emotional experience. One significant session with Suzie late in treatment included her boyfriend and two friends from the chronic fatigue support group. At the end of the session, Suzie announced her resolve to drop out of the group, saying, "This group just isn't meeting my needs. I want to maintain my friendships, but I need to focus on my exercise program now." Several weeks later, she also broke up with her boyfriend, who had refused treatment for his alcoholism. At 1-year follow-up, Suzie had a new boyfriend, a new job, and only the occasional headache.

Family members of somatizing patients often worry about both the physical well-being and the unhappiness of their symptomatic loved ones. Because of this concern, family members may provide important support for therapy, especially in the early phases when patients may be most resistant. Suzie's sister and mother brought her to the early sessions because they worried "that she might die if we don't try everything." In reality, the life span of somatizing patients is no shorter than that of the general population (Coryell, 1981). However, the life of the patient and the lives of other family members can be dominated by physical symptoms, interpersonal struggle, and an excess of medical care.

Smith, Monson, and Ray (1986) found that a psychiatric consultation coupled with recommendations for the primary care physician reduced the medical costs of patients with somatization disorder by 53%. In an early experiment in integrated collaborative care, Huygen (1982) found that referrals to a family therapist in his office resulted in much less overutilization of medical services. In a study of 292 adults in an HMO, Law and Crane (2000) found a 21.5% reduction in health care utilization. A prospective study of children born extremely premature compared with children carried full-term at age 4.5 years found that those premature children who had experienced early hospitalizations and pain were likely to develop somatizing disorders if their parenting was also "nonoptimal" (Grunau, Whitfield, Petrie, & Fryer, 1994). It is easy to see how some parents who experience the trauma of a premature infant might develop inappropriate parenting strategies in response to common childhood aches and pain and how medical family therapy might correct this and prevent the development of later problems. Several uncontrolled studies found family therapy to be successful with somatizing adults (Hudgens, 1979) and children (Mullins & Olson, 1990).

CLINICAL STRATEGIES FOR TREATING SOMATIZING PATIENTS AND THEIR FAMILIES

Collaborate During the Referral Process

Most somatizing patients who easily accept a referral to a mental or behavioral health specialist by definition do not have a serious somatizing problem. The contract for treatment early on is with the referring physician. The patient and family members are usually somewhere between skeptical and actively resistant to seeing a therapist, so the referral usually requires creativity, patience, and extra energy on the part of the physician or nurse practitioner and the therapist. Much of the work for the therapist with these referrals involves consulting with the referring clinician, as early in the process as possible, to build a close collaborative relationship, and planning for a warm handoff whenever possible. The following suggestions can help the therapist work with the referring clinician during the referral of a somatizing patient.

Empathize

First, allow the physician to express the frustration he or she typically feels by the time the referral is made. Empathize with the physician about how difficult it is to tolerate the uncertainty of managing these patients medically. As every primary care practitioner knows, somatizing patients can develop serious diseases like any other patient. The physician always feels he or she is walking a fine line in terms of not missing an important medical diagnosis and yet not playing into the somatizing behavior and giving the patient an expensive biomedical workup for an emotionally based problem.

Collaborative Treatment

Suggest an integrated treatment approach in which physician and therapist have regular and continued involvement with the patient and family (see Figure 11.3). Some physicians may want to "dump" these patients after a long series of frustrating encounters; therapists can be tempted to assume responsibility. Emphasize the importance of the physician's role in evaluating and reassuring the patient and family about any new or intensified symptoms, especially while therapy is progressing. Success is most likely if both professionals continue to see the patient on a regularly scheduled basis so they do not have to become symptomatic to be seen. This understanding often prevents the physician from withdrawing. It may also help the physician to view the patient's demands for a "cure" as demands for continued caring (Kaplan, Lipkin, & Gordon, 1988).

For patients who have medically unexplained symptoms and are not at the severely somatizing end of the continuum, explore the psychosocial stressors in their lives, their "unheard agendas." These patients may also respond to meditation, yoga, and therapies such as mindfulness-based stress reduction to shift perceptions of their physical experience and compassionately engage their suffering. Mindfulness principles can be integrated into couple or family therapy as well (Gehart & McCollum, 2007).

Ask for Support

Ask the physician to support the referral actively with the patient and the family. Ongoing support from the physician is often crucial to the success of the referral. For an example illustrating the importance of this support, see Taplin, McDaniel, and Naumburg (1987). It should be suggested, however, that the physician not promise too much while trying to convince the patient to accept the referral. Rather, he or she may say something like,

> My colleague is a therapist with a special interest in working with patients who have mysterious medical problems. Many patients and their families have found working with her to be helpful. You and I have tried many things; I would like you to see her and find out if she can be helpful as you try to live with these symptoms and regain some of your enjoyment of life.

Meet Conjointly When Appropriate

For severely somatizing patients who are resistant to the referral, a warm handoff or a joint session (or sessions) with the physician, the patient, and the family may be especially important to success of the behavioral healthcare treatment. Somatizing cases can be similar to those referred by the courts in that the motivation for treatment is typically much higher in the referring person than in the patient. Joint sessions allow the physician to express direct support for the family to seek therapy. In the context of such support, the sessions also allow the patient and family to demystify the therapist and the therapy experience and enhance the development of trust. Frequently after one session with both providers, the family is willing to see the therapist on its own. For physicians and therapists with a special interest in collaboration around somatizing patients, tough cases may be treated effectively and efficiently by the therapist and physician acting as a cotherapy team throughout treatment. For an example of this approach, see McDaniel, Campbell, Hepworth, and Lorenz (2005).

Some patients are more likely to require long-term medical family therapy, rather than brief behavioral health consultations. Although long-term therapy is costly, the expense pales in contrast to the cost of unnecessary tests, procedures, and hospitalizations. The following case of Mr. Crane falls at the severely somatizing end of the spectrum. Because these patients experience significant suffering, are very frustrating for the medical team, and drive health care costs skyward as they search for a biomedical answer, we describe this case in some detail, dividing it into early, middle, and late phases of treatment. We illustrate clinical strategies that can be used with less challenging somatizing problems.

> Mr. Crane, a 63-year-old retired plumber, was active until diagnosed with prostate cancer. Mrs. Crane had a history of bilateral breast cancer in remission. Dr. Gale, a family physician, was attached to Mr. Crane and his wife. "He reminds me of my father," she said in referring him to the therapist.
>
> Dr. Gale had not pursued some early diagnostic testing when Mr. Crane became symptomatic and so felt guilty when the cancer was found. Once the diagnosis was made, Mr. Crane quickly had surgery. After surgery, there was some confusion about whether Mr. Crane required radiotherapy. The surgeon first told them that Mr. Crane was "cured" and then reversed this and told them that he needed radiation. Mr. Crane had a psychotic episode in the hospital in reaction to some pain medication. He had no previous psychiatric history, and his mental status cleared when the medication was withdrawn.
>
> During the radiation treatment, Mr. Crane became profoundly depressed and had to be psychiatrically hospitalized for a week. His psychiatrist reported that the patient had been catatonic and would not be responsive to psychotherapy.
>
> The referral for family therapy was made by the primary care physician 6 months after surgery. At that time, the physician said Mr. Crane was fixated on his scar, reporting soreness and a conviction that the surgeon had not removed all the cancer. The therapist had two phone conversations with the physician about this patient, mostly listening to the physician talk about her guilt over not picking up symptoms of the cancer earlier. The therapist also learned the patient had other somatic complaints and was extremely reluctant to see another mental health specialist. His problem, he said, was his cancer, not his mental state. The referral was easier than some, however, because the couple had a long-standing and close relationship. The patient agreed to go to therapy at the urging of his wife and his physician.

EXTEND JOINING DURING THE EARLY PHASES OF TREATMENT

The joining phase with somatizing patients like Mr. Crane is typically lengthy because of the patients' caution, distrust, and reluctance to acknowledge any emotional aspects of their illness. Communicating respect to these patients is of utmost importance, in part because of their experiences with frustrated medical providers. It can take months to develop a mutually agreeable contract.

Early in treatment, patients often wish to schedule sessions far apart, hoping that a biomedical cure will occur in the meanwhile. Sometimes a medication metaphor will facilitate negotiations about when to return: "You need to come frequently enough so that you're experiencing a therapeutic dose." This period, when the patient or family is highly resistant to therapy and will not (or cannot) discuss their emotional lives, can seem slow moving. A systems approach, with close collaboration with the medical providers and a large dose of patience and persistence, can often be successful in helping these families through this phase.

The most important technique in joining with these patients is some acceptance of their definition of the problem. Many early sessions are characterized by patients trying to convince themselves, their families, and especially their therapists that they do not need therapy because the symptoms represent a *medical* problem. The following are strategies that can help therapists deal with this presentation.

Focus on Symptoms

It is important for the therapist not to be intimidated by the patient's numerous symptoms; in fact, focus on them in the session by listing them on poster paper, having the patient draw pictures of physical problems, and generally soliciting information about the symptoms. Also ask the patient to keep a symptom diary outside the session to help with assessment of the illness. The symptom diary may be formatted so that physical symptoms are recorded on the left side of the page, and life events and emotional reactions on the right. This format foreshadows recognition of the interweaving of physical and emotional processes. Family members who are involved in the patient's illness may also keep a diary about their observations of the patient.

Elicit the Illness Story

Solicit the patient's and each family member's descriptions and diagnosis of the problem. Hear their story and their experiences with the symptoms, the illness, and the medical system. Work to understand the meaning of the symptom for each person. The patient and the family members all need to have the experience of feeling understood.

Collaborate With the Family

Use a collaborative approach that emphasizes the unknown, mysterious aspects of the patient's illness. Begin to enlist the patient and family help in discovering what seems to yield even small improvements and what seems to make symptoms worse.

Solicit the patient's and family's strengths and areas of competence. These can be useful resources for treatment. Patients with somatic fixation and a history of deprivation or abuse need a huge dose of support.

Note the extent to which the family's health beliefs are consistent with or different from those of the physician, health care team, and therapist. During the course of treatment, the goal is to work toward explanations of the symptoms that are mutually acceptable to the patient, family, medical team, and psychotherapist.

Generate a Genogram

Use a genogram first to take a family medical history. Gather information about any transgenerational meaning for the patient's symptoms by asking, "Has anyone else in the family had an illness that in any way resembles this one?" Mullins and Olson (1990) found modeling to be a significant factor in the development of somatizing disorders in children.

Over time ask about recent stressful life events. When the trust level has increased, assess the patient and family for childhood abuse, deprivation, unresolved grief, substance abuse, and workaholism or other forms of overfunctioning.

Identify Role Changes

Listen for how the illness may have changed the typical roles or balance of power in the family. In one couple, both members' somatizing behavior brought them together after an affair threatened their marriage. In another, the illness gave the husband a "job" as a patient when he had been at loose ends after retirement. In another family, the wife's illness forced the husband to help with housework and parenting after years of his wife's overfunctioning at home and working on the family farm.

Use Medical Language

During the early phase, use medical language and physical interventions, such as relaxation tapes, exercise, and attention to sleep and diet. Many of these interventions become family projects and represent a healthier perspective on the body. At a minimum, the therapist must work to have family members support, or at least not sabotage, these interventions.

Refrain From Emotional Language Early in Treatment

Emotional language, reframes, and in-depth emotional exploration are premature during this phase. The therapist must wait for the family and the patient to signal their readiness. Frequently, important aspects of family history are withheld for months until the family is ready and able to discuss them. This should be respected.

Tolerate Uncertainty

In addition to monitoring the biomedical status of the illness, stay in touch with what is not known about the illness; at times biological components to the problem emerge and require biomedical treatment. Like the physician, the therapist must communicate that he or she does not fully understand the symptoms, does not have a quick answer or pill that will solve the problem, and is able to tolerate the uncertainty while continuing to work on various aspects of the patient's problem.

> In the early phase of treatment, Mr. Crane attended therapy with his wife but believed it to be "a waste of my time and your time, doc." He was polite but not engaged. On a few occasions when Mrs. Crane was unable to attend a session, it was difficult to maintain a conversation with Mr. Crane except when listing and describing his symptoms. He fixated and perseverated on several symptoms and gave monosyllabic answers when asked about any other topic. He kept a symptom diary that was highly repetitive and had a few paragraphs a day on the left side for physical symptoms and only an occasional word on the right side for stressful events or emotional reactions.
>
> Mr. Crane believed his symptoms were due to a recurrence of his prostate cancer, a recurrence that physicians were unable to detect. Mrs. Crane believed her husband's symptoms were related to anxiety and not cancer. She frequently reassured him that he was OK and that the doctors were trustworthy.
>
> Mrs. Crane drew from her own experience with cancer to cope with her husband's illness. At one time, after her mastectomy, she became depressed for 6 months and withdrew from her family and her community. She felt the same was happening to her husband. After several months, Mr. Crane compared his illness with his father's experience in his last years when he seemed to be deeply depressed. His father did not recover emotionally before a heart attack resulted in his death. (See Figure 11.4 for a genogram of the Crane family.)

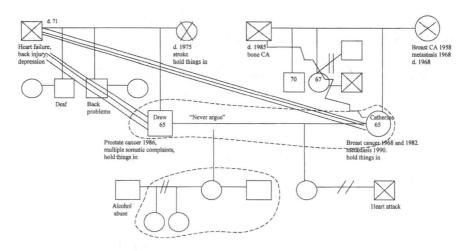

Figure 11.4. The Crane family.

Mr. Crane had been close to his father, who was kind and also "held things in." He was less close to his mother. Mrs. Crane had been physically abused by her father. She said she married her husband because of his family, especially his father. Both Mr. and Mrs. Crane agreed that they never fought—Mr. Crane because he admired that in his father, Mrs. Crane because she was determined to have a different kind of household than the one in which she was raised.

Mr. and Mrs. Crane had many strengths. They had two grown sons and several grandchildren, all living out of state. They described their marriage as close and were supportive of each other, although they had kept separate bedrooms for years. Both seemed to have an uneasy, uncomfortable relationship with their own and each other's bodies. Mr. Crane had been especially active in the community before his retirement, going to church and visiting with sick friends. He was action oriented and had not been successful in filling his leisure time after retirement.

The couple was likeable, although they exhibited somewhat flat affect, anxious moods, and appeared rather passionless. Mr. Crane was able to use a relaxation tape that focused on breathing to ease the discomfort he felt at the site of his surgical scar. He did not respond to other muscle relaxation tapes, but his wife used them.

PERSIST THROUGH THE MIDDLE PHASE OF TREATMENT

The middle phase of treatment with a severely somatizing family can extend for as long as 6 months to several years. During this phase, it is important to judge progress in the patients by monitoring changes in their level of functioning rather than in their symptoms. Symptom-free living (a "cure") occurs occasionally but is unlikely in these patients. More realistic goals involve a decrease in symptoms and an increase in functioning in areas such as work and family relationships. Several strategies are commonly useful during this phase of treatment.

Negotiate a Definition

Work toward a mutually acceptable definition of the problem. This is frequently accomplished by listening for and suggesting language that can bridge physical and emotional explanations, as in this series of examples:

> "Mr. Crane, it sounds as if your body has been under a tremendous amount of *stress* given all you and your wife have been through in the past several years. You have a sensitive body, and these symptoms seem to act as *warning signals* to you. We must learn to pay attention to them and understand what they are trying to tell us."

> "Your husband's heart attack is a serious matter, Mrs. Gonzola. And now, 6 months later, you lose your grandson in this terrible accident. You must feel as if your heart is broken. We must have your physician evaluate your chest *pain*, and we all must evaluate the effects of the other painful experiences you have had recently."

> "Mr. Easterly, it is as if your body is no longer sick but has sustained some internal *scarring* as a result of all you have been through. We must work to protect these scars and your other old wounds so that you may continue to live your life with the least amount of distress possible."

Express Curiosity

Express curiosity about and help the patient and family determine their individual responses to stressful life events and chronic difficulties. Introduce the possibility of both physical and emotional responses. Continue with the diaries to help the patient and family members begin to differentiate physical from emotional sensations.

Introduce Emotional Language

Once bridging terms have been mutually agreed on, slowly use emotional language for emotional experience and gradually have sessions that become less somatically fixated. Examples of emotional language are described in the later phases of Mr. Crane's case.

Reinforce Engagement and Explore Risk

Help family members to reinforce each other's interest and attempts at a higher level of activity and engagement in relationships and to withhold reinforcement for symptomatic behavior.

Explore the risk of change by asking how family life would be different if the patient's symptoms disappeared or improved. When somatizing is a chronic problem, the risk of change is most substantial. For the couple who both began somatizing behavior after facing a marital crisis because of the husband's affair, both members of the couple felt their illness helped them reestablish their priorities and brought them closer together. They were fearful of what might happen if they became well enough to return to work and interact more with friends outside the family. Also, the husband stopped a substantial drinking habit because of his illness; both worried he would resume it if he got better. It was important to address these issues in the middle phase of treatment.

Avoid Psychosocial Fixation

Avoid psychosocial fixation by using an integrated biopsychosocial approach. Continue to refer patients to their physician or nurse practitioner when they have a new or different symptom. The best interventions with somatically fixated patients are those that combine the biomedical and the psychosocial—that is, biomedical interventions that make psychological sense and psychological interventions that make biomedical sense (McDaniel, Campbell, Hepworth, & Lorenz, 2005). Collaboration with and information from the health care team make these interventions most likely. Mr. Brown, discussed earlier in this chapter, was clearly embedded in unresolved grief about the deaths of two babies. Each time grief over the deaths was mentioned in couples therapy, the husband described an increasing number of physical symptoms. Finally, a conjoint session with the physician was held in which the physician read the babies' death certificates line by line, and the medical significance of each sentence was discussed. This intervention took an hour and was the first time the couple was able to converse about the loss. They had many questions about what had happened. The session was a turning point in the treatment.

Occasionally during the middle phase of treatment, a power struggle between the patient and family and the physician may escalate as the patient continues to be symptomatic and fires the physician (or team of physicians). In these cases, the treatment team has been disrupted, and the therapist may be the only one providing continuity of care for the patient. When the problem with the physician is unresolvable, the therapist may refer the patient to a team that has experience in treating somatizing patients—in listening and setting limits in the context of a caring relationship.

Very slowly Mr. Crane began to believe that his symptoms might not be life-threatening. He saw his surgeon and his oncologist, who continued to tell him that there was no recurrence of his cancer. His diary began to have more entries on the right side. He also discussed his commitment to church and how he felt peaceful and calm when attending a service.

Mr. Crane began to describe his problem as one of "anxiety" and joked about how he always focused on the worst-case scenario. He also began describing "discomfort" in his surgical scar as evidence of overactivity, rather than as a recurrence of his cancer. The therapist also suggested he consider it a signal that something was bothering him and that he had to figure out whether it was physical or emotional. Early in this process of relabeling, Mr. Crane pressed the therapist for solutions to his "anxiety," much as he had pressed his physicians for solutions to his somatic symptoms. The therapist maintained her uncertainty about his illness but affirmed a belief in his ability to function better if he and his wife collaborated in finding a treatment plan that could work for him.

Mrs. Crane began to use the same language to describe her husband's problems. They agreed that Mr. Crane did not have enough to do and that he became "depressed" when sitting around and "worrying about his illness." She suggested he again take up woodcarving as a hobby, which he soon did. Therapy focused on increasing Mr. Crane's level of activity. Mrs. Crane agreed to make his favorite meal on days when he was able to visit his old bowling buddies. It was also agreed that when Mr. Crane was feeling bad, he needed to be quiet. Therefore, he would retire to his room rather than lying in the living room, where his wife tried to nurse him back to health.

The therapist slowly began to talk with this couple about giving themselves permission to recognize negative feelings, disagree, express themselves, and still feel safe with each other. This process occurred in conjunction with paying tribute to Mr. Crane's father, who bore his anger and disappointments in silence. Both Mr. and Mrs. Crane began to question whether his father's depression in his last few years might have been related to his inability to talk about what bothered him. Over time, Mrs. Crane began to distinguish between "healthy discussions," as they called their arguments, and the abuse that seemed to characterize any conflict in her childhood home.

Mr. Crane's functioning fluctuated considerably for much of this phase of treatment. Each time he experienced a new symptom, he returned to his physician. During one phase he became angry at the surgeon, who he believed had "lied" to him about getting all the cancer out. He considered going to another doctor but decided against it after discussing his complaints with the surgeon.

At another point in treatment when he had fixated for a particularly long time on his scar, the primary care doctor and the therapist held a joint session to evaluate the problem. The patient was encouraged both to return to his oncologist for another evaluation and to pray more. The fixation eased within weeks.

Before retiring, Mr. Crane had been an avid gardener. During this phase of treatment, Mr. Crane started with one tomato plant (which threatened to die on several occasions) and moved to a small plot with a variety of vegetables during the next season. These vegetables provided an invaluable metaphor for treatment. The first tomatoes from the first plant were enjoyed and greeted with great fanfare by the couple and the therapist.

As Mr. Crane began functioning better, several sessions focused on the risks of his improvement. As with many cases, the couple agreed that the illness had brought them closer together. It had also given Mr. Crane a "job." The couple discussed what they would need to do to remain close if he was not so ill. They also discussed some hobbies and volunteer activities he could engage in to keep him active and entertained. The therapist agreed that Mr. Crane seemed to be the kind of person who is happiest when he is busy. However, she cautioned the couple to move slowly on these new projects and to pay attention to how he was feeling so as not to aggravate his "scar."

REINFORCE CHANGE IN LATER PHASES OF TREATMENT

In the early and middle stages of treatment, the therapist explores the risk of change, and the patient learns to regard his or her symptoms as "warning signals" or as communications about a problem that needs attention. Once the patient and family are functioning better, the therapist can help the patient feel a greater sense of control over the symptoms by exploring at length what makes them worse. Family members may act as consultants about what they observe. Successful completion of these experiments means that termination may be considered. As in all medical family therapy cases, ending a course of treatment involves returning the patient to the care of the primary care clinician and the rest of the team. In somatizing cases, it is important to remain available to the family (and the team) should the need arise. When somatization is a long-standing, pervasive coping style, it is not unusual for the therapist to see the patient or family again for a period of treatment when they encounter some new transition or stress. The medical family therapist is part of the primary care team, available when needed. Usually there is increased somatizing behavior, but the therapist and family are able to focus much more quickly on the emotional aspects of the problem. The following strategies for the late phase of treatment for somatization are often helpful.

Predict Setbacks

As the patient begins to have fewer and fewer symptoms, expect and predict setbacks. In one case where difficulties were not predicted, a patient became symptomatic while the therapist was on vacation. The patient called her family physician, who provided reassurance about her newest ovarian tumor fear but did not ask her to come in. The patient ended up seeing her obstetrician and finally felt slightly relieved. When the therapist returned, the therapist told the patient that it was great the patient only had to go through this process once (a huge improvement over the past). However, the patient might have been spared some of the disappointment if the therapist had predicted problems as the patient began to improve. Predictable setbacks can occur when a patient's family member or friend receives a new diagnosis, when someone important dies, or as a result of any significant stress.

WRITE A "PRESCRIPTION FOR ILLNESS"

A "Prescription for Illness" details what the patient and each member would have to do to bring back the patient's symptoms or make them worse. For one family's "Prescription for Headaches," the patient said she would have to deny she had any problems, fight every possible battle with her husband, not keep in touch with her parents, stop exercising, and not get enough sleep. Her husband said he would have to ignore his wife except when she was sick, not talk to her about what he was thinking or how he was feeling, and leave all the child rearing to her. Their 10- and 12-year-old boys said they would have to keep yelling and fighting even when their mother asked them to calm down.

Terminate Slowly and Remain Open to Future Consultation

Consult with the primary care physician about the timing of terminating this episode of care. Make sure the patient has an appointment with the physician or nurse practitioner soon after stopping therapy.

See the family once a month, then once every 3 months, until the family and the rest of the health care team agrees to stop. It is easy to remain available if working on-site, but set the expectation that future contacts are likely to be "consultations" (Wynne, McDaniel, & Weber, 1986) rather than another course of therapy, unless an entirely new issue arises. Such was the case with the Cranes.

> As he improved, Mr. Crane raised the possibility of stopping treatment. At first, Mrs. Crane opposed him as she feared he would again become incapacitated. In response to her concern, the therapist helped the couple to write a "Prescription for Mr. Crane's Pain and Anxiety." They each agreed that what could make his symptoms worse were inactivity, lack of exercise, not seeing a trusted physician regularly, not talking honestly to each other, and the onset of a new illness. The therapist suggested that they do an experiment to see if they could make the symptoms worse by intentionally not talking to each other the next time one of them was annoyed about something. The couple was unable to complete the assignment because they kept teasing each other about not talking whenever an annoyance arose.
>
> After this experience, with Mrs. Crane's support, the therapist scheduled the sessions for once every 3 months for a year and then terminated. Both Mr. and Mrs. Crane had regular appointments with their family physician during this time. The physician reported to the therapist that he saw no increase in symptoms or decrease in functioning, so both agreed it was time to stop the therapy.
>
> The Crane family was not seen for about a year, until they were referred because of Mrs. Crane's depression after she received a diagnosis of metastatic cancer. With this news, Mr. Crane's functioning improved even more as he was needed to take care of his wife. His wife described her diagnosis as "shock therapy" for her husband. The couple was seen once every month or two to support them and keep their communication open during this stressful period. After an initial block in their communication, the terminal illness brought them even closer. They were able to talk about their joys and their sorrows, Mrs. Crane talked about her fears about death, and Mr. Crane talked about his fears about life without her.
>
> After Mrs. Crane's death, Mr. Crane experienced an acute recurrence of some of his symptoms as had been predicted, but he was also aware of his intense feelings of grief. The intensified somatic symptoms lasted only about 3 weeks and remitted within 2 months as he successfully reorganized his life.

CHALLENGES FOR THERAPISTS TREATING SOMATIZING FAMILIES

"The somatizing patient confronts us continuously with our own vulnerability to physical illness, the aging process, deterioration, and ultimate death" (Chabot, 1989, p. 133). This is perhaps true for all medical family therapy, but it is especially true in work with somatizing patients, whose fears about illness and death are intense. The somatizing patient often expresses the family's fears of dying, fears of living, and general unease with uncertainty of any kind. Therapists who enjoy working with these patients must develop spiritual and emotional resilience to be able to confront these basic challenges of living. The therapist may also be able to help the physician and medical team feel more comfortable in the face of their uncertainty about the symptoms. When the treatment team can move forward in the face of uncertainty, it provides a model for the family about remaining active while acknowledging and living with the unknowns of life.

In addition to challenging the therapist on an existential level, the somatizing patient and family also frequently challenge the therapist on a technical level. As mentioned earlier, the joining phase can be difficult and extended, and require patience on the part of the therapist. It is easy to get pulled into a power struggle over whether the patient's symptoms are entirely organic or not. Focusing on the symptoms and the family's explanations diminishes this problem. Some parts of treatment can be tedious while the patient's language about emotional life remains impoverished. Curiosity about the symptoms as metaphors can help the therapist through this period.

Collaboration with the medical team can also be an important outlet for support. We regularly bring somatizing patients to a consulting group of physicians and therapists (McDaniel et al., 1986) when the therapist's experience has been alternating among satisfaction, hope, frustration, and boredom. Sometimes the difficulty is a "boring" family; sometimes it is frustration with the treatment team. The support and the input of others with differing points of view usually help the therapist to try new strategies and bring new energy to the case.

Although working with somatizing patients and their families almost always includes phases of frustration or difficulty, it is also intellectually stimulating and personally rewarding. This work is important conceptually because it occurs precisely at the interface of our struggles to understand the constructs we label *mind* and *body*. Patients are often extremely grateful to find someone who "understands" and someone who can help them better negotiate the medical system. It is poignant to experience the patient and the family as they begin to develop a language and an ability to experience emotional events. With these developments come more significant connections with the therapist and, more important, with each other. Sessions can move from flat, sterile, biological discussions to warm, humorous, and expressive exchanges. These experiences are a testimony that medical family therapy can make a difference in people's lives.

12

THE EXPERIENCE OF GENOMIC MEDICINE: A NEW FRONTIER

For Sally, the question of genetic testing arose when she went to her internist for a physical at age 23, 6 months after her mother died of breast cancer. The internist learned that Sally's mother was only 45 at the time of her death and that her mother's sister, Sally's aunt, had survived breast cancer at age 34 (see Figure 12.1). Only 5% to 10% of breast cancers are genetic, but having two first-degree relatives with the disease, as Sally did, increased the risk that these disorders were genetically linked (Easton, Ford, & Bishop, 1995). Knowing this, the internist became activated and insisted on a referral for Sally for genetic testing.

Sally was still in the midst of intense grieving over the loss of her mother. A young woman, she was distraught after her visit with the internist and did not accept the referral for genetic counseling, nor did she return to her care. From a traditional biomedical perspective, this intervention by the internist was entirely reasonable and evidence based. From a biopsychosocial perspective,

http://dx.doi.org/10.1037/14256-012
Medical Family Therapy and Integrated Care, Second Edition, by S. H. McDaniel, W. J. Doherty, and J. Hepworth

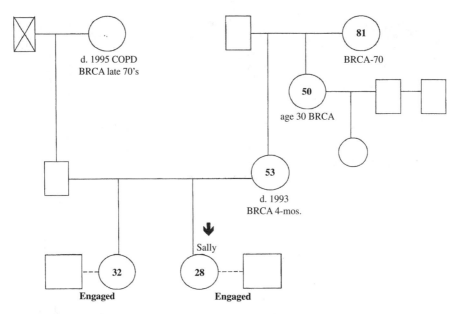

Figure 12.1. Decision making about breast cancer genetic testing. COPD = chronic obstructive pulmonary disease.

it was premature. Any risk to Sally was unlikely to occur immediately, and her emotional state prevented her from being able to absorb this new information. She needed an integrated, collaborative, biopsychosocial approach with a health professional who could support her through the grief process, slowly help her integrate the possibility of her own risk, and decide what to do about it.

Over time, this did happen in medical family therapy, in collaboration with Sally's new primary care physician, geneticist, and genetics counselor. After a year of counseling with her new husband, Sally decided to continue increased surveillance for breast cancer (e.g., regular breast examinations, frequent mammograms) but to not have genetic testing. She was consumed with wanting to start a family. Her way of coping with uncertainty was to put aside the genetic testing and focus on those elements of her health that she felt she could control.

As Sally's story illustrates, the burgeoning science of genomics blurs the boundary between health and illness. *Genomics* is the interaction of all human genes with each other and their interactions with the environment. Cracking the human genetic code has brought increased awareness that almost all diseases and disorders have a genetic component, not only in terms of their causes but also in terms of susceptibility and resistance, prognosis, progression, and response to treatment.

The implications for medical family therapy are far-reaching. Genetic conditions are, by definition, family conditions and deserve a family systems perspective on diagnosis and intervention (McDaniel, Rolland, Feetham, & Miller, 2006). In addition, genetic testing has opened a Pandora's box of psychosocial and ethical challenges for the patient and the family. This chapter begins with basic information about genomics—single gene and more common genetic conditions. We then explore the phases of patient and family experience with genetic conditions, from becoming aware in the pregenetic testing phase, to gaining the information through genetic testing, and integrating the results as patients and families move toward long-term adaptation (Rolland, 2006). We discuss the importance of collaboration with what can be numerous other professionals involved with these patients, and the opportunities for medical family therapists to participate in the evolution of this exciting new area of medicine.

GENETIC RISK AND GENETIC CONDITIONS

Because information about genetic conditions is expanding rapidly, the experience of facing genetic risk or a genetic condition is like facing a shifting landscape. Any psychosocial intervention must be flexible to accommodate emerging knowledge that affects genetic testing, diagnosis, and treatment. Medical family therapy must also be sensitive to the psychosocial demands of a particular genetic condition and the unique experience for each patient and family.

Some diseases elicit strong feelings of anticipatory loss. These include traditional single gene disorders with a high likelihood of development, high severity, known timing in the life cycle, and no effective treatment. Huntington's disease is an example in which a positive genetic test is diagnostic for developing the disease (unless one dies early of some other cause). A newly diagnosed patient knows the approximate timing of onset at midlife, and the probable course of the disease. For some, acquiring this kind of genetic risk information can be emotionally debilitating, especially if the prognosis is grim and seemingly beyond control. For others, learning that a disease has a predictable course helps them focus on priorities and life planning (Rolland, 2005).

Most common disorders such as diabetes and heart disease have complex multiple gene and environmental interactions that are not yet well understood. These multifactorial genetic illnesses are much more variable or less likely to develop than the single gene disorders. Prevention and treatment are available, and the trajectory is uncertain in terms of onset, course, and outcome. A positive genetic test for these mutations is a statement about risk or probability of developing the disease; it is not a diagnosis. Preventive steps, when available, may help foster a sense of mastery in meeting a biological challenge or lessening its impact. For these types of conditions, the experience of genetic risk knowledge is quite different from that of traditional genetic disorders.

Psychosocial and systemic assessment and interventions for families at risk for genetic disorders are in the early phase of clinical innovation and discovery. Most have yet to be studied scientifically for their effectiveness. What does it means to know one's mutation status for a familial illness? What interventions support healthy individual and family coping with this information? A 2002 review concluded that most patients, across conditions, are not significantly distressed or clinically disturbed after testing positive for the gene (Lerman, Croyle, Tercyak, & Hamann, 2002). However, each person's response is shaped by previous life experience, family health beliefs, family illness experience, past or current mental health problems, as well as the seriousness of the potential illness and whether there are effective treatments.

BECOMING AWARE: THE PREGENETIC TESTING PHASE

The first awareness that the family may have a heritable illness can dawn in many different ways—from popular media, from a physician, in a science class, from a family member with a new diagnosis. It can come at a time of transition in the family life cycle, such as when considering marriage or having a baby. It happens with a backdrop of strengths, stories, losses, and other psychosocial challenges of life. Patients turn to their primary care physicians, geneticists, or genetic counselors to gain more information about the illness and understand their possible risk. A skill for medical family therapists is understanding the potential genetic condition in the context of family illness history, illness meanings, and life transitions.

Dealing with familial illness risk is not a rational process; data alone will not produce healthy decision making. Miller (1995, 2006) studied the way people cope with genetic testing and genetic information. She described two kinds of coping. The first is like Sally's avoidant behavior in our opening example, which Miller called *blunting behavior*. Blunting is distracting from, delaying, or avoiding what may be threatening cues. People with blunting behavior may minimize or avoid genetic information, denying its importance. A more extreme example involved a man who tested positive for the gene but lied to his family about his results. He used blunting behavior to cope with his anxiety. Most people with blunting behavior minimize such that they never seek genetic testing or therapy. They do not seek information as a form of coping and undergo testing or therapy only when brought in by family members or when their disease process becomes so significant that the denial doesn't work anymore. Their minimizing behaviors may require confrontation.

What is the expected outcome if prevention or intervention does not occur? Genetic and nongenetic family members (e.g., a spouse) may help increase these patients' concern and support them through screening, genetic testing, or surveillance during the nonsymptomatic phase.

The second style of coping with health information is *monitoring behavior*, which involves scanning for and amplifying threatening cues. People with monitoring behavior tend to feel more anxious and vulnerable to disease. They seek information, but with the danger of becoming overwhelmed by it. The implications for medical family therapy are that people using monitoring styles of coping benefit from targeted information and support. Family members, especially non–genetically linked family members such as a spouse, can be useful in recording important information during genetic counseling and providing support to decrease anxiety in their loved one.

Sometimes genetic testing is not available or revealing of a disorder. For example, Lynn, a 33-year-old woman who came to medical family therapy with Greg, her 45-year-old boyfriend, was referred by her geneticist, Dr. Shin. Lynn has a rare, progressive genetic condition that has resulted in blindness and difficulty with balance. She badly wanted to marry and have children. The single biggest reason that adults say they want to choose to get tested for the genetic condition is to know for the sake of their children, present or planned. Greg was divorced and said he loved Lynn but only wanted to marry and have children if he could be assured that they have better than even chances that Lynn would not pass along the gene(s) for her disorder. Greg lived in a rural community and commuted to work an hour away in a city. He envisioned a blind wife with balance problems trying to care for an infant who might also have special needs, with him miles away. The meaning of the illness to this couple was interwoven with their transition to marriage. In extreme monitoring mode, Lynn had $30,000 worth of genetic tests at genetics centers across the country, without any conclusive diagnosis. The couple and their physicians were focused on diagnosis and a degree of certainty that was not available. As can happen in cancer treatment, the geneticists wanted to try one more test, but nothing was illuminating.

The sheer expense this couple had put out was amazing. With each failed test, the strain on their relationship increased. By the time they were seen in medical family therapy, Lynn was begging Greg to adopt an optimistic viewpoint about their future. Greg held firm, based on his temperament, his preferred coping strategies, and his past failed marriage. He wanted more certainty this time around.

The couple had lost their nonillness identity; they were overly focused on the genetic tests and not dealing with the reality of their relationship. As in all medical family therapy, collaboration with other health professionals is key. The geneticist and medical family therapist shared their mutual frustration. Although a specific plan did not emerge from this phone call, the couple came to therapy changed after seeing Dr. Shin. They said the physician explained the risk using new and different language, and they now understood that it was unlikely that any test would provide the information they wanted. They found this both disappointing and a relief. The rest of the session involved exploring more about their relationship and the possibility of marriage while being more uncertain of the future than is typical of couples planning a wedding.

Over three sessions, Greg withdrew more and more. It became obvious that he did not want to marry and that this was only in part due to Lynn's genetic condition. Lynn was heartbroken but glad for the clarification as the deadlock seemed as if it could have gone on endlessly. In a postsession phone call, Dr. Shin said to the medical family therapist,

> I listened to how you talked about the couple and the illness, and realized that I needed to express the risk to them in a different way. The standard way of communicating about genetic risk was leading this couple to think we'd eventually find the answer.

Collaborating allowed these professionals to unhinge this couple from their problem and, in this case, from each other. Medical family therapists can work with primary care physicians, geneticists, and genetic counselors to provide psychoeducation and support to patients and families considering genetic testing.

GAINING THE INFORMATION: THE GENETIC TESTING AND POSTTESTING PHASE

The decision to have genetic testing typically provokes a personal crisis, and often a family one. Family members must learn about the illness, who is at risk, and who to include in decision making, and then decide whether to test, not to test, or defer the decision altogether. This means considering the implications of genetic testing results for those who test positive as well as those who test negative. Once tested, the knowledge is permanent. This is similar to how people often felt about being tested for HIV in the 1980s and 1990s before good medications were available. They tried to imagine whether it would be beneficial to learn of their status, and often their expectations about how they would respond did not correspond to their feelings following a test result.

Lisa was a 48-year-old woman who was diagnosed with colorectal cancer, first at age 22 and then age 44. She was successfully treated both times. She went for genetic testing because so many of her family members had had the disease.

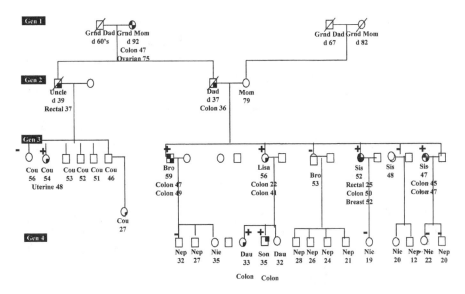

Figure 12.2. Pedigree of a family with colorectal cancer mutation. Bro = brother; Dau = daughter; Grnd = grand; Nep = nephew; Nie = niece; Sis = sister.

The patient's family history is shown in the pedigree, a genogram-like tool used by geneticists to track genetic disorders and mutations. (See Figure 12.2. Darkened pie shapes within the circles or squares depict a cancer diagnosis.) A dramatic case because it occurs in a large family, this pedigree illustrates the variety of issues that can be experienced across a number of smaller families. Lisa's father was only 36 when he became symptomatic with colon cancer. He had a history of alcoholism. Lisa's mother had pressured her father to go to the doctor for several months but, using blunting behavior, he resisted. Her mother had a history of panic disorder, exacerbated by the father's cancer diagnosis. Neither mother nor father explained the nature of the illness to their six young children. The father died tragically young, a year later.

It was not until Lisa was diagnosed with colon cancer at age 22 that the family began to consider a hereditary susceptibility to colorectal cancer. Lisa was the mother of a young child, increasing the emotional trauma of the diagnosis and treatment. The diagnosis also made it clear that two sets of cousins might be affected by a genetic mutation—the children of her father and the children of her uncle. The two extended families had not spoken for several years since a family business dispute erupted between their fathers. However, it became clear that more information needed to be collected about previous generations and shared between the families. In addition to their paternal grandmother, who was diagnosed with colon cancer at 47, Lisa's father's brother had colon cancer diagnosed at 39. Lisa's was the first case of colorectal cancer in Generation III, and the fourth case of known early-onset colorectal cancer in the family. Because of the increased risk of ovarian cancer with this mutation, the patient and her next-younger sister requested prophylactic oophorectomies and scheduled their surgeries at the same time to provide each other mutual support.

Lisa's older brother then was diagnosed with colon cancer at age 47. He reconnected with his siblings and cousins after many years of bitter unresolved conflict. The experience of genetic testing motivated him to reach out to distant siblings and cousins and share information as well as support. In addition, he feared for his children and the other children in the next generation. He began an active educational campaign for these cousins and strongly endorsed genetic testing. This campaign created tension with his two youngest sisters, who were reluctant for their children to be burdened with this worry in their early 20s. Undaunted, Lisa and her next-younger sister prioritized information sharing and informed decision making in all their conversations with family members.

Lisa's youngest sister's cancer diagnosis came in the midst of a particularly troubling time in her marriage. She feared her husband's anger about their financial problems and worried about making genetic testing available to her children. In fact, testing was provided free as part of a study.

Many families with a genetic condition have theories or beliefs about who is likely to inherit the responsible mutation. The medical family therapist worked to surface this family's hypotheses: that the mutation alternated such that if the oldest did get it, the next one wouldn't, the next would, and so on; other family members believed (as is common) that those bearing a physical resemblance to an affected member means one will have the mutation; some believed, half humorously, it might relate to whether they had a crooked pinkie finger; still others believed that those with the strongest religious faith would test positive for the genetic condition as they could best manage the suffering.

When genetic testing became available, a family meeting was held to inform all members about the mutation and available testing. Health professionals at the meeting included the geneticist, the genetic counselor, and two medical family therapists (because of the family's size). Out of a potential 37 family members, 28 attended, representing four generations and the two extended families of the deceased brothers. Information about the mutation was provided by a video, followed by education by the geneticist and genetic counselor. Then one of the medical family therapists facilitated an hour-long discussion about the meaning of the mutation and genetic testing to individuals and the family. The therapists urged family members to respect individual differences in decision making. They also asked about previously successful coping styles in dealing with stressful decisions. The discussion was videotaped and shared, along with the informational video, with those who could not attend and wished to view them.

At the end of the first meeting, the family was offered follow-up meetings at an interval that was appropriate to their needs. They requested quarterly family meetings, which continued for 2 years. Drawing on the work of Gonzalez, Steinglass, and Reiss (1989) on psychoeducational groups for patients with chronic illness, the first 15 to 20 minutes of these meetings started with the geneticist communicating any new research or information and answering questions about the colorectal genetic mutation. He left, and the medical family therapists worked to increase family support and constructive communication and deal with issues of loss for the final hour.

The family argued over whether others had the right to ask about genetic testing results, with some feeling that being asked was a form of caring and others feeling intruded on unless they offered the information themselves. The family reported that the mood of holiday and birthday gatherings changed significantly as family members shifted the focus of conversation away from children's school and sporting accomplishments to recent screenings, genetic testing, prophylactic surgeries, or future health concerns. The medical family therapists encouraged the family to return to their usual rituals and routines so that genomics did not overshadow these celebrations.

Before genetic testing for the colorectal mutation, family members felt anxious about having a heightened risk for this cancer and felt pressure to undergo regular surveillance by colonoscopy. All went in the early years, then about half stopped going, wanting to avoid any bad news. However, when DNA testing became available, seven of 12 cousins took advantage of it. One chose testing without telling his siblings or cousins because, unaffected with cancer at 56, he suspected he lacked the family mutation and felt guilty about testing negative when his brother and so many of his cousins were testing positive.

Two sisters, unlike most of their generation, were not having regular colonoscopies and generally coped using blunting behavior. After much coaxing, the two agreed to genetic testing. Their DNA tests revealed no mutations. The youngest son of Lisa's uncle declined testing even though it was provided free as part of the study, and he also dissuaded his children from testing, apparently finding the prospect too threatening. The year after this decision, his daughter was diagnosed with late-stage colon cancer at the age of 27, a wrenching outcome for the family.

For members of Generation III who had genetic testing and tested positive, the testing of their children was a far more emotional topic than their own testing. Had they transmitted the mutation to future generations? As to Generation IV, many preferred not to think about the issue, feeling "too young" to confront mortality so squarely. Some older members of that generation decided only to have colonoscopy surveillance. One related the decision to her fitness to have children, feeling that "if I test positive, I can't have children." Although prenatal diagnosis was available, she did not find pregnancy termination acceptable because of her religious beliefs.

The diagnosis of cancer in a female cousin at age 27 suddenly made the risk of early-onset cancer dramatically clear to Generation IV. The fact that the cancer was inoperable when diagnosed made it doubly threatening. It also revealed that her father, who had refused genetic testing, was a mutation carrier. The father became depressed and withdrawn with the news. Generation IV began seeking more active surveillance and genetic testing.

Testing of the next generation was especially difficult for Lisa. Two of her three children were found to have the mutation, the only ones to test positive in Generation IV on this side of the family. "The risk is not 50:50 for our family!" she lamented. Her daughters expected to test positive because they look like their mother. (One did test positive, and one did not.) Her son expected to test negative because he looks like his father, but he agreed to have DNA testing to please his mother. When he tested positive, it shattered the family myth of resemblance. The oldest daughter proceeded with a colonoscopy immediately after testing positive; cancer was identified and surgically removed. The family struggled to balance the burden of carrier status with the relief of catching a cancer diagnosis much sooner than it otherwise would have been detected. This family felt vindicated for their "knowledge is power" position.

Two of the cousins requested individual psychotherapy as a result of issues presented in the family meetings. One brother attended a few sessions to address issues related to guilt of passing on the genetic mutation to his children. Lisa continued in longer term individual and couples therapy focused on the multiple challenges of managing the genetic condition in her family as well as unresolved conflict and loss from many years of a troubled marriage and childhood trauma.

INTEGRATING THE RESULTS: LONG-TERM ADAPTATION

The long-term adaptation of families with knowledge of genetic mutations remains to be studied. At the request of a breast cancer genetics researcher, two medical family therapists developed a 6-week psychoeducational group for women who had tested positive a year earlier in his study (Speice, McDaniel, Rowley, & Loader, 2002). The group was composed of nine women, including two sisters and one woman and her niece. They ranged in age from 32 to 60. Three were nonsymptomatic, and six already had survived cancer.

The format of the groups was similar to that described earlier for the extended family meetings for those at risk for familial colorectal cancer; they also bear some resemblance to the medical groups visits that are common in primary care. The first 15 minutes of each group was spent with the geneticist and genetic counselor answering questions and communicating any new information about the gene, the disease, or its treatment. The next 75 minutes were on topics developed by the women themselves in the first session, which included family reactions to genetic testing—their partners, their children, and their extended families; disclosure—who in the family is also at risk, who to tell and when; confidentiality with insurers and in the workplace; their own emotional reactions and coping strategies; body image; and relationships with physicians.

The sessions were emotionally intense. The women were initially hesitant but then quickly bonded with each other as they discovered their shared experiences and felt understood in this way for the first time. They felt a powerful sense of communion in a situation that had left them feeling quite alone. Many issues related to facing one's mortality, including spouses who distanced themselves or children who became angry at their own potential vulnerability. One woman was distressed at the conflict and cutoff that occurred when, after her urging, her adult son tested positive for both BRCA1 and two genetic mutations, increasing his daughters' chances of carrying one or more of the mutations and eventually developing cancer. Her son's wife said, "Now when I look at my daughters, I see death on their faces. I'm angry at what you've done to our future." Most of the women in the group had taken prophylactic measures, such as preventive mastectomies, that they believed would prolong their lives. The woman whose son quit talking to her said, "I'm glad I had the testing, because it's education that's keeping me alive. For me it's important, but now I feel guilty that I pushed so hard with my kids."

The women in this group were functioning well in their lives. Given the breast cancer in their families, they expected to have the mutation. They all received good pregenetic test counseling. However, 100% of these women said that they vastly underestimated what it would mean to them to know they were positive for the breast cancer mutations.

Long-term adaptation takes on different meaning when confronted by traditional, single gene disorders, such as Huntington's disease. For example, Jill is the wife of Joe, whose family has a history of Huntington's. Jill first presented alone, requesting support for herself and couples therapy. Joe had been in individual therapy for some time, mostly focused on work-related issues. They were referred by the couple's internist.

Jill was sad in the session as she discussed her love for her husband and her fears for his health. Jill and Joe had two children, ages 12 and 9 (see Figure 12.3). As it happened, both were adopted after a long and painful period of infertility. When Joe's mother was diagnosed with Huntington's disease, Jill said, for the first time they both felt the infertility was a blessing. At least they did not have to worry about their children having the disease.

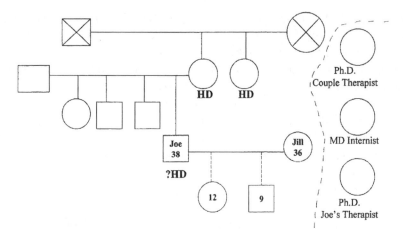

Figure 12.3. A couple facing Huntington's disease.

Jill reported that their physician told the couple, without any obvious cause, that she felt it was unlikely Joe had inherited the disease. When the therapist called the physician, she admitted that she had been positive with the couple about Joe's chances to escape Huntington's, saying rather sheepishly, "Well, I just really don't want him to have it." The physician was clearly relieved to have both these patients in psychotherapy and agreed to work together as they moved toward a decision on genetic testing.

In the individual session, Jill wept as she spoke about being hyper-vigilant and then annoyed whenever Joe's behavior was out of line, from twitching while asleep to forgetting his keys. She monitored him closely, saying, "I ask myself every time, 'Are these problems normal husband and wife issues, or does Joe have Huntington's?'" Genetic testing would provide an answer to that question. However, after several individual and couples sessions, Jill and Joe came to the conclusion that although they had a loving and com-mitted relationship, they wanted to strengthen their marital communication before going through testing. They worked for 2 years to increase their sense of agency and communion. At the end of that time, the couple said they were functioning much better and decided together that they did not want to go through testing. They would rather not know.

As mentioned, Huntington's is progressive, terminal, and there is currently no treatment. For some, the uncertainty is worse; for others like Joe and Jill, the knowledge is worse. Given the prognosis for Huntington's disease, perhaps it is not surprising that studies show significant discrepancies for at-risk people between their intentions to get tested and their actual testing behavior. In one study, only 10% to 20% of individuals at risk for the disorder actually sought genetic testing (Craufurd, Dodge, Kerzin-Storrar, & Harris, 1989), whereas several studies of large families with known breast cancer mutations found test uptake of 35% to 43% (Lerman, Croyle, Tercyak, & Hamann, 2002). The most interesting and robust studies on psychosocial aspects of genetic testing find that it is the *perceived* risk, rather than the scientific risk, that influences behavior, decision making, and the emotional outcome after testing (Lerman, 2002). It is the *meaning* people make of these data, not the data themselves, that affects how they respond and what they do about it.

Four years after this course of medical family therapy, Jill and Joe called for an appointment. They came because Joe had finally gotten tested and they were having trouble adjusting to the results: He was negative! They talked about all the behaviors and issues they had attributed to Huntington's that now belonged to Joe or to their relationship. Jill had to adjust to having a partner who may live a long and healthy life. They were amazed at how difficult it was to absorb the good news. Joe talked about how he now has to take responsibility for losing his keys or other behaviors that both he and his wife attributed to likely Huntington's. Jill, for her part, had to become accustomed to the likelihood that her husband would live a long time. Several medical family therapy sessions were spent rewriting their family narrative, which changed significantly as a result of this genetic test.

COLLABORATING WITH A GENETIC HEALTH CARE TEAM

The most effective and comprehensive approach for the care of people with genetic disorders and their families involves collaboration among an interdisciplinary genetic health care team that includes primary care physicians and nurse practitioners; geneticists; genetic counselors; specialists such as surgeons, diabetologists, and pulmonologists; and clergy with medical family therapists. Figure 12.4 describes how a patient with the suspicion of a genetic disorder might encounter health professionals, from a continuity relationship with a primary care clinician, medical family therapist, or clergy, to periodic contact with a geneticist, genetic counselor, and medical or surgical specialist or subspecialist. The bidirectional arrows between professionals indicate the importance of communication and collaboration for optimal team functioning.

Primary care clinicians and medical family therapists may have both longitudinal and contextual knowledge of a patient and family that is directly relevant to identifying and understanding the meaning of genetic information to a patient and a family. The genetic specialty team (geneticist, genetic counselors, and nurses) has a more focused role of providing genetic counseling, diagnosis, and education. The primary care clinician cares for their overall, long-term health needs. A medical specialist may treat the genetic disorder.

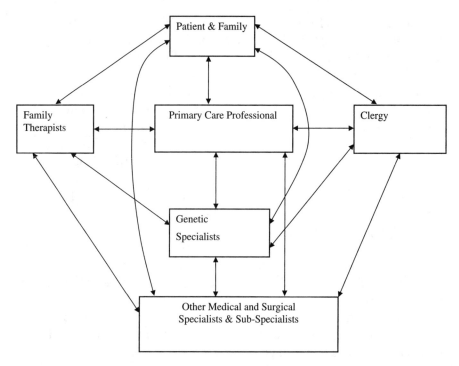

Figure 12.4. The health care team for genetic disorders. From *Individuals, Families, and the New Era of Genetics: Biopsychosocial Perspectives* (p. 531), edited by S. M. Miller, S. H. McDaniel, J. S. Rolland, & S. L. Feetham, 2006, New York, NY: W. W. Norton & Company. Copyright 2006 by W. W. Norton & Company. Adapted with permission.

The medical family therapist supports family strengths to manage stress at various stages of the process, from considering genetic testing to challenges presented by the illness.

This work is emotionally challenging for geneticists, genetic counselors, and medical family therapists alike. For one, we all have genetic mutations, even if most of us are unaware of what they are. It was only at his funeral that we discovered the geneticist who referred the women in the breast cancer mutation group himself was diagnosed with melanoma during the same year that he made this referral. The women were not the only ones suffering.

Similarly, while taking a genetics course, a medical student found that both her grandmother and her aunt had the genetic mutation for breast cancer. Because of her interest in biomedicine, she was tested at age 23. She tested positive as well, then took an emotional nosedive, unprepared for the psychosocial aspects of having the information. For the medical family therapist as well, this work raises issues about how much one wants to know, comfort with uncertainty, and biological connections with other family members. It is a humbling experience. None of us knows for sure how we would handle the emotional crucible experienced by the patients described in this chapter.

CONCLUSION

The science of genomics is far ahead of our understanding of the human experience with these biotechnical interventions. This is the place where biology, ethics, and psychosocial responses collide. Medical family therapists are especially well-trained to deal with genetic concerns because of their family and relationship implications. We can make important contributions to helping families with decision making, coping with uncertainty, and integrating genetic information into their existing identities. We also can make important contributions to helping other genetic health professionals understand the complex patient and family experience, and we can augment their medical knowledge with ethical, emotional, and interpersonal considerations when dealing with genetic conditions.

13

CAREGIVING, END OF LIFE CARE, AND LOSS

Caregiving is not easy. It consumes time, energy, and financial resources. It sucks out strength and determination. It turns simple ideas of efficacy and hope into big question marks. It can amplify anguish and desperation. It can divide the self. It can bring out family conflicts. It can separate out those who care from those who won't or can't handle it. It is very difficult. Caregiving is also a defining moral practice. It is a practice of empathic imagination, responsibility, witnessing, and solidarity with those in great need. It is a moral practice that makes caregivers, and at times even the care-receivers, more present and thereby fully human. (Kleinman, 2009, p. 293)

Families caring for their ill or elderly members has always been part of life. What is new in the United States is the significant growth of professional and lay information about family caregiving, reflecting a cultural recognition of the importance and needs of those who provide care. This burgeoning includes information about family supports and resources,[1] formal recognition by medical communities, and legislative supports in the United States, like the Family Medical Leave Act (1993) and the National Family Caregiver Support Program (2000).

The reality is that more than 65 million people, or 29% of the U.S. population, provide care for a chronically ill, disabled, or aged family member

---

[1]Many nonprofit associations are devoted to caregiving; websites and blogs provide information and support to patients and families experiencing all kinds of diseases. See, for example, the website of the National Family Caregivers Association (http://www.nfcacares.org).

http://dx.doi.org/10.1037/14256-013
Medical Family Therapy and Integrated Care, Second Edition, by S. H. McDaniel, W. J. Doherty, and J. Hepworth

or friend during a year and spend an average of 20 unpaid hours per week doing so (National Alliance for Caregiving in collaboration with the AARP, 2009). The same surveys indicate that more than two thirds of caregivers are women and two thirds of all caregivers are employed outside the home. The emotional, social, economic, and health pressures on these families are impressive. It is no surprise that caregiving stress is a frequent presenting concern to medical family therapists, who can help families attend to issues of burden, loss, mourning, and death.

The medical community is also recognizing the increasing role of caregivers as important parts of treatment teams. The American College of Physicians, the largest U.S. medical specialty organization, with the endorsement of nine other medical organizations, issued a position paper on ethical guidance to develop mutually supportive patient–physician–caregiver relationships (Mitnick, Leffler, & Hood, 2010). This landmark article noted how traditional medical ethics has focused on the patient–physician relationship in isolation from family and social relationships. The guidelines highlight communication and information strategies that are supportive and inclusive of caregivers, with hallmarks including the following:

- Respect for patients' dignity, rights, and values should guide all interactions.
- Physician accessibility and excellent communication are fundamental for support.
- Caregivers are recognized as sources of continuity, information, and care and require support for maximum quality of life.
- Caregivers who are health care professionals should not be expected to function in professional capacities but be supported as caregivers.

These ethical guidelines highlight that there are potential tensions when caregivers, patients, and health care clinicians differ in their expectations for care. The guidelines also identify the importance of family roles, particularly boundary challenges that can occur when family members are also health professionals. This chapter describes some of the significant pressures for families who care for adults coping with significant chronic illness, disability, terminal illness, and advanced age. We present clinical strategies for working with the spouses, partners, adult children, and other family members who provide care for their loved ones. Because caregiving is especially important at the end of life, this chapter also considers the impact of loss and death and describes strategies to help families support one another at times of bereavement.

THE EXPERIENCES OF CAREGIVERS

Geena, a 56-year-old administrator, initiated therapy with a medical family therapist when her husband, Carl, retired because of small strokes and a cardiac condition. The strokes appeared to result in cognitive impairments, but consultations with multiple specialists, neurologists, and psychiatrists led to no clear diagnosis or prognosis. Geena's presenting emotion was frustration—frustration at the health care system that could provide no clear answer or treatment; frustration at her husband for his cognitive lapses, his decreasing abilities, and lack of interest in fighting for his health; and frustration at others who did not understand how difficult her life had become.

For more than 4 years, Geena continued monthly therapy sessions. Initially, she was an advocate for her husband with the health care teams, pushing them to provide tests and possible answers. Over time, her sense of both agency and communion grew. She learned to better accept the difficulty of uncertainty and acknowledged her husband's progressive decline, as well as his diagnosis of dementia. Geena expanded her emotional statements beyond frustration to loss, grief, powerlessness, sadness, and isolation. One of her most difficult daily experiences, she said, was "to have him there in body, but to no longer have him there." As she accepted that there was no cure, she also learned to provide better care—for him and for herself.

Through her work with a medical family therapist, Geena created life structures to support both of them for what may be many more years of significant caregiving. She arranged for Carl to attend a day-care program for adults with dementia so that she could continue to work. She worked part time, so that she had 2 days each week when he was in care and she had some time off. She used to be frustrated when he did not seem to be able to participate in simple conversations with others. She would make explanations for him but no longer feels she must "cover" for him with friends and family. She is less likely to take his angry outbursts as personal attacks, and she also provides clear feedback and helps him limit those outbursts. Geena and Carl regularly visit her brother and sister-in-law, who live in a warmer state, and Geena and Carl's adult children and grandchildren stay with Carl for days at a time so Geena can take mini-vacations with women friends. Geena acknowledges that she is doing the right things for her husband and that she will be able to look back and know she stepped up. For that, there is some satisfaction; still, it is very hard.

These multiple conflicting feelings of caregivers become the core discussions in medical family therapy. Caregivers are often told that they are strong or noble. They also are the recipients of suggestions about how they could do things differently. Friends say, "Call if there is anything I can do."

Yet many caregivers are reluctant to burden others and wait for the offers of specific help, which often do not come.

Even when family and friends are confidants, caregivers may not feel free to disclose how difficult, frustrated, tired, or lonely they feel. Therapists can encourage them to accept the full gamut of their ambivalent feelings and also consider options for care and respite for themselves and their family member. Sometimes medical family therapy with caregiving families includes the person with illness or disability. Sessions for caregivers only are also common because they need to speak honestly, without worrying about hurting their ill family member (McDaniel & Pisani, 2012).

Caregivers: The Hidden Patients

The physically well member is often a "hidden patient" whose needs or suffering is not expressed directly to professionals. Health care clinicians are taught to encourage self-care for caregivers, reminding them that it is frequently "a marathon, not a sprint." But the more observable and present needs of an ill person can lead therapists, as well as the caregivers themselves, to minimize the caregiver's needs, particularly for those caregivers who seem to be coping fairly well.

Yet the deleterious medical and psychological consequences of long-term family caregiving on caregivers are well documented (Schulz & Beach, 1999), including increased risk for depression, poorer physical health, and mortality. Women, especially, have unreasonable and unhealthy expectations that they should manage the roles alone (McDaniel & Cole-Kelly, 2003). When the caregiver is in the workforce, the stress is multiplied.

With dementia, stress is particularly great, including the amount of work (caregiver burden) and conflicted feelings related to balancing the caregiving and other roles (caregiving strain; Hunt, 2003; Ory, Hoffman, & Yee, 1999). Chronically ill elderly spouses caring for a spouse with Alzheimer's dementia, for example, have a 63% higher mortality than peers with the same illnesses who are not caregivers (Schulz & Beach, 1999). Loneliness and isolation increase because caregivers are unable to continue social activities and friends often do not know how to respond. In Vachon et al.'s (1977) study, widows described a "social death" as friends drifted away throughout the lengthy terminal phase of their husbands' cancer.

Caregiver support programs, fortunately, can make a difference. For example, caregiver support programs can effectively delay the institutionalization of a loved one with Alzheimer's dementia (Mittelman, Haley, Clay, & Roth, 2006). The REACH program (Schulz et al., 2003), which uses structured sessions with trained facilitators and focuses on problem-solving skills and support, showed modest but significant benefits for caregivers, as well as improved relationships between caregivers and their family member. Medical family therapists should be leaders or resources for these groups. Some medical family therapists find that such participation is an important way of building a medical family therapy practice.

Family psychoeducation groups provide information and support for those coping with a range of illnesses (Gonzalez & Steinglass, 2002; Steinglass, 1998) or for specific illnesses such as cancer (Kim & Givern, 2008), chronic pain (Lemmens, Eisler, Heireman, Van Houdenhove, & Sabbe, 2005) or asthma (Wamboldt & Levin, 1995). Many multiple family group programs include multiple sessions that enable families to learn about illnesses, coping styles, and receive support from others experiencing similar conditions. Attendance at sessions may have community-building benefits but can be difficult logistically. Even a 1-day, multiple-family group program for families with a child with cancer has been beneficial in reducing stress symptoms of family members. The Surviving Cancer Competently Intervention Program focuses on improving communication about cancer and its treatment and altering family beliefs (Kazak, 2005; Kazak et al., 1999).

Caring for adult children with illness or disability has particular burdens. Mr. and Mrs. Keith, a couple in their early 60s, cared for their son, Dan, age 29, who had a rare, painful form of severe arthritis. In a wheelchair, the young man sometimes was able to do things for himself. Other times his parents needed to use a lift to help move him from bed to wheelchair or bedside commode. At one hospitalization, Dan asked his physician to help him talk with his father about Mr. Keith's increasing anger and verbal abuse to him and his mother. The physician asked a medical family therapist to lead the family meeting, in which the father hotly denied that he yelled or threatened.

As the therapist talked about the stress on caregiver families, the family described how the father's anger had worsened during the past year or two. Mr. Keith responded well to the metaphor of a frog that stays in increasingly hot water because it becomes gradually accustomed to more heat. He seemed to soften as he agreed that in his case the stress had gradually increased, as had the expression of his frustration and anger. When he was informed that between 40% and 70% of caregivers have clinically significant depressive symptoms (Family Caregiver Alliance, 2006), Mr. Keith agreed to a depression screening, medication, and initiation of marital therapy to address the unhelpful patterns of communication that had developed in response to the stress and his depression.

The use of statistics in this example is a strategy to help normalize the stress of caregiving. It is especially valuable for clients such as Dan's father, who was initially resistant to any psychological intervention for himself. Families are more likely to consider care when they realize that their responses are not unique. Families can be better informed that stress, and even depression, is a common response to uncommon conditions.

Families with adult children, like Dan, anticipate caregiving responsibilities that can go on for decades. This is equally true for young spouses when their partners have nonfatal but severe illness or trauma-related disabilities. Not only must they balance the needs of the ill or disabled person with the needs of other family members, they must also make long-term arrangements for care when the caregivers can no longer provide it. Families need significant support as they face difficult decisions about future living situations for the loved one, willingness of other family members such as adult siblings to participate or assume care, and legal arrangements to ensure care over time.

Long-term illness and disability result in many kinds of loss for the patient and the family. When the person does die, especially after a long period of caregiving, the family must adjust to this final loss, as well as to the absence of caregiving. They move on to a period of bereavement.

The End of Caregiving—Helping Families Cope With Loss

Medical family therapists assist patients and families anticipating or experiencing loss, encouraging families to consider their options proactively and to assist one another with their pain. To help families, medical family therapists must consider the cultural meanings of illnesses, unique family explanatory models, and hesitancies about dealing with death. Walsh and McGoldrick's (1991) edited book was the first family therapy book that dealt with families' experiences of loss from death. Much more has been written since that time (Boss & Carnes, 2012; McGoldrick & Walsh, 2004), but some therapists still find it difficult to initiate discussions about death and loss.

Our cultural reluctance about dealing with death is mirrored in our use of language. Phrases such as "passed away," "gone on," and "no longer with us" help avoid the uncomfortable acknowledgment. If therapists are reluctant to broach discussions of loss, families will follow their lead and avoid the painful but important conversations. Psychiatrist Elisabeth Kübler-Ross (1969) challenged these cultural patterns of avoidance. She encouraged health care providers and general audiences to face their discomfort, discuss death with those who are dying and surviving, and use language that reflects the reality of death. Kübler-Ross (1975) described a social worker's recognition of the avoidance:

> One of the main reasons why many of us avoid any talk of death is the awful and unbearable feeling that there is nothing we can say or do to comfort the patient. I had a similar problem in working with many aged and infirm clients in the past years. I always felt that old age and sickness was so devastating, that although I wanted to communicate hope to them, I only communicated despair. It seemed to me that the problem of

illness and death was so insolvable and therefore these people could not be helped. (p. xvi)

Oncologists, whose medical specialty requires that they deal with death, also can compartmentalize their grief over the death of patients (Granek, Tozer, Mazzotta, Ramjaun, & Krzyzanowska, 2012). The physicians described a tension between being close enough to patients to care about them but being distant enough to avoid the pain of loss. *Denial* and *dissociation* were noted as coping strategies, as was their tendency to withdraw from patients as they became closer to death.

Many medical professionals react to death of others with at least two responses. Death represents that unwanted recognition of one's own mortality. However, death of a patient also carries a sense of professional failure for many, even when the death could not be prevented. Thus, it is understandable that medical professionals often hide behind life-sustaining technology rather than face the emotions of impending loss. Fortunately, the increased use of palliative care and hospice services helps to mediate this tension and provides much needed care for families.

In a speech to an annual meeting of hospice teams, a long-term medical director (Zagieboylo, 2012) noted that when asked, most people claim to want to die suddenly and painlessly, in their sleep. He noted that a sudden death of this nature may be good for the person who dies, but it often leaves family members wishing they had the opportunities that were lost. For those with a more chronic course, hospice work enables the person who is dying, as well as the family, to be more intentional about their choices and what they want to share with one another.

Medical family therapy also provides opportunities for families to be intentional whenever possible. It helps families face the full spectrum of challenges throughout caregiving and loss. Yet it is not easy clinical work. Just as caregiving is hard on families, therapists must be prepared to work with caregivers and families throughout some of the most painful periods of their lives. Kleinman's (2009) comments about caregiving providing "opportunities for witness and solidarity with those in great need" (p. 293) are also true for therapists. With families experiencing loss, we have the opportunity to "be more present and more fully human." The remainder of this chapter identifies clinical strategies and offers examples to help caregivers and families negotiate these challenges of caregiving and, when the time comes, bereavement and loss.

CLINICAL STRATEGIES TO HELP CAREGIVERS

Exhibit 13.1 outlines clinical strategies to help caregivers. These are discussed in detail in the following subsections.

EXHIBIT 13.1
Clinical Strategies to Help Caregivers

Provide psychoeducation and link families with resources.
Normalize changes in family dynamics.
Facilitate agency for patients and families.
Help families tolerate ambiguity.
Help families share caregiving roles.
Help families deal with unfinished emotional concerns.
Inquire about spirituality and encourage rituals.
Help families face the inevitability of death.
Share the family's loss.

Provide Psychoeducation and Link Families With Resources

By the time caregivers come to therapy, they generally feel they are failing or at least not coping well with what should be normal life transitions. We cannot underestimate the power of a therapist reminding caregivers that they are not unusual in being overwhelmed with stresses and concerns and that their work is particularly difficult. Caregiving is not something that we learn in school. Kleinman (2009), a noted medical anthropologist who wrote about caregiving before he became a caregiver, noted the absence of preparation:

> I learned to be a caregiver by doing it, because I had to do it; it was there to do. I think this is how most people learn to be caregivers. . . . But of course this is also how parents, especially mothers, learn to care for children. (p. 293)

Caregivers may find it helpful to consider what happened many generations ago, when families lived closer to relatives and neighbors, when women generally did not work outside of the home, when caregiving was shared by many, and most significantly, when people with disability and significant chronic illnesses did not live as long, or did not have complicated care procedures and schedules. Therapists can help families realize that they are taking on more responsibilities, and for a longer time, than did generations that preceded them. That awareness is often helpful as people question why they find the role strains and burdens so difficult.

Medical family therapists will not need to know all resources that can be useful for families during caregiving and loss, but we can encourage families to investigate family support groups, websites, and local resources. A list of general organizations that support families can help families get started (see Exhibit 13.2). Families can benefit from meeting with social workers and case managers to learn about and negotiate the multiple programs and resources for which they may be eligible.

Therapists should ask about the family experiences with these resources. It is important to note that not all clients will always find these experiences to be positive. A spouse of a woman with dementia felt, for example, that support groups are depressing because they are full of families who care for family members in advanced stages. Nevertheless, encouraging families to consider respite services, or partial in-home health care, facilitates agency in how they manage care while also helping caregivers sustain themselves over the long term. Therapists can motivate families to continue to include others—to accept the help of others and also do the hard work of asking others to help. The connection with others—communion—supports families to maintain their roles over time.

Normalize Changes in Family Dynamics

Caring for an ill family member changes the relationships among the family. Lovers become nurses, and adult children give directions to their parents. Yet the lovers are not solely nurses, and the adult children will always be the children of the parent. So the relationships are complicated and fraught with ambiguity. They change over time as well. One day the wife with advanced breast cancer who has become used to her husband assisting her with toileting will say that she does not want him to be her nursemaid because she wants to protect him. Or an elderly parent with dementia, who has been sanguine for months about his son's managing his finances, will demand to see his checkbook, and an ugly argument will ensue.

Illness and the stress of caregiving lead not only to role reversals but also to exacerbation of earlier family interaction patterns. It is not uncommon for an elderly parent to prefer the advice of an adult child who lives two states away over the care of the adult child who provides more regular visits and care. Or the sister of the man with pancreatic cancer may feel that her brother's wife does not communicate with her enough. The son who lives far away may fly in and critique the care systems or his sister's decisions. These can reflect people's concern that they are not included, their guilt that they live at a distance, their genuine interest in helping, the recapitulation of sibling patterns from preteen years, or all of these. The stress leads to complicated patterns at a time of heightened family emotions. These patterns occur in a context of a family with its own historical, ethnic, and gendered culture. Context includes verbalized and unsaid perspectives about previous history and concerns about loyalty, inclusion, and equity.

Sophisticated medical family therapists can provide unique opportunities for individuals to disentangle their projections, fears, and emotions and, more important, for families to meet and do this together. This is not always easily resolved but is facilitated when therapists encourage ways for more family members to participate, perhaps through Internet communications, phone, or flexible session times when geographically dispersed family members visit.

Facilitate Agency for Patients and Families

Medical family therapists can assist patients and families in making choices about medical care and communicating their needs to their medical professionals. *Shared decision making* is a process in which clinicians inform and involve patients and families in their care choices. Many families have little experience negotiating care with medical professionals, and although they may have clear ideas about what they want, they may be reluctant to provide input, even when asked. Medical family therapists can help families identify their preferences and approach their providers.

Shared decision making, as generally used in health care contexts, refers to negotiation among the patient and family and the health care team. Seldom is the family a unified decider, however. When families have choices, individual members will differ. The stress of the decision-making context can activate family dynamics, resulting in family conflicts that play out, for example, over how to care for Mom. A common scenario occurs when an adult sibling who has lived on the opposite coast flies in and seems to challenge many of the care decisions that were negotiated with the siblings who live closer. Health care teams become triangulated when family members in conflict try to align the team with their position. The team does not know who to communicate with, or avoids the conflict, such that the intrafamily conflict expands to one that includes the full health care team. This is prime time for medical family therapy interventions within the family and, when possible, inclusion of members of the health care team.

Families enhance agency with open discussions about living wills and clear directions about limits for technological care. Advance directives specify what medical technology is desired during a terminal illness, and health care proxy and power of attorney documents clarify who, other than the patient, is authorized to make necessary medical decisions. With advance discussion, families may avoid the pain experienced by the family we describe next (Hepworth & Harris, 1986).

Ms. Bellum's 63-year-old brother was on life support equipment after his liver cancer had quickly metastasized to his brain, causing large masses and a stroke. His EEG indicated no brain activity, and the family and physicians had agreed to remove the life-sustaining system. However, Ms. Bellum felt that hospital personnel had forced her to be more involved with his death than she desired. In an interview following her brother's death, Ms. Bellum stated:

> [The nurse] kept saying "well, look at him. It is part of accepting it." And I will never forget these things. . . . It was like follow the dots to me. This is where you go to do this, and here we go to do this, and there was no human touch to it. I'm sure she [the nurse] is used to doing this—helping families through this, whatever, the dying process—But to me it was like "well here is our new family and we are going to help you deal with this, and then let's hurry on because we have another family." (Hepworth & Harris, 1986, p. 14)

In this situation, the hospital had implemented a protocol in an attempt to help families. Yet Ms. Bellum remembered the situation as one that removed her choice:

> And I think in order to handle death you have to feel that you are part of it . . . I don't think you should be forced to see someone like that . . . you want to remember him [differently] . . . I think I was being told what to think and to feel and that you'll accept it better if you see him this way. And I don't think you will. I mean I think you sort of know what you can handle. (Hepworth & Harris, 1986, p. 14)

Medical family therapists can help families determine what they can handle and how they want to provide care. Some families choose to provide full care for a severely ill or dying family member at home. Others engage aides, partial day cares, or skilled nursing care settings. Each of these options results in different kinds of stresses for families, whether it is the inability to obtain relief from continuous care, guilt from not always being with the patient, or the stress of travel required to visit the ill relative.

It can be a difficult process for families to learn how to be involved in medical management and to identify how much they want to be involved. The process requires family members to consider honestly their values, beliefs, and priorities. Medical family therapists can be instrumental in facilitating these significant decisions and providing support after decisions are made. Agency is enhanced if a family comes to a decision through negotiation and honest sharing of feelings. Even with great loss, they can recognize that they used this time to consider their values and know that they did not "follow the dots" but responded in ways that they chose.

Help Families Tolerate Ambiguity

Acknowledging ambiguous loss and tolerating uncertainty is adaptive for successful response to chronic illness (Boss & Couden, 2002). Yet Gonzalez, Steinglass, and Reiss (1987) stated that family patterns formulated in response to illness demands are often adhered to rigidly: "It is as if the family believes that any adjustments to the precarious structure of its coping with the illness will bring the whole house down" (p. 2). It is the uncertainty of prognosis or the inability to predict behavior or symptom level that leads to extensive stress. Learning to tolerate the ambiguity and uncertainty is a skill that enables successful caregiving (Boss, 2011). Families need to be flexible enough to accept uncertainty but organized enough to be effective in obtaining information and managing their environment. This is a difficult balance, and one that can be addressed through conversation about how willing family members are to tolerate uncertainty and consider changes in their interactions.

Sometimes therapy can help remove some stressful ambiguity and facilitate communication that has been blocked. Eva, a 78-year-old Italian American woman with metastatic ovarian cancer, did not want to disclose the extent of her cancer to her adult children. The children met with the physician and said they knew their mother was dying, that they wanted to acknowledge it with her, but that she focused solely on how she was going to get better. They wanted to have more "real and intimate" conversations with her but did not know how to do so. After consultation with a medical family therapist, the physician talked first with the patient and explained how worried her children were and that her professional advice was that the adult children would be less stressed if they knew more details of their mother's care. The physician described how this might be something the mother could do for her children. Eva agreed to meet with the children, the physician, and the therapist.

The physician discussed how they all hoped that Eva's health would improve, but they also knew that the cancer was extensive and that it was likely that Eva's life would be significantly shortened. The therapist noted how much the family cared for each other and how they showed their care by protecting each other from hard subjects. A daughter described how she loved her mother and wanted to be able to help her more during this hard time, and Eva agreed that that would be nice. In this situation, the unacknowledged secret had been a barrier between the patient and her family at the very time when all parties were feeling most distressed and vulnerable. Opening up the possibility that they could show their love in ways other than being protective allowed them to have more frank family discussions and include Eva's adult children in decisions about the next stage of care.

Help Families Share Caregiving Roles

The acute stress of illness often means that people jump in and provide care and don't spend much time thinking about how it can be better shared. It is important that the patient, family members, and medical team discuss what kinds of care are needed, who provides each form of care, and how decisions about care are made. When possible, families should arrange caregiving responsibilities so that all family members and friends who wish to be involved in direct care have that opportunity. This is hard work, even for families in which decisions are generally easily made. It is not uncommon, however, for the stress of these decisions to activate past family discord, exemplified by the following case.

Grace Larkman, a 92-year-old widow, was diagnosed with Parkinson's disease. In the previous year, she had begun to experience symptoms of forgetfulness and confusion but had maintained her goal of independent living. Five children and many grandchildren lived within a 1-hour drive and visited frequently. As Ms. Larkman deteriorated, the oldest daughter, Emily, took primary responsibility for her mother's shopping, light cleaning, and daily help. Eventually Emily complained to the physician about the difficulties of managing both her mother's life and her own life. When asked if care could be shared, Emily told the physician that her siblings were not responsible enough to provide care consistently. It took the physician a few visits to convince Emily to meet with her siblings, the physician, and the medical family therapist.

Three visits were held with the five adult siblings. Ms. Larkman attended the first session but was quite disoriented and did not attend subsequent sessions. During the brief therapy, all siblings expressed interest in participating in care but stated that they felt that Emily did things on her own without including them. The therapist did not mention that this was a classic pattern of over- and underfunctioning. The therapist also did not blame Emily for acting like a martyr or tell the siblings they had abdicated care. Instead, the therapist focused on how effective Emily had been and how that had been effective for the early stages of care. The other siblings were able to express their respect for Emily's hard work. The therapist then added that the family care was going to continue and that everyone probably wanted to be involved with decisions and with specific care roles.

The therapist also said that this change for more shared care would be hard. On the basis of experience with other families, the therapist could describe how it was hard for those not previously involved to know what to do or how to help, especially when it seemed like one person or subgroup had a plan. It was hard for the person who previously had provided primary care because it meant that that other family members performed care activities differently from how the primary person might have preferred. Two follow-up sessions helped the adult children identify how they each could participate more and how they could use a daily e-mail to one another to share observations and communicate logistics.

Eighteen months later, Ms. Larkman entered the hospital and died from her illness. While visiting their mother in the hospital, the siblings again met with the therapist and stated how pleased they had been to provide care for their mother during her illness. Certainly they mourned her death, but their joint care had enabled each of them to say goodbye throughout the year. They were also better able to turn to each other for support during their loss.

This case demonstrates two important clinical perspectives for medical family therapists. First, the family needs to be viewed from a nonpathological perspective, and second, the focus is on meeting the family's immediate needs. If the therapy of the Larkman siblings had addressed how they had abdicated responsibility to one sister or how the sister controlled access to care, the family would have resisted change. By focusing on the immediate goal of involving all in care and by minimizing history, the siblings were able to meet their mother's needs quickly. Moreover, the joint care of the mother throughout the year changed the family dynamics as the siblings were all involved and felt more equal to each other. The care of their mother during her terminal illness allowed them to work through some previously unresolved issues, defused potential unresolved grief reactions after her death, and positively affected the future relationships of these family members.

Family conflicts are often exacerbated by the intense stress of terminal illness and are not always alleviated as neatly as the Larkman case. Unfortunately, surviving family members frequently respond to perceived inequities in caregiving or bequests by turning against each other. The conflicts often are repeated family patterns but also may reflect projected anger about having to say goodbye. For some families, it is easier to show rage than sadness.

By meeting a few times with families anticipating or experiencing bereavement, medical family therapists can help limit later family discord. Therapists can facilitate discussion of mourning, describe the kinds of unacceptable feelings that may exist, and discuss the consequences of not acknowledging sadness. Families can recognize each other's contributions and the ways they supported one another during the illness. Family therapists and physicians can remind families about the biological realities of the illnesses and help them limit blame toward each other.

Medical family therapy underscores the importance of creating ways for family members to say goodbye to each other. By caring for the ill person and each other, removing disrupting emotional barriers, and creating meaningful rituals, families have the opportunity to say goodbye. When families can come together, it is sometimes possible to help them use the immediacy of the crisis not only to create meaningful connections but also to modify earlier family patterns.

Help Families Deal With Unfinished Emotional Concerns

The stress of illness often brings up painful or unresolved grief from past losses, particularly traumatic losses, like death of a child, other recent losses, or those where there were questions about causality or quality of medical care. The unresolved grief often manifests itself in distancing or separation from one another. For patients with terminal illness, acknowledging the inevitability of death allows families to "balance their emotional ledger" (Boszormenyi-Nagy & Spark, 1973). Even dying patients who have experienced extended estrangements from family may feel an urgency to reconnect (Walker, 1991). This reconnection does not require that family members share all their past resentments with each other, but it does permit members to consider what is important to say and what is important to let go.

For example, when Maureen Farr knew that she would probably die from breast cancer, she talked with the therapist about some of the conflicts she had experienced with her mother. This discussion allowed Maureen to tell her mother that it had not always been perfect but that she knew she had always been loved. She decided that although her mother's perceived favoritism toward a sister still angered her, she did not need to tell her mother how hurt she had been by the slights. Maureen was pleased that she expressed her concerns to her mother in ways that helped them feel more forgiveness and closeness.

Family members manage losses according to family experiences and myths. Medical family therapist John Byng-Hall (1991) reported that during bereavement, families tend to engage in scripts that repeat past family patterns and may inadvertently lose the opportunity to be truly intimate with one another. Byng-Hall suggested that the intensity of emotions generated during grieving can be used to help family members alter their structure. They may elect corrective scripts that change previous painful patterns and identify treasured memories that allow them to change the family legacy about loss (Bowen, 1991). The dying person has the singular opportunity to pass on hopes for the future and suggestions about how he or she would like to be remembered.

Inquire About Spirituality and Encourage Rituals

One way to enhance agency during chronic illness and bereavement is to help families incorporate their own rituals and spiritual values. Some families may be unaware that they have special beliefs or practices, and the process of selecting desired rituals helps them consider what could be comforting. For some, religious practices provide structured customs for mourning and burying the dead. Other families are not comforted by religious customs or may be reluctant to use conventional rituals, perhaps because they have not been actively involved with a religious group.

After an untimely death of an adult daughter, Evelyn chose to have the funeral at a church. An elderly uncle initially was critical of Evelyn's decision because the family had not attended the church for many years. The pastor was responsive to the mother and agreed that a church service was part of the extended family experience and an appropriate way to respond to their sorrow. Evelyn and the extended family received much comfort from the service, which represented their belief that they were connecting their daughter to the family members who had lived before. Her uncle was surprised by his own appreciation of the church rituals and was grateful that a church service had been chosen.

Rituals are valuable for marking a loss. Family members may be encouraged to go to grave sites of deceased members or create a marker ceremony or "unveiling," as is traditional in the Jewish faith. Rituals also become important during caregiving as a way of creating connection and comfort. One woman sung her ailing husband to sleep every night with a song that they had both sung in a community theater group. She felt connected to him, remembering a time when he was able to participate in the group. He felt reassured by her presence, even though he was sleeping in a hospital bed in a separate room.

Rituals can honor the past, alter the present, and enable the future (Imber-Black, Roberts, & Whiting, 2003) and should be chosen carefully to be meaningful for each family. Therapists can ask families how they will change a holiday celebration, for example, to acknowledge a terminal illness as well as the holiday. A young adult man died in his late 20s from a long-term debilitating illness, 4 months before his brother's wedding. Because some wedding guests had not traveled for the funeral, the family wanted to acknowledge their loss at the wedding. At the wedding dinner, the groom gave a special toast to his deceased brother, and another sibling responded by saying that she knew that their brother would have been pleased at the groom's good fortune.

When therapists help families choose their rituals, the family should guide the creative process. Bagarozzi and Anderson (1989) recommended leaving some details of the proposed rituals undecided. In the family having a wedding soon after the loss of the son, the therapist and engaged couple discussed making a toast at the wedding. It was not decided whether the sibling would respond. In other families, members may meet to agree about where to scatter ashes, for example, but not plan the details of what each will say. By remaining fully responsible for making their practices their own, families devise rich and meaningful acknowledgments.

Help Families Face the Inevitability of Death

Determining when to stop treatment is a patient and family decision taken in consultation with the medical team that can allow family members to directly help their dying family member be more comfortable. Acknowledgment of the inevitability of death also allows families to share their concerns and plans.

Patients with cancer are often placed in the position of choosing to "stop treatment" or to begin a new or different round of chemotherapy or radiation. There is a balance between being optimistic and seeking care and participating longer than a patient can tolerate the discomfort. Families who are physically near may more easily understand the patient's decision not to try another round of chemotherapy. Family members who live farther away or those who have a very different belief in what should be done may have a hard time accepting the patient's choice.

These differences sometimes erupt in conflict, which can lead to long-term discord. Years after losses, it is possible to hear statements such as, "You let Dad stay on a ventilator longer than he ever would have wanted," or "Don't talk to me about cancer treatments. You weren't even willing to let your sister try any new drugs." Medical family therapists help families realize that their understanding of each other's positions and negotiations are important for the immediate care of their family member as well as the long-term health of their family.

Share the Family's Loss

Close to the time of death, medical family therapists should be flexible about ways in which they can be available to families. Therapists may be most helpful if they are willing to meet families in different settings, such as home or hospital, are available for telephone support, and allow the family to decide about timing for future meetings. Families should also have the opportunity to meet with the therapist and physician after the death.

Medical family therapists can also support grieving medical team members. Although the medical family therapist is part of the treatment team, she or he can be the catalyst for encouraging team members to discuss their responses to a particular family and loss. Our physician colleagues have expressed gratitude about our availability to them at these times.

Just as families find it difficult to say goodbye, therapists may have difficulty with the loss of a dying client. Medical family therapists working with terminally ill patients and families should have professional peer support to discuss their feelings of sadness, loss, and helplessness. Therapists can also carefully express these feelings briefly with the families, making sure that families do not need to take care of the therapist. Therapists and physicians may choose, in consultation with the family, to attend funerals or memorial services, which may be healing for both families and professionals.

One of us worked with a family and patient who eventually died of AIDS. When arriving at the funeral, the mother of the young woman asked the therapist and the patient's nurse practitioner to read poems during the service. Some therapy training emphasizes tight boundaries, but this was a time for flexibility. Clearly, the inclusion of the nurse practitioner and the medical family therapist was meaningful for the family, and for the professionals as well.

Medical family therapist Barry Jacobs (2007) described how he frequently "goes incognito" to funerals of patients. Confidentiality of the patient's role as a client extends into death. There may be some family members who know and acknowledge the therapist, but frequently therapists minimize their own reactions and then must cope with their personal loss by speaking with colleagues rather than the community of mourners.

Working with patients and families experiencing loss changes the therapeutic relationship. Therapists and families share intense emotions surrounding loss and usually develop deep respect for one another. Just as families can use the experience of loss to grow closer, more honest, and more appreciative of life, therapists, too, may grow from their experiences of loss.

The Legacy of Caregiving and Loss

Although their roles are stressful, caregivers also report satisfaction in their roles. A review of this research (Kramer, 1997) noted that caregivers generally feel useful and appreciated. In a study of African American caregivers of family members who had suffered strokes, many caregivers described how, after the stroke, they felt more connected to their families, a concept that Pierce (2001) described as coherence. In younger couples in which a spouse required caregiving, both members of the couple reported being closer, stating that caregiving strengthened their relationship (Gordon & Perrone, 2004).

Fred, a patient who knew he was at the end of his life, wrote words that he hoped we would publish. He wanted people to know that there were positive aspects for caregivers, but also for patients who could show care to their families:

> With things as they are, I have been the recipient of much care and profound support. My Spirit is filled with gratitude knowing that I am deeply loved—especially by my wife and children. At some level I always knew that they loved me. I didn't really understand until now how strong that love bond was. So I live life in a constant state of gratitude and knowing, knowing that each hour brings joy—or pain. But now I have a clear mission: That mission is to seek out and find ways to support them as they help

me through the challenges as we walk the path between declining health and living life.

In therapy sessions, caregivers have the opportunity to express their stresses, concerns, and losses. When these emotions are expressed, there is also opportunity for reflection about positive aspects of caregiving. Medical family therapy provides an opportunity for caregivers to consider the full continuum of emotions, including recognition of the choices they have made, the ways in which they supported their family member, and how they contributed to the family legacy about loving and caring for others (Piercy & Chapman, 2001).

> We have each gone through feelings of loss, anger and frustration. We have been marked by a special kind of pain. But we have also experienced a deepening sense of responsibility, gratitude for all that we had lived through together, love, solidarity, and a shared sensibility that we have resisted what is beyond our control and are, individually and collectively, more for it. (Kleinman, 2009, p. 292)

III

CONCLUSION

14

HOW MEDICAL FAMILY THERAPISTS CAN CONTRIBUTE TO THE TRANSFORMATION OF HEALTH CARE

The longer we practice and teach medical family therapy, the more we see it as not just a treatment modality but also as a contribution to the transformation of health care. People the world over want to be treated as a whole person in the context of their family and community. Health professionals and administrators are searching for models that improve quality, cost, and patient experience. This quest for humane, comprehensive, and integrated care is a global one, in places as disparate as Germany, Argentina, Finland, Israel, China, and Japan. Medical family therapy has much to offer in this time of clinical innovation, financial uncertainty, cultural diversity, and scientific advance. In terms of health care economics, the time is right. A crisis is coming if we don't act to change health care in a major way. Here is the summary of the situation by American health care leader Don Berwick and his colleague Andrew Hackbarth (2012):

> No matter how polarized politics in the United States have become, nearly everyone agrees that health care costs are unsustainable. At almost

http://dx.doi.org/10.1037/14256-014
Medical Family Therapy and Integrated Care, Second Edition, by S. H. McDaniel, W. J. Doherty, and J. Hepworth

277

18% of the gross domestic product (GDP) in 2011, headed for 20% by 2020, the nation's increasing health care expenditures reduce the resources available for other worthy government programs, erode wages, and undermine the competitiveness of U.S. industry. Although Medicare and Medicaid are often in the limelight, the health care cost problem affects the private sector just as much as the public. (p. 513)

And that's just the cost factor. There is also a consensus in the United States that we are not getting the quality of health care we need from the excessive amount of money we are spending. The problems range from failure to apply effective treatments in some areas to overtreatment in others, along with health disparities in prenatal services and other central domains of health care (Yong, Saunders, & Olsen, 2010). There is now agreement that we lack effective coordination of the services we do provide (Medicare Payment Advisory Commission, 2007).

If there is acceptance of the need for change, there is little political consensus about the reforms needed to improve quality and access while reducing costs of health care. That consensus may emerge in future years, but in the meantime we want to highlight the contributions that systems-trained psychotherapists can make to transforming health care. In other words, what can we do on the ground while the public and political leaders sort out the direction for the macro-organization of the health care system? Indeed, if we don't innovate on the ground, no reshuffling of payment and delivery systems will provide high-quality and affordable health care to the population.

SYSTEMIC THINKING

More than anything else, the problems with health care stem from bifurcated thinking and can only be solved with systemic thinking. Philosopher Alfred North Whitehead (1926) coined the term *fallacy of misplaced concreteness* to describe the mistake of missing the whole for the part, or abstracting an individual entity from its context, and then thinking we understand what's going on. Of course, great scientific gains can be made by focusing only on the parts of a person (e.g., the cellular functioning of genes), but these gains soon hit their limit when the whole person is lost. Once broken up, Humpty Dumpty can't be put back together again. Lack of coordination in care delivery is a direct outgrowth of seeing health itself as consisting of separate boxes: different organ systems served by different specialists, individuals separated from their families, families separated from their communities, and societal and cultural influences seen as outside of health care's orbit.

Medical family therapists and other systems-trained professionals bring a different intellectual and clinical tradition to our fragmented care system—but only if we resist siloing ourselves as specialists in working with family members of people with medical illness. That's what happened with clinical social work in the early 20th century when social workers were relegated to the adjunctive role of working on "social problems" of patients, with the "real" health treatment being done by medical professionals. Social work's historical focus on the individual in social context did not penetrate the medical system. The pressures for specialization continue in the 21st century, but now there is a counteracting trend in integrated care settings and patient-centered medical homes, where all team members are expected to focus on whatever medical, psychological, and social challenges are preventing the patient from achieving her or his health goals. As Hodgson, Lamson, Mendenhall, and Crane (2012) argued, medical family therapists are ideally positioned to transcend silos and make a real difference in this emerging team-oriented health care system.

UNDERSTANDING AND WORKING WITH MULTIPLE PERSPECTIVES

At one level, focusing on the whole patient and working in collaborative teams are obvious goals; there are few advocates for impersonal, fragmented care. The challenge is to translate these general ideals into every practice; the key is the ability to take multiple perspectives, a mind-set and skill that medical family therapists are especially prepared to bring to health care. Multiple perspective taking means simultaneously understanding, honoring, and working with the different needs, views, emotions, and claims of all of the stakeholders in health care encounters—especially patients and families, but also clinicians, administrators, and the larger community. It means understanding everyone's resources for solving a problem and everyone's vulnerability in the situation. In a team working with a patient who is struggling with diabetes, the patient brings resources and vulnerabilities; making these visible is a core contribution a medical family therapist can bring to patient-centered care. Likewise, seeing the resources and vulnerability of family members is at the heart of family-oriented care. These two perspectives are often lacking not because the medical providers don't care about patients and families, but because their perspective on health care is often constrained by their training, their incentives, and their current environment.

From a systems perspective, for example, medical providers bring their own vulnerabilities and resources to working with patients with diabetes. Increasingly, they are being held accountable for achieving metabolic control for their patients, but without the time and skill set to help motivate, support, and educate them. Systems-trained therapists can bring an empathic understanding of these struggles, as well as tools such as motivational interviewing, while looking for collaborative ways to bring forth the best resources of these professionals in helping their patients. This kind of perspective taking across disciplines has not been a hallmark of professional work. Rather, the opposite has often been true, with turf battles, struggles over hierarchy, and disputes about the best way to care for patients marring the potential for collaboration.

Key competencies that medical family therapists bring to team building include

- listening deeply to team members in the same way we do to patients and families;
- building relationships of trust over time;
- negotiating among players about how to work together, with respect for everyone's contributions;
- attending to issues of hierarchy, including bringing out voices of the less powerful; and
- looking at one's own role in whatever ongoing challenges the team is experiencing, and working on change starting with one-self rather than reflexively assigning responsibility elsewhere.

Ultimately, systemic perspective taking in health care is an ethical responsibility, not just a professional strategy. This is most clear when it comes to patients and families: They are persons with worth and dignity, with needs for agency and communion, and not just medical "problems" to be diagnosed correctly and treated effectively. It's also true with other members of the team, however. In Kantian ethical terms, they are not just means to an end of good care for patients. They are ends unto themselves: Each member of the team has worth and dignity, as well as desires for agency and communion in the work setting. There are real consequences for patient care when health care professionals feel disregarded or exploited.

SYSTEMIC LEADERSHIP IN HEALTH CARE

When medical family therapists make themselves valuable with their systemic skills in a health care setting, management and other leadership possibilities open up. It is an opportunity to influence change in the larger system. Although now the stakeholders multiply and the need for a systemic vision is even greater, we have found that the basic clinical skill set of a medical family therapist is invaluable. Here are three core skills that transfer to larger systems:

- *Managing one's own anxiety inside the system.* Rabbi and family therapist Edwin Friedman (1985) defined leadership as "nonanxious presence." This requires the ability to read one's feelings and respond rather than react in the presence of stress, threat, and conflict.

- *Facilitating effective communication across stakeholders and sub-systems.* A medical family therapist knows how to become "meta" to multiple perspectives while taking these perspectives into account. This is Peek's (2008) "three-world view," simultaneously taking into consideration the needs and constraints of the clinical world, the operations world, and the financial world and knowing the languages of each.

- *Avoiding scapegoating of individuals or parts of the system.* A good systems principle is that all chronic organizational conflicts are larger than personalities and are maintained by interactions that reflect power, history, and communication patterns involving multiple stakeholders. Medical family therapists are trained to resist the intuitive appeal of blaming complex structural problems on the scapegoat du jour.

Other leadership skills, such as visioning and strategic planning, are accessible through mentoring and formal training programs for people interested in health care management positions. Although they take focused effort to acquire, these skills are less difficult to learn than the self-of-leader and interpersonal skills that systems-oriented therapists already bring to the table.

LOOKING OUTSIDE OF HEALTH CARE DELIVERY SYSTEMS

Future resource demands for care are highlighting the limitations of provider-centered models of health care—another reason not to regard medical family therapy narrowly as only a clinical practice specialty that involves team consultation. A truly systemic perspective views health as something that people create together in families and communities, not just as active inside exam rooms and hospitals. Health care becomes the work of "we the people," not "we the professionals serving the rest of the people." Collaborative care becomes more than provider teams; it becomes a form of engagement with communities as agents of their own health care.

Unfortunately, the community part of health has been handed over to an underfunded public health sector. As important as the work of public health professionals is, clinicians who work with ill people and their families have the opportunity to become deeply connected with a community and develop trust with community groups. The Active Member Project in St. Paul, described in Chapter 6, is an example of an initiative that views the clinic as a locus for a community of health, not just a center for the delivery of professional services. When Active Members gather in the clinic kitchen to teach each other how to cook healthy meals, and when others go for walks in the nearby neighborhood, they are doing the work of community health care in addition to promoting their own health. Medical family therapists who catch the spirit of democratic health care can bring a much needed skill set to working with groups of patients, providers, and other community members outside of traditional service delivery.

Outside of these face-to-face engagement projects, there are opportunities for advocacy and public planning to change the environment in which communities do health care. This might involve new walking or bike paths, a local farmer's market, and partnering with parents to bring healthier menus to the schools. Medical family therapists can bring their systemic understanding to these forms of advocacy, emphasizing the importance of building relationships of trust across community groups and with political leaders.

CONCLUSION

We encourage current and future generations of medical family therapists to take up the mission of transforming health care. This will mean participating in shaping the evolving vision of family-oriented care delivered by collaborative teams. It will also mean being true to a relational, systems way of thinking and acting that never strips people and organizations from their contexts, never reduces our role to that of reimbursed service provider to consumer–patients, and always probes and pushes our care systems to achieve their highest purposes in a democratic, inclusive nation. Although we must work to influence the political and market forces that disrupt or promote these goals, we believe that transforming health care at the ground level will require creativity and boldness that will not come from above. In the words of South African poet June Jordan (1978), "We are the ones we have been waiting for."

APPENDIX: PROFILES OF MEDICAL FAMILY THERAPISTS IN PRACTICE

The everyday practice of medical family therapy has come a long way since the early 1990s, when most medical family therapists were in academic primary care settings, teaching residents and doing collaborative health care. The principles of medical family therapy are increasingly part of the skill set of systems-oriented psychotherapists in specialty medical practices, community-based primary care, large urban hospitals, and rural clinics, along with traditional mental health practices in which therapists collaborate across settings with medical providers. Medical family therapists work with populations ranging from pediatrics to end of life. In this Appendix, we profile eight medical family therapists working successfully and innovatively in medical practices settings. We interviewed these therapists about their work setting, their clinical practice, and their collaboration. We also asked about their strengths and those of their colleagues, the challenges they face, and the pearls of wisdom they want to pass on.[1] Inevitably, there is overlap in the challenges and their ways of successfully managing these challenges, but they bring distinctive perspectives as well. In addition to offering individual profiles, this chapter synthesizes take-home learnings from this talented group of medical family therapists.

HELEN COONS IN A WOMEN'S HEALTH CENTER

Helen Coons is a clinical health psychologist who works with a range of women's issues in several settings. Part of her time is spent at the University of Pennsylvania at Penn Health for Women, a multispecialty health group that offers primary care, obstetrics, gynecology, and reproductive health services; she also works with a breast cancer surgeon. This allows her to see women across the life span from ethnically diverse populations who exhibit a broad range of relational, sexual, and medical issues.

A typical day of practice includes several appointments with a variety of patients, issues, and collaborating clinicians, including physicians, nurse practitioners, physical therapists, and surgeons. Women are referred for a range of reasons, from helping them understand options for surgery, chemotherapy,

[1]Our appreciation to Samantha Zaid for her terrific work on conducting the interviews and working on the profiles. Thanks to the clinicians—Olivia Chiang, Helen Coons, Sarah Dellinger, David Driscoll, Carl Greenberg, Kristie Jewitt, Carol Podgorski, and Nancy Ruddy—for their stories.

and radiation, to helping them cope with emotional, cognitive, and sexual and physical effects.

Coons sees two primary strengths in her workplace. First, the practice views physical, emotional, relational, and sexual needs as important. Her colleagues have a commitment to having psychological services in meeting the biopsychosocial needs of the patients. Second, the practice views the individual patient in the context of relationships. She identifies several other positive characteristics of the practice:

- good communication skills,
- competent crisis management,
- flexibility,
- respecting one another's skills and professions,
- genuine caring about patients,
- patients who feel connected to providers, and
- an emphasis on patients' voices being heard at all levels.

Dr. Coons also identifies her personal traits that contribute to successful collaboration. She sees herself as flexible, respectful to her colleagues, and available. She is clear about what she contributes to the team, knows her own boundaries, and works effectively. She also notes that without support from the highest university levels, including the director of women's health, administrators, and office managers, the practice would not be as successful in their efforts to collaborate.

Challenges include that not all providers support a biopsychosocial model in general or relate to Coons personally. She isn't always available for collaboration because of the size of the practice. Communication can be difficult at times because Coons travels across locations and does not have access to the electronic medical record. In response to these challenges, Coons has focused on consulting with those who are most willing to collaborate, remain flexible, and try to think outside the box when necessary. She remembers that collaboration is mostly about relationship building, which takes time and patience.

---

1. It's about relationships: building them, maintaining them.

Bill Clinton ran a successful campaign for president with the slogan, "It's the economy, stupid!" In medical family therapy, "It's the relationship, stupid!" As medical family therapist Helen Coons indicated in her interview, "Collaborative therapists take the time to build effective relationships, and they know what they can offer." Each relationship with a colleague will be different, just as each clinical relationship is different. Some health professionals will tentatively test out whether you can help them manage one of their own difficult patients, and if you succeed, will engage you some more. Others will want to get you know you in the break room at lunch before involving you with their patients. Some might jump right in and want to fill your caseload. In all cases, it's about the relationship you have with these team members. Keep in mind that a casual encounter in the hallway can be as important to building relationships as a formal, sit-down consultation. Showing care and compassion to colleagues gives them a sense that their patients might benefit from these qualities. A helpful clinical observation gives them a sense that their patients might benefit from having you as a team member. Once formed, these collaborative relationships need the same tending over time required by other relationships, including ongoing support and attention to breaches and challenges that inevitably come.

OLIVIA CHIANG IN AN URBAN HOSPITAL PEDIATRIC CLINIC

Olivia Chiang is a clinical psychologist who practices at primary care pediatric clinic run through a large nonprofit general hospital that serves patients from pregnancy and birth to age 22. She works mostly with low-socioeconomic-status, African American, and Puerto Rican patients in teams with pediatric faculty and residents from the University of Rochester. Her varied work includes seeing patients, teaching, consulting, and supervising psychology fellows and medical family therapy postdocs. Chiang describes her role as collaborator and gatekeeper for mental health services. Often her collaborations are "curbside consultations" or electronic chart notes in which she is able to do a quick assessment and give clinicians the information they need to deal with that situation in the moment. Never a dull moment, the following are among the responsibilities that comprise her day:

- complete evaluations,
- call schools,
- recommend services,
- call lawyers,
- do family therapy,
- meet with nurse practitioners and pediatricians regarding medications and treatment collaborations,
- receive traditional referrals from pediatricians on behavioral problems,
- chart sessions and phone calls,

- facilitate community education meetings, and
- collaborate with other medical systems.

Chiang notes several strengths of her workplace. The providers know one another well: All work together, eat together, and are side by side in all of their work. As a team, they prioritize being available both for consultation and for patients. They are flexible and organized. Whatever their areas of expertise, everyone values a biopsychosocial approach. Each professional makes time for collaboration.

When asked to describe how she contributes to the success of her workplace, Chiang said that she is also flexible, organized, and has clear priorities. She believes that the medical needs of the patient come first, and that means humble collaboration.

Chiang identifies three main challenges in her setting. Because the practice has grown so much, space in the hospital is a problem. There is stigma for many low-income patients about seeing a counselor. Her medical setting is not designed to help with patients' basic needs, which for her means a lot of social service referrals.

In response to these challenges, Chiang has made adjustments that allow for her to see more people at the necessary pace. She has developed strong collaborative relationships with schools, courts, and broader legal systems that save time as well. Her collaborators in these agencies know her and can anticipate her requests. Last, because of the collaboration and education that have been done in this setting, the providers use Chiang and her colleagues' services more efficiently and effectively. They already know how to do a basic safety plan, for example, so this leaves time for her to address other things efficiently.

---

2. Flexibility with clinical time is key.

Perhaps therapists work in 1-hour blocks because Sigmund Freud did! It's tempting to turn this into an ethical matter—good care requires uninterrupted 50- to 60-minute sessions. We know one clinic where the collaborative practice never took off because the therapists would not be flexible with their clinical time. Olivia Chiang learned to vary her time with patients and families in an urban pediatric center with a large population of high-needs children and families. Although sometimes it might be a 60-minute assessment, often her sessions are what she calls "25- to 30-minute hours" that allow her to see more patients. Close collaboration with team members and with school and other community systems makes these briefer sessions effective. Like other medical family

---

therapists, Chiang learned the value of brief 5-minute "meet and greet" conversations to foster successful referrals from a clinician, as well as 10- to 15-minute brief consultations about some behavioral health issue. Here's how she describes the change: "We used to have a 50% show rate; now upon referral I go in the room with the physician, meet the patient, explain how to check in, do a brief assessment, and let them know what to expect when they come back. This has increased the referral rate, and the show rate is now 70% to 80%. Patients clearly are influenced by a positive comment, a blessing, by their physician. Chiang commented, "When they come to meet me, my patients often report how their doctor likes me, and that matters." These comments demonstrate how important the team relationship is to whether patients access a medical family therapy referral.

DAVID DRISCOLL IN A MIDDLE-CLASS PEDIATRICS PRACTICE

David Driscoll works in a hybrid private practice—incorporating both on- and off-site features of collaborative care—with four other psychologists who share a focus on children, adolescents, families, and pediatric care. They have a traditional private practice as well as a satellite office is in a pediatric group practice. When he rotates to the pediatric clinic, Driscoll's typical day is varied and always interesting. Upon arriving, he goes to the nurses' station to see what's going on for the day. There is a list with a number of pediatricians who want to check in with him about things that have come up in the past few days. He does face-to-face consultations with the pediatricians and has 50-minute psychotherapy hours with several patients. Mostly the collaboration is informal, but the collaboration is always followed up with formal documentation in the patient's file. A typical day of collaboration also includes taking triage phone calls from parents.

Driscoll sees a number of positive assets in his workplace:

- The pediatricians demonstrate "incredible professionalism."
- The practice is patient- and family-centered.
- The practice anticipates the needs of modern families and is committed to meeting those needs.
- The professionals are public about their collaboration; the team operates transparently with kids and families.

The clinicians in Driscoll's collaborative practice focus on family strengths. They stress the importance of the family's perspective about how to solve a problem. They are careful to work through less intensive interventions before resorting to more intensive ones, aiming for the greatest outcome with minimal intervention. Driscoll's behavioral health partners share call as a team to be available to their pediatric colleagues 24 hours a day, 7 days a week. The pediatricians are available to the psychologists on the same 24/7 basis. Driscoll describes this characteristic as being of primary importance to their successes as a health care team.

In terms of strengths, Driscoll says that maintaining personal connections with every physician is his way of contributing to the successes at his workplace.

There are also challenges in this setting:

- finding collaborative therapist colleagues who want to do this interesting but challenging work,
- uncompensated time for collaboration,
- maintaining confidentiality around so many providers, and
- the demanding nature of a chaotic environment.

Despite these challenges, Driscoll believes that the privilege of working on site with pediatricians and families far outweighs any difficulties. He copes with challenges by setting limits on his own availability and using the team call system, having a good referral system, and being clear about collaborative expectations when inviting someone to be part of the team.

---

3. It takes time to get in and become accepted.

Collaborative work takes patience. It's not like being hired at a mental health clinic where once your name is on your door, patients show up. Unless the medical family therapist is lucky enough to join a setting with a long track record of integrating behavioral health professionals, it can feel more like acclimating to a foreign culture with a different language and strange ways. First it feels like being a tourist, then a long-term visitor, and finally like a citizen of the land. At the start, the medical system may buzz along seemingly oblivious to your existence. It's what David Driscoll calls a "chaotic environment." But over time, we can all demonstrate our worth to clinicians who care about offering the best care to their patients. They will move from polite smiles as they race past you to telling you they couldn't practice without you. It takes confidence to wait for this process to unfold. Medical family therapy is not for those who need instant appreciation, although over time it is deeply rewarding.

SARAH DELLINGER: INTERN AT A FAMILY MEDICINE RESIDENCY

Sarah Dellinger is a prelicensed marriage and family therapist, previously an intern at the University of Washington family medicine residency. Her interest in medical family therapy came from connecting with a professor in her master's program who was passionate about the field. She found the medical setting to be exciting and a good fit.

In the residency program, physicians see the patients and then refer them to Dellinger or her colleagues. Whoever is next on the list for an opening takes the referral. Dellinger has patients scheduled in a traditional 50-minute psychotherapy hour, and she also schedules brief time slots with residents as needed. Collaboration takes place in common rooms, offices, and hallways, but given the various schedules of the physicians, Dellinger also proactively collaborates with e-mails, phone calls, and sometimes stepping out of the therapy room to find the physician to address a pressing need. She has found that her relationship with the attending faculty physician is crucial: If that physician supports her role, she and the residents and other providers work well together.

When collaborating with the health care team, Dellinger keeps her focus on one central question: "How can we get this person well in the most productive way?" This generally means accessing the right resources in a timely manner. Dellinger reports that her team does take the time to care about each patient as a person, which makes her excited about her work, but she takes nothing for granted. She reports being "kind of pushy" and making collaboration happen with physicians and the attending by being persistent.

One of the important traits most of her colleagues share is openness to collaboration and support of her role. Although some individual clinicians may not fully appreciate her role, there is an overall structure that supports collaboration, with therapists, nutritionists, physical therapists, and other clinicians all working together for patient health. The practice values the biopsychosocial approach and actively refers patients to one another when an overlapping issue is outside one's area of expertise.

The two main challenges to collaboration are the varied interest of individual providers and the geographic issue that the therapists' and physicians' offices are in different parts of the building, which limits easy access. Dellinger's main strategy for these challenges is to keep approaching providers, even when they seem resistant to collaboration. She asks for advice rather than forcing her perspective. She spends time standing in hallways and in the on-call room to increase her availability. She introduces and reintroduces herself to the physicians, describes how she is working with a patient, asks for their thoughts, and tries to engage them as much as possible. This persistent approach has increased collaboration significantly over time.

4. Use multiple forms of communication.

Therapists are trained in private, sit-down, face-to-face communication—a kind of communication that happens infrequently in medical settings. Many therapists learn to write extensive assessments and treatment plans, which most of their medical colleagues won't have time to read. Effective family therapists use whatever communication channels are available. As Sarah Dellinger observes, sometimes communication takes place in common rooms, offices, and hallways when there are no patients in hearing range. She is proactive with e-mails and phone calls, and in urgent situations, she does something that therapists in traditional settings never do: She steps out of the therapy room to track down the doctor for an immediate consult. In all of these forms of communication, brevity is the coin of the realm. One of us recalls an encounter with a family physician, coat on to rush off to the hospital, who pulled him into a room and asked for input on a patient she was to see that day. The patient was a middle-aged woman who was overweight, diabetic, and not taking care of herself. Instead of asking for more background information that was not feasible at the moment, or saying that there was not enough time for a consult, the medical family therapist asked one question: "Who is worried about her health right now—you and her, or just you?" The physician smiled, shook hands, and said, "Thank you. That's right. I'm the only one who's worked up about this right now. Gotta run."

CAROL PODGORSKI IN A LONG-TERM CARE CENTER

Carol Podgorski has worked for more than 25 years in a public, long-term care facility with more than 500 long-term care beds and services for patients ranging from newborns to the elderly. She has been a medical family therapist there since 2003. Most patients are economically impoverished because of injury, genetics, or other life misfortune. Her position involves coordination, supervision, and patient care and fits with her passion for geriatric care. She has remained impressed with the compassionate care her setting offers.

A typical day of collaboration for Podgorski includes working with physicians, nurses, nurse practitioners, social workers, dieticians, or therapists. An intensive referral process includes talking with team members about ongoing care plans for resident patients, reading progress notes, talking with the resident, completing a comprehensive intake, developing a new treatment plan, and cross-checking the plan with the team informally or formally at a team meeting.

Podgorski sees a number of strengths in her workplace:

- It offers compassionate care.
- Family consultation services have the resources and time to get to know residents' stories; they help humanize the residents in the charts and to the team.
- Knowing the residents helps them to individualize effective treatment plans.
- Her team can help other staff members understand residents and help families understand changes in their functioning.
- A team approach helps eliminate splitting so all team members can pursue the same goals with common, reasonable expectations.

Podgorski identifies that her success in this setting is enhanced because she respects all the other clinicians, and she offers an overall or humble stance that helps foster positive collaboration. She believes that her colleagues value family approaches and accept many definitions of family. Family therapy services are designed to be a consultation service to the care team, which allows Podgorski and her colleagues to be a "neutral resource" for the care team, the residents, and the families.

A unique challenge for this long-term setting relates to sexual intimacy. There is a privacy room for conjugal visits or weddings, and some residents have shared rooms. However, some staff dislike any sexual activity by the consenting residents and are unwilling to talk about it or deal with it. Different units, and even different staff on the same unit, have different practices with regard to sexual issues. Residents' needs for sexual intimacy are a primary reason for referral to the family therapist. Sometimes there are other value differences between the therapists and the care team. For example, some nurse managers have ways of dealing with behavioral problems that the therapists see as punitive but are viewed by others on the care team as appropriate responses to a difficult resident. For Podgorski, responses to these challenges are rooted in communication. She emphasizes increased communication about policies and procedures, brainstorming for alternatives, and then approaching the care team with recommendations while remaining open to feedback.

---

5. Collaboration requires comfort with not always being the central player.

The best medical family therapists project confidence in their skills and contributions but also are humble about being another member of a team that has a broader mission than behavioral health. This work is

---

not for those who need immediate acceptance from their colleagues. We have to learn more about the medical culture than most of our colleagues will learn about our professional culture. In emphasizing the "nonexpert" stance, Carol Podgorski stresses the downside of the defensive expert stance in which the therapist continually asserts the value of his or her behavioral health expertise. There are cases in which behavioral issues are at play, but the team is focused on biomedical issues. The therapist speaks up, and the team doesn't shift its approach. Rather than take this as an affront, a seasoned medical family therapist supports the team while waiting for an opportunity make a difference at a later point.

Similarly, on organizational matters, the team may be implementing an electronic medical record system without considering the special Health Insurance Portability and Accountability Act privacy requirements with mental health records. How the therapist speaks up about this is important: Ideally, he or she approaches this with a tone of helping the team see something being overlooked rather than from a stance of "nobody around here takes my world seriously." For the foreseeable future, the "bio" in "biopsychosocial" will be more prominent than the psychosocial in many medical settings; working constructively and not pitting the psychosocial against the biomedical enhances the impact of the medical family therapist.

CARL GREENBERG IN A CANCER CLINIC

Carl Greenberg is a marriage and family therapist in Washington state, on salary in a private specialty cancer care practice with 20 physicians, six midlevel practitioners, and three family therapists. He has been involved with this cancer clinic for 28 years, through building relationships, networking, and a series of collaborative opportunities.

In a typical day, Greenberg sees patients referred by physicians or nurses. He goes to the electronic medical record or the referring clinician for information about the patient. Once he sees the patient, he routes an electronic assessment form to the physician, closing the communication loop. Greenberg and his therapist colleagues are also available on an emergency basis. Other levels of collaboration include in-service trainings for physicians and staff and working with patient advocates, nurses, and schedulers. Collaboration is systemwide. There are often curbside consults in hallways, with appropriate safeguards for confidentiality. Greenberg says that if he is visibly accessible to the medical providers, they will make use of him. He also provides mediation between departments of the organization when conflict arises.

Strengths in this workplace start with the clinicians' commitment to comprehensive, innovative, compassionate, and integrative care. They provide care whether community members can afford it or not. Greenberg also sees openness to collaboration; care starts with the assumption that the providers are a team, with strengths to help one another. Greenberg and his team are visible not only to the oncologists but also to the surgeons, nurses, and everyone else involved with patients.

When it comes to his own strengths, Greenberg begins with his experience: 14 years in a family practice residency and 28 years of practice in the field. Second, the members of this organization created a position for Greenberg because they wanted him there; they knew he could walk the two worlds of medical health culture and mental health culture.

Rather than functioning as a hierarchy, Greenberg's group is a collaborative team with complementary strengths. Administrators also make it a good practice in which to work. The practice recognizes that both patients and professionals have emotional and spiritual needs in addition to their medical needs. Greenberg also attributes successful collaboration to the availability of the physicians: They take the time.

Greenberg notes four major challenges in working in this context:

- communicating across locations and within busy practices,
- working with patients who have complex challenges,
- recognizing that some physicians are better at collaboration than others, and
- acquiring important medical knowledge as a nonmedical professional.

Responses to these challenges have included logistical changes for better access to one another, and working through issues together as they come up. For Greenberg, working in the medical culture is both challenging and exciting. He says, "Don't be afraid of the physicians; they are people with stresses too. But there's something they value about our work as therapists, and you don't need to be afraid to say, 'I can help you.'"

---

6. We have to get comfortable with medical concepts, language, and culture.

As Carl Greenberg puts it, "We need to learn to talk medical talk. It's important to do this, but not easy." In professional training, everyone develops a sense of when information is "my area" or "not my area." In mental health training, a patient's diabetes is usually a black box

---

diagnosis—it's a factor in the patient's life but not something to understand in any detail. We generally don't pay attention to whether the diabetes is Type I or Type II, treated with insulin injections or only with medication, controlled or uncontrolled, with complications or not, managed adequately by the patient or not, a source of family friction or support? Medical family therapists have to develop familiarity with these medical details. We also have to learn a host of cultural factors in medicine such as the physician's sense of responsibility for the patient's diabetes, and new systemic factors such as financial rewards and penalties for the health care teams based on medical outcomes for their patients.

KRISTIE JEWITT IN A REPRODUCTIVE ENDOCRINOLOGY CENTER

Kristie Jewitt is a marriage and family therapist in a reproductive endocrinology specialty clinic, connected with the University of Rochester Medical Center, which specializes in treating infertility. Approximately 75% of the patients are underserved women of low socioeconomic status from multiple ethnic backgrounds, many whom also have chronic mental health issues. The other 25% are women and couples from middle to upper socioeconomic status backgrounds who are struggling to get pregnant. Jewitt's position was desired by the physicians and is funded for a variety of duties. As a "complimentary service" to their health care (i.e., part of their bundled payment), patients don't need to worry about funding, making extra phone calls, going to a new building, signing releases, or having medical records transferred. The practice sees the therapists as an integral piece of the medical care to which all patients are entitled.

A typical day of Jewitt's practice includes several layers of collaboration:

- reviewing depression and anxiety assessments from intake packets,
- reaching out to patients who need further assessment,
- individual and group psychotherapy or psychoeducation sessions,
- discussions with physicians before and after appointments,
- addressing behavioral and mental health treatment plans for physicians,
- calling or writing notes to patients in need of support,
- conducting workshops for staff members about their own concerns and about the psychosocial needs of the patients,
- updating the team on patient progress and treatment, and
- writing a quarterly newsletter to all patients—those that use the behavioral health services and those who don't.

Jewitt notes that the clinic physicians and administrators are always open to hearing suggestions, and they trust the behavioral health team enough to give them latitude to try new things. Through both formal and casual collaboration, the patient is treated as a whole. By seeing the big picture, the team can better meet the needs of the patients, and the patients feel this too. This requires humility and openness to integrating other providers' perspectives and views.

Jewitt's assets that have helped her in this collaborative environment include the following:

- being tolerant of differences in the medical context;
- being patient but persistent;
- working hard at creating genuine relationships; and
- moving slowly and cautiously at first, and taking time to observe, identify needs, ask questions, and then offer feedback.

Jewitt sees her colleagues as ready, wanting, and welcoming to a behavioral health team, and willing to contribute respectful and useful feedback. In addition, the tone of this practice is one of respect and kindness; it is a prevention-focused practice that anticipates patients' needs.

Bridging the medical and behavioral health cultures is a challenge in Jewitt's setting. Language, pace, and expectations for outcomes are all different. Handling this challenge requires flexibility on both sides; for example, instead of a standard 45- to 50-minute session, a patient may need a 20-minute session followed by an ultrasound. It's hard to match pace and energy when clinicians have trained differently, but it can be done if everyone is willing to adapt.

---

7. There are predictable challenges.

Kristie Jewitt emphasizes the special challenge of integration into a medical practice if the practice leaders don't value your work. She says she can't stress enough that it can take years to be fully integrated. Even then, some clinicians will keep you at arm's length because they don't understand what you offer.

The second challenge mentioned by all of the therapists we interviewed is the busy, sometimes chaotic environment of many medical settings. As Jewitt notes, your patient may need a procedure in 20 minutes, so that's all the time you have for today. Managing time pressures like this is not part of most therapists' training.

The third challenge is the lack of an integrated payment system. As Jewitt notes, most medical and mental health treatments are "piece

---

work," paid separately and not as an integrated whole. The behavioral health professional has to assign a separate diagnosis for the service to be compensated. This picture may change in the evolving health care system, but for now the mind–body split is enshrined in payment systems.

The fourth challenge is the lack of reimbursement for collaboration. One of the reasons collaborative communication so often occurs on the fly is that time for it is off the books—no one gets paid for talking together about how to better manage the patient's care. The good news is that in the emerging patient-centered medical home, some innovative settings place an emphasis on team meetings, and they arrange for coverage under umbrella contracts with payors. The related trend toward paying for outcomes and not just for visits and procedures is a positive one for collaborative practice, as long as we can demonstrate that collaboration does lead to better health outcomes and cost savings.

The fifth challenge is the tremendous differences across health care systems. Although some nations have coherent health care systems, the United States has been a hodgepodge ranging from traditional fee-for-service in small physician-owned practices to large for-profit care systems with their own hospitals and outpatient clinics, to integrated prepaid networks such as Kaiser Permanente, and university health care systems where most medical training and research occurs. In some medical family therapy contexts, the patient pool may have dozens of insurance providers, whereas in others, nearly everyone is on Medicaid or Medicare. Then there are those with no health care insurance. This variety makes it difficult to develop consistent practices for medical family therapists that cut across health care systems.

The last challenge is differences across professional mental health disciplines. For starters, some disciplines are reimbursed by Medicare and other major insurers, but others are not. Turf battles among mental health disciplines for space and prominence in behavioral health do not help the cause of integrated, collaborative care. In our experience, medical and nursing professionals do not care about the degree or pedigree of the behavioral health professional, only about their competence in helping patients and the team.

NANCY RUDDY IN SEVERAL FAMILY MEDICINE CLINICS

Nancy Ruddy is a licensed clinical child psychologist and marriage and family therapist who has worked in multiple family practice clinic settings from Rochester, New York, to southern and northern New Jersey. In these settings, she has provided both outpatient and inpatient work. Her client populations have ranged from a culturally diverse, inner-city patient groups to an upper-middle-class, suburban group. Currently she provides psychotherapy and education in a Family Medicine residency in northern New Jersey. She began this work as an intern in clinical child psychology, which later turned into a faculty position in family medicine.

A typical day for Ruddy involves the following:

- mentoring, providing one-on-one time with a family medicine resident in teaching and case consultation;
- administrative responsibilities (faculty meetings, curriculum design, recruitment);
- resident education on chronic disease management;
- collaboration, which involves consultation and seeing and helping patients with residents;
- ongoing psychotherapy with patients after a physician referral;
- formal and informal teaching activities; and
- cotherapy in physicians' appointments to help bridge the patient into behavioral health services.

Ruddy sees a combination of strengths and challenges at the different places she has worked as a medical family therapist. At some sites, collaboration is easy, particularly when there is grant or institutional support for this kind of work. At other sites, a lack of emphasis on a biopsychosocial model and limited importance placed on collaborative work makes cooperation between medical and mental health professionals difficult. Because medical and mental health practitioners are typically not trained together, they sometimes do not grasp the importance of collaborative work with one another. Ruddy states that one of the biggest challenges is that, "You can be collaboratively minded, but you cannot do it alone. Without [other] collaborators, you can't do it. There is strong geographical and cultural variability in how hard it is to make that work." In addition, current insurance billing does not have a code for collaboration.

Despite the challenges, Ruddy sees many characteristics of her work environments that contribute to the success of collaborative work, including professional awareness of both medical and mental health fields, belief in the importance of collaboration to improve patient care, emphasis on the importance of continuity of care, professional flexibility, good referral resources for specialty care, and allowing extra time with patients. Collaboration, in Ruddy's opinion, is vital for creating a satisfying work environment and offering the best patient care possible: "Being collaborative makes clinical work more fun and productive. You aren't isolated; the left hand knows what the right hand is doing. It promotes optimal care."

8. This is very satisfying work.

Nancy Ruddy captures a theme that came across clearly in our interviews with medical family therapists and in our own experience: This is gratifying work. Despite all of the challenges, medical family therapy in a collaborative setting is a high-reward activity for those who can handle the complexity. You have a sense of being part of a team doing important work. You feel valued by both patients and colleagues because you are helping both. You see patients and families who would never come to you as a therapist in independent practice. You get to be part of life and death moments, sharing the tears and joy with your colleagues. There is rawness in this work, a rough and tumble that makes traditional therapy work seem, in retrospect, a bit staid. But these rewards only come to the persistent and to those who put relationships first. In Nancy Ruddy's words, "It's a little like religion; it's an act of faith at first."

CONCLUSION

Writing about the contexts of medical family therapy early in the second decade of the 21st century is a bit like writing about new communication technologies. The ground is shifting in front of us as we look at it. The health care system of the future will likely differ in important ways from the current one. Some of these changes may make medical family therapy more appealing and feasible in health care settings; a chief example would be reimbursement for time spent in collaborative interactions. Another is tying reimbursement to patient satisfaction and outcomes. Other changes might make this work more difficult, say, by simply squeezing short-term costs out of the system through reducing payments and cutting providers who don't do procedures.

Whatever changes come, we believe that the principles articulated in this Appendix will remain central to the work of medical family therapists. In any system, fragmented care is poor care, and collaborative, patient- and family-centered care is good care. This will be true across the settings described here and in many others such as the health care home, end of life care, and genetic counseling, to name just three. Wise medical family therapists will have a flexible toolkit and adapt to new opportunities rather than specialize in one area with which they are comfortable. Innovative contexts of the future are likely to emphasize the patient experience and patient outcomes, which medical family therapists can help improve, along with the provider experience, a realm that medical family therapists and similarly trained professionals can also enhance. They are stimulated and fulfilled in their work. And they help their colleagues feel good about their own work. It's a road for traveling together.

REFERENCES

Agency for Health Care Research and Quality. (2012). Patient centered medical home resource center. Retrieved from http://www.pcmh.ahrq.gov/portal/server.pt/community/pcmh__home/1483

Alderfer, M. A., & Kazak, A. E. (2006). Family issues when a child is on treatment for cancer. In R. T. Brown (Ed.), *Comprehensive handbook of childhood cancer and sickle cell disease: A biopsychosocial approach* (pp. 53–74). New York, NY: Oxford University Press.

Alderfer, M. A., Navsaria, N., & Kazak, A. E. (2009). Family functioning and post-traumatic stress disorder in adolescent survivors of childhood cancer. *Journal of Family Psychology, 23*, 717–725. doi:10.1037/a0015996

Allen, L. A., & Woolfolk, R. L. (2010). Cognitive behavioral therapy for somatoform disorders. *Psychiatric Clinics of North America, 33*, 579–593. doi:10.1016/j.psc.2010.04.014

American Psychiatric Association. (2000). *Diagnostic and statistical manual of mental disorders* (4th ed.; text rev.). Washington, DC: Author.

American Society for Reproductive Medicine. (n.d.). *State infertility insurance laws.* Retrieved from http://www.asrm.org/insurance.aspx

American Society for Reproductive Medicine Ethics Committee. (2004). Informing offspring of their conception by gamete donation. *Fertility and Sterility, 81*, 527–531. doi:10.1016/j.fertnstert.2003.11.011

American Society for Reproductive Medicine Practice Committee. (2008). Definitions of infertility and recurrent pregnancy loss. *Fertility and Sterility, 90*(Suppl. 5), S60. doi:10.1016/j.fertnstert.2008.08.065

Andersen, T. (1984). Consultation: Would you like co-evolution or referral? *Family Systems Medicine, 2*, 370–379.

Anderson, H., & Goolishian, H. (1988). Human systems as linguistic systems: Preliminary and evolving ideas about the implications for clinical theory. *Family Process, 27*, 371–393.

Angell, M. (2004). *The truth about the drug companies: How they deceive us and what to do about it.* New York, NY: Random House.

Antonovsky, A. (1979). *Health, stress, and coping.* San Francisco, CA: Jossey-Bass.

Apostoleris, N. H. (2000). *Integrating psychological services into primary care in an underserved community: Examining the referral process for on-site mental health services.* Philadelphia, PA: Northeast Regional Conference of the Society of Teachers of Family Medicine.

Aveyard, P., Massey, L., Parsons, A., Manaseki, S., & Griffin, C. (2009). The effect of transtheoretical model based interventions on smoking cessation. *Social Science & Medicine, 68*, 397–403. doi:10.1016/j.socscimed.2008.10.036

Bacon, L., & Aphramor, L. (2011). Weight science: Evaluating the evidence for a paradigm shift. *Nutrition Journal, 10,* 1–13. Retrieved from http://www.nutritionj.com/content/10/1/9

Badr, H., & Taylor, C. L. (2009). Sexual dysfunction and spousal communication in couples coping with prostate cancer. *Psycho-Oncology, 18,* 735–746. doi:10.1002/pon.1449

Bagarozzi, D., & Anderson, S. (1989). *Personal, marital and family myths: Theoretical formulations and clinical strategies.* New York, NY: Norton.

Bagchi, D., & Preuss, H. G. (Eds.). (2012). *Obesity: Epidemiology, pathophysiology, and prevention* (2nd ed.). New York, NY: CRC Press. doi:10.1201/b12261

Bakan, D. (1966). *The duality of human existence: An essay on psychology and religion.* New York, NY: Rand McNally.

Baker, L. (1987). Families and illness. In M. Crouch & L. Roberts (Eds.), *The family in medical practice* (pp. 97–111). New York, NY: Springer-Verlag.

Baker, L., Wagner, T. H., Singer, S., & Bundorf, M. K. (2003). Use of the Internet and e-mail for health care information: Results from a national survey. *JAMA, 289,* 2400–2406. doi:10.1001/jama.289.18.2400

Balint, M. (1957). *The doctor, his patient, and the illness.* London, England: Churchill Livingstone.

Barrett, M. S., & Berman, J. S. (2001). Is psychotherapy more effective when therapists disclose information about themselves? *Journal of Consulting and Clinical Psychology, 69,* 597–603. doi:10.1037/0022-006X.69.4.597

Barsky, A. J. (1979). Patients who amplify bodily sensations. *Annals of Internal Medicine, 91,* 63–70.

Barsky, A. J., Orav, E. J., & Bates, D. W. (2005). Somatization increases medical utilization and costs independent of psychiatric and medical comorbidity. *Archives of General Psychiatry, 62,* 903–910. doi:10.1001/archpsyc.62.8.903

Baslet, G., & Hill, J. (2011). Brief mindfulness-based psychotherapeutic intervention during inpatient hospitalization in a patient with conversion and dissociation. *Clinical Case Studies, 10,* 95–109. doi:10.1177/1534650110396359

Bateson, G. (1979). *Mind and nature: A necessary unity.* New York, NY: Hampton Press.

Benazon, N. R., Foster, M. D., & Coyne, J. C. (2006). Expressed emotion, adaptation, and patient survival among couples coping with chronic heart failure. *Journal of Family Psychology, 20,* 328–334. doi:10.1037/0893-3200.20.2.328

Bennett, K. K., Compas, B. E., Beckjord, E., & Glinder, J. G. (2005). Self-blame and distress among women with newly diagnosed breast cancer. *Journal of Behavioral Medicine, 28,* 313–323. doi:10.1007/s10865-005-9000-0

Benyamini, Y., Gozlan, M., & Kokia, E. (2005). Variability in the difficulties experienced by women undergoing infertility treatments. *Fertility and Sterility, 83,* 275–283. doi:10.1016/j.fertnstert.2004.10.014

Berg, C. A., & Upchurch, R. (2007). A developmental-contextual model of couples coping with chronic illness across the adult life span. *Psychological Bulletin, 133*, 920–954. doi:10.1037/0033-2909.133.6.920

Berge, J. M. (2009). A review of familial correlates of child and adolescent obesity: What has the 21st century taught us so far? *International Journal of Adolescent Medicine and Health, 21*, 457–483. doi:10.1515/IJAMH.2009.21.4.457

Berge, J. M., & Patterson, J. M. (2004). Cystic fibrosis and the family: A review and critique of the literature. *Families, Systems, & Health, 22*, 74–100. doi:10.1037/1091-7527.22.1.74

Berwick, D. M., & Hackbarth, A. D. (2012). Eliminating waste in health care. *JAMA, 307*, 1513–1516. doi:10.1001/jama.2012.362

Berwick, D. M., Nolan, T. W., & Whittington, J. (2008). The triple aim: Care, health, and cost. *Health Affairs, 27*, 759–769. doi:10.1377/hlthaff.27.3.759

Bhatt, A., Tomenson, B., & Benjamin, S. (1989). Transcultural patterns of somatization in primary care: A preliminary report. *Journal of Psychosomatic Research, 33*, 671–680.

Blackmore, E. R., Cote-Arsenault, D., Tang, W., Glover, V., Evans, J., Golding, J., & O'Connor, T. G. (2011). Previous prenatal loss as a predictor of perinatal depression and anxiety. *The British Journal of Psychiatry, 198*, 373–378. doi:10.1192/bjp.bp.110.083105

Blais, M. A., Balty, M. R., & Hopwood, C. J. (2010). *Clinical applications of the Personality Assessment Inventory*. New York, NY: Routledge.

Blank, T. O. (2005). Gay men and prostate cancer: Invisible diversity. *Journal of Clinical Oncology, 23*, 2593–2596. doi:10.1200/JCO.2005.00.968

Blechman, E., & Brown, K. D. (Eds.). (1988). *Handbook of behavioral medicine for women*. New York, NY: Pergamon Press.

Blount, A. (1998). *Integrated primary care: The future of medical and mental health collaboration*. New York, NY: Norton.

Blount, A., Schoenbaum, M., Kathol, R., Rollman, B. L., Thomas, M., O'Donohue, W., & Peek, C. J. (2007). The economics of behavioral health services in medical settings: A summary of the evidence. *Professional Psychology: Research and Practice, 38*, 290–297. doi:10.1037/0735-7028.38.3.290

Bohlmeijer, E., Prenger, R., Taal, E., & Cuijpers, P. (2010). The effects of mindfulness-based stress reduction therapy on mental health of adults with a chronic medical disease: A meta-analysis. *Journal of Psychosomatic Research, 68*, 539–544. doi:10.1016/j.jpsychores.2009.10.005

Boivin, J. (2003). A review of psychosocial interventions on infertility. *Social Science & Medicine, 57*, 2325–2341.

Boivin, J., Appleton, T. C., Baetens, P., Baron, J., Bitzer, J., Corrigan, E., . . . European Society of Human Reproduction and Embryology (2001). Guidelines for counseling and infertility. *Human Reproduction, 16*, 1301–1304. doi:10.1093/humrep/16.6.1301

Boivin, J., Griffiths, E., & Venetis, C. A. (2011). Emotional distress in infertile women and failure of assisted reproductive technologies: Meta analysis of prospective psychosocial studies. *British Medical Journal, 342*, d223. doi:10.1136/bmj.d223

Bodenheimer, T., Wagner, E., & Grumbach, K. (2002). Improving primary care for patients with chronic illness. *JAMA, 288*, 1775–1779.

Boss, P. (2011). *Loving someone who has dementia: How to find hope while coping with stress and grief.* San Francisco, CA: Jossey-Bass.

Boss, P., & Carnes, D. (2012). The myth of closure. *Family Process, 51*, 456–469. doi:10.1111/famp.12005

Boss, P., & Couden, B. A. (2002). Ambiguous loss from chronic physical illness: Clinical interventions with individuals, couples, and families. *Journal of Clinical Psychology, 58*, 1351–1360. doi:10.1002/jclp.10083

Boszormenyi-Nagy, I., & Spark, G. (1973). *Invisible loyalties: Reciprocity in intergenerational family therapy.* New York, NY: Harper & Row.

Boszormenyi-Nagy, I., & Spark, G. M. (1984). *Invisible loyalties: Reciprocity in intergenerational family therapy.* Levittown, PA: Brunner/Mazel.

Bowen, M. (1991). Family reactions to death. In F. Walsh & M. McGoldrick (Eds.), *Living beyond loss: Death in the family* (pp. 79–92). New York, NY: Norton.

Boxer, A. S. (1996). Infertility and sexual dysfunction. *Infertility & Reproductive Medicine Clinics of North America, 7*, 565.

Boyte, H. C. (2004). *Everyday politics.* Philadelphia: University of Pennsylvania Press.

Boyte, H. C., & Kari, N. N. (1996). *Building America: The democratic promise of public work.* Philadelphia, PA: Temple University Press.

Brownell, K. D., Kelman, J. H., & Stunkard, A. J. (1983). Treatment of obese children with and without their mothers: Changes in weight and blood pressure. *Pediatrics, 71*, 515–523.

Bruch, H., & Touraine, A. B. (1940). Obesity in childhood: V. The family frame of obese children. *Psychosomatic Medicine, 2*, 141–206.

Buchbinder, M. A., Longhofer, J., & McCue, K. (2009). Family routines and rituals when a parent has cancer. *Families, Systems, & Health, 27*, 213–227.

Burns, L. H. (1987). Infertility and boundary ambiguity. *Family Process, 26*, 359–372. doi:10.1111/j.1545-5300.1987.00359.x

Bursztajn, H., Feinbloom, R., Hamm, R., & Brodsky, A. (1981). *Medical choices, medical chances: How patients, families, and physicians can cope with uncertainty.* New York, NY: Dell.

Butler, M., Kane, R. L., McAlpine, D., Kathol, R. G., Fu, S. S., Hagedorn, H., & Wilt, T. J. (2008, October). *Integration of mental health/substance abuse and primary care* (Evidence Report/Technology Assessment No. 173; AHRQ Publication No. 09-3003). Rockville, MD: Agency for Healthcare Research and Quality.

Butler, P. (2003). Assisted reproduction in developing countries—facing up to the issues. *Progress in Reproductive Health, 63*, 1–8.

Butryn, M. L., & Lowe, M. R. (2008). Dieting: Good or bad? In J. G. Golson & K. Keller (Eds.), *Encyclopedia of obesity* (pp. 184–187). Thousand Oaks, CA: Sage.

Byng-Hall, J. (1991). Family scripts and loss. In F. Walsh & M. McGoldrick (Eds.), *Living beyond loss: Death in the family* (pp. 130–143). New York, NY: Norton.

Cain, B., & Patterson, A. (2001). *Double-dip feelings: Stories to help children understand emotions* (2nd ed.). Washington, DC: Magination Press/American Psychological Association.

Callahan, D. (1991, May 7). *Caring and curing: Striking the right balance*. Plenary address at the Annual Meeting of the Society of Teachers of Family Medicine, Philadelphia, PA.

Cameron, J. K., & Mauksch, L. B. (2002). Collaborative family healthcare in an uninsured primary-care population: Stages of integration. *Families, Systems, & Health, 20,* 343–363. doi:10.1037/h0089509

Campbell, T. L. (1986). *Family's impact on health: A critical review and annotated bibliography* (No. DHHS Publication No. 86-1461). Washington, DC: U.S. Government Printing Office.

Campbell, T. L. (2003). The effectiveness of family interventions for physical disorders. *Journal of Marital and Family Therapy, 29,* 263–281. doi:10.1111/j.1752-0606.2003.tb01204.x

Campbell, T. L., & McDaniel, S. H. (1987). Applying a systems approach to common medical problems. In M. Crouch (Ed.), *The family in medical practice: A family systems primer* (pp. 112–139). Berlin and Heidelberg, Germany: Springer-Verlag.

Campbell, T. L., & Williamson, D. (1990). Presentation at a meeting of the American Association for Marriage and Family Therapy–Society of Teachers of Family Medicine Task Force for Family Therapy and Family Medicine, Washington, DC.

Candib, L. M. (1999). *Medicine and the family: A feminist perspective*. New York, NY: Basic Books.

Cella, D. F., & Najavits, L. (1986). Denial of infertility in patients with Hodgkin's disease. *Psychosomatics: Journal of Consultation Liaison Psychiatry, 27,* 71. doi:10.1016/S0033-3182(86)72747-3

Centers for Disease Control and Prevention. (2008a). *Health, United States, 2008.* Washington, DC: U.S. Government Printing Office.

Centers for Disease Control and Prevention. (2008b). *National Health Interview Survey, 2008.* Retrieved from http://www.cdc.gov/nchs/nhis/nhis_2008_data_release.htm

Centers for Disease Control and Prevention. (2009). *Overweight and obesity.* Retrieved from http://www.cdc.gov/obesity/data/trends.html

Centers for Disease Control and Prevention. (2010a). *CDC's Healthy communities program.* Retrieved from http://www.cdc.gov/healthycommunitiesprogram/overview/index.htm

Centers for Disease Control and Prevention. (2010b). *National diabetes fact sheet.* Retrieved from http://www.cdc.gov/diabetes/pubs/estimates07.htm#3

Centers for Disease Control and Prevention. (2010c). *Smoking and tobacco. Data and statistics: Fast facts.* Retrieved from http://www.cdc.gov/tobacco/data_statistics/fact_sheets/fast_facts/

Centers for Disease Control and Prevention. (2011). *Infertility FAQ's.* Retrieved from http://www.cdc.gov/reproductivehealth/Infertility

Centers for Disease Control and Prevention. (2013). *Asthma.* Retrieved from http://www.cdc.gov/nchs/fastats/asthma.htm

Chabot, J. (1989). Treating the somatizing patient: Countertransference, hate, and the elusive cure. *Psychotherapy in Private Practice, 7,* 125–136. doi:10.1300/J294v07n02_11

Chandra, A., Martinez, G. M., Mosher, W. D., Abma, J. C., & Jones, J. (2005). Fertility, family planning and reproductive health of U.S. women: Data from the 2002 national survey of family growth. *Vital Health and Statistics, 23,* 1–160.

Charon, R. (2001). Narrative medicine. *JAMA, 286,* 1897–1902. doi:10.1001/jama.286.15.1897

Chassin, L., Presson, C. C., Rose, J., Sherman, S. J., Davis, M. J., & Gonzalez, J. L. (2005). Parenting style and smoking-specific parenting practices as predictors of adolescent smoking onset. *Journal of Pediatric Psychology, 30,* 333–334. doi:10.1093/jpepsy/jsi028

Chen, T. H., Chang, S. P., Tsai, C. F., & Juang, K. D. (2004). Prevalence of depressive and anxiety disorders in an assisted reproductive technique clinic. *Human Reproduction, 19,* 2313–2318. doi:10.1093/humrep/deh414

Chlebowski, R. T., Anderson, G. L., Gass, M., Lane, D. S., Aragaki, A. K., Kuller, L. H., . . . Prentice, P., for the Women's Health Initiative Investigators. (2010). Estrogen plus progestin and breast cancer incidence and mortality in postmenopausal women. *JAMA, 304.* doi:10.1001/jama.2010.1500

Christakis, N. A., & Fowler, J. H. (2007). The spread of obesity in a large social network over 32 years. *The New England Journal of Medicine, 357,* 370–379. doi:10.1056/NEJMsa066082

Christakis, N. A., & Fowler, J. H. (2008). The collective dynamics of smoking in a large social network. *The New England Journal of Medicine, 358,* 2249–2258. doi:10.1056/NEJMsa0706154

Christian Apologetics & Research Ministry. *What does the Bible say about artificial insemination?* Retrieved from http://carm.org/what-does-bible-say-about-artificial-insemination

Clark, P. (2009). Resiliency in the practicing marriage and family therapist. *Journal of Marital and Family Therapy, 35,* 231–247. doi: 10.1111/j.1752-0606.2009.00108.x

Cohen, L., Zilkha, S., Middleton, J., & O'Donnahue, N. (1978). Perinatal mortality: Assessing parental affirmation. *American Journal of Orthopsychiatry, 48,* 727–731. doi:10.1111/j.1939-0025.1978.tb02577.x

Cohen, S. (2004). Social relationships and health. *American Psychologist, 59,* 676–684. doi:10.1037/0003-066X.59.8.676

Cohen, S., Janicki-Deverts, D., & Miller, G. E. (2007). Psychological stress and disease. *JAMA, 298,* 1685–1687. doi:10.1001/jama.298.14.1685

Cole-Kelly, K., & Hepworth, J. (1991). Performance pressures: Saner responses for consultant family therapists. *Family Systems Medicine, 9,* 159–164. doi:10.1037/h0089225

Combrinck-Graham, L. (1985). A developmental model for family systems. *Family Process, 24,* 139–150. doi:10.1111/j.1545-5300.1985.00139.x

Cook, C. (1990). The gynecologic perspective. In N. Stotland (Ed.), *Psychiatric aspects of reproductive technology* (pp. 51–65). Washington, DC: American Psychiatric Press.

Cooke, N. J., Salas, E., Kiekel, P. A., & Bell, B. (2004). Advances in measuring team cognition. In E. Salas & S. M. Fiore (Eds.), *Team cognition: Understanding the factors that drive process and performance* (pp. 83–106). Washington, DC: American Psychological Association. doi:10.1037/10690-005

Coons, H. L., Morgenstern, D., Hoffman, E. M., Striepe, M. I., & Buch, C. (2004). Psychologists in women's primary care and obstetrics-gynecology: Consultation and treatment issues. In R. Frank, S. H. McDaniel, J. H. Bray, & M. Heldring (Eds.), *Primary care psychology* (pp. 209–226). Washington, DC: American Psychological Association.

Coryell, W. (1981). Diagnosis-specific mortality: Primary unipolar depression and Briquet's syndrome (somatization disorder). *Archives of General Psychiatry, 38,* 939–942. doi:10.1001/archpsyc.1981.01780330097012

Council of Academic Family Medicine. (2012). *Behavioral health addendum to the joint principles of the patient-centered medical home.* Leawood, KS: Author.

Covington, S. N. (2006). Infertility counseling in practice: A collaborative reproductive healthcare model. In S. N. Covington & L. H. Burns (Eds.), *Infertility counseling: A comprehensive handbook for counselors* (2nd ed., pp. 493–507). Cambridge, England: Cambridge University Press.

Coyne, J. C., & Anderson, B. J. (1988). The "psychosomatic family" reconsidered: Diabetes in context. *Journal of Marital and Family Therapy, 14,* 113–123. doi:doi:10.1111/j.1752-0606.1988.tb00726.x

Coyne, J. C., & Smith, D. A. (1994). Couples coping with a myocardial infarction: Contextual perspective on patient self-efficacy. *Journal of Family Psychology, 8,* 43–54. doi:10.1037/0893-3200.8.1.43

Coyne, J. C., Wortman, C. B., & Lehman, D. R. (1988). The other side of support: Emotional overinvolvement and miscarried helping. In B. H. Gottlieb (Ed.), *Marshalling social support: Formats, processes, and effects* (pp. 305–330). Newbury Park, NY: Sage.

Crane, D. (1986). The family therapist, the primary care physician, and the health maintenance organization: Pitfalls and opportunities. *Family Systems Medicine, 4,* 22–30.

Craufurd, D., Dodge, A., Kerzin-Storrar, L., & Harris, R. (1989). Uptake of presymptomatic predictive testing for Huntington's disease. *The Lancet, 334,* 603–605. doi:10.1016/S0140-6736(89)90722-8

Creed, F. (2010). Is there a better term than "medically unexplained symptoms?" *Journal of Psychosomatic Research, 68,* 5–8. doi:10.1016/j.jpsychores.2009.09.004

Cummings, N., Dorken, H., Pallak, M. S., & Henke, C. (1990). *The impact of psychological intervention on healthcare utilization and costs.* San Francisco, CA: The Biodyne Institute.

Czyba, J. C., & Chevret, M. (1979). Psychological reactions of couples to artificial insemination with donor sperm. *International Journal of Fertility, 24,* 240–245.

Dakof, G. A., & Liddle, H. A. (1990, August). *Communication between cancer patients and their spouses. Is it an essential aspect of adjustment?* Paper presented at the American Psychological Association Annual Meeting, Boston, MA.

Danaei, G., Ding E. L., Mozaffarian, D., Taylor B., Rehm, J., Murry, C. J., & Ezzati, M. (2009). The preventable causes of death in the United States: Comparative risk assessment of dietary, lifestyle, and metabolic risk factors. *PLoS Med, 6*(4), e1000058. Retrieved from http://www.plosmedicine.org/article/info:doi/10.1371/journal.pmed.1000058doi:10.1371/journal.pmed.1000058

DeFrain, J. (1991). Learning about grief from normal families: SIDS, stillbirth, and miscarriage. *Journal of Marital and Family Therapy, 17,* 215–232. doi:10.1111/j.1752-0606.1991.tb00890.x

deGruy, F., Columbia, L., & Dickinson, P. (1987). Somatization disorder in a family practice. *The Journal of Family Practice, 25,* 45–51.

de Ridder, D., Geenen, R., Kuijer, R., & van Middendorp, H. (2008). Psychological adjustment to chronic disease. *The Lancet, 372,* 246–255. doi:10.1016/S0140-6736(08)61078-8

de Vries, K., Degani, S., & Eibschita, I. (1984). The influence of the post-coital test on the sexual function of infertile women. *Journal of Psychosomatic Obstetrics & Gynaecology, 3,* 101–106. doi:10.3109/01674828409017453

Didonna, F. (Ed.). (2009). *Clinical handbook of mindfulness.* New York, NY: Springer. doi:10.1007/978-0-387-09593-6

Dietzen, J. (2010, October 7). What does the church say about artificial insemination? *Catholic Courier.* Retrieved from http://www.catholiccourier.com/commentary/other-columnists/what-does-church-say-about-artificial-insemination/?keywords=artificial%20insemination&tag=&searchSectionID=

Doherty, W. J. (1988). Implications of chronic illness for family treatment. In C. Chilman, E. Nunnally, & F. Cox (Eds.), *Chronic illness and disability* (pp. 192–210). Newbury Park, CA: Sage.

Doherty, W. J. (1995). The why's and levels of collaborative family health care. *Family Systems Medicine, 13,* 275–281.

Doherty, W. J., & Baird, M. (1983). *Family therapy and family medicine: Towards the primary care of families.* New York, NY: Guilford Press.

Doherty, W. J., Baird, M., & Becker, L. (1987). Family medicine and the biopsychosocial model: The road toward integration. *Marriage & Family Review, 10*, 51–69. doi:10.1300/J002v10n03_03

Doherty, W. J., & Campbell, T. (1988). *Families and health*. Newbury Park, CA: Sage.

Doherty, W. J., & Carroll, J. A. (2002). The citizen therapist and family-centered community building. *Family Process, 41*, 561–568.

Doherty, W. J., & Colangelo, N. (1984). The family FIRO model: A modest proposal for organizing family treatment. *Journal of Marital and Family Therapy, 10*, 19–29. doi:10.1111/j.1752-0606.1984.tb00562.x

Doherty, W. J., Colangelo, N., & Hovander, D. (1991). Priority setting in family change and clinical practice: The family FIRO model. *Family Process, 30*, 227–240. doi:10.1111/j.1545-5300.1991.00227.x

Doherty, W. J., & Harkaway, J. E. (1990). Obesity and family systems: A family FIRO approach to assessment and treatment planning. *Journal of Marital and Family Therapy, 16*, 287–298. doi:10.1111/j.1752-0606.1990.tb00849.x

Doherty, W. J., & McDaniel, S. H. (2010). *Family therapy*. Washington, DC: American Psychological Association.

Doherty, W. J., McDaniel, S. H., & Baird, M. A. (1996). Five levels of primary care/behavioral healthcare collaboration. *Behavioral Healthcare Tomorrow, 5*, 25–27.

Doherty, W. J., & Mendenhall, T. J. (2006). Citizen health care: A model for engaging patients, families, and communities as coproducers of health. *Families, Systems, & Health, 24*, 251–263. doi:10.1037/1091-7527.24.3.251

Doherty, W. J., Mendenhall, T. J., & Berge, J. M. (2010). The Families and Democracy and Citizen Health Care Project. *Journal of Marital and Family Therapy, 36*, 389–402.

Doherty, W. J., & Peskay, R. E. (1993). Family systems and the schools. In S. L. Christianson & J. C. Connolly (Eds.), *Home-school collaboration* (pp. 1–18). Washington, DC: National Association of School Psychologists.

Doherty, W. J., & Whitehead, D. (1986). The social dynamics of cigarette smoking: A family FIRO analysis. *Family Process, 25*, 453–459. doi:10.1111/j.1545-5300.1986.00453.x

Domar, A. D., & Prince, L. B. (2011, October). Impact of psychological interventions on IVF outcome. *Sexuality, Reproduction, &. Menopause, 9*, 26–32.

Domar, A. D., Rooney, K. L., Wiegand, B., Orave, I. J., Alper, M. M., Berger, B. M., & Nikolovski, J. (2011). Impact of a group mind/body intervention on pregnancy rates in IVF patients. *Fertility and Sterility, 95*, 2269–2273. doi:10.1016/j.fertnstert.2011.03.046

Domar, A. D., Smith, K., Conboy, L., Iannone, M., & Alper, M. (2010). A prospective investigation into the reasons why insure united states patients drop out of in vitro fertilization treatment. *Fertility and Sterility, 94*, 1457–1459. doi:10.1016/j.fertnstert.2009.06.020

Driscoll, W. D., & McCabe, E. P. (2004). Primary care psychology in independent practice. In R. G. Frank, S. H. McDaniel, J. H. Bray, & M. Heldring (Eds.), *Primary care psychology* (pp. 133–148). Washington, DC: American Psychological Association.

Druley, J. A., Stephens, M. A., & Coyne, J. C. (1997). Emotional and physical intimacy in coping with lupus: Women's dilemmas of disclosure and approach. *Health Psychology, 16*, 506–514. doi:10.1037/0278-6133.16.6.506

Dym, B., & Berman, S. (1986). The primary health care team: Family physician and family therapist in joint practice. *Family Systems Medicine, 4*, 9–21. doi:10.1037/h0089687

Easton, D. F., Ford, D., & Bishop, D. T. (1995). Breast and ovarian cancer incidence in *BRCA1*-mutation carriers: Breast cancer linkage consortium. *American Journal of Human Genetics, 56*, 265–271.

Ebbesen, S. M., Zachariae, R., Mehlsen, M. Y., Thomsen, D., Højgaard, A., Ottosen, L., . . . Good, B. (2009). Stressful life events are associated with a poor in-vitro fertilization (IVF) outcome: A prospective study. *Human Reproduction, 24*, 2173–2182. doi:10.1093/humrep/dep185

Edelmann, R., Humphrey, M., & Owens, D. (1994). The meaning of parenthood and couples' reactions to male infertility. *British Journal of Medical Psychology, 67*, 291–299. doi:10.1111/j.2044-8341.1994.tb01797.x

Edwards, T. M., Patterson, J., Vakili, S., & Scherger, J. E. (2012). Healthcare policy in the United States: A primer for medical family therapists. *Contemporary Family Therapy: An International Journal, 34*, 217–227. doi:10.1007/s10591-012-9188-4

Eisenberg, L. (1979). Interfaces between medicine and psychiatry. *Comprehensive Psychiatry, 20*, 1–14. doi:10.1016/0010-440X(79)90054-3

Elkaim, M. (1990). *If you love me, don't leave me: Constructions of reality and change in family therapy.* New York, NY: Basic Books.

Ell, K. (1996). Social networks, social support and coping with serious illness: The family connection. *Social Science & Medicine, 42*, 173–183. doi:10.1016/0277-9536(95)00100-X

Ell, K., Katon, W., Xie, B., Lee, P. J., Kapetanovic, S., Guterman, J., & Chou, C. P. (2010). Collaborative care management of major depression among low-income, predominantly Hispanic subjects with diabetes: A randomized controlled trial. *Diabetes Care, 33*, 706–713. doi:10.2337/dc09-1711

Engel, G. L. (1977). The need for a new medical model: A challenge for biomedicine. *Science, 196*, 129–136. doi:10.1126/science.847460

Engel, G. L. (1980). The clinical application of the biopsychosocial model. *The American Journal of Psychiatry, 137*, 535–544.

Epstein, L. H., Valoski, A., Wing, R. R., & McCurley, J. (1990). Ten-year follow-up of behavioral, family-based treatment for obese children. *JAMA, 264*, 2519–2523. doi:10.1001/jama.1990.03450190051027

Epstein, R. M., & Peters, E. (2009). Beyond information: Exploring patients' preferences. *JAMA, 302*, 195–197.

Epstein, R. M., Quill, T. E., & McWhinney, I. R. (1999). Somatization reconsidered: Incorporating the patient's experience of illness. *Archives of Internal Medicine, 159*, 215–222. doi:10.1001/archinte.159.3.215

Epstein, R. M., Shields, C. G., Meldrum, S., Fiscella, K., Carroll, J., Carney, P., & Duberstein, P. (2006). Physicians' responses to patients' medically unexplained symptoms. *Psychosomatic Medicine, 68*, 269–276. doi:10.1097/01.psy.0000204652.27246.5b

Fagundes, C. P., Bennett, J. M., Derry, H. M., & Kiecolt-Glaser, J. K. (2011). Relationships and inflammation across the lifespan: Social developmental pathways to disease. *Social and Personality Psychology Compass, 5*, 891–903. doi:10.1111/j.1751-9004.2011.00392.x

Family Caregiver Alliance. (2006). *Fact sheet: Caregiver health*. Retrieved from http://www.caregiver.org/caregiver/jsp/content_node.jsp?nodeid=1822

Fiddler, M., Jackson, J., Kapur, N., Wells, A., & Creed, F. (2004). Childhood adversity and frequent medical consultations. *General Hospital Psychiatry, 26*, 367–377.

Flegal, K. M., Carroll, M. D., Kit, B. K., & Ogden, C. L. (2012). Prevalence of obesity and trends in the distribution of body mass index among US adults, 1999–2010. *JAMA, 307*, 491–497. doi: 10.1001/jama.2012.39

Fletcher, J. M., Frisvold, D., & Tefft, N. (2010). Taxing soft drinks and restricting access to vending machines to curb child obesity. *Health Affairs, 29*, 1059–1066. doi:10.1377/hlthaff.2009.0725

Forkner-Dunn, J. (2003). Internet-based patient self-care: The next generation of health care delivery. *Journal of Medical Internet Research, 5*(2), e8. doi: 10.2196/jmir.5.2.e8

Foy, R., Hempel, S., Rubenstein, L., Suttorp, M., Seelig, M., Shanman, R., & Shekelle, P. G. (2010). Meta-analysis: Effect of interactive communication between collaborating primary care physicians and specialists. *Annals of Internal Medicine, 152*, 247–258. doi:10.1059/0003-4819-152-4-201002160-00010

Frank, A. W. (2004). *The renewal of generosity: Illness, medicine, and how to live*. Chicago, IL: University of Chicago Press.

Frankel, R., Quill, T., & McDaniel, S. H. (Eds.). (2003). *The biopsychosocial approach: Past, present, and future*. Rochester, NY: University of Rochester Press.

Frankel, R. M., & Inui, T. S. (2006). Re-forming relationships in health care. Papers from the Ninth Bi-Annual Regenstrief Conference. *Journal of General Internal Medicine, 21*(Suppl. 1), S1–S2. doi:10.1111/j.1525-1497.2006.00301.x

Franko, D. L., Thompson, D., Affenito, S. G., Barton, B. A., & Striegel-Moore, R. H. (2008). What mediates the relationship between family meals and adolescent health issues. *Health Psychology, 27*(Suppl. 2), S109. doi:10.1037/0278-6133.27.2(Suppl.).S109

Franks, M. M., Peinta, A. M., & Wray, L. A. (2002). It takes two: Marriage and smoking cessation in the middle years. *Journal of Aging and Health, 14,* 336–354. doi:10.1177/08964302014003002

Franks, M. M., Shields, C. G., Lim, E., Sands, L. P., Mobley, S., & Boushey, C. J. (2012). I will if you will: Similarity in married partners' readiness to change health risk behaviors. *Health Education & Behavior, 39,* 324–331. doi:10.1177/1090198111402824

Freeman, E. W., Boxer, A. S., Rickels, K., Tureck, R., & Mastroianni, L., Jr. (1985). Psychological evaluation and support in a program of in vitro fertilization and embryo transfer. *Fertility and Sterility, 43,* 48–53.

Freeman, T., & Golombok, S. (2012). Donor insemination: A follow-up study of disclosure decisions, family relationships, and child adjustment at adolescence. *Reproductive Biomedicine Online, 25,* 193–203. doi:10.1016/j.rbmo.2012.03.009

Frey, J., & Wendorf, R. (1984). Family therapist and pediatrician: Teaming up on four common behavioral pediatric problems. *Family Systems Medicine, 2,* 290–297.

Friedman, E. (1985). *Generation to generations.* New York, NY: Guilford Press.

Friedman, E. (1991, June). *Managing crisis: Bowen theory incarnate.* Audiotape of a presentation at a Family Systems Theory Seminar, Bethesda, MD.

Ganley, R. M. (1986). Epistemology, family patterns, and psychosomatics: The case of obesity. *Family Process, 25,* 437–451. doi:10.1111/j.1545-5300.1986.00437.x

Gehart, D. R., & McCollum, E. E. (2007). Engaging suffering: Towards a mindful re-visioning of family therapy practice. *Journal of Marital and Family Therapy, 33,* 214–226. doi:10.1111/j.1752-0606.2007.00017.x

Gilden, J. L., Hendryx, M., Casia, C., & Singh, S. P. (1989). The effectiveness of diabetes education programs for older patients and their spouses. *Journal of the American Geriatrics Society, 37,* 1023–1030.

Gjerdingen, D., Crow, S., McGovern, P., Miner, M., & Center, B. (2009). Stepped care treatment of postpartum depression: Impact on treatment, health, and work outcomes. *Journal of the American Board of Family Medicine, 22,* 473–482. doi:10.3122/jabfm.2009.05.080192

Glantz, M. J., Chamberlain, M. C., Liu, Q., Hsieh, C. C., Edwards, K. R., Van Horn, A., & Recht, L. (2009). Gender disparity in the rate of partner abandonment in patients with serious medical illness. *Cancer, 115,* 5237–5242. doi:10.1002/cncr.24577

Glanz, K., Rimer, B. K., & Viswanath, K. (Eds.). (2008). *Health behavior and health education: Theory, research, and practice* (4th ed.). San Francisco, CA: Jossey-Bass.

Glaser, R., & Kiecolt-Glaser, J. K. (2005). Stress-induced immune dysfunction: Implications for health. *Nature Reviews. Immunology, 5,* 243–251. doi:10.1038/nri1571

Glenn, M. (1987). *Collaborative health care: A family-oriented model.* New York, NY: Praeger.

Gold, D. R. (2008). Vulnerability to cardiovascular effects of air pollution in people with diabetes. *Current Diabetes Report, 8,* 333–335.

Gold, K. J. (2010). Marriage and cohabitation outcomes after pregnancy loss. *Pediatrics, 125*, e1202–e1207. doi:10.1542/peds.2009-3081

Goleman, D. (2006). *Emotional intelligence.* New York, NY: Bantam.

Golombok, S., Blake, L., Casey, P., Roman, G., & Jadva, V. (2012). Children born through reproductive donation: A longitudinal study of psychological adjustment. *Journal of Child Psychology & Psychiatry,* doi: 10.1111/jcpp12015

Gonder-Frederick, L. A., Cox, D. J., & Ritterband, L. M. (2002). Diabetes and behavioral medicine: The second decade. *Journal of Consulting and Clinical Psychology, 70*, 611–625. doi:10.1037/0022-006X.70.3.611

Gonzalez, S., & Steinglass, P. (2002). Application of multifamily groups in chronic medical disorders. In W. McFarlane (Ed.), *Multifamily groups in the treatment of severe psychiatric disorders* (pp. 315–340). New York, NY: Guilford Press.

Gonzalez, S., Steinglass, P., & Reiss, D. (1987). *Family-centered interventions for people with chronic disabilities: The eight-session multiple family discussion group program.* Washington, DC: Center for Family Research, Department of Psychiatry and Behavioral Science, George Washington University Medical Center.

Gonzalez, S., Steinglass, P., & Reiss, D. (1989). Putting the illness in its place: Discussion groups for families with chronic medical illnesses. *Family Process, 28*, 69–87. doi:10.1111/j.1545-5300.1989.00069.x

Gordon, P. A., & Perrone, K. M. (2004). When spouses become caregivers: Counseling implications for younger couples. *Journal of Rehabilitation, 70*, 27–32.

Gorin, A. A., Wing, R. R., Fava, J. L., Jakicic, J. M., Jeffery, R., & West, D. S. (2008). Weight loss treatment influences untreated spouses and the home environment: Evidence of a ripple effect. *International Journal of Obesity, 32*, 1678–1684. doi:10.1038/ijo.2008.150

Gottman, J. M., & Katz, L. F. (1989). Effects of marital discord on young children's peers interaction and health. *Developmental Psychology, 25*, 373–381. doi:10.1037/0012-1649.25.3.373

Granek, L., Tozer, R., Mazzotta, P., Ramjaun, A., & Krzyzanowska, M. (2012). Nature and impact of grief over patient loss on oncologists' personal and professional loves. *Archives of Internal Medicine, 1426*, 1–3.

Greenson, R. (1965). The working alliance and the transference neuroses. *The Psychoanalytic Quarterly, 34*, 155–181.

Greil, A. L. (1997). Infertility and psychological distress: A critical review of the literature. *Social Science & Medicine, 45*, 1679–1704. doi:10.1016/S0277-9536(97)00102-0

Griffiths, F., Lindenmeyer, A., Powell, J., Lowe, P., & Thorogood, M. (2006). Why are health care interventions delivered over the Internet? A systematic review of the published literature. *Journal of Medical Internet Research, 7*, e10. Retrieved from http://www.jmir.org/2006/2/e10

Grunau, R. V., Whitfield, M. F., Petrie, J. H., & Fryer, E. L. (1994). Early pain experience, child and family factors, as precursors of somatization: A prospective study

of extremely premature and full-term children. *Pain, 56,* 353–359. doi:10.1016/
0304-3959(94)90174-0

Hagedoorn, M., Kuijer, R. G., Buunk, B. P., DeJong, G. M., Wobbes, T., &
Sanderman, R. (2000). Marital satisfaction in patients with cancer: Does support
from intimate partners benefit those who need it most? *Health Psychology, 19,*
274–282. doi:10.1037/0278-6133.19.3.274

Haley, J. (1976). *Problem solving therapy.* San Francisco, CA: Jossey-Bass.

Hämmerli, K., Znoj, H., & Barth, J. (2009). The efficacy of psychological interventions
for infertile patients: A meta-analysis examining mental health and pregnancy
rates. *Human Reproduction Update, 15,* 279–295. doi:10.1093/humupd/dmp002

Hanafin, H. (2006). Surrogacy and gestational carrier participants. In S. N. Covington
& L. H. Burns (Eds.), *Infertility counseling: A comprehensive handbook for counselors*
(2nd ed., pp. 370–386). Cambridge, England: Cambridge University Press.

Harkaway, J. E. (1983). Obesity: Reducing the larger system. *Journal of Strategic &
Systemic Therapies. Journal of Strategic & Systemic Therapies, 2,* 2–14.

Harkaway, J. E. (1986). Structural assessment of families with obese adolescent girls.
Journal of Marital and Family Therapy, 12, 199–201. doi:10.1111/j.1752-0606.1986.
tb01639.x

Harp, J. (1989). *Physicians' expectations of therapists.* Rochester, NY: Family Programs,
University of Rochester Department of Psychiatry.

Harris, M. A., Antal, H., Oelbaum, R. Buckloh, L. M., White, N. H., & Wysocki, T.
(2008). Good intentions gone awry: Assessing parental "miscarried helping"
in diabetes. *Families, Systems, & Health, 26,* 393–403. doi:10.1037/a0014232

Harvey, J. H. (2002). *Disenfranchised grief.* Champaign, IL: Research Press.

Haynes, A. B., Weiser, T. G., Berry, W. R., Lipsitz, S. R., Breizat, A. H., Dellinger,
E. P., . . . & the Safe Surgery Saves Lives Study Group. (2009). A surgical safety
checklist to reduce morbidity and mortality in a global population. *The New
England Journal of Medicine, 360,* 491–499. doi:10.1056/NEJMsa0810119

Hecker, L., Martin, D., & Martin, M. (1986). Family factors in childhood obesity.
American Journal of Family Therapy, 14, 247–253. doi:10.1080/01926188608
250644

Helgeson, V. S. (1994). Relation of agency and communion to well-being: Evidence
and potential explanations. *Psychological Bulletin, 116,* 412–428. doi:10.1037/
0033-2909.116.3.412

Hepworth, J. (1997). The two-way mirror in my therapy room: AIDS and families.
In S. H. McDaniel, J. Hepworth, & W. J. Doherty (Eds.), *The shared experience
of illness: Stories of patients, families, and their therapists* (pp. 163–172). New York,
NY: Basic Books.

Hepworth, J., Gavazzi, S., Adlin, M., & Miller, W. (1988). Training for collaboration:
Internships for family-therapy students in a medical setting. *Family Systems
Medicine, 6,* 69–79.

Hepworth, J., & Harris, L. (1986, November). *Changing metaphors for the healthcare process: A model of coordinated care*. Paper presented at the Annual Meeting of the National Council on Family Relations, Dearborn, MI.

Hepworth, J., & Jackson, M. (1985). Healthcare for families: Models of collaboration between family therapists and family physicians. *Family Relations, 34*, 123–127.

Hill, C. E., Helms, J. E., Tichenor, V., Spiegel, S. B., O'Grady, K. E., & Perry, E. S. (1988). Effects of therapist response modes in brief psychotherapy. *Journal of Counseling Psychology, 35*, 222–233. doi:10.1037/0022-0167.35.3.222

Hill, C. E., & Knox, S. (2001). Self-disclosure. *Psychotherapy: Theory, Research, Practice, Training, 38*, 413–417. doi:10.1037/0033-3204.38.4.413

Hobbs, N., Perrin, J., & Ireys, H. (1985). *Chronically ill children and their families*. San Francisco, CA: Jossey-Bass.

Hodgson, J., Lamson, A., Mendenhall, T., & Crane, R. (2012). Medical family therapy: Opportunities for workplace development in healthcare. *Contemporary Family Therapy, 34*, 143–146.

Holmes, T. H., & Rahe, R. (1967). The social readjustment rating scale. *Journal of Psychosomatic Research, 11*, 213–218. doi:10.1016/0022-3999(67)90010-4

Homish, G. G., & Loendard, K. E. (2005). Spousal influence on smoking behaviors in a US community sample of newly married couples. *Social Science & Medicine, 61*, 2557–2567. doi:10.1016/j.socscimed.2005.05.005

Hopwood, P., Lee, A., Shenton, A., Baildam, A., Brain, A., Lalloo, F., . . . Howell, A. (2000). Clinical follow-up after bilateral risk reducing ("prophylactic") mastectomy: Mental health and body image outcomes. *Psycho-Oncology, 9*, 462–472. doi: 10.1002/1099-1611(200011/12)9:6<462::AID-PON485>3.0.CO 2-J

Horowitz, J. I., Galst, J. P., & Elder, N. (2010). *Ethical dilemmas in fertility counseling*. Washington, DC: American Psychological Association. doi:10.1037/12086-000

House, J. S., Landis, K. R., & Umberson, D. (1988). Social relationships and health. *Science, 241*, 540–545. doi:10.1126/science.3399889

Hu, F. (2008). *Obesity epidemiology*. New York, NY: Oxford University Press. doi:10.1093/acprof:oso/9780195312911.001.0001

Hudgens, A. (1979). Family-oriented treatment of chronic pain. *Journal of Marital and Family Therapy, 5*, 67–78.

Hughes, P. M., Turton, P., & Evans, C. D. (1999). Stillbirth as risk factor for depression and anxiety in the subsequent pregnancy: Cohort study. *British Medical Journal, 318*, 1721–1724. doi:10.1136/bmj.318.7200.1721

Hunt, C. K. (2003). Concepts in caregiver research. *Journal of Nursing Scholarship, 35*(1), 27–32. doi:10.1111/j.1547-5069.2003.00027.x

Hunter, C., Goodie, J., Oordt, M., & Dobmeyer, A. (2009). *Integrated behavioral health in primary care: Step-by-step guidance for assessment and intervention*. Washington, DC: American Psychological Association.

Huygen, F. J. A. (1982). *Family medicine: The medical life history of families*. New York, NY: Brunner/Mazel.

Hymowitz, N., Schwab, M., McNerney, C., Schwab, J., Eckholdt, H., & Haddock, K. (2003). Postpartum relapse to cigarette smoking in inner city women. *Journal of the National Medical Association, 95*, 461–474.

Imber-Black, E. (1988). The family system and the health care system: Making the invisible visible. In F. Walsh & C. Anderson (Eds.), *Chronic disorders and the family* (pp. 169–183). New York, NY: Hayworth. doi:10.1300/J287v03n03_11

Imber-Black, E. (1989). Ritual themes in families and family therapy. In E. Imber-Black, J. Roberts, & R. Whiting (Eds.), *Rituals in families and family therapy* (pp. 47–83). New York, NY: Norton.

Imber-Black, E. (1993). *Secrets in families and family therapy*. New York, NY: Norton.

Imber-Black, E., Roberts, J., & Whiting, R. A. (2003). *Rituals in families and family therapy*. New York, NY: Norton.

Integrated Behavioral Health Project. (2009). *Partners in health: Primary care/county mental health collaboration*. San Francisco, CA: Author. Retrieved from http://www.ibhp.org/uploads/file/IBHP%20Collaborative%20Tool%20Kit%20final.pdf

Jacobs, B. (2007). Reliable witness: What it takes to be with your clients to the end. *Psychotherapy Networker, 31*, 35–39, 56.

Jadva, V. (2003). The experiences of surrogate mothers. *Human Reproduction, 18*, 2196–2204.

Jadva, V., Murray, C., Lycett, E., MacCallam, F., & Golombok, S. (2003). Surrogacy: The experiences of surrogate mothers. *Human Reproduction, 18*, 2196–2204. doi:10.1093/humrep/deg397

Johnson, B., Ford, D., & Abraham, M. (2010). Collaborating with patients and their families. *Journal of Healthcare Risk Management, 29*(4), 15–21. doi:10.1002/jhrm.20029

Johnson, S. K. (2008). *Medically unexplained illness: Gender and biopsychosocial implications*. Washington, DC: American Psychological Association. doi:10.1037/11623-000

Johnson, S. M. (1996). *The practice of emotionally focused marital therapy: Creating connection*. Hove, England: Brunner-Routledge.

Johnson, S. M., Bradley, B., Furrow, J., Lee, A., & Palmer, G. (2005). *Becoming an emotionally focused therapist: The workbook*. New York, NY: Routledge.

Johnson S. M., & Whiffen, V. E. (Eds.). (2005). *Attachment processes in couple and family therapy*. New York: Guilford Press.

Jordan, J. (1978). *Poem for South African women*. Retrieved from http://www.junejordan.net/poem-for-south-african-women.html

Kaplan, C., Lipkin, M., & Gordon, G. (1988). Somatization in primary care: Patients with unexplained and vexing medical complaints. *Journal of General Internal Medicine, 3*, 177–190. doi:10.1007/BF02596128

Kassirer, J. P. (2005). *On the take: How medicine's complicity with big business can endanger your health*. New York, NY: Oxford University Press.

Kathol, R. G., Butler, M., McAlpine, D. D., & Kane, R. L. (2010). Barriers to physical and mental condition integrated service delivery. *Psychosomatic Medicine, 72*, 511–518. doi:10.1097/PSY.0b013e3181e2c4a0

Katon, W. (1985). Somatization in primary care. *The Journal of Family Practice, 21*, 257–258.

Katon, W., & Russo, J. (1989). Somatic symptoms and depression. *The Journal of Family Practice, 29*, 65–69.

Katon, W., & Unutzer, J. (2006). Collaborative care models for depression: Time to move from evidence to practice. *Archives of Internal Medicine, 166*, 2304–2306. doi:10.1001/archinte.166.21.2304

Katon, W., Von Korff, M., Lin, E., Walker, E., Simon, G. E., Bush, T., . . . Russo, J. (1995). Collaborative management to achieve treatment guidelines: Impact on depression in primary care. *JAMA, 273*, 1026–1031. doi:10.1001/jama.1995. 03520370068039

Katon, W. J. (2009). Collaborative care: Evidence-based models that improve primary care depressive outcomes. *CNS Spectrums, 14*(Suppl. 14), 10–13.

Kazak, A. E. (2005). Evidence-based interventions for survivors of childhood cancer and their families. *Journal of Pediatric Psychology, 30*, 29–39. doi:10.1093/jpepsy/ jsi013

Kazak, A. E., Kassam-Adams, N., Schneider, S., Zelikovsky, N., Alderfer, M. A., & Rourke, M. (2006). An integrative model of pediatric medical traumatic stress. *Journal of Pediatric Psychology, 31*, 343–355. doi:10.1093/jpepsy/jsj054

Kazak, A. E., & Noll, R. B. (2004). Child death from pediatric illness: Conceptualizing intervention from a Family/Systems and public health perspective. *Professional Psychology: Research and Practice, 35*, 219–226. doi:10.1037/0735-7028.35.3.219

Kazak, A. E., Simms, S., Barakat, L., Hobbie, W., Foley, B., Golomb, V., & Best, M. (1999). Surviving cancer competently intervention program (SCCIP): A cognitive-behavioral and family therapy intervention for adolescent survivors of childhood cancer and their families. *Family Process, 38*, 176–191. doi:10.1111/ j.1545-5300.1999.00176.x

Kellner, R. (1986). *Somatization and hypochondriasis*. New York, NY: Praeger-Greenwood.

Kellner, R., & Sheffield, B. (1973). The one-week prevalence of symptoms in neurotic patients and normals. *The American Journal of Psychiatry, 130*, 102–105.

Kessler, D. A. (2009). *The end of overeating: Taking control of the insatiable American appetite*. New York, NY: Rodale Books.

Kessler, R., & Stafford, D. (2008). Primary care is the de facto mental health system. In R. Kessler & D. Stafford (Eds.), *Collaborative medicine case studies: Evidence in practice* (pp. 9–24). New York, NY: Springer.

Keye, W. R. (2006). Medical aspects of infertility for the counselor. In S. N. Covington & L. H. Burns (Eds.), *Infertility counseling: a comprehensive handbook for counselors* (2nd ed.; pp. 20–36). Cambridge, England: Cambridge University Press.

Kiecolt-Glaser, J. K., Loving, T. J., Stowell, J. R., Malarkey, W. B., Lemeshow, S., Dickinson, S. L., & Glaser, R. (2005). Hostile marital interactions, proinflammatory cytokine production, and wound healing. *Archives of General Psychiatry, 62*, 1377–1384. doi:10.1001/archpsyc.62.12.1377

Kim, Y., & Givern, B. (2008). Quality of life of family caregivers of cancer survivors. *Cancer, 112*(Suppl. 11), 2556–2568. doi:10.1002/cncr.23449

Kleinman, A. (1988). *The illness narratives: Suffering, healing and the human condition.* New York, NY: Basic Books.

Kleinman, A. (2009). Caregiving: The odyssey of becoming more human. *The Lancet, 373*, 292–293. doi:10.1016/S0140-6736(09)60087-8

Kleinman, A., Eisenberg, L., & Good, B. (1978). Culture, illness and care: Clinical lessons form anthropological and cross-cultural research. *Annals of Internal Medicine, 88*, 251–258.

Klonoff-Cohen, H., Chu, E., Natarajan, L., & Sieber, W. A. (2001). Prospective study of stress among women undergoing in vitro fertilization or gamete intra-fallopian transfer. *Fertility and Sterility, 76*, 675–687. doi:10.1016/S0015-0282(01)02008-8

Kowal, J., Johnson, S. M., & Lee, A. (2003). Chronic illness in couples: A case for emotionally focused therapy. *Journal of Marital and Family Therapy, 29*, 299–310. doi:10.1111/j.1752-0606.2003.tb01208.x

Kraft, A. D., Palombo, J., Mitchell, D., Dean, C., Meyers, S., & Schmidt, A. W. (1980). The psychological dimensions of infertility. *American Journal of Orthopsychiatry, 50*, 618–628. doi:10.1111/j.1939-0025.1980.tb03324.x

Kramer, B. J. (1997). Gain in the caregiving experience: Where are we? What next? *The Gerontologist, 37*, 218–232.

Krasner, M. S., Epstein, R. M., Beckman, H., Suchman, A. L., Chapman, B., Mooney, C. J., & Quill, T. E. (2009). Association of an educational program in mindful communication with burnout, empathy, and attitudes among primary care physicians. *JAMA, 302*, 1284–1293. doi:10.1001/jama.2009.1384

Kroenke, K., Spitzer, R. L., deGruy, F. V., Hahn, S. R., Linzer, M., Williams, J. B., . . . Davies, M. (1997). Multisomatoform disorder: An alternative to undifferentiated somatoform disorder for the somatizing patient in primary care. *Archives of General Psychiatry, 54*, 352–358.

Kroenke, K., & Swindle, R. (2000). Cognitive-behavioral therapy for somatization and symptom syndromes: A critical review of controlled clinical trials. *Psychotherapy and Psychosomatics, 69*, 205–215. doi:10.1159/000012395

Krugman, P., & Wells, R. (2006). The health care crisis and what we can do about it. *New York Review of Books.* Retrieved from http://www.nybooks.com/archive/2006/mar/23/the-heatlh-care-crisis-and-what-to-do-about-it/0

Kübler-Ross, E. (1969). *On death and dying.* New York, NY: Macmillan.

Kübler-Ross, E. (1975). *Death: The final stage of growth.* Englewood Cliffs, NJ: Prentice-Hall.

Kuijer, R. G., Ybema, J. F., Buunk, B. P., de Jong, G. M., Thijs-Boer, F., & Sanderman, R. (2000). Active engagement, protective buffering, and overprotection: Three ways of giving support by intimate partners of patients with cancer. *Journal of Social and Clinical Psychology, 19*, 256–275. doi:10.1521/jscp.2000.19.2.256

Kumanyika, K. S. K., & Brownson, R. C. (2007). *Handbook of obesity prevention: A resource for health professionals*. New York, NY: Springer.

Kushner, K., Bordin, E., & Ryan, E. (1979). Comparison of Strupp and Jenkins' audiovisual psychotherapy analogues and real psychotherapy interviews. *Journal of Consulting and Clinical Psychology, 47*, 765–767.

Lalwani, S., Timmreck, L., Friedman, R., Penzias, A., Alper, M., & Reindollar, R. H. (2004). Variations in individual physician success rates within an in vitro fertilization program might be due to patient demographics. *Fertility and Sterility, 81*, 944–946. doi:10.1016/j.fertnstert.2003.04.005

Latzer, Y., Edmunds, L., Fenig, S., Golan, M., Gur, E., Hochberg, Z., . . . Stein, D. (2009). Managing childhood overweight: Behavior, family, pharmacology, and bariatric surgery intervention. *Obesity, 17*, 411–423. doi:10.1038/oby.2008.553

Law, D. D., & Crane, D. R. (2000). The influence of marital and family therapy on healthcare utilization in a health maintenance organization. *Journal of Marital and Family Therapy, 26*, 281–291. doi:10.1111/j.1752-0606.2000.tb00298.x

Lee, T. Y., & Sun, G. (2000). Psychosocial response of Chinese infertile husbands and wives. *Archives of Andrology, 45*, 143–148. doi:10.1080/01485010050193913

Leff, J., & Vaughn, C. (1985). *Expressed emotion in families*. New York, NY: Guilford Press.

Leff, P. (1987). Here I am, Ma: The emotional impact of pregnancy loss on parents and healthcare professionals. *Family Systems Medicine, 5*, 105–114. doi:10.1037/h0089703

Leiter, M. P., Frank, E., & Matheson, T. J. (2009). Demands, values, and burnout: Relevance for physicians. *Canadian Family Physician, 55*, 1224–1225.

Lemmens, G., Eisler, I., Heireman, M., Van Houdenhove, B., & Sabbe, B. (2005). Family discussion groups for patients with chronic pain. *ANZJFT: The Australian and New Zealand Journal of Family Therapy, 26*, 21–32.

Leppert, P. C., & Pahlka, B. (1984). Grieving characteristics after spontaneous abortion: A management approach. *Obstetrics and Gynecology, 64*, 119–122.

Lerman, C., Croyle, R., Tercyak, K., & Hamann, H. (2002). Genetic testing: Psychological aspects and implications. *Journal of Consulting and Clinical Psychology, 70*, 784–797.

Levie, L. H. (1967). An inquiry into the psychological effects on parents of artificial insemination with donor sperm. *The Eugenics Review, 59*, 97–107.

Lewis, M. A., & Rook, K. S. (1999). Social control in personal relationships: Impact on health behaviors and psychological distress. *Health Psychology, 18*, 63–71. doi:10.1037/0278-6133.18.1.63

Lin, E. H., Katon, W., Von Korff, M., Tang, L., Williams, J. W., Jr., Kroenke, K., . . . & IMPACT Investigators. (2003). Effect of improving depression care on pain and functional outcomes among older adults with arthritis: A randomized controlled trial. *JAMA, 290,* 2428–2429. doi:10.1001/jama.290.18.2428

Livneh, H. (2009). Denial of chronic illness and disability: Part II. Research findings, measurement considerations, and clinical aspects. *Rehabilitation Counseling Bulletin, 53,* 44–55. doi:10.1177/0034355209346013

Lorenz, L. S. (2011). A way into empathy: A "case" of photo-elicitation in illness research. *Health: An Interdisciplinary Journal for the Social Study of Health, Illness and Medicine, 15,* 259. doi:10.1177/1363459310397976

Ludwig, D. S., & Kabat-Zinn, J. (2008). Mindfulness in medicine. *JAMA, 300,* 1350–1352. doi:10.1001/jama.300.11.1350

Lurie, S. J., Schultz, S. H., & Lamanna, G. (2011). Assessing teamwork: A reliable five-question survey. *Family Medicine, 43,* 731–734.

Manne, S., & Badr, H. (2008). Intimacy and relationship processes in couples' psychosocial adaptation to cancer. *Cancer, 112*(Suppl. 11), 2541–2555. doi:10.1002/cncr.23450

Manne, S. L., Norton, T. R., Ostroff, J. S., Winkel, G., Fox, K., & Grana, G. (2007). Protective buffering and psychological distress among couples coping with breast cancer: The moderating role of relationship satisfaction. *Journal of Family Psychology, 21,* 380–388. doi:10.1037/0893-3200.21.3.380

Manne, S. L., & Zautra, A. J. (1989). Spouse criticism and support: Their association with coping and psychological adjustment among women with rheumatoid arthritis. *Journal of Personality and Social Psychology, 56,* 608–617. doi:10.1037/0022-3514.56.4.608

Marshall, C. A., Larkey, L. K., Curran, M. A., Weihs, K. L., Badger, T. A., Armin, J., García, F. (2011). Considerations of culture and social class for families facing cancer: The need for a new model for health promotion and psychosocial intervention. *Families, Systems, & Health, 29,* 81–94. doi:10.1037/a0023975

Matthews, R., & Matthews, A. (1986). Infertility and involuntary childlessness: The transition to nonparenthood. *Journal of Marriage and the Family, 48,* 641–649.

Mayo Clinic Staff. (2012, September 9). *Infertility. Causes.* Retrieved from http://www.mayoclinic.com/health/infertility/DS00310/DSECTION=causes

McCall, C., & Storm, C. (1985). Family therapists and family therapy programs in hospital settings: A survey. *Family Systems Medicine, 3,* 143–150.

McCartney, C., & Wada, C. (1990). Gender differences in counseling needs during infertility treatment. In N. Stotland (Ed.), *Psychiatric aspects of reproductive technology* (pp. 141–154). Washington, DC: American Psychiatric Press.

McCubbin, H. I., & Patterson, J. M. (1982). Family adaptation to crises. In H. I. McCubbin, A. Cauble, & J. Patterson (Eds.), *Family stress, coping and social support* (pp. 26–47). Springfield, IL: Thomas.

McCubbin, H. I., & Patterson, J. M. (1983). The family stress process of adjustment and adaptation. In H. I. McCubbin, M. B. Sussman, & J. M. Patterson (Eds.), *Social stress and the family* (pp. 7–38). New York, NY: Hayworth Press.

McDaniel, S. H. (1987). Trapped inside a body without a voice: Two cases of somatic fixation. In S. H. McDaniel, J. Hepworth, & W. J. Doherty (Eds.), *The shared experience of illness: stories of patients, families, and their therapists* (pp. 274–290). New York, NY: Basic Books.

McDaniel, S. H. (1994). Within-family reproductive technologies as a solution to childlessness due to infertility. *Journal of Clinical Psychology in Medical Settings, 1*, 301–308. doi:10.1007/BF01991074

McDaniel, S. H. (1995). Collaboration between psychologists and family physicians: Implementing the biopsychosocial model. *Professional Psychology, 26*, 117–122.

McDaniel, S. H. (2005). The psychotherapy of genetics. *Family Process, 44*, 25–44. doi:10.1111/j.1545-5300.2005.00040.x

McDaniel, S. H., Bank, J., Campbell, T. L., Mancini, J., & Shore, B. (1986). Using a group as a consultant. In L. C. Wynne, S. H. McDaniel, & T. Weber (Eds.), *Systems consultation: A new perspective for family therapy* (pp. 181–198). New York, NY: Guilford Press.

McDaniel, S. H., Beckman, H. B., Morse, D. S., Silberman, J., Seaburn, D. B., & Epstein, R. M. (2007). Physician self-disclosure in primary care visits: Enough about you, what about me? *Archives of Internal Medicine, 167*, 1321–1326. doi:10.1001/archinte.167.12.1321

McDaniel, S. H., & Campbell, T. L. (1986). Physicians and family therapists: The risks of collaboration. *Family Systems Medicine, 4*, 4–8.

McDaniel, S. H., Campbell, T. L., Hepworth, J., & Lorenz, A. (2005). *Family-oriented primary care* (2nd ed.). New York, NY: Springer-Verlag.

McDaniel, S. H., Campbell, T. L., & Seaburn, D. (1989). Somatic fixation in patients and physicians: A biopsychosocial approach. *Family Systems Medicine, 7*, 5–16. doi:10.1037/h0089761

McDaniel, S. H., & Cole-Kelly, K. (2003). Gender, couples, and illness: A feminist analysis of medical family therapy. In T. J. Goodrich & L. Silverstein (Eds.), *Feminist family therapy* (pp. 267–280). Washington, DC: American Psychological Association.

McDaniel, S. H., & Fogarty, C. T. (2009). What primary care psychology has to offer the patient-centered medical home. *Professional Psychology: Research and Practice, 40*, 483–492. doi:10.1037/a0016751

McDaniel, S. H., & Hepworth, J. (2003). Family psychology in primary care: Managing issues of power and dependency through collaboration. In R. Frank, S. H. McDaniel, J. Bray, & M. Heldring (Eds.), *Primary care psychology* (pp. 113–132). Washington, DC: American Psychological Association.

McDaniel, S. H., & Hepworth, J. (2004). Family psychology in primary care: Managing issues of power and dependency through collaboration. In R. G. Frank, S. H. McDaniel, J. H. Bray & M. Heldring (Eds.), *Primary care psychology* (pp. 113–132). Washington DC: American Psychological Association.

McDaniel, S. H., Hepworth, J., & Doherty, W. (1992). *Medical family therapy: A biopsychosocial approach to families with health problems*. New York, NY: Basic Books.

McDaniel, S. H., Hepworth, J., & Doherty, W. (1995). Medical family therapy with somatizing patients: The co-creation of therapeutic stories, *Family Process, 34*, 349–362.

McDaniel, S. H., Hepworth, J., & Doherty, W. J. (1997). *The shared experience of illness: Stories of patients, families, and their therapists*. New York, NY: Basic Books.

McDaniel, S. H., & Pisani, A. (2012). Family dynamics and chronic disabilities. In R. C. Talley & J. E. Crews (Eds.), *Multiple dimensions of caregiving and disability* (pp. 11–28). New York, NY: Springer.

McDaniel, S. H., & Rolland, J. (2006a). *Medical family therapy participates in the genomic revolution*. Washington, DC: American Association for Marriage and Family Therapy.

McDaniel, S. H., & Rolland, J. (2006b). Psychosocial interventions for patients and families coping with genetic conditions. In S. Miller, S. H. McDaniel, J. Rolland, & S. Feetham (Eds.), *Individuals, families, and the new era of genetics: Biopsychosocial perspectives* (pp. 173–196). New York, NY: Norton.

McDaniel, S. H., Rolland, J., Feetham, S., & Miller, S. (2006). "It runs in the family:" Family systems concepts and genetically-linked disorders. In S. Miller, S. H. McDaniel, J. Rolland, & S. Feetham (Eds.), *Individuals, families, and the new era of genetics: Biopsychosocial perspectives* (pp. 118–138). New York, NY: Norton.

McDaniel, S. H., & Speice, J. (2001). What family psychology has to offer women's health: The examples of conversion, somatization, infertility treatment, and genetic testing. *Professional Psychology: Research and Practice, 32*, 44–51. doi:10.1037/0735-7028.32.1.44

McEwan, K. L., Costello, P., & Taylor, P. (1987). Adjustment to infertility. *Journal of Abnormal Psychology, 96*, 108–116. doi:10.1037/0021-843X.96.2.108

McGoldrick, M., & Walsh, F. (Eds.). (2004). *Living beyond loss: Death in the family*. New York, NY: Norton.

McHale, J. P., & Lindahl, K. M. (Eds.). (2011). *Coparenting: A conceptual and clinical examination of family systems*. Washington, DC: American Psychological Association. doi:10.1037/12328-000

McLean, N., Griffin, S., Toney, K., & Hardeman W. (2003). Family involvement in weight control, weight maintenance, and weight-loss interventions: A systematic review of randomised trials. *International Journal of Obesity, 27*, 987–1005. doi:10.1038/sj.ijo.0802383

Medicare Payment Advisory Commission. (2007). *Report to the Congress: Promoting greater efficiency in medicare*. Washington, DC: National Academies Press.

Meltzer, D., Chung, J., Khalili, P., Marlow, E., Arora, V., Schumock, G., & Burt, R. (2010). Exploring the use of social network methods in designing health care quality improvement teams. *Social Science Medicine, 71*, 1119–1130.

Menning, B. (1977). *Infertility: A guide for the childless couple*. Englewood Cliffs, NJ: Prentice Hall.

Mermelstein, R., Lichtenstein, E., & McIntrye, K. (1983). Partner support and relapse in smoking-cessation programs. *Journal of Consulting and Clinical Psychology, 51*, 465–466. doi:10.1037/0022-006X.51.3.465

Miall, C. E. (1994). Community constructs of involuntary childlessness: Sympathy, stigma, and social support. *Canadian Review of Social Anthropology, 31*, 392–421.

Miller, S. M. (1995). Monitoring versus blunting styles of coping with cancer influence the information patients want and need about their disease. *Cancer, 76*, 167–177. doi:10.1002/1097-0142(19950715)76:2<167::AID-CNCR2820760203>3.0.CO;2-K

Miller, S. M. (2006). The individual facing genetic issues. In S. Miller, S. McDaniel, J. Rolland, & S. Feetham (Eds.), *Individuals, families, and the new era of genetics: Biopsychosocial perspectives* (pp. 79–117). New York, NY: Norton.

Miller, W., & Rollnick, S. (2002). *Motivational interviewing: Helping people change* (2nd ed.). New York, NY: Guilford Press.

Minuchin, S. (1974). *Families and family therapy*. Cambridge, MA: Harvard University Press.

Minuchin, S., Rosman, B., & Baker, L. (1978). *Psychosomatic families: Anorexia nervosa in context*. Cambridge, MA: Harvard University Press.

Mitnick, S., Leffler, C., & Hood, V. (2010). Family caregivers, patients and physicians: Ethical guidance to optimize relationships. *Journal of General Internal Medicine, 25*, 255–260. doi:10.1007/s11606-009-1206-3

Mittelman, M. S., Haley, W. E., Clay, O., & Roth, D. L. (2006). Improving caregiver well-being delays nursing home placement of patients with Alzheimer's dementia. *Neurology, 67*, 1592–1599. doi:10.1212/01.wnl.0000242727.81172.91

Morisky, D. E., Levine, D. M., Green, L. W., Shapiro, S., Russell, R. P., & Smith, C. R. (1983). Five year blood pressure control and mortality following health education for hypertensive patients. *American Journal of Public Health, 73*, 153–162. doi:10.2105/AJPH.73.2.153

Morse, D. S., McDaniel, S. H., Candib, L. M., & Beach, M. C. (2008). "Enough about me, let's get back to you": Physician self-disclosure during primary care encounters. *Annals of Internal Medicine, 149*, 835–837.

Moynihan, R., & Cassels, A. (2005). *Selling sickness: How the world's biggest pharmaceutical companies are turning us all into patients*. New York, NY: Nation Books.

Mullins, L., & Olson, R. (1990). Familial factors in the etiology, maintenance, and treatment of somatoform disorders in children. *Family Systems Medicine, 8*, 159–175. doi:10.1037/h0089230

Munk-Olsen, T., Laursen, T. M., Pedersen, C. B., Lidegaard, O., & Mortensen, P. B. (2011). Induced first-trimester abortion and risk of mental disorder. *The New England Journal of Medicine, 364,* 332–339. doi:10.1056/NEJMoa0905882

Myers, M. (1990). Male gender-related issues in reproduction and technology. In N. Stotland (Ed.), *Psychiatric aspects of reproductive technology* (pp. 25–35). Washington, DC: American Psychiatric Press.

Nachtigall, R. D., Tschann, J. M., Quiroga, S. S., Pitcher, L., & Becker, G. (1997). Stigma, disclosure, and family functioning among parents of children conceived through donor insemination. *Fertility and Sterility, 68,* 83–89. doi:10.1016/S0015-0282(97)81480-X

National Academy for State Health Policy. (2010). *A tale of two systems: A look at state efforts to integrate primary care and behavioral health in safety net settings.* Retrieved from http://www.nashp.org/publication/tale-two-systems-look-state-efforts-integrate-primary-care-and-behavioral-health-safety-net

National Alliance for Caregiving, in collaboration with the American Association of Retired People. (2009, November). *Caregiving in the U.S. 2009.* Bethesda, MD: Author. Retrieved from http://www.aarp.org/relationships/caregiving/info-12-2009/caregiving_09.html

National Institute of Mental Health. (2012). *Antidepressant medications for children and adults.* Retrieved from http://www.nimh.nih.gov/health/topics/child-and-adolescent-mental-health/antidepressant-medications-for-children-and-adolescents-information-for-parents-and-caregivers.shtml

Neese, L. E., Schover, L. R., Klein, E. A., Zippe, C., & Kupelian, P. A. (2003). Finding help for sexual problems after prostate cancer treatment: A phone survey of men's and women's perspectives. *Psycho-Oncology, 12,* 463. doi:10.1002/pon.657

Noble, E. (1987). *Having your baby by donor insemination.* Boston, MA: Houghton Mifflin.

Noffsinger, E. (2009). *Running group visits in your practice.* New York, NY: Springer.

Noyes, R. W., & Chapnick, E. M. (1964). Literature on psychology and infertility. *Fertility and Sterility, 15,* 543–558.

Nutting, P. A., Miller, W. L., Crabtree, B. F., Jaen, C. R., Stewart, E. E., & Stange, K. C. (2009). Initial lessons from the first national demonstration project on practice transformation to a patient-centered medical home. *Annals of Family Medicine, 7,* 254–260. doi:10.1370/afm.1002

Ockene, J. K., Nuttall, R. L., & Benfari, R. S. (1981). A psychosocial model of smoking cessation and maintenance of cessation. *Preventive Medicine, 10,* 623–638. doi:10.1016/0091-7435(81)90052-9

Okasha, A., Saad, A., Khalil, A., El Dawla, A., & Yehia, N. (1994). Phenomenology of obsessive-compulsive disorder: A transcultural study. *Comprehensive Psychiatry, 35,* 191–197. doi:10.1016/0010-440X(94)90191-0

Ory, M. G., Hoffman, R. R., & Yee, J. L. (1999). Prevalence and impact of caregiving: A detailed comparison between dementia and nondementia caregivers. *The Gerontologist, 39,* 177–186. doi:10.1093/geront/39.2.177

Palazzoli, S. M., Boscolo, L., Cecchin, G., & Prata, J. (1980). The problem of the referring person. *Journal of Marital and Family Therapy, 6,* 3–9.

Paris, M., & Hogue, M. (2010). Burnout in the mental health workforce: A review. *The Journal of Behavioral Health Services & Research, 37,* 519–528.

Park, E. W., Tudiver, F., Schultz, J. K., & Campbell, T. (2004). Does enhancing partner support and interaction improve smoking cessation? A meta-analysis. *Annals of Family Medicine, 2,* 170–174. doi:10.1370/afm.64

Patterson, J. M. (1988). Chronic illness in children and the impact on families. In C. S. Chilman, E. W. Nunnally, & F. M. Cox (Eds.), *Chronic illness and disability, families in trouble series* (2nd ed., pp. 69–77). Newbury Park, CA: Sage.

Patterson, J. M. (1989). A family stress model: The family adjustment and adaptation response. In C. N. Ramsey (Ed.), *Family systems in medicine* (pp. 95–118). New York, NY: Guilford Press.

Patterson, J. M. (2002). Integrating family resilience and family stress theory. *Journal of Marriage and Family, 64,* 349–360.

Patterson, J. M., & Garwick, A. W. (1994). The impact of chronic illness on families: A family systems perspective. *Annals of Behavioral Medicine, 16,* 131–142.

Patterson, J. M., Peek, C. J., Heinrich, R. L., Bischoff, R. J., & Scherger, J. (2002). Mental health professionals in medical settings: A primer. New York, NY: Norton.

Payne, S. (2006). *The health of men and women.* Malden, MA: Polity.

Peek, C. J. (2008). Planning care in the clinical, operational, and financial worlds. In R. Kessler & D. Stafford (Eds.), *Collaborative medicine case studies: Evidence in practice* (pp. 25–38). New York, NY: Springer.

Peek, C. J. (2011). *A collaborative care lexicon for asking practice and research development questions.* Retrieved from the Agency for Healthcare Research and Quality website: http://www.ahrq.gov/legacy/research/collaborativecare/collab3.htm

Perez, M. A., Skinner, E. C., & Meyerowitz, B. E. (2002). Sexuality and intimacy following radical prostatectomy: Patient and partner perspectives. *Health Psychology, 21,* 288–293. doi:10.1037/0278-6133.21.3.288

Peters, E., Lipkus, I., & Diefenbach, M. A. (2006). The functions of affect in health communications and in the construction of health preferences. *Journal of Communication, 56*(Suppl. 1), S140–S162. doi:10.1111/j.1460-2466.2006.00287.x

Peterson, B. D., Newton, C. R., & Rosen, K. H. (2003). Examining congruence between partners' perceived infertility-related stress and its relationship to marital adjustment and depression in infertile couples. *Family Process, 42,* 59–70. doi:10.1111/j.1545-5300.2003.00059.x

Petok, W. (2006). The psychology of gender-specific infertility diagnoses. In S. N. Covington & L. H. Burns (Eds.), *Infertility counseling: a comprehensive handbook for counselors* (2nd ed., pp. 37–60). Cambridge, England: Cambridge University Press.

Phillips, K. A. (2008). Somatization disorder. In R. S. Porter & J. L. Kaplan (Eds.), *The Merck Manual Home Health Handbook.* Whitehouse Station, NJ: Merck Sharp & Dohme.

Pierce, L. L. (2001). Coherence in the urban family caregiver role with African American stroke survivors. *Topics in Stroke Rehabilitation, 8,* 64–72. doi:10.1310/V5A2-6RKD-GJ9U-AMWC

Piercy, K. W., & Chapman, J. G. (2001). Adapting the caregiver role: A family legacy. *Family Relations, 50,* 386–393. doi:10.1111/j.1741-3729.2001.00386.x

Pigeon, Y., & Khan, O. (2013). *Leadership lesson: Tools for effective team meetings.* Retrieved from the American Association of Medical Colleges website: http://www.aamc.org/members/gfa/faculty_vitae/148582/team_meetings.html

Pratt, K. J., & Lamson, A. (2009). Clinical update: Childhood obesity. *Family Therapy, 8,* 36–48.

Pratt, K. J., Lamson, A. L., Collier, D. N., Crawford, Y. S., Harris, N., Gross, K., . . . & Saporito, M. (2009). Camp Golden Treasures: A multidisciplinary residential summer camp promoting weight-loss and a healthy lifestyle for adolescent girls. *Families, Systems, & Health, 21,* 116–124.

Pratt, K. J., Lamson, A. L., Lazorick, S., White, C. P., Collier, D. N., White, M. B., & Swanson, M. S. (2011). Conceptualising care for childhood obesity: A three-world view. *Journal of Children's Services, 6,* 156–171.

Prochaska, J. O., Butterworth, S., Redding, C. A., Burden, V., Perrin, N., Leo, M., . . . Prochaska J. M. (2008). Initial efficacy of MI, TTM tailoring and HRI's with multiple behaviors for employee health promotion. *Preventive Medicine, 46,* 226–231. doi:10.1016/j.ypmed.2007.11.007

Prochaska, J. O., & Velicer, W. F. (1997). The transtheoretical model of health behavior change. *American Journal of Health Promotion, 12,* 38–48. doi:10.4278/0890-1171-12.1.38

Prouty Lyness, A. M. (2004). *Feminist perspectives in medical family therapy.* New York, NY: Haworth Press.

Pyle, S. A., Haddock, C. K., Hymowitz, N., Schwab, J., & Meshberg, S. (2005). Family rules about exposure to environmental tobacco smoke. *Families, Systems, & Health, 23,* 3–15. doi:10.1037/1091-7527.23.1.3

Quill, T. E. (1985). Somatization: One of medicine's blind spots. *JAMA, 254,* 3075–3079. doi:10.1001/jama.1985.03360210091038

Rainville, F., Dumont, S., Simard, S., & Savard, M. (2012). Psychological distress among adolescents living with a parent with advanced cancer. *Journal of Psychosocial Oncology, 30,* 519–534. doi:10.1080/07347332.2012.703765

Ranjan, R. (2011). *Social support and health.* Toronto, Canada: University of Toronto Press.

Regier, D. A., Narrow, W. E., Rae, D. S., Manderscheid, R. W., Locke, B. Z., & Goodwin, F. K. (1993). The de facto US mental and addictive disorders service system: Epidemiologic catchment area prospective 1-year prevalence rates of disorders and services. *Archives of General Psychiatry, 50,* 85–94.

Reiss, D. (1981). *The family's construction of reality.* Cambridge, MA: Harvard University Press.

Reiss, D., Gonzalez, S., & Kramer, N. (1986). Family process, chronic illness, and death: On the weakness of strong bonds. *Archives of General Psychiatry, 43*, 795–804. doi:10.1001/archpsyc.1986.01800080081011

Reiss, D., & Kaplan De-Nour, A. (1989). The family and medical team in chronic illness: A transactional and developmental perspective. In C. J. Ramsey (Ed.), *Family systems in medicine* (pp. 435–444). New York, NY: Commonwealth Fund.

Robinson, P. J., & Reiter, J. (2007). *Behavioral consultation and primary care: A guide to integrating services.* New York, NY: Springer Science. doi:10.1007/978-0-387-32973-4

Rohrbaugh, M. J. (2001). Brief therapy based on interrupting ironic processes: The Palo Alto model. *Clinical Psychology: Science and Practice, 8*, 66. doi:10.1093/clipsy.8.1.66

Rohrbaugh, M. J., Shoham, V., Trost, S., Muramoto, M., Cate, R. M., & Leischow, S. (2001). Couple dynamics of change-resistant smoking: Toward a family consultation model. *Family Process, 40*, 15–31. doi:10.1111/j.1545-5300.2001.4010100015.x

Rolland, J. (1984). Toward a psychosocial typology of chronic and life-threatening illness. *Family Systems Medicine, 2*, 245–262. doi:10.1037/h0091663

Rolland, J. S. (1988). Family systems and chronic illness: A typological model. In F. Walsh & C. Anderson (Eds.), *Chronic disorders and the family* (pp. 148<en163). New York, NY: Hawthorn Press. doi:10.1300/J287v03n03_10

Rolland, J. S. (1994). *Families, illness, & disability: An integrative treatment model.* New York, NY: Basic Books.

Rolland, J. S. (2006). Living with anticipatory loss in the new era of genetics: A life cycle perspective. In S. M. Miller, S. H. McDaniel, J. S. Rolland, & S. L. Feetham (Eds.), *Individuals, families, and the new era of genetics* (pp. 139–172). New York, NY: Norton.

Rolland, J. S., & Williams, J. K. (2005). Toward a biopsychosocial model for 21st century genetics. *Family Process, 44*(1), 3–24. doi:10.1111/j.1545-5300.2005.00039.x

Rosenberg, T., & Pace, M. (2006). Burnout among mental health professionals: Special considerations for the marriage and family therapist. *Journal of Marital and Family Therapy, 32*, 87–99. doi:10.1111/j.1752-0606.2006.tb01590.x

Rosman, B., & Baker, L. (1988). The "psychosomatic family" reconsidered: Diabetes in context—a reply. *Journal of Marital and Family Therapy, 14*, 125–132. doi:10.1111/j.1752-0606.1988.tb00727.x

Roy-Byrne, P. P., Craske, M. G., Stein, M. B., Sullivan, G., Bystritsky, A., Katon, W., . . . Sherbourne, C. D. (2005). A randomized effectiveness trial of cognitive-behavioral therapy and medication for primary care panic disorder. *Archives of General Psychiatry, 62*, 290–298. doi:10.1001/archpsyc.62.3.290

Ruddy, N. B., Borresen, D. A., & Gunn, W. B. J. (2008). *The collaborative psycho-therapist: Creating reciprocal relationships with medical professionals*. Washington, DC: American Psychological Association.

Ryder, A. G., Yang, J., Zhu, X., Yao, S., Yi, J., Heine, S. J., & Bagby, R. M. (2008). The cultural shaping of depression: Somatic symptoms in China, psychological symptoms in North America? *Journal of Abnormal Psychology, 117,* 300–313. doi:10.1037/0021-843X.117.2.300

Sabatelli, R., Meth, R., & Gavazzi, S. (1988). Factors mediating the adjustment to involuntary childlessness. *Family Relations, 37,* 338–343.

Sadler, A., & Syrop, C. (1987). *The stress of infertility: Recommendations for assessment and intervention*. Family stress. Rockville, MD: Aspen.

Saleh, R. A., Ranga, G. M., Raina, R., Nelson, D. R., & Agarwal, A. (2003). Sexual dysfunction in men undergoing infertility evaluation: A cohort observational study. *Fertility and Sterility, 79,* 909–912. doi:10.1016/S0015-0282(02)04921-X

Salmon, P., Dowrick, C. F., Ring, A., & Humphris, G. M. (2004). Voiced but unheard agendas: Qualitative analysis of the psychosocial cues that patients with unexplained symptoms present to general practitioners. *The British Journal of General Practice, 54,* 171–176.

Sander, E. P., Odell, S., & Hood, K. K. (2010). Diabetes-specific family conflict and blood glucose monitoring in adolescents with Type 1 diabetes: Mediational role of diabetes self-efficacy. *Diabetes Spectrum, 23,* 89–94. doi:10.2337/diaspect.23.2.89

Sargent, J. (1985). Physician-family therapist collaboration: Children with medical problems. *Family Systems Medicine, 3,* 454–465.

Schulte, I. E., & Petermann, F. (2011). Familial risk factors for the development of somatoform symptoms and disorders in children and adolescents: A systematic review. *Child Psychiatry and Human Development, 42,* 569–583. doi:10.1007/s10578-011-0233-6

Schulz, R., & Beach, S. R. (1999). Caregiving as a risk factor for mortality: The caregiver health effects study. *JAMA, 282,* 2215–2219. doi:10.1001/jama.282.23.2215

Schulz, R., Burgio, L., Burns, R., Eisdorfer, C., Gallagher-Thompson, D., Gitlon, L. N., & Mahoney, D. F. (2003). Resources for enhancing Alzheimer's caregiver health (REACH): Overview, site-specific outcomes, and future directions. *The Gerontologist, 43,* 514–520. doi:10.1093/geront/43.4.514

Schutz, W. C. (1958). *FIRO: A three-dimensional theory of interpersonal behavior*. New York, NY: Holt, Rinehart & Winston.

Schwartz, L. (1991). *Alternatives to infertility*. New York, NY: Brunner/Mazel.

Scott, J. L., Halford, W. K., & Ward, B. G. (2004). United we stand? The effects of a couple-coping intervention on adjustment to early stage breast or gynecological cancer. *Journal of Consulting and Clinical Psychology, 72,* 1122–1135. doi:10.1037/0022-006X.72.6.1122

Seaburn, D., Lorenz, A., & Kaplan, D. (1992). The transgenerational development of chronic illness meanings. *Family Systems Medicine, 10,* 385–394.

Seaburn, D. B., Lorenz, A. D., Campbell, T. L., & Winfield, M. A. (1996). A mother's death: Family stories of illness, loss, and healing. *Families, Systems, and Health, 14,* 207–221.

Seaburn, D. B., Lorenz, A. D., Gunn, W. B., Jr., Gawinski, B. A., & Mauksch, L. B. (1996). *Models of collaboration: A guide for mental health professionals working with health care practitioners.* New York, NY: Basic Books.

Seaburn, D. B., Morse, D., McDaniel, S. H., Beckman, H., Silberman, J., & Epstein, R. M. (2005). Physician responses to ambiguous patient symptoms. *Journal of General Internal Medicine, 20,* 525–530. doi:10.1111/j.1525-1497.2005.0093.x

Seligman, M. (1988). Psychotherapy with siblings of disabled children. In M. D. Kahn & K. G. Lewis (Eds.), *Siblings in therapy* (pp. 167–189). New York, NY: Norton.

Shapiro, S. (1988). Psychological consequences of infertility in critical psychophysical passages in the life of a woman. In J. Offerman-Zuckerberg (Ed.), *A psychodynamic perspective* (pp. 269–289). New York, NY: Plenum Medical.

Shields, C. G., Finley, M. A., & Chawla, N. (2012). Couple and family interventions in health problems. *Journal of Marital and Family Therapy, 38,* 265–280. doi:10.1111/j.1752-0606.2011.00269.x

Shields, C. G., Wynne, L., & Sirkin, M. (1992). Illness, family theory, and family therapy: I. Conceptual issues: The perception of physical illness in the family system. *Family Process, 31,* 3–18.

Shindel, A., Quayle, S., Yan, Y., Husain, A., & Naughton, C. (2005). Sexual dysfunction in female partners of men who have undergone radical prostatectomy correlates with sexual dysfunction of the male partner. *Journal of Sexual Medicine, 2,* 833–841. doi:10.1111/j.1743-6109.2005.00148.x

Shirazi, M., & Subhani, J. (n.d.). What does Islam say about artificial insemination? In *Religious questions answered: Logic for Islamic rules* (Chap. 72). Retrieved from http://www.al-islam.org/falsafa/75.htm

Shoham, V., Butler, E. A., Rohrbaugh, M. J., & Trost, S. E. (2007). Symptom-system fit in couples: Emotion regulation when one or both partners smoke. *Journal of Abnormal Psychology, 116,* 848–853. doi:10.1037/0021-843X.116.4.848

Siegel, D. J. (2010). *Mind sight.* New York, NY: Bantam Books.

Smeenk, J. M., Verhaak, C. M., Eugster, A., van Minnen, A., Zielhuis, G. A., & Braat, D. D. (2001). The effect of anxiety and depression on the outcome of in-vitro fertilization. *Human Reproduction, 16,* 1420–1423. doi:10.1093/humrep/16.7.1420

Smith, G. R., Monson, R., & Ray, D. (1986). Psychiatric consultation in somatization disorder. *The New England Journal of Medicine, 314,* 1407–1413. doi:10.1056/NEJM198605293142203

Speck, R., & Attneave, C. (1972). Network therapy. In A. Ferber, M. Mendelsohn, & A. Napier (Eds.), *The book of family therapy* (pp. 637–665). New York, NY: Science House.

Speice, J., McDaniel, S. H., Rowley, P., & Loader, S. (2002). A family-oriented psycho-education group for women found to have a BRCA mutation. *Clinical Genetics, 62,* 121–127. doi:10.1034/j.1399-0004.2002.620204.x

Sperry, L. (2009). *Treatment of chronic medical conditions: Cognitive-behavioral therapy strategies and integrative treatment protocols* (pp. 173–188). Washington, DC: American Psychological Association. doi:10.1037/11850-012

Sperry, L. (2011). *Family assessment: Contemporary and cutting-edge strategies* (2nd ed.). New York, NY: Routledge.

Starr, P. (1994). *The logic of health-care reform.* New York, NY: Penguin.

Staton, J. (2009). *Making the connection between healthy marriage and health outcomes: What the research says.* Retrieved from the National Healthy Marriage Resource Center website: http://www.healthymarriageinfo.org/resource-detail/index.aspx?rid=3371

Steinglass, P. (1998). Multiple family discussion groups for patients with chronic medical illness. *Families, Systems, & Health, 16,* 55–70. doi:10.1037/h0089842

Steinglass, P., Bennett, L. A., Wolin, S. J., & Reiss, D. (1987). *The alcoholic family.* New York, NY: Basic Books.

Steinglass, P., & Horan, M. (1988). Families and chronic medical illness. In F. Walsh & C. Anderson (Eds.), *Chronic disorders and the family* (pp. 127–142). New York, NY: Haworth Press.

Steinglass, P., Temple, S., Lisman, S., & Reiss, D. (1982). Coping with spinal cord injury: The family perspective. *General Hospital Psychiatry, 4,* 259–264. doi:10.1016/0163-8343(82)90083-4

Stern, D. (2004). *The present moment in psychotherapy and everyday life.* New York, NY: Norton.

Stotland, N. (1990). *Psychiatric aspects of reproductive technology.* Washington, DC: American Psychiatric Press.

Strosahl, K. (1994). New dimensions in behavioral health primary care integration. *HMO Practice, 8,* 176–179.

Stuart, R. B., & Jacobson, B. (1987). *Weight, sex, and marriage.* New York, NY: Norton.

Sturm, R., & Gresenz, C. R. (2002). Relations of income inequality and family income to chronic medical conditions and mental health disorders: National survey. *British Medical Journal, 324,* 20–23. doi:10.1136/bmj.324.7328.20

Sullivan, H. S. (1974). *Schizophrenia as a human process.* Oxford, England: Norton.

Suls, J. M., Davidson, K. W., Kaplan, R. M. (Eds.). (2010). *Handbook of health psychology and behavioral medicine.* New York, NY: Guilford Press.

Sunderam, S., Chang, J., Flowers, L., Kulkarni, A., Sentelle, G., Jeng, G., & Macaluso, M. (2009). Assisted reproductive technology surveillance—United States, 2006.

Morbidity and Mortality Weekly Report, 58, October 2011. Retrieved from the Centers for Disease Control and Prevention website: http://www.cdc.gov/mmwr/preview/mmwrhtml/ss5805a1.htm?s_cid=ss5805a1_e

Sutton, G. C. (1980). Assortative marriage for smoking habits. *Annals of Human Biology, 7*, 449–456. doi:10.1080/03014468000004561

Taplin, S., McDaniel, S., & Naumburg, E. (1987). A case of pain. In W. Doherty & M. Baird (Eds.), *Family-centered medical care: A clinical casebook* (pp. 267–275). New York, NY: Guilford Press.

Taylor, H. (2010). The Harris Poll #149. Retrieved from http://www.harrisinteractive.com/NewsRoom/HarrisPolls/tabid/447/mid/1508/articleId/648/ctl/ReadCustom%20Default/Default.aspx

Thelen, E., & Smith, L. B. (1994). *A dynamic systems approach to the development of cognition and action.* Cambridge, MA: Massachusetts Institute of Technology.

Thernstrom, M. (2010, December 29). Meet the twiblings. *New York Times Magazine, 15.*

Totman, R. (1979). *Social causes of illness.* New York, NY: Pantheon Books.

Troxel, W. M., & Matthews, K. A. (2004). What are the costs of marital conflict and dissolution to children's physical health? *Clinical Child and Family Psychology Review, 7*, 29–57. doi:10.1023/B:CCFP.0000020191.73542.b0

Uchino, B. N. (2004). *Social support and physical health.* New Haven, CT: Yale University Press.

Umberson, D. J., & Montez, J. K. (2010). Social relationships and health: A flashpoint for public policy. *Journal of Health and Social Behavior, 51*, 54–66.

U.S. Department of Health, Education, and Welfare. (1979). *Healthy people: The surgeon general's report on health promotion and disease prevention* (DHEW Public Health Service Publication No. 79-55071). Washington, DC: U.S. Government Printing Office.

U.S. Department of Health and Human Services, Health Resources and Services Administration. (2008). Women in health profession schools, women's health USA 2008. Washington, DC: U.S. Government Printing Office. Retrieved from http://mchb.hrsa.gov/whusa08/popchar/pages/107whps.html

U.S. Office of Technology Assessment. (1988). *Infertility: Medical and social choices.* Washington, DC: U.S. Government Printing Office.

Vachon, M. L., Freedman, A., Formo, A., Rogers, J., Lyall, W. A., & Freeman, S. J. (1977). The final illness in cancer: The widow's perspective. *Canadian Medical Association Journal, 117*, 1151–1154.

van Eijk, J., Grop, R., Huygen, F., Mesker, P., Mesker-Niesten, J., van Mierlo, G., . . . Smits, A. (1983). The family doctor and the prevention of somatic fixation. *Family Systems Medicine, 1*, 5–15. doi:10.1037/h0090180

van Orden, M., Hoffman, T., Haffmans, J., Spinhoven, P., & Hoencamp, E. (2009). Collaborative mental health care versus care as usual in a primary care setting: A randomized controlled trial. *Psychiatric Services, 60*, 74–79. doi:10.1176/appi.ps.60.1.74

Vera, M., Perez-Pedrogo, C., Huertas, S. E., Reyes-Rabanillo, M. L., Juarbe, D., Huertas, A., . . . Chaplin, W. (2010). Collaborative care for depressed patients with chronic medical conditions: A randomized trial in Puerto Rico. *Psychiatric Services, 61,* 144–150. doi:10.1176/appi.ps.61.2.144

Verhaak, C. M., Lintsen, A. M., Evers, A. W., & Braat, D. D. (2010). Who is at risk of emotional problems and how do you know? Screening of women going through IVF treatment. *Human Reproduction, 25,* 1234–1240. doi:10.1093/humrep/deq054

Vilchinsky, N., Dekel, R., Leibowitz, M., Reges, O., Khaskia, A., & Mosseri, M. (2011). Dynamics of support perceptions among couples coping with cardiac illness: The effect on recovery outcomes. *Health Psychology, 30,* 411–419. doi:10.1037/a0023453

von Bertalanffy, L. (1976). *General system theory: Foundations, development, applications.* New York, NY: George Braziller.

Wagner, E. H., Austin, B. T., Davis, C., Hindmarsh, M., Schaefer, J., & Bonomi, A. (2001). Improving chronic illness care: Translating evidence into action. *Health Affairs, 20*(6), 64–78. doi:10.1377/hlthaff.20.6.64

Walker, E. A., Unutzer, J., Rutter, C., Gelfand, A., Saunders, K., Von Korff, M., . . . Katon, W. (1999). Costs of health care use by women HMO members with a history of childhood abuse and neglect. *Archives of General Psychiatry, 56,* 609–613. doi:10.1001/archpsyc.56.7.609

Walker, G. (1991). *Systemic therapy with families, couples, and individuals with AIDS infection.* New York, NY: Norton.

Walsh, F. (1998). *Strengthening family resilience.* New York, NY: Guilford Press.

Walsh, F. (2009). Spiritual resources in family adaptation to death and loss. In F. Walsh (Ed.), *Spiritual resources in family therapy* (2nd ed., pp. 81–102). New York, NY: Guilford Press.

Walsh, F., & McGoldrick, M. (1991). *Living beyond loss: Death in the family.* New York, NY: Norton.

Waltzer, H. (1982). Psychological and legal aspects of artificial insemination (A.I.D.): An overview. *American Journal of Psychotherapy, 36,* 91–102.

Wamboldt, M. Z., & Levin, L. (1995). Utility of multifamily psychoeducation groups for medically ill children and adolescents. *Family Systems Medicine, 13,* 151–161. doi:10.1037/h0089356

Wang, W., & Taylor, P. (2011). *For millennials, parenthood trumps marriage.* Retrieved from the Pew Research website: pewresearch.org/pubs/1920/millenials-value-parenthood-over-marriage

Weardon, A. J., Tarrier, N., Barrowclough, C., Zastowny, T. R., & Rahill, A. A. (2000). A review of expressed emotion research in health care. *Clinical Psychology Review, 20,* 633–666.

WebMD. (n.d.). *What are the success rates for IVF? Infertility and in-vitro fertilization.* Retrieved from http://www.webmd.com/infertility-and-reproduction/guide/in-vitro-fertilization?page=2

Weingarten, K. (2010). Reasonable hope: Construct, clinical applications, and supports. *Family Process, 49,* 5–25. doi:10.1111/j.1545-5300.2010.01305.x

Weingarten, K. (2012). Sorrow: A therapist's reflection on the inevitable and the unknowable. *Family Process, 51,* 440–455. doi:10.1111/j.1545-5300.2012.01412.x

White, D. (1990, November 16–18). Letter. *USA Weekend,* 9.

White, M., & Epston, D. (1990). *Narrative means to therapeutic ends.* New York, NY: Norton.

Whitehead, A. N. (1926). *Science and the modern world.* New York, NY: Cambridge University Press.

Whitehead, D., & Doherty, W. J. (1989). Systems dynamics in cigarette smoking: An exploratory study. *Family Systems Medicine, 7,* 264–273. doi:10.1037/h0089784

Willerton, E., Dankoski, M. E., & Martir, J. F. S. (2008). Medical family therapy: A model for addressing mental health disparities among Latinos. *Families, Systems, & Health, 26,* 196–206. doi:10.1037/1091-7527.26.2.196

Williamson, D. (1991). *The intimacy paradox.* New York, NY: Guilford Press.

Wimberly, S. R., Carver, C. S., Laurenceau, J. P., Harris, S. D., & Antoni, M. H. (2005). Perceived partner reactions to diagnosis and treatment of breast cancer: Impact on psychosocial and psychosexual adjustment. *Journal of Consulting and Clinical Psychology, 73,* 300. doi:10.1037/0022-006X.73.2.300

Wood, B. L., Miller, B. D., Lim, J., Lillis, K., Ballow, M., Stern, T., & Simmens, S. (2006). Family relational factors in pediatric depression and asthma: Pathways of effect. *Journal of the American Academy of Child and Adolescent Psychiatry, 45,* 1494–1502. doi:10.1097/01.chi.0000237711.81378.46

Wood, B. L., Watkins, J., Boyle, J., Noguiera, J., Zimand, E., & Carroll, L. (1989). The "psychosomatic family" model: An empirical and theoretical analysis. *Family Process, 28,* 399–417. doi:10.1111/j.1545-5300.1989.00399.x

Wood, L. M., Klebba, K. B., & Miller, B. D. (2000). Evolving the biobehavioral family model: The fit of attachment. *Family Process, 39,* 319–344. doi:10.1111/j.1545-5300.2000.39305.x

Wood, L. M., Lim, J., Miller, B. D., Cheah, P., Zwatch, T., Ramesh, S., & Simmens, S. (2008). Testing the biobehavioral family model in pediatric asthma: Pathways of effect. *Family Process, 47,* 21–40. doi:10.1111/j.1545-5300.2008.00237.x

World Health Organization. (2001). *From bench to bedside: Setting a path for translation of improved sexually transmitted infection diagnostics into health care delivery in the developing world.* Geneva, Switzerland: WHO/TDR Wellcome Trust.

World Health Organization. (2012). *Health topics: Chronic diseases.* Retrieved from http://www.who.int/topics/chronic_diseases/cn

Wright, L. M., Watson, W. L., & Bell, J. M. (1996). *Beliefs: The heart of healing in family health and illness.* New York, NY: Basic Books.

Wynne, L. C. (1989). Family systems and schizophrenia: Implications for family medicine. In C. N. Ramsey (Ed.), *Family systems in medicine* (pp. 1–4). New York, NY: Guilford Press.

Wynne, L. C., McDaniel, S. H., & Weber, T. T. (1986). *Systems consultation: A new perspective for family therapy.* New York, NY: Guilford Press.

Wynne, L. C., Shields, C. G., & Sirkin, M. I. (1992). Illness, family theory, and family therapy: I. Conceptual issues. *Family Process, 31,* 3–18. doi:10.1111/j.1545-5300.1992.00003.x

Yong, P. L., Saunders, R. S., & Olsen, L. (Eds.). (2010). *The healthcare imperative: Lowering costs and improving outcomes.* Washington, DC: Medicare Payment Advisory Commission.

Young, K. M., Northern, J. J., Lister, K. M., Drummond, J. A., & O'Brien, W. H. (2007). A meta-analysis of family-behavioral weight-loss treatments for children. *Clinical Psychology Review, 27,* 240–249. doi:10.1016/j.cpr.2006.08.003

Zabin, L. S., Hirsch, M. B., & Emerson, M. R. (1989). When urban adolescents choose abortion: Effects on education, psychological status, and subsequent pregnancy. *Family Planning Perspectives, 21,* 248–255. doi:10.2307/2135377

Zagieboylo, R. (2012, May). Keynote address at the Masonic Care Hospice Annual Memorial Service, East Hartford, CT.

Zito, J. M., Safer, D. J., dosReis, S., Gardner, J. F., Boles, M., & Lynch, F. (2000). Trends in the prescribing of psychotropic medications to preschoolers. *JAMA, 283,* 1025–1030. doi:10.1001/jama.283.8.1025

Zolbrod, A., & Covington, S. N. (1999). Recipient counseling for donor insemination. In S. N. Covington & L. H. Burns (Eds.), *Infertility counseling: a comprehensive handbook for counselors* (pp. 325–344). Cambridge, England: Cambridge University Press.

INDEX

Chawla, N., 168

Chiang, Olivia, 285–287

Childhood cancer, 201

Childhood chronic illness, 195–212. *See also specific diseases or conditions*
  challenges for families with, 202–204
  developmental issues with, 43–44, 198
  families' levels of risk with, 196–197
  and family dynamics that influence health, 199–202
  fear of "contagion" with, 198
  grief over loss of imagined future with, 197–198
  grief over "normal" childhood loss with, 197
  parental guilt with, 197
  prevalence of, 195–196
  special assessment issues in, 204–208
  special collaboration issues in, 211–212
  special treatment issues in, 208–211
  and vulnerability to health professionals' opinions, 198–199

Children
  adult, caring for, 259
  born of surrogacy, 191
  chronic illness in. *See* Childhood chronic illness
  desire for, 169, 170
  development issues in dealing with, 43–44
  with donor insemination origins, 187
  family dynamics that influence health of, 199–202
  illness in couple's child, 154–156
  obesity in, xxiv, 137

Christakis, N. A., 139

Chronically Ill Children and Their Families (Hobbs, Perrin, and Ireys), 202–203

Chronic disease management, 80

Chronic illness/disease/disability, xix. *See also specific diseases or conditions*
  in adults, 196
  characteristics of, 31–34
  in children. *See* Childhood chronic illness
  impact on families, 29–31
  joint sessions for, 68
  knowledge of, 15–16

learning from, 51–52
losses with, 90
patient-centered medical homes for, xxiv–xxv
positive aspects of, 51–52
prevalence of, 29, 30, 129–130
professionals' roles in treating, 71
psychosocial typology of, 21, 31–32
subpar care for, xxi
and therapeutic quadrangle, 23
therapist's knowledge of, 15–16

Chronic/maintenance phase of illness, 32, 33
  central task of, 24
  communion in, 14
  family response to, 19–20
  social system in, 23–24

Chronic pain
  professionals' roles in treating, 71
  support for coping with, 259

Citizen health care, 115–124
  citizen health care homes, 121–124
  defined, 115
  Department of Indian Work FEDS program, 117, 119
  key implementation strategies for, 117, 118
  main principles of, 115–116
  principles of, 116
  Students Against Nicotine and Tobacco Addiction, 120–121

Citizen health care homes, 121–124

Citizen models of partnership, 111–115

Clinical area, split between financial and operational areas and, 6–7

Clinical health care–larger community split, 7

Clinical social work, 279

Clinical strategies, 27–52
  to attend to developmental issues, 43–44
  and characteristics of chronic illness, 31–34
  for childhood chronic illnesses, 208–211
  for couples, 156–167
  to elicit family illness history and meaning, 35–37
  to enhance family's sense of communion, 50

Emotions
    expressed, 164
    impact of infertility treatment on, 171
    intensity of, 85
    normalizing, 40, 84, 88
    unfinished, 269
Empathetic validation, 100
Empathic presence with family,
        maintaining, 50–51
Empathy, 95, 224
Employers, health care costs for, xxiii
Empowerment of patients/families, 109,
        210–211
End of life care, 256
    creating ways to say goodbye,
        268–269
    sharing, 267–268
Engagement
    active, in couples, 162
    collaborative care as form of, 281
    community. *See* Community
        engagement
    consumer, 121
    in families of somatizing patients,
        232
Engel, G. L., 9, 96
Enmeshment, 200
Entry into adult world, obesity in
        children and, 142
Environmental tobacco smoke (ETS),
        132
Epstein, R. M., 42–43
Erectile dysfunction, in infertile men,
        180
Ethical issues
    in infertility counseling, 172
    with new reproductive technologies,
        184
    with preimplantation genetic
        diagnosis, 189
    in supporting caregivers, 256
ETS (environmental tobacco smoke),
        132
Expectations
    about illness, 36
    about length of treatment, 80
    of caring for couple's parents, 153
    in couples therapy, 156–158
    with infertility, 172
Expressed emotion (EE), 164

Extended families, communion
        among, 14
Externalizing illnesses, 45

FAAR (family adjustment and adapta-
        tion response) model, 21, 203
Failure
    feelings of, 167
    infertile men's sense of, 180
Fallacy of misplaced concreteness, 278
Families
    communication within, 41–42
    communication with medical
        providers and patients, 42–43
    health and illness impact of, 6,
        18–20
    and the health care system, 23–24
    obesity in, 138–139
    working with, 12
Family acute response, 19
Family adjustment and adaptation
        response (FAAR) model, 21, 203
Family and health research, therapist's
        knowledge of, 18–20
Family balancing, 189
Family continuity, biological reproduc-
        tion as centerpiece of, 170
Family dynamics. *See also* Family
        interaction
    in decision making, 264
    dysfunctional triangles, 205
    and family systems theory, 11
    normalizing changes in, 263–264
    and psychosomatic family model, 200
    and relationships with health care
        teams, 6
    that influence children's health,
        199–202
Family experiences, in couples therapy,
        156–158
Family FIRO model, 21–22
    for health behaviors, 139–142
    and sexuality, 144
Family health and illness cycle, 18–20
Family health histories, 24, 35–37
Family histories
    in couples therapy, 156–158
    with somatizing patients, 229
Family identity, nonillness, 44–45
Family illness history, eliciting, 35–37

Family interaction. *See also* Family
   dynamics
   and children's health, 199–202
   core dimensions of, 22
   and course of illness and recovery,
       30–31
   in psychosomatic family model, 200
   and smoking, 22
   and somatizing behavior, 222–223
Family life cycle, illness typology and, 21
Family Medical Leave Act (1993), 255
Family of origin medical issues, 24,
       98–99
Family problems, distinctions between
       psychological or physical
       problems and, 7–8
Family responses, positive, 49
Family stress theory, 21
Family systems theory, 11
   and FAAR model, 21
   and obesity treatment, 139–144
   of psychosomatic illness, 200
Family therapists. *See also* Medical
       family therapists
   in hospital settings, 69
   in residency training settings, 69
   systems-trained, 6, 7
Family therapy. *See also* Medical family
       therapy
   and citizen health care, 115
   general systems theory in, 11–12
   historical mistrust of medical
       approaches in, 75–76
   relationships of family and larger
       systems, 23
Farley, Tillman, 217
Fatal diseases, 32
FDIU (fetal death in utero), 175
Fear
   ambivalence about, 163
   courage vs., 89–90
   and overestimation of risk, 84
   in somatizing patients, 237
FEDS program (DIW), 117, 119
Fee-for-service environment, billing in,
       68–69
Fetal death in utero (FDIU), 175
Financial area (in health care), split
       between clinical and operational
       areas and, 6–7

Finley, M. A., 168
Finn, Holly, 169
FIRO (fundamental interpersonal
       orientations) model, 139. *See
       also* Family FIRO model
Flexibility, with clinical time, 286–287
Focus, in family FIRO model, 141
Forgiveness, guilt vs., 88–89
Fowler, J. H., 139
Framing, of illness impact, 45
Framingham Study, 139
Frank, Arthur, 95
Freezing embryos, 184
Freezing oocytes, 189
Freud, Sigmund, 286
Friedman, Edwin, 280–281
Frustration
   of caregivers, 257, 259
   in couples with health issues, 161
   in fertility treatments, 185
   of physicians with somatization,
       216–220
   with somatization, 216–218
   in treating chronically ill children,
       206–207
Functional disorder, 214. *See also*
       Somatization
Functional recurrent abdominal pain
       syndrome, 201
Fundamental interpersonal orientations
       (FIRO) model, 139. *See also*
       Family FIRO model

Gamete donation, 184, 190–191
Gavazzi, S., 103
Geenen, R., 84
Gender, selecting embryos for, 189
Gender differences
   in divorce rates, 167
   in infertility experience, 178–181
Gender issues. *See also* Men; Women
   with power and status, 104–105
   research on, 18
General Motors, xxiii
Genetic anomalies, termination of
       pregnancy and, 176
Genetic health care team, 251–253
Genetic risk/genetic conditions,
       241–242

Heritable illnesses. *See* Genomic
disorders
"Hidden patients," caregivers as, 258–260
Hierarchical models of partnership,
111–114
HIPAA (U.S. Health Insurance Porta-
bility and Accountability Act of
1996), 72
Hispanics (Latinos)
obesity among, 137
somatization in, 216
History and meaning of illness, eliciting,
35–37
HIV testing, 244
HMOs, stress of dealing with, 23
Hobbs, N., 202–203
Hodgkin's disease, infertility and,
179–180
Hodgson, J., 279
Hoffman, E. M., 66
Holmes Rahe Social Readjustment
Scale, 18–19
Homeopaths, 218
Hope, despair vs., 88
Horan, M., 29
Hormone-replacement therapy, xxiv
Hospital settings, family therapists in,
69
Hostility
in couples, 164
and illness/health outcomes, 164
House, J. S., 17
Hovander, D., 140
Hu, F., 136
Hubert H. Humphrey Job Corps Center,
St. Paul, 120
Human flourishing, agency and commu-
nion for, 14
Human genome, 22
Humility, 35
Humor, 49
Huntington's disease, genetic testing for,
241, 249–251
Huygen, F. J. A., 223
Hymowitz, N., 132
Hypertension
as nonincapacitating, 32
and obesity, 136
therapist's knowledge about, 16
Hypochondriasis, 213

Identification, in treating children with
chronic illness, 195
Illness, 78. *See also* Chronic illness/
disease/disability
in couple's child, 154–156
in couple's parents, 153–154
disease vs., 78
effects of, 83
family adaptation to, 19–20
individual responsibility for, 216
link between family and, 6
in a partner, 156
therapists' personal experiences
with, 96
typology of, 21, 31–32
Illness stories, 85–86. *See also* Emotional
themes and responses
of couples, 158–159
of families, 35–37
of somatizing patients, 227
Imber-Black, E., 23
Incapacitating illnesses, 32
Incapacitation, degree of, 32
Inclusion
as dimension of family interaction,
22, 140, 141
as obesity treatment issue, 142–143,
145
Independent practice, family therapy
referrals in, 69
Individual–family–institutional settings
split, 6
Individual–family split, 6
Infertility, 169–173, 177–193
causes of, 178
for couples, 181–182
defined, 177
experience of, 178
in men, 170–171, 179–181, 185–187
reproductive technologies for,
182–185
secondary, 182
for the therapist, 182
within-family solutions for, 190–192
in women, 170, 179, 187–190
Infertility rates, 170–171
Insemination, 183–186
Insurance coverage, of infertility
treatments, 184

Insurance providers
  in current delivery system, 24
  stress of dealing with, 23
Integrated care, 54
  defined, 54
  in health care home model, xxv
  levels of, 60
  for somatization disorder, 223
  "warm handoff" in, 65
Intergenerational intimidation, 97
Internet
  and clinician–patient relationships,
      109–110
  consultations via, 66
  online support communities, 46
Interpersonal neurobiology, 23
Intervention(s). *See also* Clinical
      strategies
  for obesity, 138–139
  providing chart notes copy as, 74
  with somatizing patients, 228–229,
      232
  and success of in vitro fertilization,
      190
Intimacy. *See also* Sexual intimacy
  in couples, 166
  as dimension of family interaction,
      22, 140, 141
Intimate relationships, individual–
      family split in, 6
Intimidation, intergenerational, 97
Intracytoplasmic sperm injection,
      185–186
In vitro fertilization (IVF), 172
  cost of, 184
  defined, 188
  for female infertility, 188–190
  genogram with, 182–183
  psychological interventions and
      success of, 190
  success rate with, 188
Ireys, H., 202–203
Ironic processes, 163–164
Isolation
  as emotional response to illness,
      92–93
  from mental health colleagues,
      103
IVF. *See* In vitro fertilization

Jacobs, Barry, 272
Jacobson, B., 144
Jewitt, Kristie, 294–296
Johns Hopkins, xix
Johnson, Susan, 84
Joint sessions, 67–69, 75, 225–226
Jordan, June, 282
Juvenile arthritis, 196

Kaiser Permanente, 296
Kaplan De-Nour, A., 23, 24
Kari, Nancy, 115
Katz, L. F., 19, 199–200
Kazak, A. E., 196
Kellner, R., 220, 222
Kennedy, Edward, 89
Kennedy, John F., 91
Kiecolt-Glaser, J. K., 19
Kleinman, A., 78, 216, 255, 261, 262,
      273
Knowledge base (for medical family
      therapists), 15–24
  families and the health care system,
      23–24
  family and health research, 18–20
  and knowledge of self, 24–25
  major chronic illnesses and
      disabilities, 15–16
  new brain research, 22–23
  new genetics, 22
  research in behavioral medicine and
      social sciences, 16–18
  systems theories about families and
      health, 20–22
Kraft, A. D., 179
Kramer, N., 20–21
Krugman, Paul, xxii
Kübler-Ross, Elisabeth, 260–261
Kuijer, R., 84

Lamson, A., 279
Landis, K. R., 17
Language
  medical, 293–294
  and somatizing behavior, 222,
      228–229, 231
  when dealing with death, 260
Language barriers, in consultation,
      78–79

Reiss, D., 20–21, 23, 24, 44–45, 247, 266
Relaxation training, with infertility, 172
Releases, for collaboration, 72–73
Relief, burden vs., 89
Religious traditions
    and fertility, 169, 170
    and preimplantation genetic diagnosis, 189
    and reproductive technologies, 184, 186
Renewal, loss vs., 90
Reproduction issues, 169–193
    clinical strategies for, 192–193
    infertility, 169–173, 177–182, 185–193
    pregnancy loss, 169, 171–177
    reproductive technologies, 169, 171, 174, 182–185, 189
Reproductive stage (in life cycle), 170
Reproductive technologies, 169, 171, 182–185
    for infertility, 172
    with IVF implications, 189
    and new categories of pregnancy loss, 174
    success of, 184
Research, therapist's knowledge of, 16–20, 22–23
Resentment
    in couples therapy, 160–161
    in professionals dealing with childhood chronic illness, 212
    when caring for aging parents, 154
Residency training settings, 69
Resilience
    couples therapy focus on, 166–167
    defined, 167
    while living with illness, 20
Resonance, of therapist with patient/family struggles, 100
Resource model, 29
Resources, for caregivers, 262–263
Responsibility for care, clarifying, 31
Rheumatoid arthritis, 21
Rigidity
    of patterns in response to illness, 266
    in psychosomatic family model, 200

Rituals
    during caregiving, 270
    in chronic illness and bereavement, 269–270
    in end of life care, 268–269
Rochester General Hospital, 66
Rohrbaugh, M. J., 132, 163, 164
Role clarity, 31, 103
    in patient-centered medical home model, 106–108
    for therapist, 105–106
Roles
    of behavioral health consultants, 63–65
    in caregiving, 263
    clarifying, 31, 103
    in families of somatizing patients, 228
    in joint sessions, 67
Rolland, J. S., 21–23, 31–32, 161
Rollnick, S., 134
Roosevelt, Franklin, 91
Rosman, B., 20, 200
Ruddy, Nancy, 296–298

Sadler, A., 184
Sadness, in pregnancy loss, 174
Salud Community Health Center, Denver, 66
SANTA (Students Against Nicotine and Tobacco Addiction), 120–121
Sargent, John, 81–82
Savard, M., 20
Scapegoating
    avoiding, 281
    in treating children with chronic illness, 195, 212
Schizophrenia, 164
School systems, negotiating with, 210–211
Schutz, Will, 139
Schwab, J., 132
Scope of practice, 105–106
Scott, Lee, xxiii
Secondary infertility, 182
Secondhand smoking, 132
Secrecy
    about donor insemination, 187
    as emotional response to illness, 91

ABOUT THE AUTHORS

Susan H. McDaniel, PhD, is the Dr. Laurie Sands Distinguished Professor of Families & Health, the director of the Institute for the Family in the Department of Psychiatry, associate chair of the Department of Family Medicine, and the director of the Patient- and Family-Centered Care Physician Coaching Program at the University of Rochester Medical Center, where she has been since beginning her career in 1980. Her career is dedicated to integrating mental/behavioral health into health care. Dr. McDaniel is the author of numerous journal articles and 13 books, translated into eight languages. She was coeditor of *Families, Systems & Health* for 12 years, and is now an associate editor of the *American Psychologist*. Dr. McDaniel is active in multiple professional organizations; she is on the American Psychological Association Board of Directors and the Board of the Collaborative Family Healthcare Association. She has received many awards, including the American Psychological Foundation/Cummings PSYCHE Prize in 2007, the Donald Bloch MD Award for Outstanding Contributions to Collaborative Care in 2009, the Society of Teachers of Family Medicine Recognition Award in 2011, and the Elizabeth Hurlock Beckman Award for Mentoring in 2012.

William J. Doherty, PhD, is a professor in the Department of Family Social Science at the University of Minnesota, where he directs the Minnesota Couples on the Brink Project and the Citizen Professional Center. He is also an adjunct professor in the Department of Family Medicine and Community Health. He has served as president of the National Council on Family Relations and received the Significant Contribution the Field of Marriage and Family Therapy Award from the American Association for Marriage and Family Therapy. He has authored 10 books for professionals and four books for the lay public. In addition to collaborative family health care, Dr. Doherty's professional focus is on community engagement to co-create solutions for health and social problems, and new forms of clinical practice with couples on the brink of divorce.

Jeri Hepworth, PhD, is a family therapist, and professor and vice-chair of family medicine at the University of Connecticut School of Medicine. She has taught family physicians, and primary care, psychiatry, and mental health clinicians for more than 30 years, with a focus on collaboration and team development. After completing the Executive Leadership in Academic Medicine fellowship, she is also director of faculty development programs for the School of Medicine, with a special interest in mentoring and leadership development. She is the immediate past-president of the Society of Teachers of Family Medicine, and the chair for the Council for Academic Family Medicine. Dr. Hepworth's scholarly activity has focused on families and health with expertise in psychosocial issues in medicine, and integrating behavioral health into primary care. Among her publications, she is coauthor of three books: *Medical Family Therapy*, *The Shared Experience of Illness*, and *Family Oriented Primary Care*. Dr. Hepworth enjoys leading organizational retreats, has consulted nationally and internationally, has held board and leadership positions in multiple professional associations, and serves on advisory boards of five professional journals.